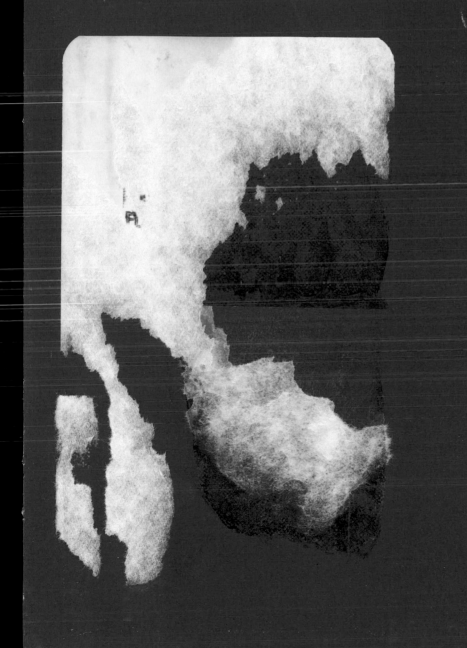

THE

OF EARL

THE MEMOIRS OF EARL WARREN

MEMOIRS
WARREN

BY CHIEF JUSTICE EARL WARREN

1977

DOUBLEDAY
& COMPANY, INC.
GARDEN CITY,
NEW YORK

92
W287m

Library of Congress Cataloging in Publication Data

Warren, Earl, 1891–1974.
The memoirs of Earl Warren.

Includes index.
1. Warren, Earl, 1891–1974.   2. Judges—United
States—Biography.
KF8745.W3A35   347'.73'2634 [B]
ISBN: 0-385-12835-5
Library of Congress Catalog Card Number 76-42842

To NINA, the best thing that ever happened to me.

CONTENTS

CONTENTS

PROLOGUE

It is the contention of many that, during his sixteen years as Chief Justice of the United States, Earl Warren was the most influential single figure for social progress in the land. It is also said that he helped to achieve this progress at the expense of judicial traditions and of certain congressional and executive prerogatives—a sacrifice which few would consider totally unbearable.

Warren, for the young or short-memoried, was long in the public eye as a district attorney (authoritatively declared in his day "the best in the land"), as an attorney general for what is now our most populous state, as the forceful and exemplary governor of that state, and as a Chief Justice who is generally conceded to rank with John Marshall and Charles Evans Hughes as one of the three greatest in the Court's history. As Chief Justice, he figured prominently in vital decisions that today affect every American. They had to do with the racial desegregation of schools, the attainment of one-person-one-vote elective parity for all, the negation of certain huge corporate mergers, protection of the constitutional rights of those suspected of crimes, and freedom of the individual to criticize public figures and policies. Warren also, of course, headed the President's Commission that investigated the assassination of President John F. Kennedy. It found no evidence of conspirators other than the man who was arrested, a finding that has never been provably contravened despite its many die-hard critics.

There have been several books and many magazine articles written about Earl Warren. They have given us *external* views of the man as he moved through these and other phases of his career.

This book, his autobiography, gives us for the first time an *interior* view. This is how he saw himself and the people and events that swirled around him during his fifty-odd years of vigorous public service.

Already the former Chief Justice, who died in 1974, is receding in our memories, and one might well ask: Of what value are his recollections today?

He was an enormously warm and genial person, a man who made friends easily in public life. The fjord-blue eyes were usually twinkling, the massively handsome face smiling. But he was firm and commanding, independent, never a man to duck hard issues, and he occasionally had to make decisions that were unpopular in many quarters, as when he played a leading part in the internment of Japanese-Americans in World War II, or guided the Warren Commission's probe of the Kennedy slaying, or reached some of his more controversial Supreme Court judgments. When he was a public official, and especially when on the court, he did not believe in undignified scuffling with his critics. He suffered them with the granite stolidity of Mount Rushmore facing a snowstorm. But he felt their peltings, and in this book he lets out a good many of his long-suppressed feelings about the charges his detractors made. His defense of the Court against those—and they ranged from President Eisenhower to the American Bar Association and the John Birch Society—who deplored its alleged tendencies to poach on other governmental preserves and aid leftist causes is just one such attraction of the book.

Another attribute of these memoirs is that anybody, whether she or he be a student of government, of the judiciary, or simply of one person's unusual effectiveness at getting the democratic process to work, can benefit from a study of Warren's methods.

Few of us have not asked today, usually with a note of wistfulness mixed with indignation, "Where are the reformist politicians we need in this post-Watergate era, the kind who are personally appealing, who are accessible to the citizenry, who never pass the buck, who are utterly incorruptible and responsive to public need, who know what they're doing and have the will and the drive to get things done?"

An impossible search? Not if more politicians modeled themselves on Warren, who set high standards in all of these regards. In state office, he held to an open-door policy and was ready to listen and act if the cause seemed worthy. In a time of much bureaucratic buck-passing, he believed in dealing directly, openly, and in a nonpartisan way with any problem. While most other politicians courted moneyed sources as an indispensable leg-up to higher office, he steadfastly refused to be obligated to any special interest. He based his ability to gain and hold office on his past performance and on the confidence of the people. That he had their support was shown by his repeated re-election. Above all, he reacted to people's needs and changing times and got things done. In this he often seemed actuated by moral rather than statutory law. Whatever, few men of this century can claim to have had such an important hand in converting the tides of social reform into applied principles of the law.

Clearly he has much to teach us if we would follow the light of democratic justice that, as former Supreme Court Justice and United Nations delegate Arthur Goldberg said, ". . . burned brightly while the torch was in his keeping."

Finally, one can read these memoirs simply for their behind-the-scenes revelations. They tell, for example, what Dwight Eisenhower in an unguarded moment told Warren he would really like to do to Communists. They tell of Warren's touchy relations with ex-President Richard Nixon over the years. They tell what arguments prevailed for the Chief Justice in the famous *Brown* case that led to the enforced desegregation of American schools. They tell what he thought of Senator Joseph McCarthy and loyalty oaths and witch hunts during the time of the nation's paranoia about the "Communist menace." They let us know why Warren changed from a district attorney who sometimes allowed suspected criminals to be intimidated under questioning by his deputies into the Supreme Court Justice who condemned such actions in the *Miranda* and other cases. They describe what he learned about the wiretapping of foreign embassies in Washington during John Mitchell's term as U. S. Attorney General. They reveal his true feelings about the compulsory relocation of Japanese-Americans which he advocated as California's attorney general. They recall the presidential campaigns in which he figured, once as a vice-presidential candidate teamed with New York's Governor Thomas Dewey. And they give us some of his thoughts on the ultimate answer to the problem of finding a workable system for world peace.

Warren's comments on these matters and many more are to be found here as a valuable supplement to the history of his time.

A word should be said about the preparation of this book. Warren worked on it from early 1970 until he died of a cardiac arrest on July 9, 1974. He worked sporadically and did not have time to finish quite all of the very rough first draft, let alone polish it.

It should be remembered, if the ensuing pages become convoluted and repetitive at times, that he was relying almost entirely on memory, at the age of eighty and more, especially in recalling West Coast days from which he was more than twenty years removed. A certain amount of editorial tinkering and checking was required, and some adjustments were made in the interest of readability and accuracy. Here and there bits of further information have been provided where they might serve to clarify a point. The rule was always to avoid changing the basic sense of what Warren wanted to say. Editorial notes are clearly indicated as such, and the original manuscript can be made available for inspection.

Readers will observe that Warren, who showed becoming modesty when in office, tends to use the personal pronoun profusely in the account that follows. Some will accuse him of pompousness and immoderate pride in his accomplishments. Others, who knew him better, will realize that he is simply being forthright, as always, though sometimes to the point of naïveté, and that his inexperience with intimate personal writing of this sort left him unaware of the means by which more subtle and professional authors may advance their own causes without seeming to.

It should also be mentioned that Warren does not indulge here in the sort of name-calling that has been attributed to him by some reporters since his death, in particular with regard to his opinion of former President Nixon. Such posthumous attributions are entirely inconsistent with Earl Warren's nonaccusatory character as we knew him during many months of close association while he was working on this book. Although he did not approve of many of the things President Nixon did, he never in our experience permitted himself to become personally abusive in expressing his views of President Nixon or anyone else. As Justice William O. Douglas has stated, "Even in private conversations he never leveled off at an antagonist or denounced him." We tend to look askance at those who say he did, now that he is gone.

What follows, then, with only superficial editorial changes, are his own words about his life, written while he was enthusiastically and productively living it to the very end.

                                                        The Editors

THE MEMOIRS OF EARL WARREN

I

A CASE OF EMOTIONAL IMPACT

The home of the Supreme Court of the United States, facing Capitol Plaza, has often been called the most beautiful building in Washington, D.C. It is indeed an awesome sight as one stands before its Grecian serenity and reads the words chiseled in white marble above the main entrance. Like the building itself, the words are inspiring. They say: "Equal Justice Under Law."

As one enters through the massive bronze doors and passes down a lofty hallway to the courtroom around which the building was designed, a feeling of solemnity and a sense of history build until the visitor arrives at the Supreme Court room itself. Inside, the stately side columns of Italian marble, the polished mahogany furnishings and the red velour hangings induce a self-imposed, respectful silence. This silence invariably prevails in deference to the cause of justice whether the Court is in session or not. Thousands of visitors come each month; on some individual days as many as twenty thousand. Yet one almost never hears a discordant sound. In the entire sixteen years that I presided as Chief Justice of the Supreme Court, I never heard an unauthorized voice raised during a session.

Rarely, in fact, did there appear to be even an air of tension in the courtroom, regardless of the importance of the case being argued or reported.

It was very different, however, on May 17, 1954.

That was the day when the historic school segregation case of *Brown* v. *Board of Education* was reported to an expectant American public. Seventeen of our states, by their own laws, had racially segregated public schools. A number of others had *de facto* segregation because of the rapid growth of ghettos which concentrated minority groups in the larger cities. The *Brown* case, when it came before the Supreme Court, challenged such discrimination in public schools as being unconstitutional.

For weeks before the announcement of our decision, the courtroom had been jammed with people; anticipation had been mounting and political writers had been hazarding all kinds of guesses as to why the opinion had been delayed from December 8, 1953, when the case had been argued, until this momentous day in May of the following year.

Contrary to speculations in the press, there had *not* been a division of opinion expressed on the Court at any time. At the weekly conference after arguments in the case, the members, conscious of its gravity and far-reaching effects, decided not to put the case to a vote until we had thoroughly explored the implications of any decision. As a result, we discussed all sides dispassionately week after week, testing arguments of counsel, suggesting various approaches, and at time acting as "devil's advocates" in certain phases of the case, but not stating our final decision until February of 1954.

At that time we voted unanimously among ourselves to declare racially segregated public schools to be unconstitutional.

Although the Chief Justice always assigns opinions when he is with the majority, I neither assigned nor pre-empted the writing of this one. Some of the senior members of the Court voluntarily suggested that I write it. The others agreeing, I did so. The opinion was submitted to the Court in conference, and, after suggestions were incorporated into it, it was officially reported, as I have noted, on May 17.

I write this at some length to emphasize that there was no dissension within the Court in connection with the *Brown* case. There was not even vigorous argument. Our decision represented the judgment of every Justice independently arrived at in the finest collegiate tradition. In my entire public career, I have never seen a group of men more conscious of the seriousness of a situation, more intent upon resolving it with as little disruption as possible, or with a greater desire for unanimity. To show how desirous we all were to present a united front, Justice Robert Jackson, who had been in the hospital for a month or so as the result of a heart attack, surprised us all by insisting on dressing and coming to the Court for the announcement. I showed concern about the danger of his overdoing, but he insisted that the case was of such importance as to call for a full Court, and he prevailed.

The lawyers and the public knew in advance that the decision must soon be reported because the usual date for adjournment of the term was not far distant.

As we Justices marched into the courtroom on that day, there was a tenseness that I have not seen equaled before or since. When I announced that I was about to report the judgment and opinion of the Court in *Brown* v. *Board of Education of Topeka, Kansas,* there was a general shifting of positions in the crowded room and a rapt attention to my words. It was not a long opinion, for I had written it so it could be published in the daily press throughout the nation without taking too much space. This enabled the public to have our entire reasoning instead of a few excerpts from a lengthier document.

In the middle of the opinion, I read:

> "We come then to the question presented: Does segregation of children in public schools solely on the basis of race, even though the physical facilities and other tangible factors may be equal, deprive the children of the minority group of equal educational opportunities? We unanimously believe that it does."

When the word "unanimously" was spoken, a wave of emotion swept the room; no words or intentional movement, yet a distinct emotional manifestation that defies description. Some of it undoubtedly was occasioned by relief that the case was decided in such a manner; some of it because of disagreement with the result; but I am sure that much of it stemmed from the word "unanimously," which flew in the face of previous news stories about dissension on the Court with regard to this case. I assume this because for weeks thereafter people would phone the Clerk's Office and demand to see the dissenting opinion. When informed that the decision was unanimous and, therefore, there could be no dissenting opinion, they would demand to know, "By what right is the dissenting opinion withheld?" or "Who outlawed dissenting opinions?"

Much has been said and written concerning this unanimity. I have been praised by many who favor the opinion for bringing it about, and I have been condemned by others who object to it. But I am entitled to neither approbation nor condemnation. The real credit for achieving unanimity, in my opinion, should go to the three Justices who were born and reared in that part of the nation where segregation was a way of life and where everyone knew the greatest emotional opposition to the decision would be forthcoming. They were Justices Hugo L. Black of Alabama, Stanley F. Reed of Kentucky, and Tom C. Clark of Texas. The others of us, while enthusiastic in our adherence to the decision and fervent in our desire for unanimity, were not in danger of being faced with animosity and harassment in our home states because of centuries-old patterns of life.

Incidentally, this was the genesis of the phrase "The Warren Court." It was coined not as a symbol of achievement or endearment, but as an indication of scorn by those who resented the decision. Since that time, it has been used in various senses. I say this advisedly because, shortly after *Brown*, Southern congressmen signed and introduced into the Congressional Record the so-called "Southern Manifesto," pledging that they would use every means at their command to overcome the *Brown* decision. Several of them told me personally that I had "stabbed them in the back." I know of no reason why they should have thought me ever to have been in favor of segregation in the first place. As far as I am aware, there was nothing in my career that would convey such an impression. I had been born and reared in California where there was no accepted policy of school segregation. I had attended public schools and the University of California, and had sat in classrooms with blacks and members of almost every minority group. I never gave it a second thought.*

As the wartime governor of California, I had integrated the National Guard shortly after its return from the War. In fact, I was one of the first, if not the first, governor to do so. I appointed some Negroes as judges. Walter Gordon, a Negro who later distinguished himself as governor of the Virgin Islands and as a United States district judge, was appointed by me to the important position of chairman of the California Adult Authority, which fixed the sentences and determined the paroles of all the prisoners in our state penitentiaries. I saw to it that Negroes and all minority groups shared in the employment benefits of our Civil Service of sixty thousand employees. All of this could hardly have been reasonably interpreted as a bias in favor of segregation.

But people do misinterpret a public figure's instincts and motivations, and I have often encountered this in my career. It has been writ-

---

* Ed. note: In the preceding the author uses the more modern and socially aware term "black," but elsewhere interchanges it with "Negro." For him, the latter was never a pejorative word; it was simply the usage of his time and in his mind carried recognition of class dignity and due respect.

ten that there was nothing in my background to presage my so-called "liberal" decisions on the Supreme Court. This notion has always been something of a mystery to me. Of course, I could well have some prejudice, as most of us do, in favor of my own consistency, but my actions have been exposed to the public constantly for more than half a century, and I feel that my views and actions in later years are but an outgrowth of the earlier ones.

Many people believe that my views on crime are radically different from those of my district attorney and attorney general days. I have been accused of being "soft on crime" and "in favor of permissiveness." Senator Joseph McCarthy once said on the floor of the Senate, "I will not say that Earl Warren is a Communist, but I will say he is the best friend of Communism in the United States."

I have also had the experience of having two presidential candidates, George Wallace and Richard Nixon, work against me and the Court over which I presided by conveying the impression that we were a menace to the internal security of the nation and pledging themselves to undo our work of sixteen years. Even the fatherly President Dwight Eisenhower was widely quoted as having said that his appointment of me as Chief Justice "was the biggest damn fool thing I ever did."

I knew he had some such opinion because we once discussed his view of the opinions of the Court which I either wrote or joined. On this occasion, President Johnson had appointed me to head the United States delegation to the funeral service of Sir Winston Churchill in London. He assigned his *Air Force One* plane for the use of the delegation, and former President Eisenhower accompanied us. Eisenhower was not a member of the delegation, but he was invited by the Churchill family to the ceremony. I do not recall how the conversation started, but Eisenhower said he had been disappointed in Justice Brennan and me; that he had mistakenly thought we were "moderate" when he appointed us, but eventually had concluded otherwise. I replied that I had always considered myself a moderate, and asked him what decisions he was referring to.

He said, "Oh, those Communist cases."

"What Communist cases?"

"All of them."

I pursued the discussion, and asked if he had read the opinions. He said he had not, but he knew what was in them. I then suggested that he must have some particular case in mind, and he said, "The Communists in California." I knew he probably meant the *Yates* case, which involved some garden variety Communists of no great importance. Ironically, he had just praised Justice Harlan, whom he had also appointed, for his moderation, so I said with some satisfaction, "John

Harlan wrote that one." He responded that it didn't make any difference who wrote it. I tried to explain that in the judging process we were obliged to judge Communists by the same rules that we applied to all others. He refused to accept this statement, and I asked him:

"What would you do with Communists in America?"

"I would kill the S.O.B.s," he said.

I was sure this remark was merely petulant rather than definitive, so I replied, "Perhaps that could be done in the Army, but it could not be done through civilian courts."

It being dinnertime, the conversation ended. It was not a pleasant session. However, I was glad that it occurred, not only because I was always fond of the general and appreciated his having given me the opportunity to serve on the Supreme Court, but also because it afforded me the first opportunity I had had in years to explain to him my views on the difference between moderation in the political process and in the judicial processes. Through politics, which has been defined as the art of the possible, progress could be made and most often was made by compromising and taking half a loaf where a whole loaf could not be obtained. The opposite is true so far as the judicial process was concerned. Through it, and particularly in the Supreme Court, the basic ingredient of decision is principle, and it should not be compromised and parceled out a little in one case, a little more in another, until eventually someone receives the full benefit. If the principle is sound and constitutional, it is the birthright of every American, not to be accorded begrudgingly or piecemeal or to special groups only, but to everyone in its entirety whenever it is brought into play. I think of this principle often because many people have said to me concerning our civil rights decisions, "I agree that everyone should have equal rights, but don't you think we are going too fast?" This is but another way of saying that moderation calls for doling out rights only a little at a time to the minority groups, the poor, the uneducated, and the otherwise underprivileged. It was this misunderstanding that was responsible for the outburst of emotion in some quarters when *Brown* v. *Board of Education* was decided.

In my more than fifty years of public service, I have been exposed to both processes, the political and the judicial, and to the interrelationship between the two, until I have what I believe is a clear concept of each in the administration of justice. In those official positions I have held, I have tried to carry this distinction in mind, and to honor both sides as essential ingredients of our governmental system. One is not born with such a concept, nor is it acquired overnight. It is an evolving thing that stems from one's experiences in life and from interpretations he or she gives them, particularly when the paths of the two processes cross.

My years on the Court were crowded with cases involving segregation, voting rights, and other civil rights, malapportionment of representative bodies, incursions on the Bill of Rights, and so forth—all of which had an emotional impact on large segments of the nation. Such cases would provoke controversy regardless of the way they might be decided. I, of course, understood that it was in the nature of the judicial process to evoke criticism because no judge can satisfy both sides, particularly in emotion-charged cases. Therefore, I never took objection to the criticism leveled at me or the Court, and made no attempt to justify publicly any of our decisions. On the other hand, I did want General Eisenhower, who had appointed me to the Court, to know from me that I had not changed my spots; that I was acting from conscience in accordance with my view of the judicial process, even though doing so resulted in unpopularity in some circles.

My first job in public service was as a clerk of the Judiciary Committee of the California State Legislature. Thereafter, I served in the City Attorney's Office of Oakland. This was followed by fourteen years as district attorney of Alameda County; then four years as state's attorney general, and later eleven years as governor of California before coming to the United States Supreme Court. They were all exciting jobs because I filled them in exciting times. All of them carried with them potentialities for controversy, unless the officeholder was willing merely to float with the tide. Such an approach never appealed to me, with the result that I was usually in controversy with some element—not personal or partisan political controversy, but what might more properly be called "issue controversy." From every such experience, I believe I learned something that could be fitted into some phase of my work as Chief Justice.

I am sure all judges realize when they assume the robe that they are not supposed to *make* the law, but are to *interpret* it as it is given to them by the Legislative Branch of the government, and to apply it to the facts of the particular case as those facts arise during the course of the proceeding. Critics of our courts complain that judges bring predilections to the bench, whereas ideally they should completely divest their minds of every experience extraneous to the case itself. This I do not believe is the true function of a judge. It is literally impossible for a person to eliminate from his reasoning process his experiences in life up to that point. I am certain that my lifetime experiences, even some of the earliest ones, have had an effect on the decisions I have rendered—not deliberatively, but because human nature compels it. A jurist's mind cannot operate in a vacuum.

Justice Oliver Wendell Holmes expressed it well when he said: "The life of the law has not been logic; it has been experience."

Because the experiences of one man who has spent almost his entire adult life in public service might be of interest to others for avoidance of or for learning from such a career, and to still others who might be interested merely in knowing what makes such an individual tick, I propose to record in the following pages a narrative of my life from my earliest days in California, in a little railroad and Wild West oil town, to the time of my retirement as Chief Justice of the United States.

II

EARLY LESSONS: *Boyhood Days*

It was my great good fortune to be born in and grow up with the most exciting and rapidly expanding state in the Union. My birth occurred only a few years after the passing of the century-old easygoing Spanish-Mexican pastoral era on the Pacific Coast. That era officially ended with, though it lingered on after, the Treaty of Guadalupe-Hidalgo, which ceded California to the United States at the conclusion of the Mexican War in 1848.

Up to that time, Los Angeles, where I was born, was a sleepy little village of a few hundred people. However, nine days before the treaty was signed, gold was discovered at Coloma, near Sacramento, some five hundred miles north of Los Angeles. Then came the deluge from every part of the world—the Gold Rush of 1849—and in two years California was admitted to the Union with a population of ninety thousand people.

While Los Angeles was not in the gold-producing area, the lackadaisical cattle business to which its landowners were committed took a spurt, and this gave the town its first of many booms. Prior to that time the cattle business had been sustained largely by the barter of hides to itinerant sailing vessels which called occasionally with their eastern and European foodstuffs, liquor and clothing materials for trade. With the influx of people to the gold fields, there was a great need for meat, and the Angelinos were ready to drive their cattle north for that purpose instead of selling only the hides at home. The value of cattle skyrocketed to unheard-of prices, and Los Angeles became an affluent little city, though more dedicated to fun and ribald living than to industry.

This lasted until the winter of 1862–63 when Southern California was visited by a great drought. Since no provision had been made for feeding livestock in such an emergency, the cattle either died of starvation or were sold only for their hides. The old Spanish owners soon lost their land to newcomers through foreclosure of extortionate mortgages that had been negotiated to sustain their carefree way of living, and for a time the city was reduced to prostration.

Then the new Anglo owners subdivided the ranches and started the first of the land booms which at different times have gripped Los Angeles. People came by the hundreds, and by the early 1870s two great railroad companies—the Southern Pacific from San Francisco in the north and the Santa Fe from San Diego in the south—fought over preferential rights-of-way for entering the city and for domination of the community, which involved access to a harbor twenty-five miles away.

It was a long and ruthless war. The Southern Pacific arrived first, and Los Angeles achieved its first rail connection with the rest of the nation in 1876. At that time, Los Angeles had a population of 16,000, but by the 1880 census it had shrunk to 11,000 because of a financial panic.

In 1885, the Santa Fe Railroad made its way into the city. Immediately, the rail company conflict was resumed in lethal fashion. An important phase of it was the rate war which centered around the passenger fare from Los Angeles to Kansas City, seventeen hundred miles away. It finally reached a point where Southern Pacific offered first-class passage to or from Kansas City for ten dollars. The Santa Fe reduced its fare to as low as eight dollars. People rushed to the city by the thousands. In two more years, the population was estimated at 80,000. There was a wild scramble for real estate, and values soared to fantastic heights, only to have the bottom drop out of the boom in 1887. In three years the population dropped from 80,000 to 50,000, according to the 1890 census.

It was at this point that I was born in Los Angeles on March 19, 1891. The entire county had but 100,000 people, and the state of California only a little over 1,000,000. By the time I was eighty, according to the 1970 census, the city alone had a population of 2,782,400, the county 6,700,000, and metropolitan Los Angeles more than 8,000,000.

ior to my birth, as I mentioned, had passed
deflation which resulted in a loss of almost half of
eople in three years.

ard L. Doheny and his partner, Charles A. Canfield,
owntown Los Angeles, and another boom was on. By
arted in 1895, there were more than five hundred pro-
the little city, and it became the most important oil field
the state.

collection of one minor event about which I often think to
remember reciting for visitors who came to our home the
their capitals and the waterways on which they were located
rm of a little ditty which my father taught me. I also
er going once to the classroom of my sister, Ethel, who was
ars older than I for that purpose. The little ditty began with
e and followed around the perimeter of the United States and
d by filling in with the interior states. The first words were, "State
Maine, Augusta, on the Kennebec River," etc. To this day, if I desire
recall the states and their capitals, I follow that format and the little
ingle which accompanied it.

I do not remember when or how I learned it, but my mother said my
father taught it to me before I was three years old. That was certainly
in keeping with his practice throughout my grammar school days. During all of those years, he always had me doing a little homework and
mathematics in advance of my class at school. But all this stopped when
I went to high school because he never studied algebra, or geometry, or
physics, or languages.

I also remember two tragic occurrences which made a lasting impression on me. One of them was my first encounter with death. The family living next door to us had a teenage daughter of whom my sister
and I were very fond. She suddenly became seriously ill. I believe it was
either polio or spinal meningitis. She suffered greatly and, because of
the proximity of the houses, we could hear her cries of pain for several
days. The doctor finally told the family he could do nothing more for
her, and in desperation they called in a Chinese herb doctor, who advised killing a chicken and placing it across her chest. He said that if
she then relaxed and fell asleep she would survive. She did not do so,
and died shortly thereafter in great pain. Her anguished cries and the
sobbing of the family after her passing gave me a lasting impression of
death. I suppose it remains in my memory so distinctly because that
was my only intimate contact with death in my entire childhood.

My father was a railroad man, a car repairman or car inspector according to his particular assignment, and, of course, he joined the other
workers when they decided to strike against Southern Pacific. We lived

The state of California during m
and is now the most populou
this growth represents the
tory.

Historians tell us th
1890s with open ga
comers who we
remember nothin
years old we moved
have only a few distinc

I do remember the colo
plaza church that had been
and secular ceremonials had bee
still in the Spanish neighborhood
where I was born. These fiestas, or "fa
colloquially called, were held quite often.
great extravaganzas with large bands, many
men on silver-decked animals, all adorned in
sure now that my childhood imagination greatly n
sity of those days, for this was not the wealthy or n
the city, and the celebrations were undoubtedly local and
in their significance.

So I suppose the dancers, singers, and horseback riders were
the music probably consisted of one or two guitars, a trumpet, an
dion, a drum, and a few dancing girls with their tambourines and ca
nets. But I am sure that my remembrance of the *colors* is no
overdrawn because the Spanish and Mexican people love multicolored
costumes and their ceremonies are marked by them. Also I am sure that
I was not mistakenly impressed by the melodious music, because I have
always enjoyed the soulful Mexican songs and have attended scores of
fiestas throughout the years to hear them. As governor, I not only attended but seized many opportunities to promote them in order to help
preserve as much as possible of the old Spanish culture which has contributed so much to the history of California.

I believe I remember discussions among my elders before we left Los
Angeles to the effect that "The boom will not last. There is nothing to
support a big city. The only thing that brings people to L.A. is the climate." But it may be that I remember such dire forecasts from conversations I heard later, because each summer, after moving away from
Los Angeles, my mother, my sister, and I would vacation there for a
week or so and would, of course, visit with friends in our old neighborhood. I might have heard the subject discussed on such occasions. It
was a topic of serious conversation throughout my early years.

only a few doors from the Ann Street School which my sister attended. One night a large group of men assembled on the school grounds, started a bonfire, and then raised a dummy on the flagpole where it hung by the neck. I have never forgotten the jeering and the sight of that body in the eerie light of the bonfire. It gave me a horror of mob action which has remained with me to this day.

The strike was a bitter one, and Eugene V. Debs, who fathered it against the Pullman Company, went to jail when his cause was lost. The strike in Los Angeles was in sympathy with the main strike, and when it also was lost, those who had left their jobs were blacklisted and could not return. Some were permitted to return under newly assumed names, I am told, but my father would not go back under such circumstances. There was no other employment available for him, so he left my mother, my sister, Ethel, and me in Los Angeles and went to San Bernardino, about ninety miles away, where he obtained a similar job on the Santa Fe Railroad. After a time, he was accepted for employment by Southern Pacific at Bakersfield, a new division point to which the repair shops had recently been moved. The railroad station and the shops for Bakersfield were really not in that city; they were about two miles distant because of the arrogance of the railroad and as a display of its power in the state.

When a line was built through the San Joaquin Valley from San Francisco about twenty years before, Bakersfield was the new county seat of Kern County and the only city at that time in the valley where it approaches the Tehachapi Mountains. When the city refused certain demands of the railroad, the city was bypassed, and a new town site, which it named Sumner, became the official station. Bakersfield was situated two miles to the east. Similar action was taken by the Southern Pacific when it passed through the adjoining county of Tulare. The county seat was Visalia, but when they also refused certain demands of the railroad, the line was laid seven miles to the west, and the shops were located at Tulare, only to be moved to Sumner a few years later.

Sumner was a little town of a few hundred people when we moved there. Just how many there were I do not know, but five years later, after oil was discovered nearby and there had been quite a boom, there were thirteen hundred. The town was built around the railroad yard and shops. There were a few stores, saloons, and small hotels, some of which were patronized by the French and Basque sheepmen who headquartered there, and the others were for the railroad men. A large percentage of the railroad men lived in hotels or rooming houses because those were the days of the so-called "boomers"—men without families who moved from one town or one railroad to another, never staying in a single place long enough to consider themselves permanent residents.

The more railroads they had worked for and the more places they had been, the greater their status as "boomers." My father was not of that type. With the exception of the time he lost his job as a result of the strike, he worked for the Southern Pacific at Los Angeles and Bakersfield from 1890 until his retirement on pension more than thirty years later.

This is an appropriate place, I believe, to tell something about my father. He was born in Haugesund, a little maritime city in southern Norway. His father was a small farmer who lived a mile or two from the city. The family emigrated to America, bringing my father, an infant of only a few months, and his brother, Ole, who was older by two years. Like so many Scandinavians, they went directly to the open spaces in the Middle West. This is characteristic of the Scandinavians, and although several million of them came to this country, very few of them landed in the ghettos of the big cities. They did not come here to participate in the industrial revolution. They chose immediately the parts of the country which were most like their native lands, so they could pursue their accustomed callings. They went to Minnesota, Wisconsin, the Dakotas, Nebraska, Iowa, and Illinois. Most of these were frontier states a century ago. My father's family located first in Leland, Illinois, and then in Eagle Grove, Iowa.

After the family arrived in this country, two more sons, Burton and Enoch, were born. Enoch died in infancy. When my father was four years old and still living in Leland, his mother died. Some time thereafter, my grandfather remarried, moved to Eagle Grove, and the family grew rapidly, with eight more children—five boys and three girls. Neither the size nor the affluence of the farm grew with the family, my grandfather being in increasingly poor health, and the home was neither spacious enough nor sufficiently compatible for the older boys. They were parceled out—Burton, the youngest of the three, to collateral relatives with whom he lived until he was of age, and my father and Ole to neighboring farmers where they did chores for their board, room, and schooling.

My father went to school through the seventh grade, and then he and his brother Ole went to Chicago. Exactly when they went there and how long they were there I do not know, but I do know that while there Ole contracted a galloping form of tuberculosis and died in my father's arms on a Christmas Eve. Having lost the one most near and dear to him and being broke in a strange city, my father later told me, he then swore that as long as he lived he would never be broke again; that no matter how little he earned he would save something. That became the guiding principle of his life. He would say, "Earl, saving is a habit like drinking, smoking, or spending. Always save some part of what you earn." From Chicago, he went to Minneapolis and there married my mother. My sister, Ethel, was born there. They then moved to California, first to San Diego and then to Los Angeles.

My mother also came to this country as an infant. She was two years younger than my father, and was brought to America by her parents from the province of Hälsingland, Sweden, when she was but a few months old. The family name was Hernlund. Like my father's family, they went first to Illinois, and while in Chicago their home was burned in the Great Fire of October 8–10, 1871, the fire that was started by Mrs. O'Leary's cow. The family then moved to Minneapolis where my mother went to school and at eighteen years of age married my father.

I never heard our racial background discussed until I entered politics. I do not mean to imply that my parents were deceptive about it. I just never heard the matter talked about, and that was not out of the ordinary because family background was not an important subject of discussion in our little town of Sumner. The name Warren being Anglo-Saxon and, therefore, in the realm of normality, it did not provoke much notice. However, as soon as I became district attorney of Alameda County, genealogists came to me and told me I should have my pedigree established for political purposes. I showed no interest in doing so. Finally, a lawyer of my acquaintance came to see me and urged me to do so in my own best interests. He said he had taken the liberty of looking into my ancestry, and had traced it back through the first family of Warrens of Virginia and then back a thousand years to William the Conqueror of England. He then added that his family was in the same strain. This seemed a bit pompous and unlikely to me. I replied irreverently that he was risking great danger because if he went back much further he might find his ancestors and mine hanging from palm trees and throwing coconuts at each other. This outraged him, and I am not sure that he ever forgave me. Particularly when I then told him that our ancestral family name was not Warren but was the Norwegian name of Varran, as I believe it was spelled, and had only been anglicized in the last two generations by a great-uncle and great-aunt of mine.

While writing about family names, I should add that when I entered school, I became conscious of the fact that the other children all had middle names or initials, and my sister and I had neither. So I said to my father, "Dad, how does it happen that all the other children have middle names and sister and I don't?" He thought for a moment, and then said, "My boy, when you were born I was too poor to give you a middle name." I imagine that wasn't far from the truth.

I know little of the immediate family background, but so far as I am aware they were all law-abiding Christian people. We lived two thousand miles from our nearest relatives on both my father's and my mother's side. We made but one trip to visit either during my youth, and that was when I was about ten years old. I saw my paternal grandfather in Eagle Grove only that one time and my maternal grandmother in Minneapolis on the same trip. My other grandparents were deceased at the time of my birth.

My father spoke very little about his youth. I always thought this was because it was a lonesome and unhappy one. Somehow, on reading *Oliver Twist*, I associated some of Oliver's experiences with those of my father. While he was not raised in an orphanage, as was Oliver, he was deprived of a home life as a youth and was, I am sure, nearly always very poor at that time. He felt the lack of a good education and made it a life passion to see that my sister, Ethel, and I should have one. It was a great sorrow to him that she was not able to go to college, but as a teenager she was in poor health and could not go beyond high school. She married, however, and had two children—a girl, Dorothy, who died of tuberculosis, and a son, Warren Roland Plank—and lived to the age of eighty.

Not only did my father do everything possible to keep me interested in learning, but until he was well into middle age he took correspondence courses himself in accounting and various phases of mechanics.

He maintained no close association with any of his family in the Midwest, although he did help some financially. His family, with the exception of the offspring of his half brother, Enoch, who lived in Illinois, is now extinct. Of the twelve children sired by his father, four died in infancy or youth, five never married, one married but had no children, and only my father and Enoch, both now deceased, had families. Of my father's family, my mother and sister are gone, and I am the last. My Uncle Enoch had a sizable family, but we never really became acquainted because of the distance involved.

I know little more of my mother's family, all of whom remained in or close to Minneapolis, where she was reared. Her home life as a girl, although not affluent, was a happy one, and her relations with her sisters and brother were affectionate, but only in correspondence. While I had a number of cousins, the only one I have really seen more than two or three times is Anna Powers, the oldest daughter of my mother's oldest sister.

So it will be seen that when we moved to Sumner (or Bakersfield, to which it later was annexed) we were alone in a new and distant community.

There were few cultural facilities or activities in our little town. There was a small school which I later attended, a little Methodist church, and a lodge room where some social gatherings were held. But the place where the townspeople gathered most often was the railroad station. Every evening one passenger train would arrive from Los Angeles in the south and another from San Francisco in the north. Both would stop for fifteen or twenty minutes for servicing and to change train and engine crews, during which time the passengers would disembark for relaxation. Whenever the weather was agreeable, a large number of the townspeople would always be there to see if they knew anybody on the train and to visit with each other. The saloons, with their open gambling, were the only clubs. They were used extensively and sometimes tumultuously by the railroaders. My father was not a patron of them, as he never smoked or drank. Both my mother and father were total abstainers; not as prohibitionists, but merely as a matter of personal forbearance.

There were no organized social or recreational activities for either school children or adults. There was no theater, nor for some years even a library. It was just a dusty frontier railroad town, connected to Bakersfield, the county seat of three thousand people, by a horse car.

Small as the town was, there were really three main groups in it. One was composed of railroad people, another of sheepmen. These last were either Basques or Frenchmen who would market and winter their sheep at Sumner, then drive them to the mountains for feed in the spring. The two elements were not antagonistic, but both were inclined to be clannish. The sheepmen lived on the south side of the railroad tracks, and the railroad people largely on the north side. Each group had its own hotels and its own activities. Practically the only social contact between the two was through the school children, as all of us went to the one school.

The third group consisted of Chinese, whom the railroad had imported as cheap labor for construction of the road and thereafter for maintenance work. There were no Chinese families. All of the workmen lived in barracks on the railroad right-of-way and kept themselves completely isolated from the community.

We lived in a little row house across the street from the shopyards. My father, a slight but wiry and tireless man, worked on the night shift as a car inspector for a number of years, then as foreman of the Bakersfield car repair shops, and finally as master car repairer for the San Joaquin division, which extended from Fresno, one hundred miles to the north, to Los Angeles, a like distance to the south. He was master car repairer until his retirement.

In keeping with his determination that I should have an education, he induced the school principal to relax the rule for entering pupils and obtained my admission when barely five instead of the customary six. I suppose he was able to do this because he had already taught me to write and do some reading prior to that time. Also for this reason, I suspect, I skipped the second grade and went directly from the first to the third grade.

This was all recalled to my attention some years ago when Mr. William Compton, superintendent of schools in Bakersfield, wrote to me at the Court and told me that in remodeling the school I attended they discovered my first grade school desk with my name scratched into the wood, and asked if I wanted it. He said the School Board refrained from publicizing it because of the likelihood of children now in school following my example and defacing their desks. Of course I wanted it. He sent it to me, and it is indeed a relic. The cast-iron base of the desk is not only rubbed smooth, but also considerably worn down by the little feet of at least sixty-five years of first-graders since I used it.

My years at grammar school were uneventful except for the fact that I was punished my first and last days there. When I entered school, my mother could not bring herself to agree to cutting the little ringlet curls that she had nurtured since my earliest childhood. As we marched through the aisles before the admiring parents who were there to see their children start their careers, one of my little classmates reached out and yanked one of my curls. According to reports, I continued the march until we were all at our proper places and seated, at which time I got up, returned to the spot where I had been humiliated, and punched my tormentor. For this, I was made to stand in the corner during the very first session. On the whole, I profited by this experience because my father then proceeded to cut my hair to relieve me of future embarrassment and possibly more severe punishment.

On the last day of school, as we were graduating from the eighth grade and ready for high school, seven of us boys committed some minor act of *lèse majesté,* and were all paddled by our principal, Mr. Leo G. Pauly. The others were older and larger than I was, and they received the brunt of the punishment. When he reached me, he gave me only two or three cuffs on the posterior. I really do not remember what we had done, but it must have been something that was fairly offensive because Mr. Pauly was a temperate man and not addicted to violent punishment. It was my pleasure many years later as governor to appoint him to fill a vacancy on the Board of Supervisors of Kern County. He was a fine public servant, and passed away only recently in his late nineties.

That little grammar school was a turbulent one. There were fully grown pupils, some as old as sixteen years and possibly even older. When I entered, they were having internal warfare. The principal's name was Taggart, and I remember the older boys gathered on the sidewalk after school calling him a "blankety-blank mule-driver," and daring him to come out of the schoolyard. Very soon thereafter Mr. Pauly succeeded him, and such troubles ended, but there was much fighting between the pupils at recess as well as before and after school. I was not in on the fighting because I was both young and small, and also I was under injunction from home not to engage in it.

Most of the boys went directly from school to work for the railroad. Very few ever went to high school. As far as I can remember, I was the first one ever to be graduated from college.

My grades were good in grammar school, and I had many extra-curricular activities of my own making. I had a job every summer from the time I was nine years old, and during the school year I often had jobs in the morning before school or after school.

My second summer job was on an ice wagon. I was a helper or "swamper" to the iceman who served the residential customers. He had a regular route that he followed each day in a covered wagon filled with large cakes of ice which he sawed, chipped, and delivered according to the needs of his clients. The smallest amounts sold were in ten-pound lots. For carrying them into homes and putting them in the icebox I received twenty-five cents a day and a ten- or fifteen-pound piece of ice for our home.

It is strange how things of the past sometimes come to light. On the occasion of my eightieth birthday, a dinner was given for me by Congressman William S. Mailliard and former Senator Thomas H. Kuchel, both of California, at the Mailliard home. At this party I met Admiral E. R. Zumwalt, Jr., Chief of U. S. Naval Operations, who told me that he came from Tulare, California. It developed that I knew his father many years ago in some political connection. I asked him if he had any relatives in Bakersfield because my first job was on an ice wagon with an Ethen Zumwalt. The admiral was not certain, but he communicated with his father who, in turn, wrote to a daughter of Ethen's, and she uncovered a family document written by Ethen over fifty years ago in which was related the portion of his career during which he drove an ice wagon in Sumner. In it, he wrote:

> Being a lad just out of my teens, I was the sole dispenser of the very necessary ice supply in the community, where the thermometer would hold sway at 110 degrees in the cooler places for days.
>
> At eleven o'clock each morning [in the year 1900], after serving the wholesale trade, I would pull my flashing red and white wagon in front of Charlie's, a popular Chinese Restaurant of the rail center, put the nose bags on my two big bays,

Patsy and Dick, and would have lunch and relax for a few minutes.

Upon returning to the wagon—and with never a miss in the three summers did he fail me—[I would find] a husky boy about nine sitting on the driver's seat with a big smile and a morning greeting of 'We are all set, Ethen.' This chap received for his services—from 8 to 9 hours, 7 days a week—25¢ a day and ice for his family.

After loading for the afternoon delivery, we made our start, with the two faithful horses to lead the way through the winding dusty streets, and we proceeded to replenish the refrigerators and homemade ice boxes . . .

A ten pound minimum piece of ice was the greater portion of our delivery, and was taken care of by the lad while I did the cutting and took care of the heavier deliveries. The populace looked forward to the coming of the ice wagon, and I often wondered if it was the ice or the smiling young lad, who always picked the larger pieces for some of the less fortunate families, or to be sure that some baby milk would be kept sweet through the long hot day.

In the middle of the third summer, the drivers asked management to put on other men to unload the ice cars when they came in at night. The ice had to be stored in a warehouse for future delivery. The unloading and the loading for the next morning's rounds were done by lamp light. The request was refused, and the crew, even though they knew that there were dozens of men available for every man quitting, walked out in a body.

I will never forget the look on Earl Warren's face when I turned my wagon over to the new driver after refusing a generous offer of the management to stay on. He climbed off the wagon and, patting the big bay on the shoulder, told the boss he would have to depend on Patsy for the rest of the summer.

I moved to Berkeley when Earl started to college, and I watched him with pride and confidence when he finished his schooling and entered the service of the City of Oakland, knowing that the community was truly fortunate in having such an honorable young man in its service.

I was happy to receive this verification of my first job because I was quite proud of it at the time and, indeed, thought it of some importance because delivering ice to homes that had no air conditioning in weather from 100 to 120 degrees was almost a humanitarian service.

After the ice-carrying job, I began working as helper to a bakery wagon driver early each morning. For that, I also received twenty-five cents a day. There wasn't any of the precious ice to take home, but there were plenty of cookies.

Then, for two successive summers, I drove a grocery wagon powered by a pair of mules. And one summer I kept books for a produce merchant. From the time I was fifteen until I was graduated from law school, I worked every summer and Christmas vacation in some depart ment of the Southern Pacific at Bakersfield—in the car shops, machine shops, baggage room, and as a caller of engine and train crews. I also delivered the Bakersfield *Californian* to East Bakersfield readers and at times sold the Los Angeles *Herald* early in the morning at the railroad station. While in high school, I coached a former Southern Pacific brakeman, who had become a bartender when he lost a foot, for the college entrance examinations which he was obliged to take in order to enter a medical school. To my delight, he passed the examinations and became a successful physician in Chicago.

I did quite well with my jobs with the exception of one or two. From an advertisement which came to our home, I believe through the mail, I undertook to sell books on the life of President William McKinley and the Boer War in South Africa. Both of these subjects had made a profound impression on me. I was greatly saddened by the assassination of President McKinley and was stirred by the courageous fight being made by the Boers. I rejoiced when, with their poorly equipped soldiers and primitive techniques, they withstood and sometimes defeated the highly trained British forces. I repeated often in my prayers at that par ticular time the declamation of William Jennings Bryan, "God grant that England shall never win."

Feeling as I did about these two dramatic events, I was sure I could sell the books about them, which were advertised in very emotional terms. But I was almost a complete failure. I sold two or three copies of each, but wore out a couple of pairs of shoes in doing so, and finally gave up in despair. I was too small and immature to be taken seriously, could not make a convincing sales talk, and was too easily put off.

Also, I was of little value on any of the mechanical jobs in the shops or in helping my father with the plumbing or installation of electrical fixtures in the houses he built. I had no interest in those jobs, and sometimes had a hard time keeping awake while holding a section of pipe or some electrical fixture to be fitted.

I functioned satisfactorily in all of my clerical or delivery jobs, how ever, and particularly as a call boy for train and engine crews. Here I was dealing with people in a meaningful way. The procedure was for the call boy to be notified whenever the time for departure of a train was scheduled. I was then required to notify in person the crew members who were to be called for that train, giving them one and one half hours to prepare for the trip and make their appearance. It was not always easy to locate them because so many were not family men, and the last place one could expect to find them was at home. Consequently, when a train was called, I would, according to custom, immediately post the information on a board kept for that purpose in the principal gambling joint in town. If they were not to be found there, I would go to some of their other haunts which, as a matter of necessity, I was obliged to learn. If they could not be located even then, I would go to their rooms in the boardinghouse or hotel.

During the time I worked in that job I never delayed a train for failure to find the trainmen, and whenever any of them was incapacitated for any cause, he was reported as sick, and another man on the list kept for that purpose was called to substitute before train time. As a result, I became quite a boy hero with the men. My reputation paid dividends later in my political career. Railroaders were mostly Democrats in later years, but when I ran for office as a Republican, the old-timers in the San Joaquin Division saw to it that I was not too badly treated by the Railroad Brotherhoods.

When I first went to work for the Southern Pacific, I was under the acceptable age, and it was necessary for me to have the consent of my father. He gave it, but only on my assurance that at the end of the summer I would leave work and go back to school. He was always concerned that I might do what so many other boys in town did—go to work for the railroad and then never finish my education. He often reminded me of a saying about railroading: "You cuss it every day, but once in it you can't get out even if you try." The "boomer" instinct was very strong, and many young men in the business simply became itinerant workers.

My father was always happy to see me have jobs; in fact, he encouraged me to do so in order to make some money. He never wanted it for family use. He wanted me to save it for my own future. This was in keeping with his way of life. He was devoted to both industry and thrift. He never spent an unnecessary dollar on himself. He lived a Spartan life, which meant a more or less Spartan life for my mother also. I always thought too Spartan for both of them, but I should be the last to complain: he adopted those habits so he would be sure that my sister and I would have a good education.

He had an abiding sense of responsibility for those in the family who might have need in the future. When he had accumulated a modest amount of money, he divided it among all the members of the family, transferring to each of his grandchildren and to my sister and me five thousand dollars. Then when my sister's husband, at forty-five years of age, died suddenly on the golf course and her daughter contracted tuberculosis, he transferred to my sister his properties that had a potential for business purposes. It was farsighted of him to do so because Dorothy, her daughter, died after six years in a tuberculosis sanatorium. He told me, and very properly so, that he was making no provision for me because I had my health and an education. When he died, his entire estate went to my mother.

In politics, I was often embarrassed when some of my friends would tell how I had worked my way through school and college and helped support the family. They did that because they knew that I had held many jobs, and they wanted to have me appear more deserving to the public, but there was not an iota of truth in it, and I gave no furtherance to the story. I did work, but that which I didn't spend, I saved for myself. My father financed my entire education and all the expenditures of the family. While he had no money for what he considered frivolities, there was always money available for any educational activity—books, music lessons, lectures. He had no interest in sports of any kind, and we never discussed them at home. I always had jobs after school or was practicing on the clarinet, which I played in the town band. I had no chance to practice regularly for any of the school teams. For a time, I played on the high school baseball team in my senior year, but lost my place when I could not practice regularly with the team because of outside jobs. I was active, but not in organized sports. I suppose that is the reason I have been an ardent fan of most sports throughout my life and why I have always encouraged my children in any sports activities they liked. I believe competitive sports are an important phase of American life.

A great deal of my free time as a boy was spent with my animals, and I had many of them—house dogs and hunting dogs, a sheep, an eagle, pet chickens, rabbits, and, above all, a burro. They were all almost human in my eyes, but my burro Jack was my friend and constant companion for years. Several of the boys in our community had burros which they obtained from sheepmen when the herders brought the sheep down from the mountains for the winter. The sheepmen did not wish to feed the burros hay all winter, and would sell them for almost nothing. Mine was, of course, an "unusual" animal, and we rode around the country in every direction; to go swimming or fishing, to chase jack rabbits with the greyhounds, to trap squirrels, or just to see what was going on.

Our little town was something like an oasis in a desert. The surrounding country was dry as a bone, and every wind would result in a dust storm. Sometimes these would last for days, and no amount of batten around the windows and door sills would keep the dust out of the houses, where it gathered sometimes even to the point of suffocation.

Although it was arid nine or ten months of the year, for a few weeks in the springtime it was a place of surpassing beauty. The entire countryside as far as the eye could see became a veritable crazy quilt of wild flowers. Great patches of golden poppies, the official flower of the state, and the blue lupines which are always associated with them dominated the picture, which was spotted with smaller patches of red, white, and yellow four-o'clocks, Indianheads, buttercups, and forget-me-nots on a carpet of grass. I can remember my father saying, as we roamed the countryside and gathered the various blossoms, "The Lord must have intended these hills for something more than these flowers for such a few days each year." And how right he was.

In 1899, oil was discovered there, and it became one of the great oil fields of the West. Still later, when irrigation became the science it now is, these barren, sterile lands were transformed into a lush agricultural area which today contributes mightily to the food and fiber production of our state.

I remember once going out into the country to see some cockfights. It was a sickening sight. The magnificent birds with steel spurs on their legs would slash at each other until one would go down and pour out his lifeblood until dead. Then the bettors, who were seated around the ring, would reach in and grab their money, after which they would make their bets on the next fight by throwing more cash into the ring to be covered.

It was cruelty personified, and I never wanted to see another exhibition of that character. I do not know why I was admitted to those fights, because they were illegal, and I do not recall knowing anyone connected with them.

I read in the paper one day that there was to be a rabbit drive. Most of the surrounding country was so dry and covered by sagebrush that nothing but jack rabbits and lizards could live on it, but wherever it was irrigated, it would grow good crops. It would also attract rabbits from miles around. Occasionally the farmers would gather on a given day and spread out in a gigantic circle. They would then converge toward the center, beating the brush and yelling until they were able to put a fence around the animals thus entrapped. The farmers would then move inside the fence with clubs and sticks, and beat the frantic rabbits to death. I never have heard such sounds. The victimized rabbits remained in my mind as babies screaming, and I could not sleep well for weeks. While the rabbits were destructive pests, it always seemed to me that there must be a better way of ridding the countryside of them. I could not witness another such sight to this day.

I saw nearly everything that went on in the surrounding country. My burro, Jack, would take me any place. We didn't need roads. We would go cross-country because there was very little to obstruct passage. I always rode bareback, and much of the time without a bridle. A slap on the side of the neck and pressure on his flanks with my feet were sufficient.

On the morning of April 19, 1903, we heard that there had been some shooting in Bakersfield and the city marshal and a deputy sheriff had been killed. That was enough information for Jack and me. Over to the scene of the shooting we went. Crowds were standing around discussing the affair, and sure enough the city marshal, the deputy, and a notorious bandit had been slain. There was much speculation about the affair, and there was even talk about lynching another deputy who had been named by the dying marshal as the killer.

It became a celebrated case. A bandit by the name of Jim McKinney, a former resident of Visalia, sixty miles north of Bakersfield, had operated for years as a desperado throughout the Southwest. He had been jailed in Hanford, a San Joaquin Valley town north of Bakersfield, but escaped and was robbing and killing in the surrounding mountains. There were wild stories concerning his activities and, of course, much talk of them in the bars of Bakersfield.

On the night of April 18, 1903, there was such a discussion going on in the bar of the Arlington Hotel at Twenty-ninth Street and Chester Avenue, the main intersection of the business district. During the course of it, a deputy marshal by the name of Al Hultse suggested that his listeners might be surprised to know that McKinney was in Bakersfield and not more than a few hundred yards from where they were drinking. Later, Deputy Hultse was followed when he left the hotel. He went to a Chinese joss house about three blocks away. Guessing correctly that McKinney was in that same building, City Marshal Jeff Packard and his deputy, Will Tibbet, entered the building the following morning, and were killed by blasts of a shotgun. Burt Tibbet, the brother of the slain deputy, then shot from behind a woodpile and killed McKinney as he peeked out of the window. The dying marshal had said it was not McKinney but Al Hultse who had shot him. Hultse was arrested later in the morning and charged with the murder of the officers.

It happened that during the previous holiday season there was a turkey shoot in the countryside north of Kern City and, of course, that was enough for Jack and me to be there. A turkey was tied to a stake by a rope that permitted him to move about six or eight feet. At a distance of some two hundred yards, shooters were permitted to try to kill the bird for fifty cents a shot. If hit, the turkey belonged to the shooter.

One man was hitting the birds quite consistently. He had a pile of them, which he soon proceeded to count. While I was looking on, he came to a smaller white one, and, glancing up at me, said, "Boy, would you like this turkey?" Of course I would, and he gave it to me.

The next fall I started high school in Bakersfield, and to get there had to pass through the courthouse square. They were then trying Al Hultse for murdering his two fellow lawmen. My curiosity took me into the courthouse, and there before the bench was the defendant. He was, as you may have guessed, the same man who had given me the turkey. The first trial resulted in a disagreement, the second in a conviction for second degree murder. But while in jail pending an appeal, Hultse slit his throat from ear to ear with a razor that had been given to him to shave with.

The murdered deputy city marshal was the father of Lawrence Tibbett, the famous baritone of the second quarter of this century. At the time of the tragedy, Lawrence was a child of six years.

There is a book written about this episode entitled *Shot Guns on Sunday* by Joseph E. Doctor. It not only tells the story of the gunplay, but gives a graphic description of Bakersfield as it was in those days. Doctor's appraisal of the affair was as follows:

> Although few, if any, of the participants and witnesses were aware of it at the time, the gory battle in the Chinese tong headquarters on Bakersfield's L Street brought to a close an epic period in the American West. Bakersfield looked on the incident as perhaps the most revolting of a series of "man for breakfast" episodes which had given the city a reputation for being the roughest and most hellish of its day, worthy successor to Virginia City, Abilene, Dodge, Deadwood, Tombstone, Bodie and other western boomtowns noted at various times for the vigor of their vice and violence.
>
> Death of Jim McKinney in the lethal blasts from the avenging shotgun of Burt Tibbet was to mark the end of the western badman as an authentic figure in American history. A chronicler of the day, writing in a Bakersfield newspaper, *The Californian*, referred to him as the last of the Old West's outlaw tradition, and expressed no regret at [his] passing.

It was, indeed, a wild and woolly city at the time I entered high school in September 1903. Oil had been discovered in the environs along the Kern River in 1899, and the boom was in full swing.

Our school was the Kern County Union High School. It was the first and only one in the county, and when I was graduated there were sixteen in our class. Only four of us went to college. The students came from all over the county, which was almost as large as the kingdom of Belgium. I was the youngest and the smallest boy in the school, and to my embarrassment, I was the only one in knee pants. For an entire year I felt humiliated, but my mother could not bear seeing me in what she considered adult clothing. This and the fact that I came from Kern City made me a sort of outlander. I was too small and immature to try out for any of the athletic teams, and was not considered a part of the group interested in other activities, which were very few, though there were some dances and parties. I did not start really to grow until the middle of my junior year, and then shot up like a weed until I was over five feet eleven at graduation, but weighed less than 130 pounds fully clothed.

I was not an inspired student. I did well in the subjects I liked, such as history, English, and French, but was lackadaisical in the others, to my lasting regret. However, it was not a particularly inspirational atmosphere. The principal was not well liked. He spied on the students, held grievances, and some of the older ones at times openly defied him.

With some exceptions, my principal heroes were the football and other athletic stars, because I was not engaged in those activities myself. I always felt that in going to high school so young I was being shortchanged in that respect. The feeling has been a lasting one with me, and I never wanted any of our children to advance faster than his or her class, because it seems to me that to do so is likely to deprive one of a sense of belonging which is very important, particularly in early life. We were of all racial and religious backgrounds and of all colors, but we had no differences on those scores; in fact, I do not remember ever thinking seriously about them.

I was not interested in the girls. They were all very nice to me, but in a more or less patronizing way because of my size and age.

I really only had one close companion, Albert Cuneo, a Kern City boy a year or two older but almost of my size. He was of a fine Italian family of eight boys and one girl. We both played clarinet in the town band, and, living only a few blocks apart, were constant companions.

As a result of my semidetachment from school activities, my student life was not particularly eventful until the day before we graduated.

Our class, in accordance with custom, arranged to have a class play. The Scribner Opera House was rented and sold out for the occasion. The play was to be held the evening before graduation. Its title was "What Became of Parker?" and I was Parker. How I was selected for or why I accepted this leading role, I will never know because I had never been effective in any dramatic capacity. I did not volunteer in class, and really did not care to recite when called upon even when I was sure of the correct answer, because I did not like the sound of my voice in such situations. But there I was as Parker. The night before the show we had the dress rehearsal, and as is usual with amateur performances we were ill prepared. Our director kept us at the Opera House until well after midnight. By the time I rode my bicycle clear across town to my home and collapsed in bed it was well along in the early morning hours. A rehearsal for graduation was scheduled for nine o'clock that morning. When morning arrived, I did not feel well, and my mother suggested that if I was to be in the play that night I should remain in bed for some more sleep. I did so, and reported at school an hour or two late. Reginald Stoner, captain of the football team, and Tim English, the fullback, both of whom had major parts in the play, had also reported late. When I came in, the principal called us to his office and accused us of conspiring to sabotage the graduation rehearsal. It was not true, and we denied it. None of us had any knowledge of the cause of the lateness of the others. He would not believe us, and told us we were expelled from school. We were astounded, for regardless of what we might have done on some other occasions to incur his wrath, we certainly were not guilty this time. He proceeded to tell us that we might go ahead with the play that night, but that we would not be permitted to graduate the next day. Then the rhetoric became somewhat heady, and he was told that there would be no play unless we were to graduate. He was unimpressed, and stuck to his decision. When we left his office, word soon got around the school, to the consternation of all.

In the middle of the afternoon, we were advised that a few hours later the County Board of Education would have a special meeting to consider the matter, and that we were supposed to be present. We complied, and told our stories, as did the principal, after which he and the Board had a long conference. In the end, the Board overruled him and reinstated us.

The play was then produced, though it started more than an hour later than the scheduled time. We were graduated the following night.

I never thought at that time that they would be naming a building for me there. But they did years later on the Bakersfield Junior College campus, which the Board of Education also supervised.

The principal did not return to the school the next term, but I do not know whether the foregoing incident had anything to do with it. I lost track of him for many years, but when he was a very old man I learned he was in a rest home in our county. I contacted him, and we discussed other things of a more pleasant nature without mentioning this one. After that we exchanged greetings on occasion until his death.

My most exciting experiences were in connection with the various jobs I held in those years. Some of them grew out of my clarinet playing. A professor, George Kuhn, gave piano lessons to my sister, Ethel, and clarinet lessons to me. Kuhn also played the piano at the Opera House and clarinet in the band. As a member of the orchestra, he received complimentary tickets to the shows, and for several years Ethel and I were the beneficiaries of two of them. We sat in the front row next to the orchestra, and saw dozens of the melodramas of that era. It was a great treat for both of us, but it did interfere sometimes with our school homework.

When I was fifteen years old, the musicians of Bakersfield decided to organize a local of the American Federation of Musicians. They needed clarinets, so my school friend Albert Cuneo and I were invited to become charter members. At the organization meeting, I served as the temporary secretary. In the town band, we played all manner of engagements—ceremonial parades, political campaign meetings, torchlight parades, and summer concerts every Saturday night at the center of the business district.

But the most colorful of these musical experiences was in 1910, after I was in college. It was the year the great Lakeview Gusher was brought in on the west side of Kern County near Maricopa, a new oil town founded in 1905. This little community was as primitive as one could imagine; it had all wooden buildings, many saloons for the size of the place, and was populated largely by men without their families, if they had any. They were rough men who had developed the oil fields of America. Early in 1910, only a short distance from the town, the Lakeview Gusher exploded into the world as one of the greatest oil wells in American history. It blew all the equipment out and spurted oil hundreds of feet into the air. It was completely out of control and blackened the countryside for miles around with a murky spray that the winds carried for great distances.

In order to exploit the possibilities of the area, the town of Maricopa staged a two-day Fourth of July celebration, and the Bakersfield band was asked to provide the music. Coincidental with this celebration was the world heavyweight championship fight between James J. Jeffries and Jack Johnson at Reno, Nevada. It was comparable in its day to the recent Joe Frazier v. Muhammad Ali matches. Jeffries, the recognized world champion, had retired undefeated in 1905. In the ensuing elimination contests, Jack Johnson came to be recognized reluctantly as the new champion, but there was always a doubt raised as to whether he could beat Jeffries. Finally, after five years of easy living and with much added weight, Jeffries agreed to come out of retirement and fight Johnson.

The only subject of conversation for two days was the fight. The Maricopa saloons were crowded night and day. There was racial ten-

sion, as Jeffries was white and Johnson black. Debates lasted throughout the night of July 3. Fanning the excitement, our band played on
street corners and from one saloon to another. Hardly anyone in town
went to bed, and none of the musicians did. In the early morning, we
all rode out in a bus to see the Lakeview Gusher. It was an open chasm
at that time, roaring like an angry surf, the black oil running over the
sides into the canyons leading from it. We were told the story of the
gusher, which was an odd one. It had been abandoned by the original
operators as a dry hole and sold for a song to others who brought the
well in. The explosion was so powerful and the loss of oil and damage
so great, it was said to be doubtful that anyone could prosper from it.

After returning to Maricopa, we had lunch and then came the fight.
It was not a great match. We received the returns not as we would
today on television or radio, but by telegraph at the end of each round.
Finally came the flash: "Johnson wins by a knockout in the fifteenth."
Jim Jeffries was only a shell of his former self and no match for the
great physique and cleverness of Jack Johnson. We bandsmen returned
to Bakersfield a tired lot, but with thirty dollars each in our pockets
after more than twenty-four hours of almost constant playing. There
had been plenty of fisticuffs all around us, but fortunately no gunplay.
We had seen oil town life in the raw.

My experience with music and musicians was pleasurable, but that
which I had in my railroad jobs was more meaningful because I was
dealing with people as they worked for a gigantic corporation that dominated the economic and political life of the community. I saw that
power exercised and the hardship that followed in its wake. I saw every
man on the railroad not essential for the operation of the trains laid off
without pay and without warning for weeks before the end of a fiscal
year in order that the corporate stock might pay a higher dividend. I
saw minority groups brought into the country for cheap labor paid a
dollar a day for ten hours of work only to be fleeced out of much of
that at the company store where they were obliged to trade. I helped
carry men to the little room called the emergency hospital for amputa-
tion of an arm or leg that had been crushed because there were no
safety appliances in the shops and yards to prevent such injuries. I knew
of men who were fired for even considering a suit against the railroad for
the injuries they had sustained. There was no compensation for them,
and they went through life as cripples. I witnessed crime and vice of all
kinds countenanced by corrupt government as I learned the habits of a
large part of the railroad men with whom I was thrown in contact. As a
train caller, I saw men rush from the pay car to the gambling houses
and never leave until they had lost every cent of their month's laborious
earnings. In those days, the company did not pay by check. Each

month the pay train would come to Bakersfield and the men would file through, receiving their pay in gold and silver. Paper money was almost unheard of there, and in most business places would not be honored. Only hard money was acceptable.

I saw conditions in many of the homes where the breadwinner had lost his earnings at the gaming tables. I became familiar with the ten- and even twelve-hour day, seven days a week. I worked many such hours myself.

The things I learned about monopolistic power, political dominance, corruption in government, and their effect on the people of a community were valuable lessons that would tend to shape my career throughout life, although I did not then foresee any such results.

Before leaving my school days, I should mention the latter days of my closest companion. When I started to high school and had an afternoon paper route for the Bakersfield *Californian,* as stated earlier, my burro, Jack, became disconsolate because of my late arrival home, and would bray for hours. My parents, knowing this would be a source of irritation for the neighbors, persuaded me that we should make some disposition of him that would enable him to be busy and happy.

About that same time I was contacted by the owner of a shoe store that carried Packard shoes. He told me he would like to have Jack for use on a conveyance to advertise those shoes. He said Jack would be kept busy and would be well taken care of in a livery stable not far from the high school. Much as I hated to sell my burro, I did, and Jack went into the advertising business. The conveyance to which he was harnessed was a giant shoe on a sort of a buggy chassis. A boy sat in the top of the shoe and with reins controlled Jack's movements. It was only a partial success because they soon found that the contraption could not go to Kern City, for Jack, if he came within a half mile of our home, would put his head in the air and run there as fast as he could. The bridle and bit could not hold him. His mouth was like iron, and his determination equally so. On arriving at our house, he would bray until my mother came out and fed him a little snack of some kind. Even then he would not leave, so they abandoned trips to that part of the community. On my way home from school, I would always stop at the livery stable and give him scraps from my lunch basket. If he was not there, I would leave them in his feed box. One day when I arrived at the livery stable, I was informed that he was dead. Poisoned, they said. They did not know by whom, but I reasoned that his constant braying for me had irritated the neighbors so much that someone had decided to put a stop to it. My sorrow at his passing remains to this day. The Southern Pacific was quite a transfer point for grain and partially refined sugar. In the transfer to other cars or to trucks, a sack would often be broken, and the workmen would not salvage the contents. I made regular visits to these delivery tracks with Jack, and I rescued for him what was left. As a result, he had both grain and sugar each evening when I came home from school. How he loved that sugar. The mere sight of me carrying an empty sack would cause him to chase me, playfully grabbing for the sack as a puppy would.

After my tempestuous high school graduation, I worked at the Southern Pacific for about two months, and in the middle of August boarded a train for Berkeley and the University of California. Neither my parents nor I knew much about the school, but it was considered by all of us as the place for me to go for the remainder of my education. I had never before been away from my parents, except for one weekend in 1907 when Albert Cuneo and I went to Los Angeles and then to Santa Barbara to see the Great White Fleet of sixteen warships that President Theodore Roosevelt sent around the world to impress everyone with our naval power. Neither of my parents was inclined to moralize greatly with me, and as I left for Berkeley my father merely said, "Well, my boy, you are going away from home. You are a man now, and I am sure you are going to act like one."

III

LATER LESSONS: *The University, the Army, the Law*

It was a long, miserable trip in those days through the valley from Bakersfield to the San Francisco Bay area in the middle of August. Many of the now-thriving cities along that route of 314 miles were then only little villages, as was East Bakersfield when we arrived there. Cultivation was spotty in an arid landscape which produced much dust as the train rolled along. There was no air conditioning, of course, and with the windows open in a temperature of 100 to 115 degrees one was hot and grimy by the time the train pulled into the Southern Pacific terminal in Oakland.

I do not recall any of my specific thoughts on that all-day trip, but I know they were mixed; some of lonesomeness at leaving home for the first time; some of anticipation combined with apprehension as to what university life would be like.

Mining was a dominant part of California's economy, and because both oil and gold were important factors in the life of Kern County, my father thought mining engineering would be a good profession for me. His opinion was fortified by the fact that the University of California at Berkeley offered an outstanding course in that subject. I am surprised that my father did not better perceive that I did not have any aptitude for things of a mechanical nature, which is so important in engineering work. He was not insistent, however, and at some stage of my youth, without any well-considered reasons, I decided to become a lawyer instead.

My concept of the law was exclusively one of courtroom advocacy. Again I cannot understand why, given my diffidence about even reciting in school, I should think of such an extroverted career. As I mentioned earlier, on my way to and from high school I rode my bicycle through the courthouse square. Often on my way home I would stop to watch some trial just to see some of the lawyers in action. I can only guess that I admired their ability to stand on their feet and speak with ease before a court and jury, an ability I did not have even in the schoolroom with my classmates.

It was with such thoughts as these that I arrived in Oakland, which was only a few miles from Berkeley, my ultimate destination. I boarded a ferryboat for San Francisco, where I had decided to spend the night. The weather was superb, and the cool sea breeze after the valley heat was exhilarating beyond description. As I stood on the bow of the ferryboat, surveying the beautiful bay and looking over to the Golden Gate, I filled my lungs with refreshing air and said to myself, "I never want to live anywhere else the rest of my life." And I have never really changed my mind.

The city of San Francisco was a sad sight to behold. Rebuilding efforts had not much changed its appearance since the tragic earthquake and fire of April 1906. Downtown, the place was a mass of rubble, with the frames of a few buildings, gutted by fire, standing skeleton-like in its midst, but its natural setting was gorgeous. The remainder of the Bay Area looked calm and peaceful, and from the activity of the ferryboats to and from the historic Ferry Building at the foot of Market Street one could sense the spirit of San Francisco rising from its ashes. It was a sight that mixed grandeur and desolation, activity and destruction, and it conveyed an atmosphere of romance and enchantment that could not escape the imagination of a teenage boy from a little San Joaquin railroad town who had just left his home for the first time.

I stayed overnight in a small, reconstructed San Francisco hotel to freshen up before taking an early ferry for Oakland and then the final trip to the University of California at Berkeley. I had breakfast at a small restaurant across from the Oxford Street entrance to the university. Then I walked through the campus and its beautiful groves of live oaks, and went directly to 2323 College Avenue, home of La Junta

Club, a block from the southern campus entrance. I had been dispatched there on the recommendation of a family friend who was a graduate member of the club. It was a local organization of the fraternity type. I arrived, of course, as a prospective member. There were still two days before registration, and all the members had not yet returned. Those who were there received me warmly and invited me to stay at the club while becoming adjusted, which I was happy to do.

While I was appraising the returning members, they were, of course, appraising me. I remember the first Sunday dinner at which the full membership was present. They were asking me about high school days. Among things I remember telling them were stories of the "cat and mouse" relationship we boys had with our principal.

He had a suspicious and accusative turn of mind, and often charged an entire class with wrongdoing when no more than one or two could have been responsible. The principal would spy on classes by various means, and so far as most of the boys were concerned it became a game of who could outwit whom. He even penalized classes for *suspicion* of cheating. It therefore became fair game, we thought, to cheat on him. And we did. When I had finished telling of my part in this childish and irresponsible behavior, the subject was not pursued. Shortly after dinner, though, one of the seniors, Herbert Whiting, asked me if I would care to have dinner with him in Oakland later that week. I, of course, accepted.

At the dinner, he brought up the matter of what I had said, and in a fatherly way told me that this was not the way things were done at the university. He said the university operated on the honor system; that there was no spying; that students were entrusted with self-government, and that they were expected to be honorable in taking examinations as in all other things. What was of equal importance, he told me that most of the professors graded students on the average of the class, and that if some of the students raised their grades by other than their own industry and ability, they were unethically raising the class average and thus injuring all the others. I was, of course, greatly embarrassed, but I can recall few times in my life when I appreciated advice more than this or when it did more for me. I was deeply touched by the kind manner in which he talked to me, and promised him I would never violate the honor system.

The club, after a few weeks, invited me to become a member, and I was the first freshman initiated. I was fortunate to have landed unwittingly with a group of fellows such as these. They were all good-to-excellent students. The university standards were high, and failure to pass a certain number of units in any semester meant being "flunked out" for the next semester. During the six years of my association with this group, not one member was flunked out, and practically all of them were graduated. None of our fellows was from a wealthy family, and a goodly number of them had worked for a year after leaving high school to acquire the funds for college. Practically all of them held jobs throughout the summer for the same reason. I also labored every summer and Christmas vacation in some department of the Southern Pacific in Bakersfield, and often brought a roommate to our home so he could work too.

Two days after my arrival on the campus, registrations for the university were opened, and I registered in the College of Political Sciences as a foundation for eventually studying law.

I must admit that I was not a serious student. I was more concerned with adequacy than profundity. I was more interested in the university as a community of lively, stimulating people than as a community of scholars. I had no intention of failing, but neither did I have a burning desire for knowledge which my parents' sacrifices for my education should have called for. It was a whole new world for me, a wonderful new world—large, dynamic, enthusiastic, friendly, and with unlimited freedom. Coming from our relatively isolated little railroad town to this vibrant community was a revelation, and moving from a graduating high school class of sixteen seniors to a record college freshman class of over nine hundred from all over the world was almost overwhelming.

I sought no leadership and achieved none in my college career. I was only mildly interested in campus politics. Occasionally I helped a friend who aspired to office, but the thought of running for office myself never crossed my mind, and I never ran either at the university or in my earlier school days. Politics was not then a preoccupation with the students at Berkeley as it has been in recent years. However, we had one municipal election which disturbed the campus as well as the city greatly. There were fights, accusations of buying votes, and all manner of charges against the candidates for mayor. Meetings were disrupted. This was in 1911, a time when there was only one Socialist mayor in the country, and that was in Milwaukee. Berkeley's mayor was a conservative corporation lawyer by the name of Beverly Hodgehead. He represented some of the large public utilities on which the campaign was focused. He was challenged by an avowed Socialist, a Methodist minister named John Stit Wilson, whose son, incidentally, was a student at the university. It was a biting campaign against what is now called "the establishment." The Socialist candidate won and, contrary to dire predictions, the heavens did not fall and tranquility soon returned to the campus and the city. Mayor Wilson was an honest man, a good mayor, and was re-elected at the end of his first term.

There were many indiscretions on the part of students during that

campaign, one of which was breaking up a campaign meeting in the
Berkeley High School auditorium by forcibly taking possession of the
stage and routing the speakers. But it was as much a lark for most of
them as breaking up an opponent's football rally, a common college
practice of that day. There was no deeply embedded bitterness in their
actions such as exists in society today, and the disruptions were soon
forgotten.

We in college at that time were living, as far as we knew, in a relatively serene society wherein there was a job for everyone with any skill.
There were no great causes to attract young people then, no great issues
to divide society, and I do not recall any of my acquaintances who
were profoundly concerned about causes or were preparing to serve any
of them. It was an age of materialism in which students were preparing
for "the good life"—a home, children, affluence, and respectability. We
did things then out of a spirit of mischievousness that today would be
considered revolutionary. Occasionally we stopped traffic on the streets,
put streetcars out of commission for hours, overrode the police by
disproportionate weight of numbers, made loud tumultuous noises until
all hours of the night, and, as I have stated, even broke up political
meetings. But it was done with a carefree attitude, devoid of hatred,
and the community accepted it for what it was—boyish exuberance and
the irresponsibility of youth.

For college students of the Sixties and early Seventies the situation is
quite different. They have hardly known a time when we have not been
in a war, cold or hot, but mostly hot. Some 50,000 young people have
been killed and more than 150,000 wounded in a Southeast Asian
conflict in which most students do not believe we should ever have participated. Millions have had their lives disjointed by the draft or the
threat of the draft. Minority youth has its own problems with what it
considers an oppressive or at best indifferent white society, and has in
some cases been driven to militant rebellion. Young people see so much
crass materialism, so much waste of our natural resources, so much corruption in government and business that it is no wonder they become
disillusioned and embittered. As one escape from their frustration and
boredom, many have succumbed to what became known as the "drug
culture," and have found relief in all sorts of hallucinatory stimulants
and depressants, just as their parents have used alcohol and tran-
quilizers.

I do not condone this. I shudder when I think of it, but I do understand why—in a society where there is so much tension and bitterness
and where adults give so much evidence of social instability—so many
young people fail to conform to patterns of conduct that are prescribed

by their elders. Especially when the elders honor those patterns more in the breach than in the observance.

Dope is not a new phenomenon. In my days in school and college, it was well known. Then it was opium, morphine, and cocaine. Opium was openly smoked by the Chinese, and it could have been available for anyone. I have watched the Chinese prepare and smoke it on many occasions while I was a schoolboy, and in San Francisco tours of the opium joints were openly advertised. Morphine and cocaine were staples of the underworld. I am sure they were not difficult to obtain, but I never heard of a boy or girl in school or college succumbing to any of them. One reason, and I believe a principal reason, is that in those days there was little of the tension of present times, no undergirding bitterness throughout society, no war for young people to die or become crippled in, and instead of frustration there was hope in the hearts and minds of youth.

I do not admire the actions of many youths today, but I do have compassion for them. They are our children, of our breed, and have grown up under our guidance, but in another world and, at that, a world not made by them but by us.

I took no active part in the Berkeley mayoralty campaign which I described earlier, although I was not displeased to see so much reaction against the status quo, which I considered a decadent influence on the life of the state—although there was by no means as much corruption or corporate domination in evidence in Berkeley as I had seen in Bakersfield. On the other hand, there was ample evidence of both evils across the Bay in San Francisco, where the mayor, the Board of Supervisors, and various public officials, utilities executives, and others were under indictment for bribery in matters ranging from prostitution to fraudulent sale of public utilities franchises. The prosecutions under these indictments were a prelude to the dynamic 1910 campaign of Hiram W. Johnson for governor of California. In that campaign he promised to, and after his election did, put an end to Southern Pacific domination of the political life of our state.

In all of this I was interested, and on municipal election night in San Francisco, together with a couple of hundred other college students, I went to that city as a watcher at the polling booths in the interest of the reform mayor and the district attorney. The latter was carrying on the graft prosecutions with Francis J. Heney as special prosecutor and Hiram Johnson as his assistant. I was assigned to a waterfront precinct south of Market Street, or "South of the Slot" as the district was colloquially called, and my job was to detect fraudulent counting. It was a rough district, and the tent used as a polling place was crowded most of the night with tough-looking characters. I had difficulty getting close enough to the table to see what was actually going on. No wrongdoing was visible to me, but throughout the night I wondered what I could have done in those intimidating surroundings even if I had seen any skulduggery.

The reform ticket won. The prosecutions dragged on until the people of San Francisco became tired of reform, and the entire movement ended in complete failure except for the conviction of Abe Ruef, the political boss and chief collector of graft. I always doubted whether even he would have been convicted had a man not shot prosecutor Heney in the courtroom during the trial, leaving his assistant, Johnson, to carry on to the end. Heney survived, and the incident had one good result. It catapulted Hiram Johnson to the forefront in a manner which resulted in his election as governor of California. There ensued an administration of reform measures never equaled in California or probably in any other state before or since.

My first three years at the university were not terribly eventful. My scholarship was fair but in no sense outstanding. I made good marks in history, political science, and English, but in the other subjects they were only passable. I never failed in any course but did receive two conditional grades—one in Greek and the other in trigonometry.

Following a mixup in my sophomore year, I was told by a counselor that I must pass a trigonometry course if I wanted to graduate on time. I was really shocked; another adviser had told me the course was not required and I had dropped it. I went directly home to the club and enlisted some friendly seniors in the engineering and science courses to help prepare me for the examination. They coached me in relays. With only about ten days left to cram, I worked incessantly night and day to the exclusion of everything else, and then went to the examination. I greatly feared that I had failed, but was given a conditional mark, a "four," which entitled me to take a re-examination. During the summer months I crammed some more, and took an oral examination before a beloved professor who had graduated with the first class of the University of California, Colonel George Edwards.

He examined me at some length, and then said, "Warren, what college are you in?"

"Social Science," I said, and he replied, "Well, then I guess you know enough trigonometry for all practical purposes," and gave me a passing mark.

It was a traumatic experience which left a mark of some kind of my memory, because to this day when I have an abnormal amount of unfinished business confronting me I occasionally take that examination over again in my sleep in a nightmarish way.

I played clarinet in the university band to satisfy my military requirements, and in my junior year marched directly behind Robert Gordon Sproul, Class of '13, who came to the band as a drum major. Bob later became president of the university. He held that position during the years of its growth into the huge multiple-campus university it now is, and was president far longer than any other man in its history to date. He was still serving in that capacity throughout my years as governor of California, and we had a very happy association. As president of the university and president of the Board of Regents, respectively, he and I had splendid relations with both the school and the public, although we did have some disturbing problems on the Board of Regents, such as the loyalty oath for the faculty, about which I shall have more to say later.

I occasionally played clarinet commercially for dances, but was not particularly enamored of dancing myself. It didn't seem to fit my way of life in college. I spent my spare time with the men of the university. Much time was wasted playing cards at La Junta Club with anyone who was so inclined, and occasionally we also played at Gus Brause's, a gathering place for students who liked companionship and beer. There was a state law against the sale of alcoholic beverages within one mile of the university, and the Brause establishment was well over a mile from it. We whiled away many an evening and occasionally an afternoon there eating, playing cards, and reading with a stein of beer in front of us. It was not a ribald place. No loud noise was permitted, and patrons usually were quiet and respectful of the old German family who operated it. We drank nothing but beer to wash down the wholesome beef and cheese sandwiches Mother Brause made for us. It was good, clean companionship, and I do not know of anyone who was hurt by it. It also worked out profitably for me, for when the old gentleman passed away, the widow and her two sons, Herman and Fritz, employed me to probate his sizable estate. This was shortly after I finished Law School. I was very grateful for their confidence, as they chose me over many budding lawyers who had spent time and money in Gus Brause's. It was on a corner diagonal to old Idora Park, the recreational center for Oakland and Berkeley in those days.

We also had another host in downtown Oakland by the name of Pop Kessler. His Rathskeller was quite a rendezvous for university students. He was a fatherly old man, and looked after us as he would his own sons. I belonged to an organization which met there once a week for dinner and to read poetry over a few steins of beer. The group will go unnamed because it has never been recorded as a university organization and does not appear in the yearbook, the *Blue and Gold*. On the other hand, it is in no sense an underground organization. It has no initiation, no ritual, no dues, no ideology—nothing but a fellowship which has lasted for seventy years. The organization still exists, and I have a son and grandson who have passed that way. Once a year at Big Game time (before the Stanford-California football game) alumni members gather with students in San Francisco and read Rudyard Kipling, Robert Service, Gelett Burgess, Bret Harte, and miscellaneous poems of other writers which have appealed to the members through the years and have been collected in a private printing. There were but two rules of conduct for the organization: no dirty stories and no arm waving. Some lifelong friendships for me were either formed or strengthened there.

I also belonged to Skull and Keys, an interfraternity organization which has been in existence for most of the life of the university. I suppose it too would be called a beer-drinking society because we had a keg of beer at each of our meetings. While I was there, we built a replica of an Egyptian tomb in which we met, read books, kept alive some college projects, and rehearsed for an annual play produced for our friends. Skull and Keys had a literary background, and Frank Norris, author of *The Octopus* and other muckraking books famous in their time, was one of its founders.

All of this may sound as though beer was a major factor in my college life, though in reality it was not. None of these fellowships was dissolute in any sense, but I must confess to having had a great liking for the companionship of students who liked to eat together, read together, and visit over a glass or two.

I was a pretty fair extracurricular reader. At that time, I was fond of Kipling, Stevenson, Dickens, Frank Norris, Upton Sinclair, and Jack London, the last three all being California authors. We knew Jack London. In the winter, some of us occasionally went to the Oakland-Alameda estuary to climb over and romance about the old Alaska packer fleet of clipper ships that fished for salmon in Alaskan waters during the summer and docked on the Alameda side of the estuary during the winter months. Across the estuary from where they were moored was a little saloon named The First and Last Chance. It was a hangout for sailors, and Jack London frequented it. We would go there, buy a glass of beer, and listen to him and the others talk about their experiences, real and imagined, in the frozen North and in the South Seas. It whetted our imagination and made Jack London's books the more exciting. Occasionally, we also went to the San Francisco waterfront. It, too, was charged with romance and adventure, but when we went there we were always in a solid group. In those days a lone stranger along the waterfront might well be sandbagged and later find himself aboard a tramp schooner on its way out the Golden Gate, "shanghaied" to fill out the crew, a common practice of that time.

I was very happy in my associations with my club brothers. They were both congenial and helpful to one another. In my junior year, we applied to Sigma Phi Society, one of the old New England college fraternities, for a charter. Sigma Phi was very conservative in the establishment of additional chapters, having only nine at that time. The prospects were not too favorable, but we encountered a number of eastern alumni brothers who resided in California and they became interested in our application. Through their efforts we were granted a chapter the following year. It became a happy association, and our chapter has done well since that time.

I was enamored of fraternity life, and still believe fraternities were very important in the life of the university in those years. Berkeley was a small city of about ten thousand people, with more than three thousand students, and the vast majority of the students came from other parts of the state. There were no dormitories, and the boardinghouses were few in number and not of a high order. Fraternities and sororities were, therefore, the closest things to a home available to the students. Generally speaking, they were not pretentious or expensive, and my own moderate budget met all of the requirements of my house. They were also good instruments through which to experiment with self-government, as they ran without university supervision. Since that time, the city has grown, private accommodations have multiplied, and the University of California, like most others, has seen the feasibility of building large dormitories. The need for "frat houses" for students has accordingly lessened. Fraternity life has encountered problems that apparently have diminished their public acceptance, but I have been so long away from any meaningful observation of them that I am hardly in a position to appraise either their present usefulness or their future.

In my senior year, I entered the University of California Law School in the first class to attend all three years in a new building called Boalt Hall. The building has become by usage, if not officially, the name of the Law School; thus graduates and students alike now say they studied law "at Boalt Hall."

My first contact with the Law School was something of a shock to me. The required courses were contracts, torts, property, criminal law and common law pleading. There was no general indoctrination of any kind. On the contrary, we worked entirely from casebooks. Only a few years prior to this time, the Harvard Law School had adopted the casebook system, and it was copied so closely at Boalt Hall that we were expected to derive our legal training solely from the cases in our casebooks.

This did not appear to me to be a practical approach to becoming a lawyer, and in order to obtain some better orientation, I sought and obtained an opportunity to spend a few hours a day in a Berkeley law office where I served papers and did anything of a nontechnical character that was asked of me. I would take my casebooks with me and read them when there was nothing in the office to occupy my time.*

My grades were not outstanding in the last two years at Boalt, but they were reasonably good, and I was graduated in routine fashion.

My father would have liked me to practice in Bakersfield. However, I could not bring myself to do so. The idea of returning there after living in the San Francisco Bay area for six years seemed to me like giving up my freedom. Then there were the long, hot Bakersfield summers which I did not like; I simply could not picture myself sweltering in a law office in that heat the rest of my life. One mildly tempting alternative was to go to Sacramento, the state capital, which appeared to me to hold out great opportunities for a young lawyer. But when I thought of trying to explain to my father that I would shun Bakersfield because of the hot summers and would settle in almost equally torrid Sacramento, I quickly abandoned that thought and decided to remain in the Bay area.

A week or so after graduation, we were admitted to practice by the District Court of Appeals in San Francisco on motion of a member of our faculty. At that time, graduates of the law schools of the University of California, Hastings, and the University of Southern California were admitted without examination. That has all been changed since, and today everyone must take a comprehensive bar examination that lasts several days. It wasn't much of an advantage at that time to be admitted on motion because the examination given was of no great significance. There was no prerequisite of a law school education in order to take it. Examinations were conducted by the District Courts of Appeal, and a crowded courtroom of applicants would all be tested in a couple of hours. There was an old story then current at law schools to the effect that the Court would ask two questions of each applicant, and if he answered either one of them correctly, he would be admitted. If the applicant gave an answer wide of the mark to the first question, the justice would say, "I am sorry, your answer is wrong. Now for your second question: What is the doctrine of Cy Pres?" (It is a rule of chartable succession in estates.) If the applicant replied, "I don't know," the justice would announce, "That is correct, you don't; and you have passed the examination."

* Ed. note: Warren does not mention that working in a law office while going to school was a violation of Boalt Hall's rules governing student behavior. He felt so strongly about the need to gain practical as well as theoretical experience that he considered it a calculated risk.

This all came back to me forcibly many years later after World War II when I was governor. During the War, many graduates of our law schools, before being admitted to practice, went into the armed forces and were not discharged for two, three, or even four years. When they returned, they found themselves confronted with the necessity of taking a grueling bar examination which was given only twice a year, in April and September. The grades were not announced until three months later. This delayed the veterans from being admitted for a year or more after their return to civilian life. They came to the Legislature, and, with my hearty approval, had a bill introduced to permit them to be admitted to practice on motion. The State Bar, jealous of its prerogatives, fought this bill zealously, and when it was on my desk after passage sent a delegation to urge me to veto it. It argued that the high standards of the bar must be preserved by requiring everyone to take its examination. They made the mistake of sending some prominent lawyers of my vintage to urge their point. Most of them, like myself, had been admitted on motion, so when they finished I asked them but two questions. First, "How were you admitted?" When they replied it had been on motion, I recalled to them that I, too, had been admitted in that way. I then asked them if they thought our admission in that manner had degraded the bar. They were, of course, indignantly speechless, so I signed the bill and took them across Capitol Park to the Sutter Club where we had lunch and thus relieved the tension.

But to return to my youthful legal career: I wanted to be in a small office where I could see everything that happened, so I accepted a position with the Law Department of the Associated Oil Company. In the department were only the counsel, Mr. Edmund Tauske, a secretary, and myself. I had hopes of leading a dynamic life in a situation of that kind, but I was soon disillusioned. Mr. Tauske was an irascible old man. The only day he was ever cordial with me was the day I was employed. Thereafter, everything was peremptory. I do not remember him ever addressing me by name. It was "Do this," "Do that," and "That can't be the law!" This last was barked when I had researched some question; then in a few days he would issue a written opinion to a company officer using my authorities exactly as I had presented them. But the thing I resented most was that whenever he had a conference with others in his office and was out of cigars, he would press the buzzer for me and on my entry would hand me some money saying, "Go downstairs to the cigar store and get me a half dozen Coronas." I often felt like saying, "Go get them yourself," but restrained myself. I would have quit in short order had I not used as references for the position the names of friends whom I did not want to let down.

I stuck with the job without rebelling for one year. Then I said to him, "Mr. Tauske, I am leaving at the end of the month." He seemed shocked and asked if I had another job, and when I said, "No," he asked if I didn't know that there were many young lawyers looking for work. When I said, "Yes," he insisted on knowing why I was leaving. I told him it was because I was not happy there; that there was no human dignity recognized in the office, and that I wanted to make another start in more congenial surroundings. He seemed hurt by my frank statement, and said, "I have had probably fifty young men work for me, and none of them ever expressed such dissatisfaction." I was bold enough to tell him that if he had treated them differently perhaps he would have needed only one instead of the fifty. When the end of the month arrived, he had made no move to hire a new man, and I again informed him that I must leave, and if he could not find a replacement, I would be glad to help him. He agreed, and when I found another young lawyer for him, I left.

A short while before leaving, I was sent to obtain an order from the chief justice of the California Supreme Court. When his secretary opened the door into his office, he rose from his chair and walked halfway across the room to meet me. He said, "Mr. Warren, I am happy to see you. What can I do for you?" I explained my mission, and he signed the order. After a few pleasant words with him, I took my leave, buoyed up because of the courtesy shown me by the highest judicial officer of the state. It made a lasting impression on me, and I said to myself that when I had an office of my own I would treat every visitor in that courteous manner. As a result, I have tried to do exactly that for the past fifty-five years. Hopefully, it has relieved tension in thousands of instances. I take particular pleasure in doing it with young people, as I have often thought it might give them a lift as it did me on that occasion.

This lesson came to me the more forcibly because my morale was extremely low on account of working conditions both at the office and at the San Francisco courthouse where I went almost daily on some minor mission. The old courthouse was still rubble from the earthquake, and the courts, with their officers, had moved into a building on Market Street which in later years became the Whitcomb Hotel (later the P.S.A.-San Franciscan). Most of the judges and their attachés were holdovers from the Southern Pacific and Abe Ruef days. Their actions reflected the low grade of politics from which they sprang, and the atmosphere surrounding them was anything but inspiring.

In leaving my position, I had no idea what I would do next. Within a few days I was told that the firm of Robinson and Robinson in Oakland was looking for a young man, and that I might get located there. I applied, was accepted, and started all over. I kept the court calendar for the entire office, was the leg man to the courthouse on minor matters, and researched cases for the senior member of the firm, Edward C. Robinson, a kindly old gentleman who later became a respected judge of the Superior Court. I found it a pleasure to go to the Oakland courthouse. The judges were courteous and hard-working, and the attachés in the County Clerk's Office were helpful to everyone. The atmosphere was strikingly different from that I had previously experienced in San Francisco. It was easy to become acquainted, particularly with young lawyers with whom I was daily thrown into contact. We developed a fine camaraderie, and because the bar association was moribund at the time, we soon formed what we called "The Young Lawyers' Club of Alameda County." There were in the neighborhood of seventy-five to a hundred members. Because I had been active in forming it, I was selected as its presiding officer. I do not recall whether the title for the position was "president" or "chairman," but it doesn't matter because it carried no powers with it, the only responsibilities being to arrange for a biweekly dinner meeting and supply a speaker. It was not a professional organization in the sense that we were concerned with the manner in which justice was being administered. It was not ideological, either. It was strictly social, its meetings enlivened by talks by various persons in the legal or political world. However, since there had not been a general business meeting of the bar association for six or seven years (its affairs having been carried on by a venerable president and an executive committee of about seven apathetic members), we decided that there should be a revival of bar activity. Accordingly we submitted a petition signed by every member of the Young Lawyers' Club requesting a general meeting of the dormant association for the purpose of electing officers and reactivating its affairs. This brought forth a spirited session. We young lawyers made several requests:

(1) That there be an annual meeting for the election of officers;

(2) That there be standing committees to study problems of the bench and bar;

(3) That there be occasional meetings for the general discussion of such matters;

(4) That the rules provide for a vice-president to function in the absence of the president.

After much discussion, these suggestions were agreed to, and, much to my surprise and embarrassment, I was elected vice president at the suggestion of the younger members. Election came only as a recognition of our group. It was not preplanned. But there I was, a lawyer less than three years out of Law School, working for a clerk's salary, and yet vice-president of the third largest bar association in California.

This was only shortly before World War I started, so my activity did not last very long. We did have a few meetings before I entered the service, one of which was a joint dinner meeting of the County Medical and Bar associations, which continued as an annual event for years. We euphemistically dubbed it a meeting of the sawbones and the jawbones.

During my two years with the firm of Robinson and Robinson, although in a subordinate and not particularly important position, I managed to supplement my meager salary by coaching a group of men for the bar examination. I was obliged to leave for the Army before they were ready to apply, but one passed the exams and later became a judge.

After I had been working for the firm a year and a half, I decided it was time to build a practice for myself. Accordingly, I joined forces with two other young lawyers who had been classmates of mine at the university, and we approached Peter J. Crosby, an older gentleman who was established in the county as a trial lawyer. He was agreeable to the idea of forming a partnership in which he would get a lion's share of the joint earnings and we would benefit from his prestige and experience. We were searching for office space when along came April 17, 1917, and America's declaration of war with Germany. Immediately my employment situation took on a different aspect.

I applied for admission to the First Officers Training Camp and prepared to enter the service. There were thousands of applications for that camp, and only five or six hundred admitted. I was not admitted, and later missed a second call for recruits at the camp when I was hospitalized for a hemorrhoid operation and then developed ether pneumonia that kept me in bed for three weeks.

By the time I left the hospital, enlistments had closed, and they were notifying the first draftees to report for service. I was not among the group, but I waived my right to rely on a lower classification number and requested to go. I was put in charge of the first ten per cent of draftees who left Oakland on September 5, 1917, for Camp Lewis, Washington, which had officially opened only the day before. We were told that we would be outfitted immediately at camp and were not to take any clothes except those we were wearing at the time. When we arrived at camp, there were no army clothes for us, and we lived almost in squalor for weeks until some new issues arrived. We were little better off as far as bed clothing was concerned, with only a light canvas tick, which we filled with straw, and two thin blankets. We were immediately started on close order drill and long marches around American

Lake four miles away, and through the forests which surrounded it. For guns to drill with, we had wooden objects fashioned after the general outlines of a gun. We dug trenches in which to simulate trench warfare, and improvised in many other ways to give the impression of being soldiers.

In these circumstances, the officers found it difficult to sustain morale. We were not permitted outside camp because of our disheveled appearance while wearing the clothes we arrived in. I remember one Saturday afternoon when our officers, all of whom had recently graduated from the First Officers Training Camp at San Francisco, conceived the idea of having a track meet in which all of us were to participate. So short were we of military supplies, there was no pistol available with which to start the races. Finally one of the recruits from south of Market Street in San Francisco produced one he had clandestinely brought with him on the train. With that, the track meet, somewhat delayed, proceeded as planned. No world records were broken.

Camp Lewis was the training ground for the 91st Division, which was recruited from the western states. Our group was assigned to Company I of the 363rd Infantry. Our captain was Frank Sever of Portland, Oregon. He was a thorough gentleman and good officer with some years of experience in the Oregon National Guard. When the company was organized, he made me his first sergeant, a job I was not ready for because I had received no actual military training even at the University of California, where two years of ROTC training was required. As I noted earlier, I escaped this by playing clarinet in the band, which was a part of the military establishment. As first sergeant, I was in charge of the administration of the company. I supervised the barracks, the mess, the supplies, and the equipment. It was a good experience because we started from scratch in everything, and because of the scarcity of most items, we were required to use considerable ingenuity in making ends meet. I did everything except soldier, as my time was spent in the orderly room while the others were drilling and receiving instruction.

Most of the time I was with the company we were under quarantine, first because we had no respectable clothing and then because of epidemics of spinal meningitis and measles. We had no meningitis in my company, but others in the regiment did, and the entire regiment was confined. We had plenty of measles. We were quarantined for them over both Thanksgiving and Christmas, while other companies were free to come and go. The regulation was that in order to be released nobody could have a new case for five consecutive days. The entire company was determined to get out for New Year's. A couple of days beforehand, two men came to me and volunteered for the "light duty" detail which would take them out into the woods and relieve them from inspection. I noticed a few telltale blotches on their foreheads, but since I was no doctor, I assigned them to that duty. We thus passed inspection with flying colors, and, to resounding cheers, were relieved from quarantine. This enabled most of our frustrated outfit to go to Tacoma or Seattle for New Year's Eve.

In January 1918, a Third Officers Training Camp was held at Camp Lewis. We were all offered an opportunity to apply, but I did not do so. The captain inquired why, and I told him it was because of my two previous experiences. He thought I should not miss the opportunity, recommended me, and I was accepted.

It was quite an ordeal for me, as I was not trained in close order drilling nor had my work in the orderly room toughened me as the outdoor exercise had most of the others.

Our companies were of one hundred men. They were thinned out by thirty-five to forty per cent during the first two and a half months of the school by the actions of what we called "benzine boards." When a cadet was "benzined," it meant that a board of officers had found he did not have the qualifications for an officer. The last week of the school, I was called to company headquarters and asked by the ranking captain if I would be willing to sit with the three captains of our company in grading remaining candidates. I demurred because I did not want to be the means of anyone failing. He promptly assured me that everyone then in the company was to graduate. He said that some of the men undoubtedly had attributes that were not readily evident to the captains, and it was this that they were interested in, not the deficiencies of any of the men. I replied that I would be willing to do this, and he then asked me to select one cadet from each of the other two squad rooms. This I did, and the three of us sat with the captains for about three days. We all were graduated and were to become officers. This was the first school in which all the cadets were certified as second lieutenants. In the others, they had been rated from second lieutenants to majors.

We were then returned to our original outfits to await travel orders. In a few weeks, we were transported across the continent by train in record time without making a stop in any large community. From the secrecy maintained, we thought we were destined for France. However, we landed in Petersburg, Virginia, and were assigned to Camp Lee, a few miles distant, to train troops as replacements overseas. There we remained throughout a miserably hot, humid summer. On several occasions when we marched troops from our company area to the rifle range for target practice we had so many heat prostrations by ten o'clock in the morning that it was necessary to break ranks and leave the men under shade trees until nine at night before marching them back to camp.

The camp was filled with second lieutenants out of the Third Officers Training Camps from various parts of the country. In every company there was a lieutenant for each squad of eight men. Each squad had its own little parcel of possibly 75×250 feet of land for close order drill, and was required to remain within that area in all its formations. I was put in charge of the orderly room, and acted very much like a first sergeant in managing the affairs of the company. Each company was given a new quota of men every month, and in thirty days was expected to prepare them for overseas duty as replacements in combat outfits. The thirty days went by so fast that it was impossible to do more than scratch the surface, particularly when they spent only the last week on the rifle range. Great numbers of these boys had never fired a gun and, when they arrived, were without military training of any kind. Our own company had many from the backwoods of West Virginia and other parts of what is now called Appalachia. Much of their third week in camp was taken up with supplying them with clothing and equipment for overseas duty. Regulations required that each soldier must have the exact number of each item before leaving Camp Lee, so each day they were asked to report what they possessed. When some of them stood around without filling out their cards and were ordered to do so, the usual reply was, "Ah cain't write, suh." Actually, there were much more than two weeks for training them to march, drill, and handle their weapons. Then we would put them on trucks and send them on their way for embarkation to France. To say that they were unprepared for combat service would be a gross understatement; within a month after their arrival in France the names of some of them would appear on the casualty lists.

This procedure was repeated month after month. It was a hard grind for the young officers, and we seldom left camp. On occasion, we would explore the old Civil War breastworks surrounding Petersburg, and dig out lead bullets that had lodged in them during the historic siege of that city by General Grant. We also went to Richmond, a few miles distant, on two or three Sundays. Our first visit there was on Memorial Day, and I remember how shocked we from Camp Lewis were because the city was bedecked with Confederate flags. They were everywhere, and not an American flag was to be seen. Most of the time it was a humdrum life for us. In the late summer, in addition to my regular duties, I attended a camp bayonet school two hours a day for six weeks. It was a rigorous course, and only one other lieutenant and I out of a class of more than fifty lost no time because of injury.

The most hair-raising month I had at Camp Lee came in September when we were hit by influenza. It took the lives of more Americans in military and civilian life than World Wars I and II combined. Over half a million died, and our camp certainly had its share of casualties. I remember when the officers of our regiment were assembled and told that Spanish influenza had come into our country at Newport News, our nearest port of entry, and that we could expect to have incidences of it at Camp Lee. We were told what the symptoms were, and what little was known about its prevention and cure. Before long it hit our camp with a fury. I believe we were almost the first cantonment in the country to be ravaged by the disease. It swept through company after company like wildfire, and the base hospital was soon bursting with thousands of patients. We were told that no one could be sent there unless the regimental doctor authorized the case as desperate. Our regiment was hit very hard, but strangely my company did not have a single case, although our barracks were close to the others and we shared the same parade ground for drill. After about two weeks, the divisional medical officers took notice of this phenomenon, studied the situation, and decided to make ours a model company. Our beds were spread out with a given distance between each. Our barracks windows were all opened, and the buildings thoroughly aired. Bedding was hung on clotheslines every morning, and other minor things thought to be hygienic were done. The doctors were no sooner well launched on this program than five cases developed in our company; then twenty-five the next day and fifty the next until we had more than a hundred and fifty cases. The overworked regimental medical officer would come once and sometimes twice a day to look at them, and when he ordered one to the base hospital we came to know that in all probability it was the last time we would ever see our comrade. The rest of the time the non-commissioned officers and I did what little could be done to make them comfortable. There were no nurses available, and our ministrations were of doubtful value except for letting victims know that somebody cared and that they were not abandoned. Nobody died in the barracks, but of those taken to the base hospital twelve succumbed. Noncommissioned officers were sent with the body to the home of the deceased and at one time most of my noncoms were away on such sad missions. Finally, the pestilence departed as unceremoniously as it had arrived.

About this time I was promoted to first lieutenant and received travel orders to Camp McArthur at Waco, Texas, for service as a bayonet instructor in the Central Officers Training Camp. I arrived on November 9, and two days later the Armistice was signed and the War was over. We spent a few weeks with little to do, the first relaxation I had experienced since my induction into the Army. It afforded me an opportunity to think of my future.

I was determined not to return to a subordinate position with a law firm. I wanted my own office, if possible, but two of my previously contemplated partners were dispersed somewhere in the Armed Forces, and I had no idea when they would return or how conditions might have changed in Oakland. So our earlier plans did not seem feasible, although I would have been happy to be associated with them. They were all good men and all ultimately became Superior Court judges of Alameda County—Peter Crosby and Chris Fox by election and Thomas Ledwich by my appointment about thirty years later.

I was discharged on December 9 and soon boarded a train for California. I went first to Bakersfield for a visit with my parents. My sister, Ethel, was married at that time and living in Oakland. It was a happy home-coming. Especially joyous was the chance to see my gentle mother, whose first letter to me in the Army had remained with me throughout my service days. In it she had written: "Earl, I cannot tell you how badly I feel about the necessity of your being in the Army, but I would feel worse had you been unwilling to be there."

After a few days at home, I went to Oakland and my sister's home. A few days after Christmas I met Leon E. Gray, a former associate of mine at the Robinson firm. He inquired what I intended to do, and I told him I was in a state of flux and had no idea at the moment. He informed me that he had recently been elected to the California State Legislature; that each assemblyman had the right to appoint one attaché at five dollars per day, and that he had not yet exercised that privilege. He thought it would be a good place for me to become readjusted and decide what I wanted to do. I asked him when he was going to Sacramento, and he replied, "Tomorrow." I thanked him, and said I would be happy to go with him.

Shortly after arriving in Sacramento, we met Charles Kasch, a contemporary fraternity brother of mine, who also had recently been elected to the Assembly from Mendocino County in the northern part of the state. He, too, had no one in mind for his attaché, and suggested that he and Gray join forces and obtain a better job for me. Gray agreed. They arranged for me to become clerk of the Judiciary Committee of the Assembly at six dollars a day. No better job could have been found for me, and I was delighted. The Legislature convened the next day, and I immediately went on the payroll, little realizing that I would from that moment, be in public service without a break until my retirement fifty years later as Chief Justice of the United States.

IV

A GREAT RESPONSIBILITY : *Years as a Deputy D.A.*

The California Legislature met in Sacramento for its biennial session on the first Monday in January 1919. After the opening ceremony, I met an older lawyer friend who had at one time been an assemblyman. I asked him what he thought of my being clerk of the Judiciary Committee.

He thought for a moment and inquired, "How old are you now, Earl?"

"Twenty-seven," I replied.

"I guess it is all right," he said. "You are probably old enough now to be disillusioned as to man-made law."

In succeeding years, I thought about this advice or admonition, whichever was intended, hundreds of times as I observed the process of legislation, the tricks of the trade, the lobbying, and what seemed to be downright corruption by some. I also saw the dedication of many to the best interests of the state.

More bills were assigned to the Judiciary Committee than to any other, and it was not long until I thought I could categorize the members as independent and forthright or as lobby-ridden or corrupt.

I was the first veteran of World War I to be employed at that session, and was still in uniform. I had found when I returned to my sister's home in Oakland that I had broadened out to such an extent that it was impossible for me to wear my prewar clothes. We had been discharged from the Army with only sixty dollars separation pay, and, being short on cash, I decided to wear my Army uniforms until I had received a few paychecks. Everybody was extremely kind to me, and I greatly enjoyed the work of the committee.

The session started off with a bang. In California, we have what is known as a bifurcated session. The first part of it is limited to thirty days, during which bills are introduced, but none except an emergency bill is considered for passage. Then there is a recess of thirty days for the people at home to make known their desires concerning the proposed legislation.

When the Legislature reconvenes for a period not to exceed 120 days, the process of reviewing a bill continues through the committees and then to the floor for final action. Rarely is any action taken at the first session, but on the very first day of this meeting resolutions to ratify the proposed Eighteenth Amendment to the United States Constitution (the liquor prohibition amendment) were introduced. They were immediately referred to committee and, with practically no serious consideration given to anything but the popular clamor engendered by the prohibitionist activities of Bishop James Cannon, Jr., and his Anti-Saloon League, they were favorably recommended and given final passage on January 1. Members who were heavy drinkers voted "Aye" vociferously for the public attention their vote would be given, but I am sure without any intention of abiding by the measure personally, as several celebrated their noble action with even more liquor than usual for the remainder of the session. This was in keeping with the hysteria that spread over the nation and caused thirty-two state legislatures to take similar action during the month of January in order to be among those states responsible for prohibition's ratification. Three days later, the thirty-sixth state of the then forty-eight ratified, and the Secretary of State announced that the Eighteenth Amendment was a part of the Constitution of the United States.

Thus we achieved prohibition, but in no sense temperance. The old open saloon went out of existence and was replaced by a hydra-headed industry of rumrunning, bootlegging, hijacking, racketeering, gangsterism, corruption of public officials, and a scofflaw attitude on the part of the general public from which we have not entirely disengaged ourselves even now.

Fourteen years later, the California Legislature, with a like burst of enthusiasm, many of the same members voting, ratified the Twenty-first Amendment which repealed the Eighteenth. It, too, fell far short of its declared purpose. The argument went that nobody wanted to bring the saloon back, that it would be forever prohibited, but that the new Amendment would simply permit people to have liquor with their meals and in their homes for social purposes without violating the law. Now, however, the liquor industry is a great organized political power, more potent than it ever was in preprohibition days. It is true that the racketeers and gangsters have turned their hands largely to narcotics, loan-sharking, stolen securities, and the infiltration of legitimate business, but the saloon has returned in virulent form, and it is often cynically said that in some states, including my own, that liquor can be bought at almost any place except the post office.

One of the great problems of our time is that of alcoholism. We are said to have millions—anywhere from six to nine—of confirmed alcoholics in the United States, with the number growing, and relatively little is being done to rehabilitate them.

When the Legislature opened in 1919, our delegation from Alameda County, of which Oakland was the county seat, included four senators and eight assemblymen. Almost the entire group, and I with them, lived at the little Sequoia Hotel on K Street, a block and a half from Capitol Park. I had only casually known three or four of them beforehand, but we all became very friendly, and they manifested an interest in my future.

I still wanted to become a trial lawyer, and, although I was nervous about speaking up in open court, I forced myself to take every opportunity to overcome it. I told them of my ambition, and Assemblyman Frank Anderson of Alameda County, with whom I formed a very warm friendship, suggested that I go into the District Attorney's Office in our county. I told him I would be delighted to do so. He conferred with the other members of the delegation, and they said they thought it could be arranged.

It happened that Ezra Decoto, our then district attorney, came to Sacramento to ask the Legislature for an additional deputy. The delegation seized upon that and told him they would be happy to create the position if he would appoint me to fill it. He told them that would be difficult for him to do because he had long before promised the next position in his office to Charles Wade Snook, the son of a former district attorney of the county. They insisted, however, that if the job was to be created, I should have it.

When I heard of this, I sought Mr. Decoto out and told him that while I would very much like to be in his office, I would not accept the position if he were under such duress. He thanked me and said he had known of me through the younger men in his office and would be happy to have me on his staff as future vacancies might occur. My friends thought I was foolish to rely on such an indefinite promise when they could have forced my appointment through at that time. It was very fortunate for me that I did wait, because, as will develop later, I entered his office in a comparatively short time, eventually became his principal assistant, and, with his blessing, succeeded him as district attorney. Snook remained with me for some years as one of my principal assistants, and many years later, as governor, I appointed both Decoto and Snook to fill vacancies on the Superior Court of Alameda County.

The legislative session was not inspirational, but it was very informative and, in some respects, exciting for me. I worked diligently and learned much about the legislative process and its relationship to the other branches of government, about the individual conduct of many legislators, and about the lobbying system in both its enlightening and its more sinister forms. By and large, I would say I learned more things to avoid than to follow. The session could not be called a part of the reform movement of Hiram Johnson. He had departed two years earlier for Washington as a United States senator, and the ardor for reform had departed with him. His successor, William Stevens, a former Los Angeles congressman, had been appointed by Johnson in 1916 to fill the vacancy created by the death of Lieutenant Governor John Eshelman, a dedicated reformer. When Johnson was elected to the Senate, Stevens succeeded to the governorship, and was elected to a full term in 1918. He was a wholesome man, but not an activist, and some of the dubious practices of pre-Johnson days were in evidence. Logrolling and lobbying were not centralized in one dominant organization like that of the Southern Pacific, but there was a triumvirate consisting of Sheriff Tom Finn of San Francisco, Mike Kelly of Oakland, the "leader" or "boss" of Alameda County, depending on whom you talked to, and Kent Parrott of Los Angeles, a politician of somewhat ominous reputation, to fill the vacuum.

Noticeable obeisance was shown them, especially by the delegations of these three largest counties of the state, which were the dominant force in the Legislature. Lobbyists on important bills were obligated to work through them, and there was a general atmosphere of awe surrounding them. Lobbyists were in profusion. Some peddled influence, some entertainment, and some undoubtedly money. Of course, there were others who came to explain bills and argue them before committees in the best tradition of honest advocacy. When a gullible lobbyist came with money for entertainment, he found many legislators ready to push him into giving parties that influenced nobody, until he was out of cash. All the big interests were represented, and they often operated in mysterious ways.

There were some legislators who were regarded as "boodlers," and who, according to a swaggering lobbyist years later, could be bought with "a steak, a potato, or a girl." Some of them would not rely entirely on lobbyists for supplementary benefits. They set up their own system through what were called "cinch bills." They would learn of the vulnerability of a certain business or profession because of public prejudice against it or because of its being on the borderline of illegality in its objectives or practices. They would then introduce a bill to outlaw or seriously handicap that business or profession in the future. There would be no serious intention to press the bill for final passage; merely an effort to make the object of the bill pay for its defeat. The next step in the procedure would be for the sponsor of the bill to let the victim of the shakedown know that he had no time to discuss the merits of the bill, but that he was relying on a Mr. X in determining how the bill should move. The implication was that if the bill were to be stopped, Mr. X must be satisfied. If the intended victim was gullible or if his operations were so sensitive that publicity would greatly hurt them, he would then contact Mr. X. The latter would state that he had almost enough votes to pass the bill and would demonstrate in devious ways the friendship existing between himself and certain other legislators. Eventually he would let it be known that for a given amount of money he would be able to kill the bill. If the payoff was made, the disposition of the money would never be known, but the bill would, of course, die quietly on file. If the victim did not pay off, it would die anyway because it was generally understood which of the bills were "cinch bills," and the authors could gather no basic support for them. Many of these bills were perennials, and would be introduced year after year, either by the same author or by shuffling them around among the small group of established boodlers. Some time after the 1919 session, the speaker of the Assembly, deploring this practice, told me he could identify as many as seventy cinch bills in that session. Observing the proceedings of the Legislature, as I was able to do for many years thereafter, I believed I could identify many of them, not seventy, but enough to convince me that there was a coterie of legislators who made their living through that practice. Members at that time received a compensation of only ten dollars per day throughout the session. I still have in mind many cinch bills and their authors, but, with one exception, I will not name them because this is not an accusatory document, and besides, some of those who followed that practice may have come to appreciate the error of their ways and changed their pattern of operations for the better.

The exception I make stems from an experience I had as district attorney, and the facts were fully reported in the press.

My chair as district attorney in 1925 was not yet warm when one of the San Francisco newspapers informed me that there was a "cinch bill" shakedown at Sacramento, that the payoff was to be in our county, and that I should take cognizance of it. They offered to provide the necessary information for the investigation, and I agreed to launch one. Because the facts were thoroughly publicized in the press at the time and because they are typical of that blackmailing practice, I shall briefly summarize them.

In 1925, there were many people in California who were anti-Oriental and who looked with favor on any restrictions placed upon the Chinese. The resurgence of the Ku Klux Klan contributed greatly to this spirit, and the Legislature itself gave evidence of condoning it. Some hostile sentiment was directed against Chinese herb doctors or "herbalists," as they termed themselves. The medical profession, of course, was unalterably opposed to them, and some of the misdemeanor provisions of the Medical Practice Act were designed against them. They were, therefore, in a tenuous situation and ripe for a "cinch bill." There was a very aggressive herbalist operating in San Francisco and Alameda counties by the name of Fong Wan. He advertised extensively, which increased the wrath of the medics, but he was also very shrewd, and although prosecuted several times was able to avoid conviction. At the opening of the legislative session, a young, first-term assemblyman from Alameda County, Edward Smith, introduced a bill, the avowed purpose of which was to make the herbalists' practice a felony. Fong Wan understandably became greatly concerned. He was not able to see Assemblyman Smith, but was referred to William Brackett, a former assemblyman and police officer of Oakland, who was then a hanger-on around the Legislature. Fong contacted him and was told the terms necessary to kill the bill. He was to provide a sumptuous banquet in San Francisco for some legislators to insure their good will, and then pay Brackett ten thousand dollars, after which the bill would be dropped. The banquet reportedly was an enjoyable affair. Following it, Wan was ready to pay the ten thousand dollars to be rid of the oppressive bill. This is where the newspaper's people came into the picture. They contacted Fong, and were told the entire story. They brought it to me because the payoff was to be made in Fong's Oakland office. It was to be made on a Sunday morning to Brackett and Senator Edgar S. Hurley, a veteran Alameda County legislator. I interviewed Fong, and we made preparations to intercept the payment. With the herbalist's permission, we wired his office for sound and had officers available to take the culprits into custody immediately after the money was passed. When the appointed time arrived, the senator and Brackett did not show up, and Fong later acknowledged that he had tipped them off. We asked him why he had done so, and he said, "I no like to catch little man like Mr. Hurley and Mr. Blackett. I like to catch big man like Mr. Smith." The fact is that the novice Edward Smith was a cat's-paw, wittingly or unwittingly, for the other two and perhaps still more of their kind who gave aid and comfort to the project by attending the banquet and otherwise. There was nothing left for me to do. The payoff didn't take place, and Fong Wan, when he learned he would not be obliged to pay the ten thousand dollars, would have nothing more to do with the authorities. The Legislature, however, took no chances of having any of its members prosecuted for attempted bribery or extortion. A special committee was established to investigate the matter, the first and only time within my memory that the Legislature ever took so much as a peek at the practice of "cinch bills," although it was cognizant of the practice over a great many years. At the hearings of the committee all of the interested parties, including Fong Wan, Brackett, Senator Hurley, and the other legislators who had attended the banquet appeared. All of them, except Fong, testified fully that they neither committed any crime nor were aware of any crime being perpetrated. The committee promptly found that there was no evidence of a crime and all were exonerated.

The added shelter provided by this rests on the fact that California has a section of its Political Code which provides that anyone who testifies before a legislative committee cannot thereafter be prosecuted for any conduct about which he has testified. Thus everyone was "in free." However, ten years later I tested the provision, and had its effect limited.

In this latter experience, we were investigating the liquor administration of the member of the State Board of Equalization who had jurisdiction over Alameda County. It was generally believed that his was not an honest administration. The only question was: Who was culpable? The Board member was a former assemblyman, and his chief enforcement officer had been a long-time attaché in the assembly. The member was well covered up, but we had good evidence against his principal subordinate, Mike Connally. He was interrogated by a legislative committee the day before the grand jury of Alameda County met to indict him. When prosecuted by us, Connally claimed that this testimony absolved him from prosecution, and went to the Court of Appeals to have it so ruled. The Court held that only those who actually are *required* to testify may claim the immunity. It held that Connally *volunteered* his testimony and, thereafter, was not so entitled. He was soon convicted and went to jail.

After World War I, most legislative bodies returned to the prewar "normalcy" that President Harding advocated. California's Legislature was no exception to that rule. There was nothing creative about this restoration of the old "nuts and bolts" ways of state and local government. However, it was a great experience for me, far better than a college course in the legislative process, and the things I learned to avoid saved me from many a pitfall later on. I also cemented a few very good friendships which had an important influence upon my later years. I became greatly obligated to Leon E. Gray, my former associate of the days with Robinson and Robinson. He not only took me under his wing at the Legislature, but obtained my appointment as a deputy city attorney of Oakland and permitted me to share private offices with him until I went to the District Attorney's Office. A relationship began with Ezra Decoto, the district attorney to whom I owe a great deal for the manner in which he moved me along in his office. I became a devoted friend of Assemblyman Frank Anderson, who was not an ambitious man himself but who had an unbounded ambition for me. We were not only friends but constant companions until his death only a few years after these events.

About the time I was finishing my work on the Judiciary Committee after the adjournment of the Legislature, Leon Gray again recommended me for a job and I was appointed deputy city attorney of Oakland. He had previously accepted a similar position, so we again served together. The job paid two hundred dollars a month with the privilege of private practice. Gray invited me to share offices with him in the Bank of Italy building, which was another benefaction to me. Ours was a unique friendship. His interest in me was almost fatherly, though he was only four or five years older. We had been acquainted at Boalt Hall but had never been social friends. We worked together in various places, and the only times I was out of a job, he had located one for me, working with him. While I soon left the City Attorney's Office, he remained to reach the top post and become city attorney. After several years of estimable service, he was appointed a Superior Court judge, where he served with distinction until his death.

I had a good general experience in the City Attorney's Office, advising city boards and officers, writing legal opinions and having a fair amount of contact with the courts. I was netting about one hundred and fifty dollars a month in private legal work with Gray, although I put little effort into building a practice. Still determined to become a trial lawyer, I looked forward to experience some day in the District Attorney's Office. The opportunity came earlier than I expected.

Up to that time, personnel in the D.A.'s Office changed very seldom. In the spring of 1920, however, Mr. Decoto called me, said he would have a vacancy on May 1st, and that I would be welcome to it if I wanted it. I asked him if he was offering it because of pressure from my friends in the legislature, and when he said he was not, I accepted with enthusiasm. It was the lowest job on the staff and paid one hundred and fifty dollars a month—about half of what I was making—but it offered an opportunity for the background I wanted, and I was completely satisfied with it.

For the first time in my legal career, I had a sense of liberation such as that which possessed me when I entered the University of California. I was in an active office, the major thrust of which was courtroom activity, with an additional variety of legal business that was challenging in its nature and offered an unlimited opportunity for participation in all of it. Mr. Decoto, the district attorney, was an honest and kindly man. Like the other California district attorneys of those days, with the exception of the one in Los Angeles County, he had no investigative staff and was merely a conduit between the activities of the sheriff and the chiefs of police at one end and the Court on the other. He was not a particularly aggressive man and did little to change the status quo, although he insisted on integrity in his office. There was never any suspicion of corruption by him or his deputies during his tenure. There were between fifteen and twenty deputies in the office at the time. Most of them were old-timers who antedated Decoto's service. It was a comfortable place for the deputies because they were expected to and did engage in private practice extensively, with no office overhead. This was expected to supplement their low salaries. Much of the divorce practice of the county was handled by them. I did not see any specific conflict of interest, but the attention given to private practice necessarily detracted from their public work, and cases were often tried without adequate preparation. Until the time I came into the office, it was rare that a deputy would leave, but in the 1920s, law practice was profitable in Oakland, and the older deputies began to depart from the office and go it on their own. This made it a propitious time for me to be there, because I paid no attention to private legal activity but was ready to work with anyone, night or day, if he wanted help on an office case. I became a sort of Jack-of-all-trades on both the criminal and civil sides. I tried criminal cases, one after another, advised Boards of Education, assisted the chief deputy in advising the Board of Supervisors, and handled lawsuits against officers of the county. It was exciting for me, every day of it, and I made quick progress. Whenever one of the old-timers would leave, Mr. Decoto would ask the chief deputy, "Who knows anything about his cases?" and the deputy would often reply, "Warren has been helping him." The district attorney would then say, "Well, let's turn his work over to Warren." I worked practically every day of the week and ordinarily five nights. In about three years and a half, I occupied one of the two equal top assistantships and was assigned to what was considered the most important job in the office, that of adviser to the County Board of Supervisors. This later proved to be of inestimable value to me. While I did not realize it then, I now have little doubt that Mr. Decoto thought this might afford me the opportunity to succeed him if he should ever resign, as the Board fills such vacancies. I had a very satisfying experience with the Board, and they relied implicitly on my opinions as to the legality of their acts. There was no phase of the county government that I was not made familiar with, but, as I went along, my duties took me more and more into the field of governmental administration and away from the trial of criminal cases.

However, I remember my first criminal case very well. On my starting day in the office, I was assigned to sit in with one of the older deputies who was prosecuting a defendant under the Criminal Syndicalism Act passed by the 1919 Legislature. I had remembered its passing through our Judiciary Committee. It was part of the hysteria after World War I, and was being used throughout the state because of hostile feelings against the militant Industrial Workers of the World (IWW). In the trials, some repulsive informers were the principal witnesses, and I recall feeling squeamish about them. The defendant was an ideological radical, but I never could believe he was a terrorist. He was convicted and sentenced to prison. There was no doubt that he violated the Criminal Syndicalism Act and was, therefore, guilty. But I never liked this statute, even though its constitutionality was sustained a few years later by the United States Supreme Court, and during my many years as district attorney I never used it as a law-enforcement weapon. There was never any hesitancy on my part about prosecuting defendants for violence or conspiracy to commit it, but I never liked the act's pertinent provision: "Any person who . . . organizes or assists in organizing, or is or knowingly becomes a member of, any organization, society, group, or assemblage of persons organized or assembled to advocate, teach or aid and abet criminal syndicalism is guilty of a felony, and punishable by imprisonment."

It is easy for some people to be carried away by an ideological approval of violence without their having any intention of inciting or participating in such action. When conviction rests upon the testimony of paid informers, injustice is likely to follow.

Years later I was, therefore, pleased as one of my last acts as Chief Justice to join an opinion invalidating acts of this character. There are other and better ways of reaching the evil complained of here.

I do not know if the defendant in that first criminal case in which I participated remembered me in later years, because my role was so slight, but when I was governor he applied for executive clemency, and when he showed exemplary conduct through the years after his release I was happy to grant him a full pardon.

During my years as a deputy, my friendship with Assemblyman Frank Anderson developed into one of constant companionship. He was in the real estate and insurance business with his father, and, being a bachelor, lived with his parents. He was a quiet, unassuming man about seven years my senior. It was a matter of comment that he never made a speech in the Legislature, and when they would say to him, "Frank, you should deliver at least one speech each session," he would say, "Nobody ever votes because of a speech, and you are just stupid if you let them call the roll on your bill before you know you have the votes."

In the fall of 1923, he became ill, and about the first of the year his doctor advised his parents that he had a terminal case of tuberculosis. This was never communicated to him, and, as such patients often are, he was cheerful and always thought and spoke in terms of being up and around in a short while. Nineteen twenty-four was an election year for him, and he discussed the prospects of the coming campaign with equanimity. The doctor said it was doubtful that Frank would be alive when the next Legislature convened, but the doctor wouldn't advise him not to run for re-election because that might destroy his morale and hasten his death. With this knowledge, his parents would not urge him to refrain from running. They finally asked me to make the decision, because they said he would undoubtedly follow any advice I might give him. Like the others, I could not bring myself to tell him that he shouldn't run. The possible implications of such advice were too serious. So I told him he should, and that I would handle his affairs until he was able to do so himself. That was precisely the advice he wanted, and I found myself launched into the first political campaign of my career. It wasn't much of a campaign. We only spent a few hundred dollars for stationery and postage, and for a few cards with a picture and a "Vote for Anderson" appeal, to be posted on telephone poles and other places in view of the public. We had a few young people carry on a letter-writing campaign, and I would give out an occasional statement in his name. Also, every few days, I would gather a few friends at his bedside and we would announce a campaign meeting at the home of Frank

W. Anderson for his re-election to the Assembly, and discuss some of the issues the district was interested in.

It was generally known that Frank was quite ill, and this news attracted seven rival candidates. However, there was no open campaign against him because of his ill health, which was freely discussed. I was not acquainted in his district sufficiently to induce people to work for him, but the courthouse reporters liked him and helped by giving him occasional space in their papers. As election day approached, I had misgivings as to my advice about his decision to run, because people were openly doubting that he would be able to serve if elected. It was a very close election, and the count fluctuated throughout the night. About 4 A.M. at the courthouse, there were but two precincts to report, and Anderson was more than fifty votes behind. Those present conceded his defeat. I insisted on waiting for those last two precincts. They were late reporting because they were two of the largest in the district. When they were counted, he had won the election by sixty votes. I immediately went to his home, awakened him about daybreak, and told him of his victory. He was, of course, overjoyed, and later in the day received the congratulations of friends who came to his bedside. On the following day, he called for his mother, and when she came, he said, "Mother, it is time to say good-bye. I am going to leave you." Without saying more, he died.

It was while I was a deputy district attorney that I met my wife, the greatest thing that ever happened to me. Up to that time I had never given any serious thought to marriage. I always considered it something for the dim future, perhaps when I was well established. But meeting her changed my whole outlook. We met at a swimming party one Sunday morning at the Piedmont Baths in Oakland. I was immediately attracted to her. Her name was Nina Elisabeth Meyers. She was a young widow who was living with and supporting her little boy Jim and her widowed stepmother. Her father, deceased, was a Swedish Baptist minister named Nils Peter Palmquist. She had herself been born in Sweden, and had come to this country, like my parents, as a babe in arms. At the time of my meeting her, she was the manager of a woman's specialty shop in Oakland. She was as busy as I was, but we found time to become acquainted and often went to dinner and the theater on Saturday evenings. We also spent a part of our Sundays together whenever possible. It wasn't long until we were thinking in terms of marriage, but we decided to wait until my income was sufficient to properly maintain a home. We were each then making about $250 per month and had no other resources to fall back on. Social patterns were different then, and I would have felt humiliated if my wife had been compelled to work.

When I was appointed district attorney on January 12, 1925, we decided to be married at an early date, but my mother, who was at my sister's home for a series of eye operations, delayed us. She also incurred a serious internal illness and had an abdominal operation, as a result of which she was for a time at death's door. When she finally was able to attend our wedding, we were married in the First Baptist Church at a quiet family service on October 14. The only outsiders present were two long-time friends who had inside information about our application for a marriage license, and were determined that we not leave the city without some celebration. When we arrived at the church, these friends, Oliver D. Hamlin, the lawyer whose position as a deputy district attorney I had succeeded to, and George C. Feldman, the manager of the county garage, were in a car across the street. They had surreptitiously assembled the entire highway patrol of the county at a discreet distance to usher us noisily wherever we were going. Seeing them in the car, I said, "All right, come on in." They did, and to this day they occasionally kid me about the "engraved invitations" they received for our wedding. More than twenty years later, I appointed Hamlin as a judge of the Superior Court. He had a distinguished judicial career, serving as a judge of the United States Circuit Court in San Francisco and as a member of the Ninth Circuit. Judge Hamlin died in December 1973. George C. Feldman died in September 1972.

After the ceremony, the highway patrol made its appearance, and with sirens wide open preceded us to the county line. We were on our way to British Columbia for a two weeks' wedding trip. Once there, we stayed at the grand old Empress Hotel in Victoria, the provincial capital on Vancouver Island. Our first evening at the hotel, we went into the immense dining room and found ourselves the only ones there. I thought at first that we had miscalculated the dinner hour, but was assured that we had not. While we ate, only a few other people came to dine. It seemed strange, as I had seen many people in the hotel's lobby and corridors during the day. On inquiry later, I was reminded that the province had partial prohibition, that there were government liquor stores, and that people could legally buy liquor and drink it in their hotel rooms, but it could not be consumed publicly in the dining room. As a result, most people simply had dinner served in their rooms.

The island, with its flowers and shrubbery, was beautiful, but the weather was atrocious. For several days, there was a constant downpour. Sightseeing was out of the question, so I finally asked Nina if she would like to see a British trial. The courthouse was quite accessible from the hotel, and she readily assented. I was happy for the opportunity because

I had been annoyed by the delays and indecisions of law enforcement in our country, and although I had never seen a British trial myself, I had become enamored of them from my reading and from discussion in conferences on crime. We were fortunate to arrive at the beginning of a trial for attempted murder. The defendant was a Chinese who admittedly had shot and wounded his wife's alleged paramour. The case was called, and the bewigged and robed judge, after a few questions addressed to the jury panel, empaneled the jury without objection from either side. The prosecution made a very brief opening statement and then proceeded with the introduction of testimony. There were three or four witnesses, the direct testimony of none of them taking more than ten minutes and the cross-examination even less. I observed how expeditious British courts were in all things as compared with our cumbersome procedures. The defendant then took the stand, and in a few minutes his testimony was closed. Both sides then rested, and the prosecutor presented his case to the jury with about a ten-minute argument. The defense counsel followed and, after reviewing the evidence for a few minutes, stated that in such cases there was an "unwritten law" which must be taken into consideration in judging the defendant. This was a reference to the argument of attorney Delmas in the notorious Harry K. Thaw case in New York. The judge took vigorous exception to the statement, and upbraided counsel severely for it, saying, "There may be such a pernicious doctrine on the other side of the border, but thank God there is none such in the British Empire." The defense counsel apologized and briefly concluded his argument. In a few well-chosen words, the judge proceeded to tell the jury that the evidence was clear and not difficult of solution. There was little doubt left in anyone's mind that he would have decided the case against the defendant. He sent the jury out for its verdict, and I commented to my bride that if we had more of this kind of expeditiousness in our country we could achieve better results in law enforcement. The jury was out about ten minutes and returned with a verdict of "Not Guilty"— precisely what could have been expected in Alameda County in that kind of case.

The first day after our return to Oakland, I came home from the office to see my wife admiring some beautiful Chinese jade jewelry. I asked her who had sent it, and she said it must have come from a friend of mine because she did not recognize the name. The card showed it was from a Mr. L. Ben. I recognized immediately that this must be Lim Ben, the biggest Chinese lottery operator in the county. Nina's possession of the gift was short-lived, for the next day I notified the foreman of the county grand jury, and, with one of its members accompanying them, two of my men located L. Ben, returned the jewelry to him, and brought back a written receipt.

As to the manner in which I became district attorney, I do not believe I had much ambition for the position until the opportunity actually presented itself. There were a number of reasons for this. In the first place, I had not taken a job in the D.A.'s Office with the intention of remaining in public service or even being there for any great length of time. I wanted the trial experience the office afforded, and I believed that about a year and a half or two years at most would equip me for the private practice I contemplated. Once there, however, I became so engrossed in the work that I lost my sense of timing, and with the constant change of duties I was continually and fascinatedly learning. Mr. Decoto put me through every phase of the work, and the time passed very rapidly. When I had been there a little more than four years, talk circulated that Mr. Decoto was about to accept a state office, and there was, of course, speculation about his successor as district attorney. Because I was one of his two top assistants, my name was mentioned as a possibility. However, I gave little thought to it even then because I was a relative newcomer to a county of a half million population, and had no real political experience or associations. Consequently, when people mentioned it to me, I brushed it off as being improbable. But finally when it appeared imminent that Mr. Decoto would be appointed to the State Railroad Commission, Supervisor John F. Mullins came to me and said I should ask the five-person board of supervisors to appoint me to the resultant D.A. Office vacancy. He said he would vote for me and that Supervisor Charles W. Heyer would also, and that I needed only one more. I told him Mr. Decoto had never told me he was leaving; that I would not try to do anything for myself while he was still in office, and that I would not be interested at all if he had someone else in mind to be the new district attorney. Mullins said there was need for speedy action because pressures were developing to "do tricks with the office." He volunteered to tell Decoto and did. The latter then called me to his office and related his conversation with Mullins. He told me he had decided to leave and would be happy to have me succeed him. He assured me I was free to take any action I desired to obtain the appointment. He suggested that I solicit the vote of Supervisor Ralph W. Richmond, a representative of the agricultural part of the county who was not beholden to the county machine headed by Mike Kelly. I was very grateful, and thanked him for his confidence in me. I then contacted Supervisor Richmond and, although it was difficult for me to do so, asked him if he would vote for me. He said he would like to because of his friendship for me; that he would inquire of some of his friends in the district, and if there was no serious objection from them, he would do so. In about a week, he said he had found no detractors and would vote to appoint me. In the meantime Supervisor Heyer, who was also an independent from an agricultural district, voluntarily told me he would vote in my favor. The word was soon around the city, and while one might think that would be the end of it, the fight was just commencing. The other two members of the Board were adherents of the Mike Kelly machine, as was Supervisor Mullins, my original supporter. It was Mullins' contention that deals were in the making to open up the city of Oakland to unlawful activities. He said, "I have been a politician all my life, and while I have done many things for purely political reasons, I will never do anything to weaken the integrity of the District Attorney's Office." Nevertheless, rumors known to him persisted to the effect that when the time came, Mike Kelly would have Mullins' vote. In order to fortify himself in his conviction that this wasn't so, Mullins said, "I have gone to the people in this city whose respect I most desire and have told them that if I submit to Kelly's pressure it will be a dishonest act."

The remaining two organization supervisors were pledged to the other candidate, Frank W. Shay, the assistant who had equal rank with me in the D.A.'s Office. A very active campaign was being made for him by the Kelly people, and there was much tension around the courthouse. A reporter there for the Oakland *Tribune*, owned by Mr. Joseph R. Knowland, a former congressman, was the unofficial manager for Frank Shay, and he used his news articles to advance Shay's cause. I knew that Mr. Knowland and his paper were not politically friendly to Kelly's organization, so without any acquaintance with him I went to his office, told him the situation, and asked if I could not get a fair break on the news from the courthouse. He assured me that I would receive it, and I believe that was the beginning of his interest in me. As the situation developed into a Kelly–anti-Kelly confrontation, he became even more concerned, and used his paper's influence as well as his own in my behalf. He had no real political organization, but could marshal forces that were in opposition to Kelly.

There was only one part considered movable in this situation, and that was Supervisor Mullins. The other two votes of mine were not doubted. But people who knew Mullins and his twenty-year allegiance to the Kelly organization could not believe that he could withstand its suasions. His district was thoroughly dominated by Kelly. It was the railroad, waterfront, industrial section of the area, and in the heart of it was a cancerous little city of three thousand people called Emeryville which purveyed every kind of vice, including gambling, prostitution, and bootlegging. It was absolutely controlled by Kelly interests, and a complacent sheriff's office that was supposed to enforce the law in small cities with no real police departments did nothing about it.

Mullins said he would not change his vote for me even if it meant the loss of his seat on the board of supervisors. His perseverance was doubted until he arose in a board meeting on January 12, 1925, and proposed my name for the district attorneyship. The vote was unanimous in my favor, though I really only had three solid supporters.

Mullins, as feared, lost his place on the board at the next election as a result. He was an ardent Roman Catholic, and when the vote had been taken, he said emotionally, "Earl Warren, you owe allegiance to no one except your God and your conscience." John Mullins was not only my original sponsor but also my most ardent supporter during twenty-five years of California politics. He lived with his gentle wife Ann in a modest apartment in Oakland, and I never returned to that city without visiting him until his death in 1968.*

* Ed. note: It might be added that Friend Richardson, then governor of California, had been impressed with Warren and wanted him in the District Attorney's Office. He is credited with helping to influence those members of the Board of Supervisors who were behind Warren, other than Mullins.

V

BROADENING MY BASE: *Years as a District Attorney*

I accepted the position of district attorney in the spirit of independence with which it was tendered by John F. Mullins on behalf of the Alameda County Board of Supervisors. It is appropriate here to say that the Board lived up to its part of the bargain. Never once did any member, or anyone on a member's behalf, suggest that I deviate from Mullins' injunction to be my own man. In everything I did I had complete freedom from political obligation.

Mike Kelly showed no bitterness. He told me after my appointment that he had nothing against me, but that he thought I was not politically entitled to the position. He reserved his animosity for Mullins, whom he fought vengefully and ousted at the next election. In that same election, he entered a candidate against me for district attorney. But while the campaign was a critical one between my opponent, Preston L. Higgins, a former deputy district attorney, and me, the Kelly forces at the courthouse did not rally against me, nor did they outwardly support me. From their attitude and the results on election day, I am of the opinion that most of them were quietly friendly to my campaign. I won the election overwhelmingly, carrying every precinct except the two representing the two county hospitals. (Since then I have learned that it is almost a political rule of thumb that patients in such institutions vote against incumbent candidates.)

Kelly did not enter an opponent against me in either of my subsequent elections in 1930 and 1935.

In accepting the position of district attorney, I realized the importance of it and knew from my experience as an assistant that there were many obstacles in the way of doing a satisfactory job. In the first place, Alameda County was big and unwieldy—third in population in the state, exceeded only by San Francisco and Los Angeles counties. It had more than half a million people. It was a seaport with a growing harbor on San Francisco Bay. It was also an industrial section of the Bay as well as its railroad center. Serving as a terminal for the three important railroads of Northern California—the Southern Pacific, the Santa Fe, and the Western Pacific—it was a cosmopolitan county with people from almost every part of the world. In addition, it was the residential "bedroom" for San Francisco, and tens of thousands of commuters rode the ferries across the Bay to work in the morning and returned at night to their homes in Oakland, Berkeley, Alameda, and smaller cities in the southern end of the county, of which there were six. These little cities had only skeleton police forces, and people looked to the county authorities to see that things did not get out of hand. The county officers, of course, were the sheriff and the district attorney. The sheriff headed the policing agency, and he was willing to handle cases of murder, robbery, and burglary, but had no stomach for such things as bootlegging, gambling, and prostitution. Yet he had the only enforcing arm capable of dealing with these illegalities. California had no state police, and the district attorney had no law enforcement officers on his staff, so it was only through moral suasion and by alerting people and calling criminal conditions to the attention of the grand jury that he could be at all effective in handling such matters. In 1925, bootlegging, rumrunning, and hijacking were in full swing, and, of course, a county like ours had its share of lawbreakers. Everyone who wanted liquor had it, and it was socially the accepted thing to serve it at parties. Consequently I—who had not been a teetotaler—felt that I could not honorably prosecute liquor violators in the daytime and then go to parties where hard drinks were served in the evening. My wife and I, so far as social activities were concerned, became almost hermits for nine years until the Eighteenth Amendment was repealed. This was often difficult, but it was made much easier by the fact that, to this day, my wife has never taken a drink. She has always insisted that, while she deplores the misery liquor has brought into so many homes, she is not a prohibitionist but merely a teetotaler. I have often wondered if my abstinence from the so-called "rotgut" liquor of those prohibition days has not, to a certain extent, been responsible for the many years of good health I have enjoyed since.

I felt reasonably well qualified to conduct the District Attorney's Office efficiently because of the four and a half years' experience Mr. Decoto had given me in every phase of the work. I realized there were weak spots in certain office procedures, and I determined to remedy them. One of them was the calendar situation. Continuances were commonly granted on request, with a resulting backlog of untried cases. I made it my business to see that this situation changed because I firmly believed that delays were the cause of many miscarriages of justice.

The California Penal Code provided that if a defendant were not tried within sixty days after his arraignment in the Superior Court, the case had to be dismissed unless the defendant consented to the delay. (Most defendants ask for or consent to continuance because it is normally beneficial to them. Witnesses may die, leave the community, or fail to remember vital facts.) My deputies were instructed not to ask for a continuance unless they had first obtained approval from me, and they were not to consent to any continuance requested by the other side without the approval of the deputy in charge of the calendar, and then only to further the cause of justice. My target for trial was thirty days from arraignment. The judges of the Criminal Division agreed to the program, so we followed through on it. For a time it was not popular with defense lawyers, but it worked, and for years we tried even the most important cases within that thirty-day period. There was no bargaining for lesser pleas in order to be rid of a backlog. The cases were tried on time, and the defendants, in a short period, were convicted or acquitted. One case will indicate how a prompt trial can help in seeing justice done. Incidentally, it was the case in which I came closer to death than at any other time in my public life—at least so far as I am aware.

A carpenter by the name of Arthur Antoine lived in Oakland with his wife, Ida, and two boys, ten and eleven years of age. They were a quiet family and were well regarded in the neighborhood, particularly the wife for the manner in which she reared her boys. One day Antoine returned from the mountains where he had been working on a construction job. Two days later he went to his neighbors and shocked them by saying that he and his supposed wife had been living together for many years but had never actually married. He said that when he arrived home this time, she told him that a former lover of hers had come to Oakland, that she still loved this man, and that she was leaving to join him. With that, she went off. Antoine sought sympathy and help from the neighbors because he was left with the boys and there was no one to take care of them while he was working.

The following day he left home again for the mountains, and in a couple of days returned with a buxom eighteen-year-old girl, saying he had married her in a little mountain town in order to have a mother for his boys. This was too much for the neighbors, and a delegation of them went to the Police Department to tell of their suspicion, which was that the wife might have been murdered. Police went to the Antoine home, examined the premises, and in the bedroom found some small splotches of human blood on the inside of the silk lamp over the head of the bed where the wife slept. They then found a hammer in the garage, and where the handle fits into the hammer, they discovered human blood. They also found on an Army surplus bag in the house a tiny piece of bone and tissue about one third the size of a little finger nail.

When Antoine came home he was questioned and gave a number of conflicting stories, all of which were checked out and found to be untrue. The police, believing they had enough evidence to justify his arrest, came to my office for a warrant. The grand jury was meeting on some other matters, so the police were told to marshal their evidence and be prepared to present it later in the day. While they were waiting to testify, a murder was reported in the city, and the police asked if they could be heard and released immediately to investigate the slaying. I suspended the business we were engaged in, and called Inspector George Burbank, a reliable member of the homocide squad, as the first witness on the Antoine case. After he was sworn, we had the following dialogue:

Q: Your name is George Burbank?
A: Yes.
Q: You are a police inspector of the city of Oakland and a member of the homicide squad?
A: Yes.
Q: As such, did you investigate the disappearance of a Mrs. Arthur Antoine?
A: Mr. Warren, I don't care to answer that question.
Q: Why?
A: Because I understand this grand jury is about to indict me.
Q: Have you done anything to be indicted for?
A: No.
Q: Then why do you believe they will indict you?
A: A voice told me.
Q: Whose voice?
A: I don't know.

Q: Have you a lawyer?
A: Yes.
Q: Would you like to be excused to confer with him?
A: Yes.
Q: You may be excused.

Burbank's police associates were told he was obviously having delusions. They asked him further questions, and were told by him that he believed his chief and I intended to frame him for the Antoine murder. In relieving him of his service revolver, they found he had a second revolver which he said he had put in his pocket to take care of me in the grand jury room. Fortunately for me, I had sensed I was dealing with a deranged man, and had not angered him in my examination. Thinking back, it was a close call.

We then introduced other testimony, and Antoine was indicted. Inspector Burbank was taken to a hospital for the mentally ill, and as far as I know never left there. The doctors asked me several times to visit him in order to see if he could forget his obsession. Each time I went, he would say, "Earl, I know you would not do any such thing to me," but five minutes after I left he was back to his old fixation.

At the time of the Antoine trial, I was met with the curious defense that this was a frame-up by my office against the defendant, and that Inspector Burbank became so conscience-stricken he was driven insane.

The jury found Antoine guilty, with a recommendation of life imprisonment. I was relieved that they did not return a capital verdict because we could not produce the body of Mrs. Antoine, and in every capital case where this occurs, doubts are raised and the affair often becomes a *cause célèbre*. He was sentenced to life imprisonment, and later on his lawyer came to me and asked if I would like to know how the crime was committed. I said I certainly would. To my astonishment, the lawyer then arranged for Antoine to make a confession. Antoine's complete story was that while working in the mountains he fell in love with the buxom girl whom he had subsequently married. He then came home and broke the news to his wife. He told her he intended to leave her and marry the girl. His wife threw herself on her bed and cried. While she was crying, he went to the garage, picked up a hammer, went back in the house, and beat her over the head until she was dead. He then put her in the bathtub, and with his boys' Boy Scout tools dissected her body into parts that would fit into the incinerator of the kitchen stove. He severed the flesh from the bones, burned the latter to a crisp, and threw the ashes into a vacant lot next to the home. He did this over a period of thirty-six hours. Then he placed the flesh in a burlap bag, threw it in the back of his car, and departed for the mountains, where he married the girl. On the way, he dumped the bag into a slough of the San Joaquin River near Stockton.

We immediately notified the Sheriff's office of San Joaquin County. They happened to be skilled in that kind of work, and their search brought up the bag intact but so rotten that it disintegrated when it was hauled aboard the boat. Inside was all that remained of Mrs. Antoine.

The thing we could not at first understand was why the lawyer, who had contended that our case was a frame-up and that the wife had merely run away with a former lover, would arrange for this confession and even join in having Antoine tell the story under oath in the courtroom before leaving for the penitentiary. We soon learned the reason. The lawyer had taken a deed to the Antoines' little home as a fee for defending him. The title to the home was in the name of both husband and wife. Such a title is called "joint tenancy," and under California law if one of the parties dies the title remains in the other's name without any probate proceedings. If the lawyer was to gain the house under his deed from Antoine, it was necessary to backtrack, because unless Mrs. Antoine was provably dead, his deed of ownership was worthless. I always wondered what went through the mind of Antoine as he passed his lawyer in the yard at San Quentin prison, where in a very few years both were confined. For we later convicted the lawyer of extorting money from a score of his clients. He would tell them he needed the money to bribe various officials, then leave them without either money or a defense.

Not much time elapsed from the day of the indictment until the remains of Mrs. Antoine were brought to light and the case solved. If we had allowed it to drag on even a few days more, it would have been too late because the burlap bag would have disintegrated completely.

In those prohibition days, bail bond brokers had a bonanza. The number of arrests made for bootlegging gave them a steady flow of business at exorbitant rates. In addition, through connections with the morals squad, they were even able to name the lawyers for certain cases and obtain a cut of the fees from disreputable ones who worked with them. Oakland jailers would hold up the release of prisoners until they patronized the bond brokers, who were given free access to prisoners while all others were denied permission to see them. Some police judges in the county even gave the morals squad blank releases to carry with them on bootlegging raids, which they in turn would fill out and deliver to the jailers when the defendant reached jail, provided the arrested person bought a bail bond from one of the preferred brokers. There was no way even of knowing whether the broker was worth the aggregate of the bonds he was responsible for.

Also, when a defendant would jump bail and fail to appear as ordered, the courts would often continue the question of bail forfeiture for an abnormal period of time in order to enable the broker to have him arrested and returned. If the Court finally forfeited bail, it had been the long-time practice of the District Attorney's Office to delay the filing of the action until the statute of limitations was about to run out. Then the Court would grant extensions of time to file an answer, with the result that many cases of bail forfeiture were several years old, and the bail bond broker was operating as if nothing had happened. To make the situation even more inequitable, it was the invariable practice of the bail bond broker to require the defendant to post collateral equal in value to the amount of the bond in addition to paying the fee for the bond. Thus, when a defendant jumped his bail, the broker had both his fee and collateral for the amount of the bond, but without paying anything to the state.

I made up my mind that this system should not continue, and wrote to each broker who was in default demanding the amount due the county. They laughed at the letter. I then wrote another telling them that if they did not pay up, my office would notify every magistrate in the county that they were not responsible bondsmen and should not be permitted to post any further property bonds. They called that a "Boy Scout" act, and instead of posting property bonds they started posting Liberty Bonds of World War I, which were authorized by statute. I was stymied for a short time, but as usually happens when anyone openly defies the law and there is a determination to enforce it, opportunity comes to the enforcer. This is because many people, through cunning, can cheat the law for a time, but it is an entirely different situation if they openly defy it.

One of the most active and corrupt of the bail bond brokers was a man by the name of Charles Meyers. He put up some Liberty Bonds to guarantee the appearance of a young man who was charged with burglary. The defendant gave Meyers a deed to his home as security. While awaiting trial, he jumped bail, and the Court declared him a fugitive. However, the Court did not declare forfeiture of the Liberty Bonds posted for his appearance. A short time thereafter, the fugitive was arrested and returned to the Court, where he pled guilty and was sentenced to San Quentin penitentiary. After he was in prison, his wife went to Meyer's office and requested a return of the deed because the bondsman had suffered no financial loss. She was told that the bail had been forfeited, and that her home had been sold. If the home was indeed sold, it amounted to grand larceny. We investigated the records, and found this to be the case. I then called the grand jury and presented the evidence. The first witness was the wife. When she entered the room, she was carrying her six-months-old baby, as beautiful a child as I had ever seen. As soon as she commenced her testimony, one of the women grand jurors offered to hold the baby for her. The child was so attractive and so good-natured that before the mother had completed her testimony every grand juror had held him for a few moments. Meyers was promptly indicted, and when he was arrested an hour or so later, it was as if the foundations of City Hall had shattered.

By next morning every delinquent bail bond broker had paid into the County Treasury every dollar he owed.*

We tried Meyers for grand larceny, but he escaped punishment because a woman from his office took the blame. She testified that the deed came into the office in the regular course of business; that she believed Meyers' bonds had been forfeited; that she did not know that the defendant had been apprehended and sentenced, and that she arranged for the sale by asking Meyers to sign the deed without apprising him as to what the property was. With this testimony and his offer to return the home, the jury gave him the benefit of the doubt and acquitted him.

Nevertheless, this incident did the job. Thereafter, throughout my years as district attorney, the bail bond brokers were as meek as lambs and we never had another scandal.

In large part this was because, at my request, the grand jury investigated the entire bail system with emphasis on its connection with the Police Department. As a result, the jailers who were working with bondsmen were removed from their posts, the morals squad was replaced, and there was a general tightening of conditions at the jail and a divorcement of the bail bond broker-jailer-unscrupulous lawyer combination. We were thus relieved of the sordid conditions that existed in so many courthouses and police departments throughout the nation.

Bail bond brokers have been leeches on our judicial system for decades, and in many cities have been a highly corrupting influence. During the Twenties, San Francisco had scandal after scandal revolving around them.

There was one other incident in the Meyers case that concerned me and, as far as I know, it has never reached the courts for judicial determination. It was the bringing of that beautiful baby into the grand jury

* Ed. note: There was another facet to Earl Warren's breaking of the scandalous bail bond system controlled by Meyers. Meyers tried to "buy" Deputy District Attorney J. Paul St. Sure in return for helping the bail bond brokers in 1925, but was completely unsuccessful.

room while his mother was to testify. The California Penal Code provides that no unauthorized person shall be allowed in the grand jury room during its sessions. Only the district attorney and the witness while he or she is testifying is entitled to be there. Even the judge who empaneled the jury is not entitled to be present. I did not think of the statute as the mother and child came in, but when the session was over and I recalled how admiringly the jury had passed the little one around, I became concerned because I could imagine no stronger influence on the jury than that demure mother telling the story of how her home had been stolen from her while her baby was being cuddled by members of the grand jury. We were not confronted with the problem in the trial court, and, because of Meyers' acquittal, there was no appeal. Nevertheless, that was the last baby we ever brought to the grand jury room.

"Bunco" games were rampant throughout the world at that time. The so-called "confidence men" were a worldwide fraternity, to be found on steamships, in railroad passenger cars, in certain hotels, and particularly in cities where they had a working arrangement with law enforcement officers. They operated in gangs, and each gang would have its own particular game. Since they connived over a wide range of jurisdictions so that the detection of only one phase of a con game would not necessarily reveal a crime, picking up the whole devious thread in various jurisdictions was often a difficult thing to do. Where the police were involved, they could easily become frustrated and abandon efforts to run down the offenders. There were a number of cities where the police chief would permit confidence men to live in that community without harassment if they agreed not to practice the game there. In ten or a dozen cities this was an accepted practice, and some chiefs openly espoused the system as a law enforcement technique. For years, Oakland, under a police chief named Walter Petersen, was one of the cities that had such an understanding.

A case in point occurred a few years before I came on the scene, and serves to illustrate the methodology of at least one type of "bunco" game. There were many others, including the money box game, in which the victim buys a box that is demonstrated as being capable of making United States currency; the horse racing game, similar in technique to that of the stock market swindle soon to be described; the sale of public structures like the Brooklyn Bridge, which was sold many times over to the gullible around the country, and many more. A favorite was the pigeon game, in which a wallet with supposedly very valuable contents is picked up and is to be shared with the victim on his establishing his financial responsibility. These examples will identify bunco practices for our purpose.

The "stock market" case in Oakland started when a wealthy Nebraska farmer boarded a Pacific Coast-bound passenger train. Before long he met a stranger on the train who told him of the possibility of making a quick fortune through some connections of the stranger's in Oakland. As the story developed, the farmer was told that a firm in Oakland was able to intercept information on stock prices by wiretapping, and that it would be possible for him to be let in on this advantage if he could confirm his financial stability. On arriving in Oakland, the stranger introduced the farmer to some of his associates who induced the visitor to withdraw several thousand dollars from his Nebraska bank. They all then proceeded to a room where the stock transactions were to take place. Incidentally, it was about a hundred yards from the police station and City Hall. There, according to agreement, the farmer was handed an amount of money equal to his own, and was authorized to buy stocks as he desired, with profits to be divided equally with his new-found friends. At first he was advised to make several small purchases, all of which almost instantly produced a substantial profit based on the supposed inside information. When the dupe became enthusiastic, he was told of big news that would return a fortune, and was persuaded to invest all he had in one big deal. But this time, of course, the so-called prior information was wrong, and the entire amount was lost. The strangers consoled him. There had been a terrible mistake. They would endeavor to find out what had caused the error and obtain restitution. At this point the farmer realized he had been "buncoed," so he went to the police. They advised him to return to Nebraska and said they would try to recover his money. Needless to say, they never did.

A few years later this same farmer again made a trip to California and met up with other members of the gang. They made the same proposition to him on the train. He went along with them as though he had never had his earlier experience. He again withdrew thousands of dollars and made arrangements for the big transaction. When he arrived at the "stock brokers," as before, and they placed in his hand the amount equal to his own, instead of waiting for the stock purchases, he knocked down some of the conspirators and ran with the money directly to the police station. He deposited all the money with the desk sergeant, requested and was given a receipt, and submitted himself to arrest. The bunco artists, of course, were in no position to prosecute him, but the corrupt police endeavored to reclaim the receipt, undoubtedly to turn it back to the bunco men. They searched the farmer and his cell, and kept him in jail for days, but in some way he had smuggled the receipt out or hidden it successfully. Eventually they were compelled to release him. Shortly thereafter he appeared at the police station with the receipt and a lawyer. The police refused to honor the receipt, and he was forced to sue to regain his money. The Court of Appeals awarded it to him.

There were other cases, of course, but this one was enough to convince me that we should have no more of this in our county. That, however, was easier to decide than to accomplish. We had no investigators or agency upon which we could thoroughly rely, and it was very difficult to put the pieces of evidence together in a manner to convince a jury because the bunco victim invariably was himself responding to some illegal plan to get something for nothing. After much thought, we came up with a procedure for prosecuting such cases that turned out to be a clincher. We knew that bunco men operated all over the country, but principally in cities where they were given protection. Most of them were old-timers and had suffered numerous arrests with few convictions. Sometimes a defendant would have a dozen arrests in one city, and the FBI record would list each of them something like this: "Arrested for grand larceny of $10,000. At a later date reduced to petty larceny; bail $500." The last entry would be, "Bail forfeited. Dismissed." This was recognizable as a pattern of police protection. In California, the Supreme Court in cases involving bunco games permitted proof of "similar offences" to establish a course of conduct which would disprove innocent intent. We decided we would show proof of several of these identical crimes from other states in order to establish that the conduct complained of in our county was not unintentional but was part of a repeated scheme to defraud. We knew it would be useless to seek the assistance of other counties and states, because they had not even prosecuted their own cases. People from my office would, therefore, go to the records to locate complaining witnesses in out-of-town bunco cases involving the con men being tried locally. We would then select a few of the best of these witnesses, and when our case came to trial we would bring them in from various parts of the country and confront the perpetrators of local fleecings with them. It worked perfectly, and after two or three such trials, bunco games of such patterned types came to an end and we were relieved of that kind of crime for the rest of my time as district attorney. This counteractive stratagem became known by bunco artists everywhere, and one of them even wrote a book on the subject and advised all such crooks to remain out of Alameda County, California.

We applied somewhat the same procedure to business frauds, particularly to oil swindles which were to repay the victims anywhere from one hundred dollars for one to a thousand for one. These were long, dull cases but were well worth diligent prosecution. Having been successful in them, we had very few more of their kind for many years.

As another illustration of how such frauds can be prevented, we tried a similar system on the sewing machine business. At that time, sewing machine companies were sending out hosts of salesmen, many of whom were really bunco men. They would go to a poor household where the housewife was using an old, dilapidated machine, and tell her that because of her popularity in the neighborhood they wanted to make her a present of one of their brand-new sewing machines if she would merely advertise it in the neighborhood by telling people how much she liked it. They would then suggest taking her old machine in and exchanging for it a brand-new one. She would, of course, sign a paper which they presented to her, and at the end of the month she would receive a bill for one twelfth the cost of the new machine. When she would protest that she had been told the machine was to be *given* to her, she was shown the contract which she had signed and it provided for monthly payments. They would then take her new machine and leave her without any, since she already had given them her old machine.

We arrested several of these agents, but the sewing machine companies would have them released on bail, and when the time of their trial came they were not to be found. We studied the situation and found that in a number of instances their companies had merely sent them to another part of the state where they engaged in the same fraudulent conduct.

Finally, I asked all of the managers of sewing machine companies in Oakland to come to my office for a meeting. They did so, and I told them what our experience had been in prosecuting such cases, and what we knew about how they had disposed of the agents involved. I then declared that this was the last time we were going to charge only the agent who made the fraudulent representations; in the future we were also going to charge the managers of the businesses with criminal conspiracy, which was a felony. We never had another case of that kind while I was in Oakland.

I had only been in office for a few months when a murder case impressed me more forcibly than before with the inherent weakness of a District Attorney's Office under our then existing system. It was by far the most important office in the county government, being the only agency responsible for the honest and efficient administration of the law in all its parts. People looked to the district attorney in that light. Yet he was not given the tools to work with. Having no investigative or enforcement agency, he was left high and dry when any alleged offense occurred that involved the integrity of the particular police agency which had jurisdiction over the matter. He was obliged to use only that evidence which the involved agency produced for him. There was at

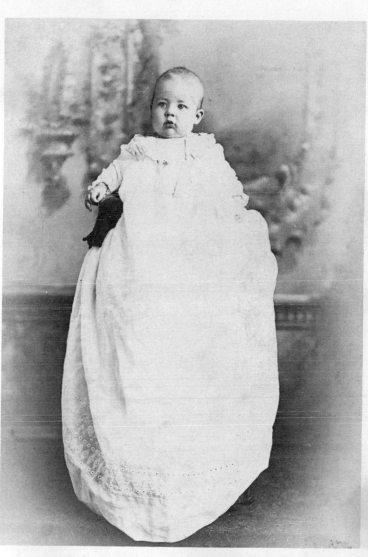

1. Earl Warren at the age of three months. A photo taken in Los Angeles. (*M. A. Wesner Studio*)

2. Mr. and Mrs. Mathias Warren with their children, Earl and Ethel. *(Lamson Studio)*

3. Early graders of Baker Street School in East Bakersfield (then known as Kern City). Earl, in the first grade, is sixth from the left in the standing front row, wearing his detested Little Lord Fauntleroy suit and ringlet curls. Mother insisted on them until too many schoolyard fights prompted their removal. *(Courtesy Bancroft Library)*

4. Eleven years old in Bakersfield.

5. The 1908 graduating class of Bakersfield High School. Earl is third from left in the front row.

6. A junior at the University of California, Berkeley, 1910.

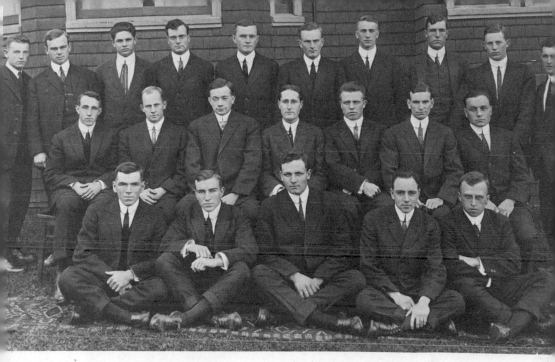

7. Members of Sigma Phi fraternity on the University of California campus in 1912. Warren is second from the right in the back row. (*A. W. Rice photo*)

8. In uniform, taken in November 1917, during World War I. Warren was then a first sergeant at Camp Lewis, Washington.

9. In 1925, at the age of thirty-three, Warren was appointed district attorney of Alameda County. His predecessor and sponsor, Ezra DeCoto, is shown congratulating him. *(Courtesy Bancroft Library)*

10. The Warren family when he was district attorney around 1937, shown in their modest Oakland home. *(Carl Bigelow, Oakland Tribune)*

11. A 1930s photo shows District Attorney Warren checking testimony with Fred Smith, principal witness in a graft trial. *(Courtesy Bancroft Library)*

12. Warren and his "raiders" moved relentlessly against bootleggers during the Prohibition years. Here the crusading D.A. and his deputy, George Helms (next to him with mustache), stand by while another deputy, Oscar Jahnsen, prepares to demolish a still. *(Courtesy Bancroft Library)*

that time no state supervision over law enforcement, and the district attorney was often left with the feeling of frustration that possesses one who has great responsibility but no power to fulfill it.

The case that so impressed me was among the very few that completely baffled us, and to this day is unsolved. It was a sordid episode, so diabolical in nature that I always thought, as did the doctors in the case, that someone having knowledge of the facts would some day, because of a gnawing conscience, make disclosures that would lead to its solution. But this never happened, and the much-publicized Ferguson murder case remains as much a mystery today as it was in 1925.

Bessie Ferguson was a beautiful, demure blonde in her mid-twenties. She lived with her mother in modest circumstances in Oakland, but was not so modest or demure in her activities. Bessie was an extortionist, and obviously a clever one because she was blackmailing a number of prominent married men on the pretense that, as a result of their secret peccadilloes, she had become pregnant by them and had borne a child. The fact is that she never bore anybody's child or even became pregnant. After her death, a doctor disclosed that he had examined her and found that she was physically incapable of giving birth. This, however, was no obstacle for Bessie because she used her sister's baby to display as her own to her victims. The prominent men, whose names need not be mentioned here, were all paying her month by month for care of the fictitious child. This apparently was all known to her mother, for one evening, according to the mother's later grand jury testimony, she asked Bessie where she was going, and Bessie replied that she was going out with Sheriff Frank Barnett of Alameda County. The mother became alarmed instantly and said, "Bessie, you leave him alone; he is too powerful for you to handle." Bessie said confidently, "Don't worry, Mother, he will pay just like the rest of them."

With her mother's protest still in her ears, Bessie left for the evening. And never returned.

The mother, greatly perturbed after two days, went to the home of the sheriff. He was working in his garden at the time, and she demanded to know where her daughter was. According to her testimony, he said, "I don't know." She then accused him of concealing her, but in an agitated way he would only repeat, "I don't know." The mother returned to her home, but made no complaint to anyone.

One evening a few days later, in the neighboring county of Contra Costa, a boy of sixteen was driving his cows home from pasture along a marsh bordering on San Francisco Bay when he discovered, hanging on a reed beside the trail, a blond curl of hair to which was attached a piece of human scalp. He took it to the police authorities, who immediately made a search of the swamp and its environs. Minute pieces of clothing and other things identified as belonging to Bessie were found, and everyone was on the alert to find her body. Then her extortionate practices were publicized. A few days later, in our county, the tender of the High Street bridge across the estuary which flows between the cities of Oakland and Alameda, sitting in his raised observation post, saw an object in the water that attracted his attention. He retrieved it, and there in a sack were most of the bones of a human being. The flesh had been removed from the bones, probably by acid, as the doctors concluded. It was the consensus that only someone with a professional knowledge of the human or animal physique could have dissected the body so skillfully. Both the upper and lower sets of teeth were in the sack, and from a chart in her dentist's office they were conclusively proved to be the teeth of Bessie Ferguson.

So a part of the mystery was solved. We knew that Bessie had been murdered, but by whom and in what jurisdiction was still undetermined. If the crime was committed near where the boy had found the curl and the scalp, jurisdiction was with the authorities of Contra Costa County. If the crime was committed near where the sack of bones was discovered, then it was in our county—but on which city's side of the estuary, Oakland's or the city of Alameda's?

Because of the difficulty of the case and the prominent people involved, none of the police agencies would greatly interest themselves. I felt the investigation could not be abandoned, so I eventually called the grand jury and presented what we had. The evidence did not lend itself to the conclusion that any of the men who admittedly were being blackmailed had committed the crime. Suspicion fell largely on Sheriff Barnett because of the grand jury testimony of the mother, but every word of it was hearsay from Bessie, and that would not be admissible in a trial. We could not connect the sheriff and Bessie at that or any other time. No indictment was returned against anyone, so the testimony was not revealed to the public. The newspapers were, of course, interested in what we had because they had been ferreting, themselves, without result. In order to allay any suspicions they might have as to what was available to us, I invited the publishers of all the papers around San Francisco Bay to meet with me, at which time I would disclose to them everything we knew about the case on condition that they would not reveal it. They consented, and to them or their designated representatives I gave the whole story. In doing so, I learned that you cannot tell things off the record to anyone or it may come back in unpredictable ways to plague you.

The next year was an election year, and it happened that the San Francisco *Examiner* started publication of an Oakland edition. One of its special writers, by the name of William Mason, was named as the new edition's publisher. On coming to Oakland, he supported my prospective opponent, Preston L. Higgins, whose campaign for district attorney he launched in an edition that revealed everything I had privately told the publishers. He wrote that a group of angry citizens was forming to compel me to prosecute the party or parties who had committed the Ferguson crime, and then proceeded to say that I had certain convincing testimony. He coupled this with the announcement that Mr. Higgins was the champion of full disclosure in the case and would oppose me at the coming election.

When I read this in the paper, I immediately made an appointment to see Mr. John Francis Neylan, chief counsel for the Hearst papers in the San Francisco Bay area. After hearing my story, he evinced outrage over the conduct of the Oakland edition's publisher and personally dictated an editorial scathingly rebuking it. He then asked me if I thought that would remedy the situation if it appeared in all the Hearst papers, of which there were four in the area. I told him it would, and thanked him for his prompt and effective response. Mr. Mason was relieved of his position and played no further part in the campaign of Mr. Higgins. The other papers in the area, the San Francisco *Chronicle*, the Oakland *Tribune*, and all of the smaller ones, as far as I can recall, supported me, and this incident, which might have been tragic to my budding political career, probably consolidated support for me as much as any other event. That was the end of my travail in the Bessie Ferguson case. We had her bones put in a preservative solution, where I believe they remain to this day—or at least they were two or three years ago—on the bare possibility that something would turn up to solve the mystery. It never did.

The case was over, but not its repercussions. Sheriff Barnett naturally was given a very unsavory reputation. His connections with vice-ridden Emeryville were widely discussed, and many people were of the belief that Bessie came to her end there. Mike Kelly abandoned the sheriff in his campaign for re-election and supported Burton F. Becker, chief of police of the little city of Piedmont. The Ku Klux Klan was riding high in Alameda County at that time, as it was in so many parts of the country. As things later developed, Becker was one of its leaders. He ran on a strict "law enforcement" platform, charged the sheriff with all kinds of shortcomings, claimed that the underworld attempted to assassinate him as he entered his garage one night just before the election, and pledged himself to wipe out all organized crime. He was elected overwhelmingly in November of 1926.

Instead of preparing to fight crime, Becker had meetings with the bootlegging, prostitution, slot machine, and Chinese lottery interests, and told each of them how they could operate and what it would cost them. This was done before he took office in January, and soon became an open secret. At the end of that month, I asked him to come to my office, where I told him what was being said in the community and how it was greatly injuring him. He brushed it off. At the end of February, I again told him that the talk was increasing and was injuring law enforcement in the county. He still persisted that complainers were just "giving me a bad time." In March I told him there was evidence that the county was opening up to more crime, and that it must stop, as it was casting reflections on all law enforcement officers. His answer this time was firm.

"You take care of your business," he said, "and I will take care of mine."

I replied, "That is exactly what I will do. I will not mention it to you again." And I never did.

However, I did not let the matter drop. I went to see Mr. Richard Carrington, publisher of the Hearst *Post-Enquirer*, who was very close to political boss Mike Kelly. I told him the day was coming when I would probably be obliged to prosecute Becker for corruption, and I did not want Mr. Kelly to think I was doing so in reprisal against him for opposing my election. He asked me if I would tell the story to Kelly, and I said I would be happy to do so. The next day we met in Carrington's office, with him, Kelly, and myself present. Upon hearing my story, Kelly said to Carrington, "Dick, I'm afraid that is true about Becker. Some of my friends have been telling me similar things. I will tell him that he must give up that kind of business. If he doesn't and gets into trouble, he can expect no help from me."

I thanked Kelly and hoped things would change, but they didn't. They became progressively worse. Slot machines started to make their appearance throughout the territory the sheriff was supposed to police, and establishments where they were installed said openly that they were protected. I announced in the press that we would destroy every machine found in our jurisdiction, and then sent some men around the county and picked up hundreds of the "one-armed bandits" and had them smashed publicly in a stamp mill close to the courthouse. We obtained a search warrant and seized a warehouse full of other machines on an order of the Court. These were destroyed in the same manner. In the small industrial city of Emeryville, we raided twenty Chinese lottery places at the same time, and arrested about fifteen hundred visitors in the process. The operators were obliged to bail them out at twenty-five dollars per person. To accomplish this job, I employed a detective agency which assigned about eighty operatives to assist some police officers I had borrowed for the occasion from some friendly departments. The raid almost ended in a tragedy at one gambling den when, as our officers with a search warrant forced their entrance into the place, a shot was fired at them. In return, one of our officers shot the pistol out of the hand of the man who had opened fire. He was only slightly wounded in the hand, but the strange part of the episode was that he was one of the detective agency's men who had been stationed inside to help with the search but who were not supposed to be armed. He said he became confused when the door was smashed open and fired accidentally. No action was taken against him, but I learned not to have jobs like that done with men who were not trained officers. Those shots in a crowded room could have killed one or more persons.

The next day I appeared before the Board of Supervisors, which was in session, and told them we had a corrupt Sheriff's Office that was disgracing every law officer in the county; that it was essential to put a stop to Becker's practices; and that, while I did not want to be a policeman, I needed about ten good investigators and a fund of thirty thousand dollars to bring the situation under control. The Board, without hesitation, granted my request, and we tackled the job with vigor. Our deputies went after the mushrooming bootleg joints and the stills that were being built. They located an enormous one in a pit under a huge barn on a hog ranch. When they left the pit for a short time during the course of their work, the still exploded and tore the roof off the barn. The explosion created an incinerator for hundreds of the poor hogs, who ran screaming into the burning building in the dark. The cause of the blast was never discovered.

At the trial of Sheriff Becker for bribery about two years later, the owners of the hog ranch testified that they had agreed with the sheriff personally to pay him four thousand dollars a month for permission to operate their still, and did in fact so pay him for two months while it was operating. They had agreed with the sheriff on the amount of alcohol it would produce, but the sheriff became suspicious that it was producing more, came to the ranch only a few days before our raid, and demanded that a meter be put on the still to determine the exact number of gallons produced as insurance against being cheated by the operators.

I disliked very much to assume this job of policing the county, but it was either that or permit the county to become a sink of organized vice and crime. If the county's authorities did not have integrity, its police departments would deteriorate comparably. There was no other choice than to do it.

The sheriff's companion and undersheriff, William H. Parker, also was a member of the Ku Klux Klan, and at the next municipal election ran for and was elected commissioner of streets of Oakland. This soon developed into a racket also. All of the paving companies that were to do business in Oakland formed what was called the Greater Oakland Construction Company. Their method of doing business was to have the commissioner of streets specify a certain type of "patent paving," which was simply a formula for mixing the gravel and asphalt in certain proportions that were supposed to result in a better pavement. The patentor would then file with the City Council an agreement to permit any successful bidding contractor to use the patent for a designated royalty. But the royalty was so high that no one who paid it could possibly compete with the members of the Greater Oakland Construction Company, who were secretly required to pay only a fraction of it. The company would then decree which of its members was to get each contract. Every company contractor except the chosen one would then routinely submit a bid higher than his. Thus there was no competitive bidding except on the surface.

For his part in this chicanery, Commissioner Parker received one-half cent per square foot of the surface to be paved as bribe money. Considering the many miles of pavement laid in the city of Oakland, this alone amounted to a sizable sum. Two of the other five commissioners, in a tangential way, were also mixed up in the racket.

It was difficult, as my small staff of investigators already was overloaded doing the sheriff's work, but we pieced this payoff scheme together with only a few missing parts when a newspaperman who was working on the story asked me when I intended to act against Parker and the combine. I told him there were some things still to be resolved; that I was obliged to be sure of my ground so it could not plausibly be charged that I was moving for political reasons, as had been done so successfully in graft trials in other places. He replied, "I can take care of that so it will be no problem. I will get Bill Parker to demand a grand jury hearing." I said if Parker demanded such a hearing that would be different.

The following morning a carefully prepared statement by Commissioner Parker appeared in the press saying he was sick and tired of my insinuations of wrongdoing by him. He demanded that I either call the grand jury, indict him, and send him to San Quentin or fully exonerate him. I immediately communicated with the foreman of the grand jury, and arranged for a session the next day. I then subpoenaed the commissioner as my first witness. He appeared, but refused to answer any questions on the ground his testimony would tend to incriminate him. I then went into the entire paving situation. It was a great scandal. Not only had they cheated on the prices charged, but they also cheated on the actual construction work by diluting the concrete mix, poorly preparing the foundation and otherwise cutting corners.

We came out of the hearing with an indictment against Parker for bribery and accusations of willful and corrupt misconduct in office against him and two other commissioners. Under California law, such an accusation takes precedence over every other matter before the courts. We set these down for hearing very soon thereafter. All three resigned their positions, which put an end to those proceedings because removal from office was the only penalty in such cases. We then were prepared to try ex-Commissioner Parker for bribery.

The grand jury heard testimony against the members of the Greater Oakland Construction Company and the "patent paving" people. Immediately almost every large law firm in the county seemed to be engaged in representing one or another of the members and the patent paving companies. By at least a common understanding, every one of them and their employees refused to testify on the ground that their testimony might tend to incriminate them. This they had a constitutional right to do, but I took the position that while they had the right to do it as individuals, to jointly bring about a complete industry blackout was a conspiratorial distortion of the right. We cross-examined them without mercy as to their reasons for refusing to testify about anything in the industry. They were relying on the fact that if all the public officials and paving industry people who were involved refused to give any evidence to the grand jury, we could not break through their conspiracy to cheat and defraud the public. They also knew that the grand jury proceedings would be secret and, therefore, the public would never know what the facts were. I was determined that this must not be permitted. Knowing that many employees of the Street Department, of necessity, had guilty knowledge of the paving frauds, the foreman of the grand jury and I, with the consent of the empaneling judge, issued a joint statement in which we said that we had no intention of prosecuting anyone who, in the course of his job, performed acts in furtherance of the illegal system; that we were interested only in prosecuting the principals and breaking up their unlawful practices, that if subordinates testified truthfully as to what happened, we would see that no harm came to them. So tight was the ring that this brought only scant results.

We then attacked the secrecy conspiracy, and I issued a statement to the effect that I would release to the public a daily transcript of the grand jury testimony. This created consternation in the paving industry, and the principal lawyers of the community quickly converged on the presiding judge of the court—not the judge in charge of the grand jury. He called the foreman to his chambers and said that if I did make public the hearings, I would find myself in jail for contempt of court. He did not make any such threat to me personally; the foreman related it to me. I told the foreman I felt secure in taking such action, that I had sufficient confidence in my twenty-five deputies to believe that they would even go to jail with me to sustain my position. I authorized him to make that known to the presiding judge. The foreman then asked me if I was sufficiently sure of my ground to risk jail, and when I responded that I was, he said, "All right, my boy, I'll stay with you until the ants carry me out the keyholes of that grand jury room."

This made me happy because when he first had been appointed foreman, we were not friendly. He was much older than I; a crusty former state senator named Frank Levitt who had represented the old race track district in Emeryville and did not look with particular favor upon my reformist regime. As soon as the grand jury was empaneled, I asked him to come to my office to discuss the work for the coming year.

"Senator," I said to him, "I know you have not been particularly friendly to my office recently, but I hope that will not prevent us from working together. We have many problems, a lot of corruption, and great difficulty in contending with the influences that sustain that corruption. I hope you will give me an opportunity to work with you in the best interests of the county. If you will afford me that opportunity, I promise you I will ferret out any facts the grand jury desires to be informed on."

Senator Levitt responded, "That is good enough for me."

So we went to work on that basis. As the months rolled by and he became fully aware of the county's criminal conditions, he became a real crusader against them. I could not have had a stronger ally, for he had a dominating personality as well as a knowledge of the sordid side of public life. This accounts for his carrying back to the presiding judge my response to the judge's threat, along with the statement that he would make no protest against my proposed action.

With that I proceeded with my announced plan to release news of the grand jury testimony, and the public knew from day to day what was transpiring.

The reason I felt secure in doing this was that while our Penal Code prohibited witnesses from disclosing the proceedings of a grand jury, it put no such limitation on a district attorney, and I felt that was consciously done in order not to handicap him in making his investigations. At all events, that was the end of the matter. My action was never protested in either the trials or appeals of any of the cases. Also, I believe this was a factor in later causing the Legislature to require all grand jury proceedings to be filed as a public document whenever an indictment was returned.

I would not recommend for today the vigorous cross-examination we gave to those prominent paving company people when they exercised their right against self-incrimination. That was more than forty years ago, when there were few guidelines for prosecutors and we were sure there was an industry-wide conspiracy to squelch by silence any attempts to root out widespread acts of corruption in city government.

The grand jury, on the testimony presented, indicted Commissioner of Streets Parker for receiving bribes; Harry Lesser, the biggest street paving contractor in Northern California and the guiding genius of the Greater Oakland Construction Company, for giving bribes; and the other members of the company for lesser crimes in connection with the bonding on their street contracts.

We were ready for trial. We had been working on it for a long time, as this unsavory situation had been developing for at least two years. I had read extensively about graft trials in other states, and how most of them had failed because it was made to appear that one political gang was merely trying to displace another. One book in particular made a deep impression on me, though I came upon it only by chance. I was in Sacramento one day during the legislative session and ran across Mr. Franklin Hichborn, an old Hiram Johnson crusader. He asked me how I was getting along on my job. I told him that I was doing all right, but was greatly concerned about a graft situation which was developing, with very little public attention being paid. He asked if I had read his book on the San Francisco graft trials of 1908 and 1909. I confessed that I had not. He said it might help me, and he would send me a copy. The book was entitled *The System*. I later received it and read it, not once, but a number of times. No book I have ever read did me as much good in my public career as that one did. It was a carefully documented account of everything that had occurred, and told how the entire reform movement in San Francisco failed because of delays in the courts. It portrayed the initiating group of high-minded liberals as receiving universal approbation. Every newspaper in the city applauded their proposed cleanup because it was generally recognized as a civic necessity. The reformists started off with a bang. The entire Board of Supervisors, seventeen in all, confessed to accepting bribes for prostitution, gambling, and the granting of franchises to street railway, telephone, water, and other public utilities companies. Numerous indictments were returned against both public and corporate officials. Then the process of delay began to work. Compliant judges issued writs of mandamus and prohibition, and granted continuances until the public became satiated. One after another of the newspapers cooled off, and then became hostile for a variety of reasons. After about two years, the complaint became prevalent that the dragged-out prosecutions were giving the city a bad name, with a net result of only one firm conviction. The person convicted was Abe Ruef, collector and distributor of much of the graft, and he was nailed only because Francis J.

Heney, the chief special prosecutor, was shot and seriously wounded in the courtroom, leaving the remainder of the trial to his fiery assistant, Hiram W. Johnson. The other indictments were washed out one way or another, and the city went back to another *laissez faire* regime of dubious character.

This had happened in other cities as well, but never to my knowledge was it documented as well as in *The System.*

I made up my mind that this would not happen in our situation if it was possible for me to prevent it. We therefore prepared for eventualities while we were still developing the evidence. When our first indictments were returned, I went to see Chief Justice William H. Waste of our Supreme Court, a man of sterling character and an excellent judge. I dared to talk to him because, as a very young lawyer, I had become acquainted with him when he was a Superior Court judge in Alameda County. I told him that we were starting what in all probability would be a series of important graft trials, and that, having read *The System,* I was fearful the same things that undercut the prosecution in San Francisco would happen to us. All but one of our Superior judges were disqualifying themselves from trying the cases, and we might be obliged to rely on the assignment of outside judges. I told him that all I was asking was expedition in handling the trials, and that if applications for special writs were made we were prepared to argue them, even on the quick notice of a telephone call. He told me he would remember this if applications were made to the Supreme Court.

We then indicted Harry Lesser, kingpin of the street paving corruption and architect of the Greater Oakland Construction Company, who immediately employed Theodore J. Roche of San Francisco, the leading trial lawyer of Northern California, and Peter J. Crosby, prominent trial lawyer of Oakland, to defend him.

History immediately started to repeat itself. Mr. Roche appeared before the chief justice one morning with a petition for a writ of prohibition to prevent the trial of his client under the indictment. The chief justice said that he thought it called for a response from me, and a hearing before the Court. He set the hearing for two o'clock that very afternoon. Mr. Roche suggested that I would not have time to prepare for it, but the chief justice said I must be prepared. He directed the clerk of the Court to so advise us. We prepared an answer, and my assistants were there at two o'clock. I was still with the grand jury. The matter was argued, and at four-thirty that afternoon the Court issued an order denying the writ. This was the last delaying tactic of that kind to confront us, and we proceeded to try the rest of our cases expeditiously.

I personally prosecuted Commissioner Parker, Sheriff Becker, one of his collectors of graft, the patent paving people, and contractor Lesser in that period. While these cases were being tried, we had others that were being prosecuted by my assistants. There was no outside help of any kind. All of the cases I tried were before our Superior Court Judge Fred V. Wood, one of the most able trial judges in the state. As previously related, the other judges of our Court disqualified themselves, a practice I very much resented because it is my belief that judges are elected to try the hard cases as well as the easy ones. And these were hard cases because they involved powerful influences in the county and were to determine its very integrity. To indicate the vice of such abdication, it is only necessary to cite what happened in two of these cases. At the time, there was a vacancy on the Court which was filled through appointment by the governor. The new judge was Edward Engs, a fine man, thoroughly conscientious, but with scant experience in the courtroom. He had enjoyed a quiet private practice largely in the field of probate law. He took the oath of office as we were about to try a half dozen of Sheriff Becker's deputies for bribery and conspiracy in a very complex matter, and as his first case Judge Engs was assigned to it. Each of the defendants had at least one lawyer, and each witness was separately cross-examined on behalf of each defendant. Naturally the case lasted for weeks. Finally the testimony and arguments ended one afternoon, and Judge Engs announced that he would instruct the jury at ten o'clock the following morning. When that time arrived the judge was not in court. A hurried telephone conversation with someone at his home informed us that he had left there with ample time to reach the courthouse. Another judge of the Court continued the case from hour to hour throughout the day, but Judge Engs never appeared, and the case was then put over until morning. On the following day, the body of the missing judge was found by a search party a half mile or so from his home in the pit of an abandoned quarry. The strain of the trial apparently had been too much for him, and on his way to court he evidently had jumped over the precipice of the quarry and landed, broken and lifeless, on the brushy ground below. Another judge had to instruct the jury, and the defendants were all convicted, but at what a price!

The other case was tried by an outside judge from one of our mountain counties. It, too, involved a number of defendants, all contractor members of the paving company. They were influential people in the community, and were represented severally by important local law firms. This trial also lasted several weeks, during which there was a reported attempt to bribe a juror. Our office felt that we had clearly proved a case, but the visiting judge, too much impressed by the array of counsel, in my opinion, advised the jury to acquit the defendants. In

California, the trial judge in a criminal case may advise the jury to acquit but cannot direct an acquittal. Believing we were right, and that a case had been proven, I directed my assistants to resist the acquittal. They argued vehemently that the judge was wrong and the defendants should be convicted. We had little hope of prevailing, but the jury was out a long time and debated the matter at great length before finally following the advice of the judge. This was the only one of the graft cases we lost. In all the others, the defendant was convicted. I was always of the belief that if a judge of our county had tried the lone exception with an appreciation of the case's importance to the public, the result would have been different.

The case against Harry Lesser was an interesting one. He was the bell cow of the paving industry in Northern California and, in my opinion, corrupted more city governments than any man I knew about in my years in California. When we indicted him, our case was not a particularly strong one. It showed probable cause, but we needed some good breaks to make his guilt crystal clear. And we got them. Once in court, everything we touched seemed to turn to gold, although we had run into great difficulties in our preparation. The foreman of the grand jury and I were both regretful that our offer of immunity in return for evidence against the principals did not produce as much as we had hoped for. None of Mr. Lesser's employees gave any assistance. We, therefore, indicted his two top employees jointly with him. We were handicapped in not having any expert engineering witnesses because none of the engineering firms with street-paving experience wanted to testify against the "contractor combine," and we could not use them. The defense had its choice of experts. Theodore Roche, Lesser's lawyer, endeavored to make it an engineering contest, and I tried to avoid that. He selected as his trump card Professor Charles Derleth, Jr., dean of the College of Engineering of the University of California. The dean had previously been employed by the City Council to report on the quality of the construction work being questioned. While he had conceded in his report that there had been deviations from the specifications for the job, he concluded that on the whole the work approximated standards of compliance followed by contractors in street-paving jobs throughout Northern California.

The dean took the stand at the beginning of court on a Thursday morning. Mr. Roche started to qualify him as an expert in his field. I immediately offered to stipulate that he was indeed an eminent engineering authority. Although the dean stated that he must be finished with his testimony before the weekend, as he was obliged to be in Chicago on Monday morning, Mr. Roche declined to accept my stipulation and for the entire day interrogated Derleth on famous engineering projects he had been associated with. On Friday, he spent most of the day asking the dean about the street-paving business in general, and the jobs involved in this case in particular. At the close of court, Mr. Roche said he realized the dean was required to be in Chicago Monday, but that he had only a very few questions for Saturday morning, as we were working a six-day week. Mr. Roche continued his direct examination until five minutes to twelve on Saturday. We could not legally extend our court session beyond noon on that day, so the judge said we might as well adjourn until Monday morning. I said that if he would let me proceed for the next few minutes I might be able to shorten the cross-examination. He said, "You may proceed."

I then picked up a copy of the report of the dean to the City Council, let him know what it was, and inquired of him: "You did report that the defendant skimped on the amount of concrete in the mix, didn't you?"

"Yes," he answered.

"And you did report that the paving was not the thickness required by the specifications, did you not?"

"Yes."

"You also found that the foundation was not adequately prepared?"

"Yes," he repeated.

"When inspecting the work a few months after completion, you found that in a number of places the pavement had cracked and there were ruts in the surface—is that not so?"

Again came the answer: "Yes."

At that moment the clock struck twelve, and I said, "That will be all, Professor. Thank you." The judge promptly adjourned the session until Monday morning. When court convened on that day, the professor, instead of being in Chicago, was present in court. Mr. Roche asked him to take the stand, where he said, "Your honor, I would like to explain my answers of Saturday."

"Your answers call for no explanation," the judge replied. "Specific questions were asked and specific answers given. You are excused, Professor."

I believe the case of the defendant was lost then and there. Ordinarily that would be as much good luck as I could expect in any case, but there was more to come.

We produced a witness who at the time the contract was being performed testified that the paving company had issued checks each week to fictitious persons characterized as "dead men," and those checks were distributed to city inspectors on the job as bribe money to obtain their consent to deviations from the specifications. He had no records to corroborate his testimony, but stuck stubbornly to the story during

three days of grueling cross-examination by Mr. Roche. He said the
timekeeper for the defendant had made the entries for the "dead men"
and had distributed the checks to city inspectors. A few days later, he
came to me and told me that in going over some old records in his
trunk the night before, he had found a book corroborating his testimony in the handwriting of the timekeeper. When the latter took the
stand for the defense, he contradicted everything my witness had said
and testified that it was a complete fabrication. On cross-examination, I
permitted him to repeat his denials, then produced the book in his own
handwriting. Thus confronted, he broke down and made a complete
confession of his wrongdoing. In all the years I was district attorney,
this was the only time I ever saw anybody change his testimony from a
denial of all guilt to a complete confession before the jury. This shortened the case greatly because the defense did not know what other incriminating evidence I might have, so no other company witnesses were
called to the stand.

As if this were not enough good fortune in one case, we found that in
a neighboring county there had been a case of bribery by Lesser and his
associates much like the one we were trying. It had been called to the
attention of the authorities there, but they had chosen to do nothing
about it. We assembled all the evidence and, employing the same technique that we used on the bunco men, we presented the case to the
jury as a "similar offense" to show a general pattern of bribery schemes
on Lesser's part. It was an even clearer case than our own. Taking all
these things together, there was no escape for Harry Lesser. He was
convicted, and was sentenced to San Quentin prison. His two employees were convicted with him, but because neither had taken the
stand and committed perjury and because there was no evidence of
their receiving any money other than their regular salaries, which were
ordinary, I suggested to the judge that justice would be done if he were
lenient with them. The foreman of the grand jury agreed with me, and
the judge imposed moderate fines instead of sending them to prison.

This ended our paving graft prosecutions. The results, I felt, were satisfactory. Imprisoned were the corrupt commissioner, the head of the
paving combine, and some of the patent paving people. Removed from
office were three of the five commissioners for willful and corrupt misconduct. The vacancies were filled by competent and honest men, and
the public in the November election abolished the commission form of
government and replaced it with the more efficient city manager-coun-
cil form, which has served the city well ever since.

Immediately after the paving indictments, we turned our attention
to the corruption sustained by the Sheriff's Office. Again we achieved
an important break at a critical time, which made our case complete.

For more than a year we had been looking for a Fred Smith, an erstwhile automobile agent who had absented himself from the community when the Sheriff Becker scandal first broke, leaving behind some complaints about his larcenous automobile contracts. While in Alameda County, he was a constant companion of the sheriff. In fact, he was recognized as Becker's agent, and in the underworld was known as his "bagman." We heard from lawbreakers that they had paid Smith money for the sheriff, but we needed him to establish that the money actually went to Becker. We had information at various times that Smith was in the Los Angeles area and were told where he was living. Showing the usual professional courtesy to the authorities in that county, my men always notified them when they went to Los Angeles to arrest Smith on a grand larceny warrant resulting from an automobile transaction. Strangely, each time they went to his home address they were advised that he had just moved.

Finally, after several such futile efforts, we were told by a newspaper reporter that he knew from a source in San Quentin prison exactly where and at what time Smith could be picked up. The price for this bit of information was that two special writers of the San Francisco *Examiner* be permitted to sit in the car with my inspectors when the pickup was made. I agreed, and we were told it would be on a Sunday at noon, on a certain street in Los Angeles. We were also told that he would be accompanied by two gunmen, and that great care must be taken to see that they did not shoot their way out of any trap.

I therefore sent two carloads of officers, and with them the two newsmen. Exactly as our information had it, Fred Smith came walking down the street at noon, flanked by a man on each side. The arresting officers' cars were maneuvered carefully to converge on the three as instantaneously as possible. At a signal, the cars stopped suddenly, and with drawn guns the officers ordered the three men to raise their hands. There was prompt compliance, and the three were searched, but no weapon was found on any of them.

Small wonder. On further investigation, it developed that Fred's two companions were ministers of the gospel. The association of the three was soon explained. A year or two before this, the Ministerial Association elected what was supposed to be a reform administration but which turned out to be equally as corrupt as the one it supplanted. How newcomer Fred Smith became a part of it, I never knew, but in accordance with his proclivities for collecting money, he had become a member of the mayor's Finance Committee. In order to appeal to the church group, he, of course, needed to have religion, which explains his being on this particular street every Sunday with two preachers coming home from worship.

I imagine the newsmen saw little of the actual arrest. Apprehensive about the possibility of a shooting, they remained, I was told, glued to the floor of the car.

Fred Smith was arrested under the warrant. The preachers were not restrained. Los Angeles authorities were not notified because, with the information that had been given us and our failures in other attempts to locate Smith, it was reasonable to assume that he would have been tipped off and would have found means of escaping a prompt return to Oakland. Instead, the officers drove north four hundred miles to San Jose, where I met them at the St. Claire Hotel. I had engaged rooms there for the purpose. When Smith was brought in, I told him he had a choice to make—that of being a witness for the prosecution in the graft investigation or a defendant in a grand larceny charge. He assured me that he would be a witness and begged me not to send him to the county jail because he said if the Becker crowd knew he had been talking to me they would kill him. He then tried some diversionary tactics to see how little I would be satisfied with, but I told him it was all or nothing. Either he would tell the true story of his relations with the sheriff or he would become a defendant. His main concern seemed to be that he might land in Becker's jail.

With his full concurrence, we kept him under wraps in a little summer home on the Russian River about sixty miles north of Oakland from that day until he testified at the sheriff's trial. As the time of the trial approached, he became ever more apprehensive about being a witness and on his return to Oakland for that purpose he announced to my assistant, Frank Coakley, that he had changed his mind. I went to Coakley's office, where Smith was, and Smith told me that he had changed his mind and would not testify. I asked him if he were sure that was the way he wanted it. When he said it was, I told Coakley to forget him as a witness and have him jailed for the larceny. I then left the room. It was only a few minutes until Coakley came to my room and said that Smith had again changed his mind and wanted to talk to me. I went back and told him I had no time to waste with him, that this was his last chance to make a choice. He said he would testify, and did so the very next day.

I did not do any of this secretly. I informed the foreman and the grand jury of every move I made. I told the trial jury in my opening statement of the choice I had given Smith. I added that he was not a reliable witness, that I would not believe him myself unless he was corroborated, and that I would not ask them to do so either. However, it was my intention to substantiate Smith, and this was done, through testimony by vicemongers who had paid off through him.

As soon as it was announced that the grand jury was investigating

Sheriff Becker, gossip around the city had it that "now is the time when Earl Warren will get even with Mike Kelly." I resented this for three reasons. First, it was not true. I had no animosity toward Kelly. Although I was not one of his organization, most of his people treated me very kindly. Second, nothing in our investigation of civic corruption had pointed toward any involvement on his part. And, third, the worst thing that could happen to our prosecutions would be to cause a belief by the public that they were politically inspired. I therefore interceded again with publisher Carrington to arrange a meeting for me with Mike Kelly in Carrington's office. The publisher agreed to the meeting, and when we had gathered I said:

"Mr. Kelly, I am thoroughly aware of the gossip around town about my seeking revenge against you. I want you to know it is untrue. Also, I want you to know that I have learned of nothing that would implicate you in any way. I can only think of one reason why I might call you as a witness before the grand jury. I propose to get Sheriff Becker on the stand and ask him if I didn't urge him personally and through you to desist from the very practices we are now investigating. If his answer is 'No,' I intend to take the stand and testify that I did. I would then feel it necessary to call upon you to corroborate me."

Kelly thought for a moment, and then said, "Don't worry, Warren, he won't deny it."

We parted on that understanding note, and neither he nor I had any occasion to regret it during the entire upheaval that followed.

My office established a clear case against the sheriff and his collectors through a succession of vice purveyors who testified that they had paid money to the sheriff or his "bagmen" to protect their illegal operations. When the testimony was concluded, I suggested that an accusation to remove the sheriff from office for willful and corrupt misconduct and indictments for bribery against both the sheriff and a collector named J. Cromwell Ormsby† would be in order. At the suggestion of one of the jurors, we took a short recess. During the break, seven of the jury members came to me and said they wanted to indict Ormsby for bribery but felt that an accusation for removal from office would be sufficient punishment for the sheriff.

I knew from records disclosed as the result of a raid on the state headquarters of the Ku Klux Klan in Los Angeles County and disclosed to law enforcement agencies throughout the state that five of the jurists as well as Becker were members of the Klan. I had no knowledge of the other two of the group, but it was a fair inference that they, too, were members. That left us one short of the necessary number to indict

† Ed. note: Ormsby had been an attorney in Los Angeles for noted evangelist Aimee Semple McPherson.

Becker. A grand jury consists of nineteen members, but one of ours had a lingering illness and did not participate in any of the investigation. The law required the affirmative vote of twelve to indict; we only had eleven.

I told the grand jury that while it was their duty to determine who should be indicted, I did not see how I could prosecute the collector who paid the bribe money to the sheriff and not prosecute the sheriff for receiving it. Nevertheless, by a vote of eleven to seven, they indicted Ormsby and filed only an accusation against the sheriff.

We then went into court and reported this action to the judge. When it had been recorded by the clerk, the judge, according to procedure, inquired of the foreman if he had anything further to report. On receiving a negative answer, he said, "Mr. District Attorney, do you have anything further?"

"Yes, your honor, I now move to dismiss the indictment against Cromwell Ormsby in the interests of justice. I do not see how in conscience I could prosecute a collector of graft for the sheriff and not prosecute the sheriff for receiving the money from him."

The judge turned to the foreman and said, "Mr. Foreman, could that possibly be the situation?" "Precisely, your honor," the foreman replied.

The judge then said, "Well, the indictment is dismissed, and the entire matter is re-referred to the grand jury for appropriate action."

The grand jury was told that we would meet in the jury room immediately. I had a subpoena issued for the sheriff to appear forthwith. He was called as our first witness. When I started to examine him, contrary to his former practice of denying everything, he exercised his constitutional right of refusing to testify on the ground that it would tend to incriminate him. Before the next witness was called, the leader of the Klan group on the jury said to me, "We are satisfied. Anyone who won't defend himself can't expect others to do it for him." He repeated this to the grand jury which determined that it needed no more testimony, and proceeded to vote unanimously to indict both the sheriff and his collector.

Before the day was over, the indictment was returned and the defendants were released on bail. The sheriff, like the city commissioners, resigned his position before the trial and under the law the coroner of the county succeeded him until the vacancy could be filled by the Board of Supervisors.

The bribery trial was spectacular only in the diversity of the graft it disclosed. Apparently no opportunity had been overlooked. The defense was neither convincing nor skillful. The sheriff denied everything, but made a bad appearance on the witness stand. The remainder of his defense was character testimony, all of which boomeranged. First, his attorneys attacked the general reputation of Fred Smith, his chief collector in the community. That suited my purpose perfectly. On cross-examination I tied their testimony about Smith's unsavory character to the period when Smith and the sheriff were constant companions. They then tried a power play to establish a good reputation for the sheriff. Relying on the custom of police officers not to testify against other police officers, the defense, without interviewing him beforehand, called James Drew, chief of police of Oakland. After establishing that he had known the sheriff for many years, they asked the question, "Do you know the general reputation of Sheriff Burton F. Becker for truth, honesty, and integrity in this community?"

The chief, after a slight hesitation, said, "I do."

"Is it good or bad?"

Agonizingly but firmly, the chief responded, "I am sorry to say, sir, that it is bad."

In spite of this disaster, Chief of Police August Vollmer of Berkeley was also called under like circumstances, and he, too, said that the sheriff's reputation was not good. No further character testimony was introduced, and the defense soon closed.

Both the sheriff and Ormsby were convicted and sentenced to San Quentin.

It was not a particularly difficult trial, but we did have some apprehension throughout. First, there was always the danger that we might have some Ku Klux Klansmen on the trial jury as we had had on the grand jury. Then there was the possible danger of violent action by the sheriff himself, a braggadocio sort who was accustomed to talking out of the side of his mouth to show his contempt and was drinking rather heavily between his indictment and the trial. He would occasionally, at some place from which he knew it would be repeated to me, say, "I am not worried about the goddamn thing. If it gets too tough, I'll give Warren half of what is in here and take the other half myself," and he would lay his six-shooter on the table or desk in front of him. His wife, in like manner, would say in women's circles, knowing it would be repeated, "We know Warren's weakness. It's those children. He had better look out for them."

Nina and I had three youngsters at the time. Naturally, these things were disturbing, but I have gone through life with the belief that a barking dog rarely bites. At times I may have relied on that belief too much, but up to this writing it has not failed me.

Becker's threats were also told to the presiding judge, and he offered to have the sheriff searched each day before court. I urged him not to do so because it would give only a modicum of security and would afford the sheriff's forces great satisfaction and even confidence if they

knew that I was frightened. I did, however, keep two men unob-
trusively close to the counsel table and their only duty was to watch the
actions of the sheriff.

Nothing untoward happened, and when the verdict of guilty was returned, he was promptly relieved of his revolver and taken to the
county jail.

This ended for a time corrupt practices by law enforcement officers
in the county, and for many years thereafter our county and the cities
which comprise it had relatively honest and efficient government.

Of course, there is an exception to every rule. The city of Alameda
was an example for a brief time in our locale. At its municipal election
of about 1936, the citizens voted in an administration that threw the
city into a turmoil. The newly elected councilmen had little conception
of their responsibilities or prerogatives. They made things worse by appointing an arrogant, irresponsible city manager by the name of B. Ray
Fritz to administer the city government. They were only in office a
short time when stories of petty thievery and other derelictions of duty
became rampant. The errant councilmen presented a solid conspiracy,
and under their manager things deteriorated rapidly. It was not a case
of underworld connections. Alameda was then strictly a residential city.
It had little more than occasional street crimes. However, theft of city
supplies and building materials, use of City Hall labor for councilmen's
homes and summer places, construction of private roads at public expense, and other irregularities began to be suspected.

One morning at breakfast I read that the members of the council
had a torrid verbal fight that resulted in a split in the administration.
Later in the morning, one of the quarreling councilmen came to my
office and told me stories of the wrongdoing of the opposing group.

The grand jury had been interested in the Alameda city situation for
some time, and we had been watching for a break-through. The
members happened to be sitting at that time, considering some routine
work. I went to the jury room and advised them of the information my
visitor had to impart. They agreed to hear him. I brought him into the
jury room where he, in anger, told his story and added that we could
get corroboration.

We immediately called as witnesses those friendly to his group. Together, they made a strong case. We sent for those complained against
and afforded them the opportunity to tell their side of the story. The
upshot of the hearing was that at the end of the second day the grand
jury returned indictments against all the members of *both* contending
forces and their city manager.

The manager was promptly tried, convicted, and sent to prison. Most
of the councilmen, each vying to be first, then wanted to resign from

their positions. We found that if they all resigned, the city charter made no provision for filling the vacancies. In order to keep a quorum, we arranged for only one member at a time to relinquish his position. Then the others would vote to install a person recommended by a cross section of civic and business leaders, who joined in an effort to restore orderly conditions to the city. One by one, the corrupt councilmen were thus replaced, and the mayor and all but two holdover members who were not involved pleaded guilty and were given county jail sentences. The speed with which this was done was the principal reason for its complete success.

Meanwhile, as a result of the Sheriff's Office convictions, the iniquitous little city of Emeryville became as quiet as a churchyard, and during my later years as district attorney presented no major problems.

The Board of Supervisors appointed the mayor of Berkeley, Mike Driver, to fill the vacancy as sheriff. He was an elderly man of sterling character who looked like a typical western sheriff of pioneer days with his long handle-bar mustache. He was known to be absolutely incorruptible, and the day he was appointed I announced that I ceased to be a policeman; that my men would in the future perform no policing action, but would rely on the sheriff as the law contemplated. For my last eight years as district attorney, we followed this policy, and conditions became progressively better. The sheriff served honorably, being elected and re-elected until his retirement, when his brother was appointed to succeed him.

I believe I should pause here to make an apology for the excessive use of the personal pronoun in relating my experiences. Such usage may be almost essential in writing an autobiography, but I have no intention of conveying the idea that it was I alone who was responsible for the successful outcome of many of these episodes. I had a staff of twenty-five lawyers, ten inspectors, a personal secretary, and a sizable clerical group. These are the people to whom credit is largely due for any success the office achieved. They were as devoted to the office as I was. They were also thoroughly loyal, and during all my years there not one leak emanated from our office. Counting the turnover, I must have had forty deputies while district attorney, and not one of them ever disgraced the office. On the contrary, they shed luster on it. Later, my chief assistant, Ralph E. Hoyt, ran for and was elected to the office when I was elected state attorney general. He served with distinction until I appointed him a Superior Court judge. J. Frank Coakley was then appointed to fill the post, and he served honorably for twenty years. I offered him a judgeship, but he was devoted to the office and decided to remain. Only recently he retired, and the office was filled by his assistant. There were so many others to whom I am particularly indebted that I dislike to mention only a few, but Warren Olney III, Charles Wade Snook, J. Paul St. Sure, Richard Chamberlain, George Helms (captain of inspectors), Oscar Jahnsen (lieutenant of inspectors), and, of course, my devoted deputy and private secretary when I was district attorney, attorney general and governor, Helen MacGregor, are some without whom there would have been little success. This is not to belittle the services of the others, because they were equally hard-working and loyal, but the list is too long. Practically all of them were young men and women, chosen for that reason. At that time, because of the low salary scale and customary permission to practice privately on the side, I had but one of two choices to make in selecting my deputies: either they had to be young lawyers who were interested in acquiring experience (as I had been myself), or old-timers who had not been particularly successful in private practice and looked upon the salary and free office service as a comfortable accommodation. I chose the former, though they had little or no experience, because they were looking for hard work, had no political connections, and had the energy to meet our tasks. This combination of attributes would give the office the independence I was determined to have. Accordingly, I announced that all vacancies would be filled with veterans of World War I, so far as they were available, and I always had two or three in reserve who were available for appointment. Also handy as a reserve pool were recent graduates of law schools, particularly of my own Boalt Hall, who saw the experience other young men were receiving in the office and offered to accept a deputyship without pay. I often seized the opportunity to hire them. Although it was a sort of internship for them, they were treated exactly the same as the others and, of course, a number of them were put on salary as vacancies occurred. Some of them remained with me throughout most of my political career. With these two pools for recruitment, I sidestepped the importunities of political forces and maintained a personal organization impervious to outside influences.

As things developed later, we needed that solidarity. In some quarters, we were called a "Boy Scout" organization, and we did have the fervency of the Scout movement, but it was effective. Since then I have often been referred to as a "crusading district attorney," but I never considered myself a crusader in any of my public positions. Public office is a great responsibility, carrying with it the duty to preserve its dignity and to use its powers so that the needs of constituents are met with efficiency, honesty, and fairness to all. This philosophy calls for a certain personal discipline, and both my wife, Nina, and I agreed to undergo it. We determined that as long as I remained in the public service, I would have no business connections that could possibly interfere.

If, in achieving our ambition to have a family of six children, it was impossible to live on the salary of the office, we decided that I would leave public service and seek more remunerative employment. Because of her good management of the home and her personal economies, we were able to have such a family without the need of my seeking outside resources during my public career. With the cooperation of our children, we were able to see them through college and into productive lives of their own. This was not easy to do, and my first test of fiscal independence came in 1926, one year after my appointment as district attorney, when I was required to run for election. A number of people offered campaign contributions. But I knew that in an election for such an office, some designing types would gladly contribute to both opposing candidates. It would, therefore, make little difference to them which side eventually won. I wanted no such obligations to donors hanging over me. My wife and I discussed the matter and decided that instead of buying the home we desired, I would invest one year's salary in my campaign and refuse *all* contributions. This I did, and with the exception of $150 donated by each of my top three assistants, this constituted my campaign fund.

Today it would be considered chicken feed, but in those days, television and radio played no part in a campaign; instead, we enrolled scores of friends to assist in a heap of letter writing. I spoke every noon at luncheon clubs, then to lodges and women's clubs in the evenings and, of course, went along with the other candidates on their nightly pilgrimages around the county, using school buildings for meeting places at which all the contending candidates spoke. The meetings were very poorly attended, but the press gave some attention to them, and it was wise for the candidates to appear. In order not to appear to favor any individual, they called on us alphabetically. As each speaker finished, he and his few adherents would leave the hall for the next meeting, and by the time we reached the W's, there was hardly anyone to talk to.

Once evening the crowd was unusually small, especially after the others had spoken and left with their followers. I was the only one on the platform, and there was only one man left in the audience. Nevertheless, I gave him my little speech, and in concluding thanked him for remaining to hear me. He replied, "You are quite welcome, but I am entitled to no credit for remaining. My name is Young, and I am the next speaker."

The campaign was a success. I achieved my complete independence, and in the elections of 1930 and 1934 did not have an opponent who necessitated any campaign expenditure on my part.

After the conclusion of the graft cases in 1930, the job was an active one but was not as emotional an experience as it had been until then.

There was no discernible corruption in the county; I had brought the trial calendar into manageable condition, and my office was so organized that I could rely on satisfactory performance in its various activities. I kept myself informed on everything that went on in the office through daily meetings at 8:30 A.M. The office was divided into five units, and I met with each of them once every week. They were the Superior Court criminal trial deputies, the Civil Division, the Oakland City Hall deputies, the deputies for the County Justices Courts, and the inspectors. Our meetings would last one hour, Monday through Friday, and on Saturday morning we would have a general meeting of all the Court House deputies and inspectors. We would discuss the pending work of the week and ways and means of achieving results. The youngest deputy in the office was free to express his opinions, and often did so to good effect. The remainder of the day I would have little contact with my deputies, except in emergencies, because we were all busy, but when the outer doors were closed at five o'clock my door was always open to them to discuss anything that concerned them. It was rare that several were not with me until six o'clock or later. This was not an easy life, but a satisfying one in that everyone knew what was going on and felt a part of the action. I could give some time to other things with a broader base, and I did.

I was particularly interested in coordinating the law enforcement agencies of the entire state to prevent the prohibition era rackets that had sprung up in so many of the eastern communities from spreading to California. In some cities, of which Chicago was a notorious example, a man could not be sure of remaining in business unless he paid tribute to some extortionate association controlled by gangsters. I was in a particularly good position to take some initiative in this field because I was chairman of the State Board of Criminal Identification and Investigation. It maintained a State Identification Bureau similar to that of the FBI (in those days the latter was not as pervasive as it is today). Also, it maintained a crime laboratory with a few experts who were available to rural sheriffs and small town police departments for help in the solution of major crimes. It also operated, through the Telephone Company, a teletype connection between the police and sheriffs' offices of the state—a new means of inter-agency communication. Finally, it was charged with the responsibility of establishing schools for the training of police. (This was an idea even preceding the FBI program of police education which has been so helpful to law enforcement throughout the years.) There was no appropriation for such a program, but I endeavored to initiate it through the universities.

I went first to the University of California, Stanford, and the University of Southern California. There was some verbal support, but the universities were willing to establish such schools only if the instruction were given by academic professors. The police showed no interest in this. At that time, there was a wide gap between police work and academia. I remember how reluctantly the idea of such schools was accepted by many of the older policemen. At that time we had a fine old gentleman, Frank Lynch, who was chief of police of Oakland. I asked him to come to my office one day to tell him about my ideas of police education in an effort to establish such a school in his department. He listened intently, and then said:

"I'm sure you must be right, Mr. Warren, but we old-time policemen who came on the force about the turn of the century had very little training. When I came on the department, I merely asked my city councilman if he could help me. He said, 'Certainly. Just report to the desk sergeant at four o'clock, and he will take care of you.' I did so, and the sergeant handed me a night stick and a revolver, told me my beat was from the City Hall on Fourteenth Street to the estuary on First Street, then west to the Point on the Bay, a distance of three miles, then back to Fourteenth and along it to the City Hall, another three miles. He said all I was required to do was to keep order in that district. I walked all night and checked in at City Hall in the morning, weary and with sore feet. I then went to Sergeant Mulqueeny, a friend of my father, and said to him, 'Sergeant, you are a veteran in the department and I am a recruit. I wonder if you can give me some advice on how to become a good police officer.' The sergeant thought for a moment, and said, 'Yes, my boy. Take care of your feet.' Now, Mr. Warren, that is all the police training we had, but I will be willing to help in any way you suggest."

This was an unusually cooperative viewpoint for an old-timer. However, there were many younger officers who could see the need for modernized training and desired it. One day when I was in Sacramento, I met Dr. Thomas W. MacQuarrie, president of San Jose State College. In a discussion of mutual problems, I told him of my trouble in interesting the universities in a practical police school. He said, "I see no difficulty there. Doctors teach medical students, lawyers teach law students, and engineers teach engineering students. There is no reason why police officers should not teach police officers. If you desire, I will work with you to develop such a school at San Jose State College." I accepted enthusiastically. Very soon thereafter we put together a faculty of outstanding police officers, laboratory technicians, and prosecuting attorneys for the purpose. Director J. Edgar Hoover of the FBI agreed to send one of his able assistants to participate, and we announced a summer course for that year. The response was tremendous. Several hundred police officers applied, many of them offering to pay their own expenses and use their vacation time in that manner. All of them could not be accommodated at once, so we had two-week terms throughout the summer. The school was considered a great success and resulted in an upsurge of morale and efficiency in law enforcement circles throughout the state.

The school continued for many years. San Jose was the first college in California to have a regular police program, and as it prospered some universities established departments of criminology. After the FBI established its national academy in 1935 and trained selected police officers throughout the country, almost every police department of any size in California set up a local school, as a result of which California law officers have been better trained, in my opinion, than those of any other state in the union.

There have been helpful by-products of this training. It brought together three law enforcement agencies—the city police, the county sheriff, and the district attorney—which previously had been disparate and envious of each other to the point of disunity. Each of these segments had, for many years, its own statewide association and its own legislative program that often conflicted with the other two. Fortunately, they all agreed that there should be no statewide police with general jurisdiction, and their representatives at the state legislature watched to see that no inroads were made against this principle.

Through the educational program, we were able to bring the various arms of law enforcement to an understanding of the fact that if we were to withstand centralization by state agencies, it would be necessary for us to make the most of our own facilities through coordination and cooperation. The result of this was that we commenced meeting together and uniting behind a single legislative program. By agreement, the management of the program centered in my office. I kept track of every bill in the Legislature affecting law enforcement and after consultation we all decided what action should be taken on each of them. It was remarkable what little difference of opinion there was among us. I kept one of my principal assistants at Sacramento throughout the legislative session, and when a hearing was set before the Judiciary committees, I would go to Sacramento and debate our case for hours at a time. We used a technique that was extremely effective. Although I made the presentation on behalf of all three law enforcement associations, we arranged whenever possible to have the district attorney, the sheriff, and the chief of police in attendance from the district represented by each member of the committee considering the bills. This moral support was most persuasive. We were not as interested in making new law as we were in preventing laws that would retard law enforcement. We fought bail bond brokers, loan sharks, and anything that would weaken our programs against organized crime. In all the years I was active in California, I do not recall any bill that became law over our opposition. Incidentally, that same program has continued, and my old District Attorney's Office still represents the law enforcement agencies at Sacramento. My former assistants, Ralph E. Hoyt and J. Frank Coakley, both carried on the program throughout their district attorneyships, which extended to 1969.

By and large, the law enforcement agencies of California have responded splendidly to the challenges presented during the years of our stupendous growth. When I became district attorney, the population of the state was about four million. Today it more than twenty million. Problems encountered in that mobility and expansion can hardly be imagined by outsiders, but our agencies have remained relatively free from scandal and have never permitted the rackets spawned by the prohibition era to become embedded in our society or in our institutions.

As I worked on this phase of my job, I became sufficiently interested in governmental affairs to want to carve out a continuing public career. While I had not deliberately sought the district attorneyship, I did aspire to and plan for the office of attorney general. I could see a great opportunity for developing it into an extremely important arm of the state government. At the time, it was considered almost a sinecure. One man had held it for thirty-six years. The salary was $5,000 a year and he had the right to practice law privately. The attorney general had approximately fifty deputies, none of whom received more than $250 a month, with a like right to practice on the side. In the years my predecessor occupied the position, it had grown like Topsy from an office of five or six people to its then size. There was no central filing system, no calendar control. Each deputy handled his own phase of the work with little supervision. There were three offices, the principal one being at San Francisco, the others at Sacramento and Los Angeles. The office had no definite law enforcement powers other than to represent the state in the appeal of criminal cases to the Supreme Court and Appellate Courts.

I advocated a plan for making the attorney general the chief law enforcement officer of the state with power to replace any sheriff or district attorney in the prosecution of any criminal case if the interests of justice so warranted. Under this plan, the attorney general would devote his entire time to the job at a salary equal to that of a justice of the Supreme Court. I also suggested that the proposal should later be implemented by the creation of a State Department of Justice adequate to the performance of the duties of the office. Many law enforcement officers indicated their agreement, and I was invited to make a speech to the American Bar Association at its meeting in Los Angeles. As far as I know, there was no such State Department of Justice in the nation at the time.‡

As vice-chairman of the State Bar Committee on the Administration of Justice, I wrote a constitutional amendment increasing the powers of the attorney general to be submitted by initiative measure to the people. At the 1934 election, it was enacted by a very substantial vote.

When it became evident that the office was to be an important one, several people indicated an interest in running for it. The incumbent was a fine old gentleman by the name of Ulysses S. Webb. He came from one of the mountain counties where he had been district attorney. He was honorable in the conduct of his office and no scandal ever touched it. I wasted no time in going to him and telling him of my ambition. I told him that I had read and heard talk about others and myself running against him, and I wanted him to know exactly what my intentions were.

"General," I said, "I do want your job, but not while you want it. I will never run against you, and as long as you seek election you may send your papers to me and I will personally circulate them for the necessary signatures. Please don't let anyone make you believe otherwise. But if you should ever decide to retire, I would appreciate it if you would advise me of your intention to do so, because I want to succeed you and would then run for the office."

He cordially thanked me, and said he would advise me in advance of any such move on his part.

About three years later, he called me to his office and said that he did not believe at his age—as I recall, it was seventy-three—he should undertake the expanded duties of the office, and that he intended to retire at the end of his term in 1938. I was therefore, under my own terms, free to contend for the office.

I had done some broadening of my base in the meantime, and had

‡ Ed. note: Contributing to Warren's conviction that statewide cooperation among law enforcement agencies was necessary were several major crimes that pointed up the need. In the early 1930s, there were two armed robberies of trains in Northern California in which the bandits made off by car after intercepting sizable amounts of the Columbia Steel Works' payroll. Both times they eluded police because there was little cooperation on the part of officers from Alameda and Contra Costa counties during the chase. This brought on a realization of the need for better intercounty planning to apprehend criminals who made getaways across county lines in an age that provided them with ever faster means of transportation.

On another occasion, in 1934, a mob broke into the Santa Clara county jail and lynched two confessed kidnappers after the pair had abducted a young man named Brooke Hart, killed him, and dumped his body off a bridge. This action, like the train robbery escapes, signaled a need to have fuller mutual assistance among city, county, and even state law enforcement agencies, especially when added manpower was required. Warren saw the Attorney General's Office as the logical hub of a statewide coordinative system, with himself at its center.

become chairman of the Republican State Central Committee. This increased my acquaintances throughout the state.*

In 1936, after a bizarre presidential primary campaign, which I will describe a little later, I was elected Republican national committeeman for California, and was made a member of the Executive Committee. All of these positions came to me almost by default after the election of Franklin D. Roosevelt, since Republican Party offices were thought to be of little value and not many prominent Republicans were seeking them during this period of general domination by the Democrats.

While I was state chairman, the 1936 presidential election came along. Apathy on the part of Republicans was manifested. Governor Alf Landon of Kansas was the hand-picked candidate of publisher William Randolph Hearst, and there were many of us in California who believed Hearst should not be dominating California Republicanism. We therefore resisted his attempt to have a slate of delegates pledged to Governor Landon. As state chairman, I conferred with many of the Republican newspaper publishers—and most California newspapers were Republican at the time. Among these publishers were Mr. Joseph R. Knowland of the Oakland *Tribune*, Mr. George Cameron of the San Francisco *Chronicle*, Mr. Harry Chandler of the Los Angeles *Times*, and heads of smaller papers. I also discussed the matter with the State Central Executive Committee, and it was agreed to submit a nonpledged delegation that would be free to make a choice at the convention—if, indeed, there was to be a choice.

We picked the most prominent Republican names in the state for the delegation. It was necessary to have someone to whom the delegation was pledged, but who would announce that he had no intention of seeking the nomination. We selected the name of Attorney General U. S. Webb. At the time, there seemed to be few problems brewing, and he agreed, but it quickly developed into an extremely controversial compaign. The state's Republican governor, Frank Merriam, joined the Hearst forces and the Landon ticket began to roll. Attorney Gen-

* Ed. note: As state chairman, Warren was asked to draw up a series of amendments to the state constitution. These included one that would put most state employees under beneficial civil service regulations that protected their jobs against shifting political winds, another that created a State Department of Justice, and the one he has already mentioned that increased the attorney general's powers, making him the chief law enforcement officer in the state, and upped his salary to $11,000. When all the amendments drafted by Warren won on the 1934 ballot, and when Frank Merriam, whose campaign he had managed, was elected governor, Warren's political stock soared. However, he took note of the fact that, for the first time in years, the Democratic vote outnumbered the Republican in California, and was sure to emphasize such terms as "nonpartisan" and "for the welfare of all the people" in hailing the new Merriam administration he had helped to bring about. The loser in the gubernatorial race that year was Upton Sinclair, with his radical EPIC plan to "end poverty in California."

eral Webb did not care to participate in a contest of such intensity, so he withdrew his name. There were no others willing to be pilloried in this struggle, and so to save the situation from complete collapse, I consented to have the delegation pledged to my name but with the public announcement that I had no presidential ambitions and would release the delegates to vote their own convictions the moment they should be elected.

The Hearst papers blasted us daily with the accusation that this was an undercover movement to nominate President Hoover. That was not true, but the idea appeared to be catching on, and I suspect Hoover was strongly in favor of such a ticket. I cannot vouch for his desires, but I know that the delegates were not named for that purpose because I was responsible for the selection of a large percentage of them, and there was no condition that they vote for Hoover attached to their selection. They were not even interrogated as to their choice. Mr. Hoover publicly stated that he did not seek nor want the nomination. Still, the Hearst papers wrote that they had taken a secret poll showing the vast majority of people favoring the nomination of Mr. Hoover. I always thought the so-called secret poll emanated entirely from the brain of one of their political writers.

Our situation appeared to be deteriorating so badly that Mr. Cameron directed that our list of delegates be published some place in every issue of the *Chronicle* until election day. One morning, to our dismay, we found it in the obituary column. I know the controversy irked Mr. Hoover greatly, because about a week before the election it was suggested that he, Mr. Knowland, Mr. Cameron, and I meet for lunch in the latter's office to discuss the worsening campaign. We met, and after some discussion, Mr. Hoover said, "Earl, you are closer to the situation than the rest of us, what do you think can be done to save it?" Naïvely, I replied that our only chance depended on a statement from him to the effect that he was not a candidate and would not accept the nomination if it were tendered to him. He became furious at me, saying that no one was going to disfranchise him, regardless of consequences. Mr. Knowland said he agreed with me, but Mr. Cameron said he thought it would be demeaning for Hoover to make such a statement and, of course, he never did. However, Mr. Cameron did authorize Chester Rowell, an original Hiram Johnson supporter, but at that time managing editor of the *Chronicle*, to say that he had talked often to Mr. Hoover about the coming convention, and he knew that he neither sought nor wanted the nomination. I did not doubt the statement, but could never understand why Mr. Hoover became so angry with me. Our relations were never the same thereafter.

A few days later, I announced that I intended to make a speech on

Mr. Hearst and his effort to dominate the Republican Party. My friends begged me not to do so, saying he would never forgive me, and that I would be starting a feud such as the one that had existed through the years between Hearst and Al Smith. But I went ahead with it and spoke on a Saturday night over a statewide radio network. I challenged his effort to dominate the Republican Party on the ground that he had never been a Republican and, secondly, that it was arrogant of him to try to control politics in California because he had publicly repudiated his California citizenship and transferred it to New York to avoid paying our taxes on his enormous income. He had fought bitterly against our state income tax and, when it was enacted, he assailed the state and established residence in New York. In the following Tuesday's balloting, to our great amazement, our ticket won by more than a hundred thousand votes. In accordance with my promise, I released the delegation from any obligation to me and left them to their own individual consciences in the selection of a presidential candidate.

We went to the convention in Cleveland. By that time, no other candidates had appeared, and our delegation therefore cast its vote unanimously for Governor Landon, who was nominated on the first ballot.

That year, 1936, was a particularly hectic one for me. In addition to run-of-the-mill affairs of the office, I was engaged in the training and organization of law enforcement agencies, in presidential politics, and in problems arising in the county because of the Depression. Then still another, more immediate, problem arose. Some of the maritime unions were dominated by extremists, and their "goon squads" operated along the waterfronts of both San Francisco and Oakland to physically intimidate any opposition. Occasionally, the trussed up body of a waterfront personality would be found floating in San Francisco Bay.

On Sunday morning, March 22, 1936, the Swain and Hoyt steamer *Point Lobos* was preparing to sail from the Alameda City side of the Oakland Estuary. The chief engineer, George Alberts, known for his resistance on his ship to Communist influences which were so prevalent in maritime circles at that time, boarded the vessel and entered his little stateroom preparatory to getting under way.

A short time later, his lifeless body was found there in a pool of blood which covered the floor. He had multiple bruises from having been beaten with a blunt instrument and several knife wounds, particularly one in the rear of his thigh which severed a vein and caused him to bleed to death in a few minutes. Some of the other injuries were also probably lethal, but would not have been as quickly so as the knife wound.

It had been close to departure time, and supposedly there were no others on the ship except the crew. But, as it afterward developed, there was a goon squad waiting for his arrival. Through information given them by members of the crew, they were able to do the job and leave the ship undetected.

Investigation at the time failed to disclose anything that would identify the killers. However, as is usual in such cases, there was much discussion along the waterfront as to the reason for the killing and as to who the murderers were. It finally developed that Earl King, the secretary and principal officer of the Oilers, Wipers and Tenders Union, had dispatched the goon squad to teach Alberts a lesson. King later stated in his own circles that he had sent the squad over from San Francisco to "tamp up" on Alberts, and they had gone a little too far and killed him.

It was learned also, through investigation, that George Wallace, a member of the union, was one of the members of the squad. A search was made for him, and he was picked up in Brownsville, Texas. He admitted that he had been sent over to Alameda by King, but claimed that he was a lookout and was not in the room when the murder took place.

It further developed that a young man by the name of E. G. Ramsay was a grievance adjuster for the union, and he had prepared the situation for the entry of the squad. A member of the crew by the name of Frank Conner was posted at a place on the ship where he could direct the members of the squad to Alberts' stateroom. When interrogated, he, too, admitted that he had done this but claimed he had no knowledge of the actual killing.

Through undercover work on the waterfront, it was learned that King was indeed the man who had dispatched the squad to the ship. Eventually, when the evidence was in shape, King, Ramsay, Conner, George Wallace, and Ben Sakowitz were indicted for the murder. Sakowitz was not apprehended for trial.

There was an uproar on the waterfront over the case, and there were accusations that I was prosecuting these men to prevent their union from obtaining an adequate contract when their existing agreement terminated in the fall. There were about sixty thousand workers on strike in the area at the time, and this, of course, was a chief subject of conversation and of union emotion. The unions had nightly radio broadcasts in which they stated that I had obtained confessions from the suspects with all manner of brutality, including strapping them into chairs and shining blinding lights in their eyes.

We proceeded to trial, and throughout the time we were trying the case, there were at least a thousand pickets around the courthouse. When the jury was brought into the building and when it left, there would sometimes be more than three thousand people there.

The judge, in order to accelerate the trial, announced that he would have night sessions, but the number of pickets was so great at night that the foreman of the grand jury told the judge the jury members were frightened at being brought to the courthouse during the night. The judge promptly terminated night sessions, and the trial was conducted during normal hours.

It took exactly a month to get a jury because all of the businessmen on the venire disqualified themselves for one reason or another—either by saying they had a fixed opinion as to the guilt of the defendants, or by saying they were against capital punishment, or for some other excuse which would automatically cause their disqualification. Finally, at the end of a month, we obtained a jury of six retired old men and six housewives. Because of the uproar in the community, the judge had the jury isolated from the public and housed in a hotel. The trial lasted for three months, and it was constantly protracted by the defense in order to confuse the issues.

During the first month of the trial, it was obvious that the jury was frightened. In the second month, they became cynical about the bombast which was constantly in evidence. In the third month, it was likewise obvious that the defense's tactics were making no impression upon them.

This was the last case to be tried in the old courthouse between Third and Fourth streets on Broadway, and as it was ending we moved to the new courthouse on Lake Merritt where the closing arguments were made.

The case was submitted to the jury, and, after three or four hours of discussion, the verdict returned was: guilty of murder in the second degree for all the defendants. George Wallace, represented by the public defender, was the only defendant to take the stand, and he was repudiated by the others. He repeated his confession, and it was well corroborated by other witnesses. There could have been no doubt about the guilt of the persons on trial, and they were sentenced to life imprisonment for their crime.

One of the known members of the murderous goon squad, Sakowitz, disappeared, but five or six years later, when we were in World War II, the Federal Government found him in the French Foreign Legion and had him returned to American Army Headquarters in Europe. Because he was under charge of murder in this case, he was sent back to the United States in custody of the provost marshal. When he arrived in

New York Harbor, presumably through the assistance of members of the same union which had brought about the killing, he escaped, and has never been heard from since.

Later Governor Culbert Olson caused the State Parole Board to release King, Ramsay, and Conner, but left Wallace in prison. I was attorney general at that time, and I criticized the governor for freeing these men, and made it one of the issues in my campaign for the governorship against him.

One of my deputies by the name of Charles Wehr, who was assisting me in the trial, died of leukemia shortly after I became attorney general. After his death, the defense charged that he had had personal and business relations with one of the women members of the jury. The Supreme Court ordered a hearing on the accusations, and the matter was assigned to Judge Hartley Shaw of Los Angeles, one of the most able and venerable Superior judges of the state. After a lengthy hearing, Judge Shaw decided the charge was not credible, and recommended that it be rejected. The Supreme Court affirmed his findings, and the case was ended. There had already been an appeal from the trial, and the Court of Appeals had unanimously affirmed the convictions.

Throughout the King trial, I worked at the office almost every night until midnight preparing for the next day. While I was away, the phone would ring at my home and when Mrs. Warren answered, someone would say, "You tell that so-and-so to lay off this case or one of those kids of yours won't be coming home from school." Of course, we were disturbed by that, but Nina and I decided that it would be worse to have the children live in fear, knowing such threats were being made, than to not tell them and take the chance of nothing happening. However, we did not totally ignore the calls. I had men watch the children from a distance while they were going to school and again when they were returning home. No attempt was made to harm them, and the children never knew that there was any danger involved.

I think this was probably as important a case as we had in the county during my time as district attorney. Since the conviction, as far as I know, there has rarely been a murder victim found in the Bay, and the injuries from goon squad activities have dropped off to practically nothing.

During the trial, I learned to have an added appreciation of the integrity of the average working man. To disprove a contention of the defense, it was necessary for me to call an entire stevedore gang to the witness stand. I put each of them on the stand and asked them about the event. For all their emotional involvement, not one of them equivocated or deviated from the truth—this in spite of the fact that the leaders of their union were publicly claiming that what I was doing was a frame-up in the interest of the shipowners to discredit the workers and prevent them from negotiating a fair contract.

The last year or two of my incumbency as district attorney were fairly routine, and I spent a good bit of time in building a base for the attorney generalship. When Attorney General Webb informed me he did not intend to seek re-election in 1938 and said I was free to contest for the position, I was ready to start.

At that time I had, I believe, the good wishes of practically all the law enforcement officers of California—the district attorneys, the chiefs of police, and the sheriffs. They supported me actively in all parts of the state. It is an irony of fate that in my last years of public service on the Supreme Court I should have had so much criticism from these very agencies.

I have never substantially changed my views about enforcement of the law, and today I am as ardent a believer in effectively upholding it as I was in those days when—as a district attorney, then attorney general, and later governor—I was a favorite in law enforcement circles. In my activities to improve the agencies involved, and particularly with regard to police education, I always urged that emphasis be placed on developing police work into a thoroughgoing profession and maintained that the best way to achieve this is to employ enlightened and fair procedures which the public would respect. I still am of that opinion, though it has cost me the wrath of some of my old colleagues who felt they were handicapped in the performance of their duties by the standards of fairness covering the treatment of suspected criminals which were established while I was on the Supreme Court.

My years as district attorney were satisfying ones. Whatever the problems that confronted us, we met them head-on, and we were successful in most of our undertakings. My staff of young people was something rarely found at that time in public office. They were selected by me personally without regard to their political persuasion, and were free to follow their political inclinations so long as they did not let them interfere with the work of the office. Although they freely supported the candidates of their choice, they were really apolitical. And there was reason for this. Young people in the universities and colleges in those days were not as politically oriented as they are today, and politics, therefore, was not a dominant influence in the lives of those who joined my organization. They soon became emotionally as well as intellectually involved in the affairs of the office, and it was one big family. Disciplinary problems were practically nonexistent, and when any problem of this kind arose it was adjusted by my more experienced assistants before it was of a proportion justifying action by me. There was no clock punching, but there were also no limits on our work. This was before the forty-hour week, and when there was work to be done we went at it until it was finished. Most of the time there was work to be done. Although I abstained from private practice myself, I did not outlaw it for my deputies. However, our public task was so demanding and so challenging that private practice was a minor factor in the affairs of the office. For some years, I personally tried many murder, bank robbery, and bribery cases, a bunco case or two, and some cases against police officers. The latter I chose to try myself rather than assign them to my deputies, who would thereby incur the ill will of the officers. Policemen, I discovered, were very organization-minded and looked with disdain on any prosecution of a fellow officer, whether he was manifestly guilty or not. It was a rugged life for me, and I gradually lost my burning desire to be frequently in the courtroom. This was particularly true after we had cleaned up the governments of the county and the city of Oakland in the messy graft trials. From that time on, with the exception of the city of Alameda episode, I believe we had as honest and well administered a local government as any metropolitan area in the country. Our work was attracting some state and national attention, and this recognition was gratifying. It was about this time that Raymond Moley, one of the architects of Franklin Roosevelt's New Deal, then an academician and director of some of the crime surveys in the nation, was quoted in the San Francisco *Chronicle* as having said, during an interview, "Do you know who is the best district attorney in the United States? Earl Warren of Alameda County."

I never made any such extravagant appraisal of our work then or since, but cannot deny the satisfaction and pleasure it gave me and my associates to have it written or said by others. Our efforts also were treated with respect by the press of our own state. I was invited as a speaker to many law enforcement conferences and was made an honorary member of various police groups, including the International Association of Chiefs of Police.

When Franklin Roosevelt was elected president in 1932, his new attorney general, Homer Cummings, invited me to sit down with a selected half dozen other law enforcement people to recommend a legislative program designed to prevent interstate criminal operations. Among the others attending was Director J. Edgar Hoover of the FBI. We were notified sufficiently in advance to come prepared with suggestions, and I came with a program worked out by the law enforcement associations of California. The conference in Washington lasted the better part of a week, and I think all of the legislative items adopted were on our California list. Congress promptly passed them, and they have served the nation well.†

In December 1934, Attorney General Cummings also held a major National Crime Conference in Washington, and at his invitation I addressed the convention. The subject of my talk was "Organizing the Community to Combat Crime." Prior to that event, as I have mentioned, the people of California, at the 1934 general election, had enacted a measure enlarging the powers and responsibilities of the attorney general and looking forward to a state Department of Justice. This was my pet project, and as vice-chairman of the State Bar Committee on the Administration, I had the opportunity to author the proposal and have it included as one of several constitutional amendments recommended by the State Bar of California and sponsored by statewide civic organizations. The people of California enacted it overwhelmingly.

I suppose if that constitutional amendment had not passed, I would have looked to other fields, because the routine of prosecuting people day after day and sending them to penitentiaries and the county jail, such as they were, was not a particularly exhilarating constant work diet. I did not find pleasure in hearing the foreman of the jury say, "Guilty as charged in the indictment," although I may have fought hard for that result. There was satisfaction, of course, in the office's accomplishments generally, but not pleasure in specific cases. It was never only the culprit who suffered. There were invariably an innocent mother or father, wife, children, brothers or sisters who were affected perhaps more than the defendant himself. And then there were the murder cases. I never heard the jury foreman say, "Guilty of murder in the first degree" without having a feeling of nausea. The taking of human life, even by the law in retribution for an unlawful killing is so awesome and gruesome that it becomes a traumatic experience for any participant in the legal tragedy.

If the great Depression of the thirties had not occurred, I believe I probably would have left the public service. I could not leave before the 1930 election because I was engulfed in the graft trials throughout most of that year, and it would have been an abdication in favor of corruption to do so. By 1934, the Depression was in full swing. There was much law business in the private sector, but clients could not pay and

† Ed. note: Among other things, Warren recommended that FBI agents be given police powers to carry weapons and make arrests, that such crimes as robbing a federal bank and interstate transportation of a stolen auto be made federal offenses, that state justice departments be created and that there be greater cooperation among all law enforcement agencies.

even well-established lawyers were hard pressed to meet their office expenses. It was no time for me to leave, so I filed and was re-elected with only token opposition. My opponent was a lawyer by the name of T. L. Christenson. He filed against me at every election as he had done against my two predecessors. He was not at all unfriendly to me, and even called me "Chief," as my associates did. His campaign consisted only of handing out a few publicity cards. One day I said to him, "T.L., why do you always file against me?" He responded, "Chief, someday in a campaign, one of you district attorneys will die and then I will be the district attorney." It was always a pleasant exercise, and some of my friends laughingly accused me of paying his filing fee just to prove to the public that I could beat someone.

During these years, my home responsibilities had greatly increased. When I was appointed to the D.A.'s Office in 1925, I was unmarried. By January 1935, I was not only married but we had the six children we had hoped for. This called for a larger home, bigger grocery bills, and other expenses that, with my salary of $7,200 a year, necessitated a very tight budget. We never would have made it had it not been for my understanding wife and the economical manner in which she managed the household. While we were getting along all right then financially, I could not forget that it would be only a comparatively few years until the children would be going to college, and no financial arrangement for that eventuality could be assured on my income. I had bought a large, old home at Depression prices, but still, after turning in my smaller home on the transaction, there was a large mortgage to be taken care of. Although we were supremely happy in our homelife and I was very much interested in the cause of law enforcement, I would have felt obliged to leave the District Attorney's Office if a more lucrative opportunity *in the law* had presented itself. But when I was offered a job as trust officer in the banking world at a greatly increased salary, I turned it down because I had no desire for any post outside the law. After the people adopted the constitutional amendment which greatly strengthened the Office of Attorney General, I found that job attractive. I felt as well prepared for the office as anyone who might seek it. During my years as head of the third largest District Attorney's Office in the state, we had organized it into an efficient unit, had eliminated court congestion, and had the trial calendar on a thirty-day basis after arraignment. We had been instrumental in keeping corruption out of the county and organized crime from gaining a foothold during the prohibition years. I had worked with the chiefs of police, sheriffs, and other district attorneys to present a common front to the crime problem, and was generally recognized as one of their leaders. I was also well known at the state legislature because of my numerous appearances there on behalf of these organizations. In other circles, there was recognition of my interest in establishing a family court in Oakland to remove minor domestic controversies from the sordid, run-of-the-mill police court world of bootleggers, thieves, drunks, pimps, and the like. I had fought for and succeeded in writing into our county charter a provision for a public defender to represent all indigent defendants. Hopefully, this public defense counsel would replace the police court hangers-on who solicited clients among the poor and then preyed upon their distressed relatives for fees they could ill afford, without regard to whether the prisoner had any defense. I had joined with some other young lawyers to establish a Legal Aid Bureau in Oakland and pay its expenses for a year or two until it could be included in the Community Chest budget. This service was for indigent persons in civil matters. Both of these aids to the needy have since prospered, and are now considered vital in the life of the community. Because at that time our superior judges had little interest in the juvenile courts over which they always presided, I had gone to the state legislature to advocate the authorization of juvenile court commissioners who would approach their work with a patient and sociological viewpoint rather than a strictly legal one, as was the practice of the judges. In this, I was not successful because too many judges, although not particularly interested in juvenile court work, were unwilling to give up any of their jurisdiction. The time was not yet ripe for it.

County jail conditions were bad in Alameda County as well as in most of the others. When we got rid of the Sheriff Becker regime, I suggested to the new sheriff, Mike Driver, that we relieve sordid jail conditions in which some prisoners were kept as long as two years in small, crowded cells with nothing to do but obtain a higher education in crime. There wasn't even any physical exercise for them. They merely stagnated there. The suggestion was that we establish a prison farm for nonviolent inmates without bars or armed guards. There they could produce vegetables for our county hospitals, and do the laundry and such other routine work around the hospitals that was necessary for their maintenance. The sheriff and the Board of Supervisors being agreeable to it, the farm was established, and, after a modest start, it developed in later years under Sheriff Jack Gleason into a nationally recognized enlightened institution. I would have gone further but the social tides weren't ready for it. Punishment, not rehabilitation, was the dominant theory of sentencing. I would have liked to release most of the nonviolent prisoners during the daytime to do work that would sustain them and their dependents, and require them to remain in custody at night, which would cover the hours when most of them usually got into trouble. Two years in the county jail, as it was then operated, was tantamount to destroying any redeeming social usefulness in a prisoner.

I had never realized before this how large California was or how difficult it could be to become known throughout the state. In trying to broaden my base, I was helped by the fact that there was a vacuum in the Republican Party, for which I had been an alternate delegate to the National Convention in 1928 and a delegate in 1932. In 1934, it was more for want of candidates than for any other reason that I was elected chairman of the State Central Committee for a two-year period. Under the law, the position had to be filled by a Northern Californian. It was during this period that we had the Hearst-Landon contest, which I have already related. Except for the interest it generated during that incident, the chairman's post was of piddling importance. Not only in our state but nationwide, the Republican Party was at the nadir of its existence, and party jobs such as mine were merely caretaking in character. I must also say that my interest in national affairs was slight, as my political views were not well formulated. I was a Republican simply because California was then an overwhelmingly Republican state. The only real division was determined by whether Republicans favored the Hiram Johnson reform wing of the party or the "Old Guard." That division was more on state than national issues, and at the time there was sentiment against widening the gap between the two factions in California.

At all events, while my accomplishments as state chairman and national committeeman were minimal, through those offices I did make friends around the state. In addition to this strictly political activity, I had some other involvements through which I gained support. I was active in the University of California Alumni Association, becoming first vice-president and later being scheduled to become president the year I first ran for governor. Through this fine organization, I made many friends in all parts of the state who were warm supporters during my subsequent campaigns. I was also for several years a research associate in the Bureau of Public Administration at the University of California at Berkeley, and became more friendly and intimate with many members of the faculty than I had as a student years before. I conducted a seminar at the bureau for prospective governmental administrators.

Though a member of several lodges, I had never held office in any of them except the Masonic Lodge, which I had joined immediately after World War I. I was elected Grand Master of Masons for California in 1935, and through that association made many more friends. There were almost 700 lodges and 150,000 members, and I knew some in every lodge. While the Masonic Order is strictly nonpolitical, friends are friends, however attained, and I have no doubt that these friendships contributed substantially to the success of many of my campaigns.

When I announced my candidacy for attorney general, I resigned my only political office as Republican national committeeman, stating that the office of attorney general was not a legitimate area for political partisanship, and that if elected it would not be so administered by me. I filed not only on the Republican and Democratic tickets but also on the ticket of the little Progressive Party, which had fewer than four thousand members, practically all of them friends of Hiram Johnson. He kept it alive as an escape hatch in case the "Old Guard" should take after him again as it had in his earlier days. It was generally understood that if Republican sentiment became anti-Johnson, he would shift his party registration to the Progressives and operate with cross-filing from that base. This was a lesson learned from the ill-fated candidacy of Mayor James Rolph, Jr., of San Francisco, the governor in 1918. The Mayor had become popular statewide during the San Francisco World Fair of 1915 because of his constant welcoming of visitors during that period. He was a Republican and filed on both the Republican and Democratic tickets. However, he gave too little attention to his own party, and received the Democratic but not the Republican nomination. The Supreme Court of California held that, having failed to receive the nomination of his own party, he could not accept that of another, so despite the fact that he had far more votes in the primary than any other candidate, he could not appear on the ballot at the final election.

I was immediately faced with a new situation. I had no money of my own to pay for a statewide campaign and, since I was running independently, there was no organizational support to look to for that purpose. Some of my friends in the San Francisco Bay area got together and raised about thirty-five thousand dollars, and that was all the money we spent on the campaign. That would hardly pay for one commercial on television these days. But it was enough to do the job, largely because of the built-in support I had from the law enforcement agencies. In all areas of the state, they helped me in many ways.

I recall one incident that was somewhat typical. The State Association of Chiefs of Police told the officials of the San Francisco World Fair of 1938 that they wanted a police building, not for administration purposes, but for exhibits. They were given tentative approval based upon whether they would produce the money for it. They had no funds for that purpose, but without any further waiting they arranged for a ground-breaking ceremony for the building, at which San Francisco Chief of Police William Quinn presided in the presence of a large delegation. Ground was broken by me and each of my six children, all of us armed with spades of appropriate size. Even three-year-old Bobby had one, as did Nina (Honey Bear), who was all of five. The news picture was an excellent one, and was given wide display throughout the state and in the campaign. The building was never constructed, but the ceremony inadvertently served as a good publicizer for me.

I was greatly assisted in my campaign by my opponents. There was no major contestant for the Republican nomination, but there were seven candidates besides myself for the Democratic nomination. They were all contending against each other, yet joined in a common plan to prevent me from obtaining Democratic approval. Accordingly, at every joint meeting, and there were many, the seven would speak for themselves, and then each in closing would say something like, "But if you cannot vote for me, vote for one of the other Democrats. Don't vote for Earl Warren because he is trying to steal our nomination." That constant advertising kept my name before the voters more than the other names combined, and I am sure it was helpful to me. In addition, I had considerable support from the press throughout the state and, when the votes were counted, I had received all three nominations—Republican, Democratic, and Progressive.

Normally this would be the end of it, because under the law my name would be the only one on the ballot for the Office of Attorney General. But in California the ballot is always open for the voter to write in the name of any person he prefers. A radical pension plan group which coveted the post would not give up on its candidate, Karl Kegley. It launched a vigorous campaign to have his name written in. The effort even reached as far as Washington, and my friend of later days, Jim Farley, made a radio speech advocating the election of "our candidate," Kegley. At every one of the ten thousand precincts in the state Kegley's campaigners were handing out pencils along with stencils of the name "Kegley," so that voters need only place the stencil over the blank space under Attorney General and trace his name with the pencil handed to them. I could not campaign against such enterprise without giving substance to it, so I totally ignored it. I spent no money and no speeches were given by or for me. Kegley rolled up the amazing number of a half million votes. The main significance of this was to show what can be done when there are zealous, well-prepared workers throughout election day at every precinct. I received over two million votes and the attorney generalship. My chief assistant, Ralph E. Hoyt, at the same election, ran for and was elected district attorney of Alameda County. He would succeed me, to my great satisfaction.

During this campaign, our family had its first tragic experience. Early in the evening on Saturday, the fourteenth of May, my father was sitting in his chair to read the evening paper, but apparently had fallen asleep. It was a warm evening, as is usual in Bakersfield at that time of the year, and the doors and windows were all open except for the screens on them. Someone came in, struck him on the head with a short piece of pipe, crushing his skull, then dragged him into the bedroom and left him there on the bed. He was in the house alone, my mother being in Oakland with my sister for a series of eye operations. The crime was discovered the next morning.

It was widely publicized in the news media, and many theories were advanced. The police department of Bakersfield did everything it could toward solving the case. Police agencies throughout the state were on the alert, and even the FBI counseled with local authorities. While my office was active in assisting the Bakersfield police, I took no part in the investigation myself. The judgment of a member of the family in such circumstances is not sufficiently objective to give proper leadership to an investigation. Also, I had confidence in those who already were conducting it. However, the murderer was never found, and, in my opinion, this was because of the casual nature and the very simplicity of the deed. Casual, simple crimes are often more difficult to solve than those that are carefully planned in furtherance of an established motive. This murder was brutal and of the blundering type, obviously without planning.

My parents' home was on Niles Street, next to the corner of Baker, the principal street of East Bakersfield. There was a gas station on the corner, thoroughly lighting the area, including the front portion of our home. The back yard was unlighted, and there were a grape arbor and some orange trees which contributed to its seclusion. With the house lighted on the inside and the doors and windows open, my father, sitting asleep in his large chair, would have been clearly observable from the rear. When authorities searched the premises after discovery of the murder, a piece of half-inch pipe about a foot long was found in the yard of our neighbor, where it could easily have been thrown from our back porch. It had blood and hair on it, indicating clearly that it was the murder weapon. On examination of our own back yard, the place where the pipe had long been partially imbedded in the soil was found and also evidence of someone having relieved himself a short distance from the place where the pipe rested. My father's wallet had been taken, but nothing else in the house had been disturbed. The murderer in escaping did not wait until he was out of the rays of light from the gas station before getting rid of the contents of the wallet, except for the money. As far as is known, the amount of currency in the wallet was small. Papers were scattered along the sidewalk for a considerable distance. The route taken by the killer was only a few blocks away from the railroad yards, where trains were coming and going around the clock.

After an investigation that was as complete as that for any unsolved murder can be, it seemed clear to me that some itinerant came into our back yard for a personal reason, and, seeing my father asleep in his chair, picked up the piece of pipe, entered by the kitchen door, smashed him on the head, took his wallet, pulled him into the darkened bedroom and fled, going through the wallet for money as he hurried off. It could well be that he went directly to the railroad and departed on a passing freight train.

This was, of course, a tragic experience for the entire family, and made my subsequent election a hollow anticlimax.

My father's death must go down in history as one of the thousands of unsolved murder cases that plague our nation each year and cause such general apprehension for the security of our loved ones, ourselves, and our homes.

VI

AGAINST ORGANIZED CRIME: *Years as an*
Attorney General

The Constitution of California provides:

> The residence and principal office of the Governor, the Attorney General and the members of the Supreme Court shall be at Sacramento.

That provision had traditionally been honored in its breach rather than its observance. When I became attorney general, the principal seat of the Supreme Court was in San Francisco and the justices, when appointed, took up their residence on San Francisco Bay. The Court sat there throughout the year except for two calendars of a few days' duration at Los Angeles and Sacramento. The main office of the attorney general and the vast majority of his deputies was in San Francisco, and he resided there. Only a token representation was stationed at Sacramento.

During the incumbency of my predecessor, an action was brought in the Superior Court by a citizen to prevent the payment of Attorney

General Webb's salary on the ground that he neither resided in nor maintained his principal office at the State Capitol. The Court conveniently held that the constitutional proviso was one which merely established venue so people would know where to initiate legal actions against the named officers and where they could be served with legal process. The decision was not appealed, and the practice of maintaining San Francisco as headquarters went undisturbed. As a result, when I assumed the office, I did not move my family to Sacramento. However, because of the legislative session which convened on the same day my term commenced, I went to the Capitol the night before and determined to be at my office early in the morning so people would know I was on the job.

I arrived shortly before opening time and was given two telephone numbers to call. One was that of Walter P. Jones, editor of the McClatchy newspapers. He was at the Sacramento *Bee*. The other was that of Joseph Stephens, president of the State Prison Board. I knew both of them well, and said to myself, "Here are two friendly calls, so I'll show them I am already in business." I called Jones first, and he excitedly asked me if I had talked to Joe Stephens. I told him I had not but that Stephens had left word for me to call him, and I intended to do so. Jones entreated me to call as soon as possible because Stephens had something of great importance that I should hear. I immediately phoned, and in a few minutes Stephens came to my office.

He was very much disturbed. Over the weekend, it seemed, he had received information to the effect that pardons were being sold through the out-going governor's office, and his private secretary, a Mark Megladdery, was the conduit through which the transactions were being handled. He asked me to see Senator David Bush, a highly respected legislator who had been a strong supporter of the governor, but who had information which he thought established corruption.

I immediately contacted Senator Bush, and shortly he was in my office corroborating the story of Mr. Stephens. I then called Oscar Jahnsen, my new chief inspector, who had come with me from my Alameda County Office, and instructed him to go to the Governor's Office and ask Mark Megladdery to see me on a matter of urgency.

Megladdery came over, and I said to him, "Mark, you have been accused of selling pardons, and I would like to talk to you about it. Are you willing to talk to me?"

"Of course, Earl," he said.

I sent for a stenographer, and for an hour or two interrogated him. He answered glibly but not truthfully, and his statements led to his ultimate undoing. He was very cocky because, at midnight the night before, the last act of out-going Governor Frank Merriam had been to appoint him a Superior Court judge of Alameda County. I called the venerable chief judge of our Superior Court, T. W. Harris, and told him the story as I had heard it from Jones, Stephens, and Megladdery. The entire matter, I said, would be submitted to a grand jury. When Megladdery later came into the Alameda County Courthouse to report for duty, Judge Harris said to him, "I know of your appointment, and having taken the oath you are now a Superior Court judge, but I have been told by the attorney general about the prison scandal, and you will be assigned no judicial work until that matter is cleared up. You may have an office but no duties to perform."

I took the matter up with the district attorney of Sacramento County. Because it involved not only the Governor's Office but some of the legislators, he was not at all interested in it. Fortunately, because Megladdery lived in Alameda County, some peripheral aspects of the matter were centered there—enough to establish jurisdiction. I immediately communicated with the county's new district attorney, my former chief assistant, Ralph E. Hoyt, and he took the case to the grand jury. Megladdery was indicted, tried, convicted, and sentenced to jail. To the great relief of the Superior Court judges of the county, all of whom had outstanding records for probity, he never sat as a judge in a single case.*

I did not displace any of my predecessor's appointees in the Attorney General's Office, but there were a few vacancies, and some of the older ones retired as the rules governing private practice became more stringent. Before this there had been few if any restrictions; for instance, deputies were accustomed to representing clients before state officers and commissions for whom the attorney general was the statutory legal

* Ed. note: In addition to Megladdery's malfeasance, Warren fell heir, as the new attorney general, to a hot potato handed him by the out-going Governor Merriam. This was the Philbrick Report, a summary of findings resulting from a grand jury investigation of legislative corruption in Sacramento. The report, written by the Sacramento district attorney's chief special investigator, Howard Philbrick, disclosed techniques by which pressure groups, through their lobbyists, bribed certain venal legislators. It also told how a few of the lawmakers themselves extorted money from persons interested in defeating their "cinch bills" which Warren has discussed earlier in this book. Chief villain in this collusion of legislators and lobbyists was Arthur Samish, a liquor lobbyist who claimed to virtually control the Legislature—until such arrogance and the exposure of a magazine article helped to bring about his downfall. Many state legislators, most of them Republicans, sought to have the Philbrick Report suppressed, but Warren soon turned it over to the new governor, Olson, and it was made public. Warren then helped in drawing up reform bills based on the report's recommendations, including one to prohibit legislators who were also lawyers from representing clients in cases where their position as state officials could influence the decision. None of the bills passed. To this day, few of the report's recommendations have been adopted by the Legislature.

adviser. This and other representations of clients that could lead to a conflict of interest were immediately prohibited by me, and as the chances of private practice while using state facilities diminished, more vacancies occurred, and I was able to reorganize the office into a manageable unit. There was no central filing system; no good system of fiscal accountability; no calendar control of litigation, and very little supervision of the work of the deputies. Each of them performed his duties almost as an independent official. I do not say this in derogation of my predecessor of thirty-six years, who was an honest man, but rather as an indication of the parsimonious manner in which the office was treated by the Legislature. More and more responsibilities were thrust on the Office with only infrequent additional deputies at paltry salaries to help with the increased workload. Things had grown in this manner through the years without a real chance to reorganize on an efficient basis.

I was determined to overcome this situation, and set about doing it immediately. It was a long, tedious job that would show no tangible results for a period of time, but it was done long before my term ended.

It seemed desirable to demonstrate immediately a use of the new responsibilities of the attorney general as the chief law officer of the state. There were a number of places where the law was being more or less openly flouted, and I decided to take them on, one by one, until they were eliminated. I had come to the conclusion that while some violators could, through cunning and device, defeat the law for a period of time, none could openly defy it if there was a concerted effort to enforce it. I chose the dog tracks to demonstrate this theory.

Dog tracks in California were clearly illegal, and they were operated in a manner to swindle the public through their unregulated gambling practices. There were only about eight counties in the state where they were permitted by the local authorities. Alameda was not one of those counties, but for some years while I was district attorney, it had been ringed by dog tracks to the north in Contra Costa County, to the west in San Mateo County, and to the east in San Joaquin County. There were a few more tracks ranging to the southern part of the state. The tracks worked together, and had seasons allocated so they would not all be running at the same time.

It happened that the only track to be open at the time I took office was the one at El Cerrito in Contra Costa County, just over the border from Alameda County. I sent my newly appointed chief criminal deputy, Charles Wehr, there to prepare a case for action. In about two weeks, he reported to me that everything was in readiness. The track was operated by John J. Jerome, commonly known as "Black Jack" Jerome because of his former activities as a hired strikebreaker. Wehr was instructed to ask Jerome to see me, and to add that it would be more in Jerome's interest than mine for him to come. Jerome arrived soon after.

"Mr. Jerome," I said, "you have been operating your track for several years, and I will give you credit for believing that you are in a lawful business because the authorities in your county have permitted you to run, but I must inform you that dog track gambling is illegal and cannot continue. It must stop. I have prepared a case, and am ready to act. If you choose to close down now, you may do so without any cost to you, but if we are obliged to proceed the hard way, it will be very expensive for you, and I believe I can assure you that in the end your operation will be closed."

He told me he thought his was a legal business, but asked if he could talk to his lawyer about it. Informed that he could, he telephoned an attorney, who soon came to my office. His name was Thomas M. Carlson, an able lawyer against whom I had been in much litigation. The two talked privately for a time, and then they returned to my office.

"Do you intend to treat all dog tracks the same?" Carlson asked. "Or are you closing Jerome's track because he is Jerome?"

I told him that in my opinion all dog tracks were illegal, and I was determined that none of them should continue in business. They conferred privately for a few more minutes, and then Carlson said to his client in my presence:

"I have known this man for many years, and if he says everyone is to be treated the same, he will do just that."

Jerome thought for a few minutes, and said, "Mr. Attorney General, will it be all right if we run until Saturday night?"

While I could not authorize him to operate what I believed to be an illegal business, I told him that this being Wednesday I undoubtedly could not be prepared to act before Saturday. They both left on a friendly note, and that night at the track they announced over the loudspeaker that they had always believed they were in a lawful business, but had been told by the attorney general this was not the fact, and they did not intend to quarrel with the law. Accordingly, they announced the track would close permanently on Saturday night. The track did close at that time, and since then there never has been a dog track operated in the state of California.

Some of the other track operators made moves indicating an intention to open, but each time I sent my chief inspector, Oscar Jahnsen, to see them and personally relate how the Jerome track was closed. He then asked, "Do you think you are tougher than Black Jack Jerome?" Leaving them to reflect on that question, he would depart. None of

them ever attempted to open, and the plants deteriorated until replaced by legitimate businesses.

I write about this operation for two reasons. First, it illustrates how
simple it is to close down any illegal business that operates openly in
defiance of the law if there is determination on the part of the responsible authority to prevent it. This one was a sizable operation. The dog
tracks with their land values, bleachers, parking spaces, and other facilities represented a great deal of money, and connected with them were a
number of shady and some thoroughly undesirable characters. However,
not one of these would stand up in open defiance of the law when it
was convincingly and uniformly brought to bear against them all.
Secondly, it shows how cheaply and with what little effort some such illicit operations can be stopped if advance preparation is adequate.

I used this direct-dealing procedure wherever possible, and often it
worked with surprising effectiveness. It saved time, manpower, and expense. Occasionally a law violator was arrogant and refused to believe
that he could be upended. In such event, it was necessary to do it the
hard way.   •

We encountered stiff opposition from the biggest open gambling operations that have ever functioned in California—the gambling ships
off the coast at Santa Monica and Long Beach harbors. There were
four of these ships, two in each harbor. In Santa Monica, there were
the *Rex* and the *Texas* and in Long Beach the *Tango* and the *Show-
boat*. The largest and most aggressive of these was the *Rex*, ostensibly,
at least, owned by Tony Cornero, a notorious rumrunner and underworld character of prohibition days. Who his other associates were, I
never was able to ascertain, but Tom C. Clark, Attorney General of the
United States and later my colleague on the Supreme Court, told me it
was money from the Al Capone crowd in Chicago. There were rumors
galore about the ownership of the others, but all we could be sure of
was that it was underworld money. Some thought control of all the
ships was the same; others that there were conflicting interests. At all
events, each of them was doing business.† The Police Departments of
Santa Monica and Long Beach were subservient to the gambling ship

† Ed. note: The *Rex* opened in May of 1938. That same year there were two
raids on the ship by officers from the Los Angeles County District Attorney's Office, the Sheriff's Office, and the Santa Monica Police Department. Owner Cornero
and others were arrested. Attempts to convict them on gambling and bookmaking
charges were thwarted by jury disagreements and by district court rulings that the
offshore gaming vessels—which moved farther offshore with each raid—were beyond
the jurisdiction of the state. After Warren took office as state attorney general on
March 20, 1939, he publicly characterized the gambling ship operations as "a great
nuisance which is drawing millions of dollars annually from legitimate trade chan-
nels."

operations, and even the major newspapers of Los Angeles carried full page ads for them at a cost of many hundreds of dollars a day and treated them charitably in their news columns. The new reform mayor, Fletcher Bowron, who had defeated the incumbent mayor in a recall election, was much against the gambling ships, but they were beyond his jurisdiction. He and I discussed them at considerable length, and I decided to put them out of business. He told me that if the county's district attorney and sheriff refused to help me he would supply the necessary city police officers to do the job, although he hoped it would not be necessary to use them beyond the city limits.

These ships were more than three miles from the shorelines of the cities of Santa Monica and Long Beach, and they relied on that fact to assert their freedom from the jurisdiction of the state of California. The two cities' harbors were quite similar in configuration. Their shore-lines were not straight, but were deeply indented in a way that permitted a ship to be anchored more than three miles from the shore of the cities but to be well within a line drawn from one to another of the headlands which determined the outer limits of the harbors. It was our thinking that the state's jurisdiction ran three miles seaward from a straight line drawn from headland to headland. In effect, this meant that these ships, in order to be beyond our jurisdiction, had to be at least ten miles out to sea from the docks where their water taxis were based. This would be impractical for them for two reasons. First, it would be too long and rough a trip for the little taxis and, second, the anchored ship in the open Pacific swells would cause so much seasick-ness that most people would lose all desire to gamble.

We had a second theory which would protect us, we believed, if the first failed. We maintained that the operation of these ships consti-tuted a public nuisance to the state of California, that they were a det-rimental enticement to our people, that they were connected up with the mainland by their water taxis, and one, the *Rex*, had set up a tele-phone line from the shore to the ship without proper authorization. We contended this all gave us the right to summarily abate the nui-sance in the same manner as if it were all on shore, regardless of how far seaward it was.

I sent Oscar Jahnsen to see Tony Cornero on the *Rex* and tell him that he must close out his operation. Jahnsen knew him from earlier days when, as a federal officer, he had arrested Cornero in a rumrun-ning affair. Cornero greeted him cordially and said, "Jahnsen, don't be silly. I have the best mouthpieces in the country, and they tell me I am legal. Come along with me, and I'll show you what we've got." Jahnsen went around the ship with him, recording everything he saw in his notebook.‡ He also made similar visits to the other ships. Cornero was the "bell cow" and because he would take no heed of our warnings, neither would they. I knew then that we had a job to do. Warren Olney III, chief of my Criminal Division (he succeeded Charles Wehr who had died suddenly from leukemia), was in charge of the job. None of us were maritime lawyers, so I sent Olney to see Vice Admiral Stanley Parker of the Coast Guard, who was stationed at San Francisco, to explore whether we would be in any legal difficulties with the federal government. Fortunately, the admiral was a lawyer and believed the gambling ships were an abomination. He enthusiastically helped us to perfect our plans. Also, to protect ourselves with the civilian agencies, we visited Mr. Ben Harrison, United States attorney, and divulged our plans to summarily abate the nuisance. He advised us we were not in conflict with any federal law.

It was a tremendous job, all the same. I felt it was necessary to raid all of the ships at the same time, because if they were owned by conflicting underworld interests and we raided only one, it would be claimed that I was putting one out of business to benefit the others. This meant a big job, calling for a number of boats and about three hundred officers. Olney and Jahnsen set about organizing a fleet. This was in July of 1939. We used four Fish and Game Commission patrol boats and rented sixteen water taxis for our "navy." We were able to muster some of the needed officers from our own ranks, even pressing lawyers into service. When plans were as complete as possible, I went to Los Angeles and asked the district attorney, Byron Fitts, and sheriff, Eugene Biscailuz, to come to my office there. I told them I was determined to close up the gambling ships and needed their help. They replied that they could not assist because they might be liable on their official bonds. Having explored that possibility, I told them that in my opinion it was without foundation. When they still insisted they could not take the chance, I told them it would then be necessary for me to invoke the new powers of the attorney general and supplant them in making the arrests and resulting prosecutions. I also told them that Mayor Bowron had promised me enough police officers to do the job if they would not do it. They then decided that they would take the chance and asked me how many men I required. I told them it could be done with one hundred and fifty from the sheriff and fifty from the district attorney. They agreed and asked when the officers would be needed. I said one o'clock that very afternoon. They balked at first, but

‡ Ed. note: Among other things, he noted that Mike Connally, a former chief investigator for the liquor administration of the State Board of Equalization and a man whom Warren had helped convict of bribery in Alameda County, was a spotter for Cornero, stationed at the gangway to see who came aboard.

finally agreed and were given the rendezvous points. Many of our own men had infiltrated the gambling ships incognito as "customers" and about two hundred men from the sheriff's and district attorney's offices were put aboard our raiding fleet.

We had served an injunction on the ships requiring them summarily to abate a public nuisance, and when they chose to disregard this notice, we took action. Target time was 3 P.M., and promptly at that hour all four ships were raided. Little resistance was offered on three of the ships, although there was some scuffling on the *Texas* when the raiding officers stayed aboard until after nightfall, and someone pulled a main light switch, causing a minor melee in the dark. But when our boats approached Cornero's *Rex*, fire hoses were turned on them to keep them away and the gangway was denied them. Our men communicated this predicament to me, and added that there were more than six hundred people aboard. I was not with the offshore raiders, but had taken some rooms at a Santa Monica beach club with Fitts and Biscailuz to watch the proceedings through field glasses.

Knowing that most of the customers on the *Rex* would want to leave soon, as they had wives, children, and jobs awaiting them, and that they would not be able easily to explain their presence on the gambling ship to concerned spouses and bosses, I gave instructions that our craft should make fast to the *Rex* near the gangway area. Then if our men could not get aboard, neither could anybody on the ship leave. In effect, we blockaded her.

Cornero held out until about three o'clock the next morning and then capitulated. Our officers took complete possession of the ship. Visitors were then permitted to leave. The gambling money aboard was confiscated, sacked, and deposited in the State Treasury. Since the ships were really barges and did not have enough power on board to navigate or even raise their own anchors, we had to cut the chains (attaching them to oil drum floats for later recovery) and the ships were then towed into port. Shortly after, by order of the Court, all of the gambling paraphernalia aboard was destroyed.

On the afternoon of the raid, I was told that a commander of the Coast Guard by the name of Greenwood had called my office and said, speaking of me, "You tell that blankety-blank to take those boats away from the *Rex* or he will land in jail." He left a telephone number to call. I thought it probably was a hoax, but found the number in the telephone book under that name. I called and asked for Commander Greenwood. After identifying myself, I repeated the exact language he was said to have used. "Yes," he agreed, "that is exactly what I said."

I replied, "Commander, before you start putting anyone in jail I would suggest that you communicate with your admiral, because he helped us work out this program."

There was a brief silence, and then he said, "Well, I'm for you fellows, but you didn't tell me anything about it."

"Perhaps we forgot to do so," I said, and the conversation ended.

Cornero employed Jerry Geisler, the most famous trial lawyer in Southern California at that time, to defend him. We obtained a permanent injunction against the ships' managements that forbade them from operating. Among other things, Cornero was sued for penalties for running water taxis as a public utility without a permit, which called for a $2,500-per-day fine.

Geisler finally came to me and said, "What do we have to do to get rid of this mess?"

I told him it was very simple. All Cornero need do for the state was to consent in writing to the confiscation of the money and gambling apparatus found on the ship, then deposit in the State Treasury the amount of money we spent on the raids after we had offered him an opportunity to close the gambling ship without any expense to either him or the state. This amounted to something over $13,000. There was also some $4,200 in taxes and a $7,500 compromise claim by the Railroad Commission to be settled. Geisler accepted, and the matter was disposed of in that manner, although Cornero also lost his ship, the *Rex*. In preparation of the case, we had discovered that, during Cornero's rumrunning days, the United States Government had assessed taxes against him of more than $100,000 which were still unpaid. With penalties for nonpayment added, the gross amount was large, and when the federal government was notified of Cornero's connection with the *Rex*, it immediately libeled the ship for the amount due. When the taxes and penalties weren't paid, the ship was sold to satisfy the claim. Eventually the *Rex* was converted back into a power ship by other owners and met an honorable end, being sunk in the Indian Ocean by torpedoes while serving as a carrier for the Allies in World War II.

I was happy to settle all the gambling ship cases in much this same manner. To have proceeded against each of the operators separately in court would have meant long and expensive trials. I was convinced of my right to summarily abate their nuisance, and that objective had been accomplished. On the other hand, the Supreme Court had never decided on my headland-to-headland theory of jurisdiction, and I was certain that issue would be raised in any criminal cases. Later, however, the California Supreme Court did sustain that theory, to my great satisfaction. Our ultimate objective of closing all the gambling ships was achieved, and I must say that, of all the raids on law violators I have known, these, as organized and executed by Warren Olney with the

help of my investigators under Oscar Jahnsen, were by far the most in-
telligently planned and successfully carried out.

One would think this was the end of gambling ships off the coast of
California, and it was for about seven years. However, a young state assemblyman named Frederick Napoleon Howser was appointed district
attorney of Los Angeles County, and he permitted Cornero, who had
again obtained possession of a vessel called the *Lux*, to re-establish it in
Santa Monica Harbor as a gambling ship. I was no longer attorney general, having been elected governor in 1942. It was not my responsibility
to close Cornero's operation, but I was determined to do so. I made
public announcement to that effect. Cornero publicly replied that anyone who interfered with his business would this time be treated as a
common pirate. I had no law enforcement agency with jurisdiction to
do the job, but I was willing, if necessary, to activate a segment of the
National Guard to prevent the gamblers' water taxis from plying between the shore and the ship. This would have effectively stopped the
operation, but I was reluctant to use the Guard for any phase of civilian
law enforcement, and as things turned out I never did in my almost
eleven years as governor.

My first step was to write a letter to President Harry Truman telling
him of the situation and of the threat made by Cornero to deal with
law enforcement as if it were piracy. I pointed out the danger involved
in raiding a ship miles at sea in such circumstances. The federal government was somewhat responsible for the situation, I argued, because it
had issued a license for the ship to operate in coastwide trade, in spite
of the fact that the vessel had no engines on it and was permanently
anchored in the harbor for the sole purpose of illegal gambling. I asked
for his assistance. In a few days, I received a telephone call from Attorney General Tom C. Clark in Washington. He said, "Governor, in relation to the letter you wrote to President Truman, give me a couple of
weeks, and I believe I can do something for you." I thanked him and
waited. Within that time, the federal government moved in on the
Lux, cut the anchor chain, towed the ship into port, and auctioned it
off for the fines assessed against it. The charge was flagrant violation of
the navigation laws.

Shortly thereafter the Congress passed an act prohibiting gambling
ships in the coastal waters of the United States. President Truman
signed the bill and ended our problems of this nature.

This did not eliminate our problems with gambling violations, however. California was not a wide-open gambling state. There was petty
gambling in a number of counties, but with the exception of bookmaking on horse races, there were really only a few flagrant operations that

gave the state a reputation for lax enforcement of gambling laws. One was at Hollywood, in the heart of the movie colony, and the other was in Palm Springs, a then budding winter resort patronized largely by people from other parts of the country, many of whom had underworld connections. Jewel and fur thieves found a bonanza there. One of the principal attractions was a large gambling establishment situated out in the desert a few miles from town, and so positioned that the operators could see and then screen everyone who came within a mile or two of the place. The district attorney of Riverside County, Earl Redwine, was anxious to have the place closed, but his sheriff, who had the only law enforcement unit in the county, would not co-operate. The hotel people and most of the merchants in Palm Springs tacitly supported the sheriff because of the attraction the gambling place had for tourists. Redwine sought our help, and after trying unsuccessfully to induce the sheriff to do his duty, I decided to supplant him and do the job ourselves. I sent Warren Olney there to work it out. The establishment was owned by the politically potent Wertheimer brothers, who had powerful connections throughout the county. The taking of the place was an exciting experience, but a raid is a raid no matter how large or difficult, and it should be sufficient to say that this gambling house was permanently closed.

Years later, when governor, I was traveling from Los Angeles to Sacramento on a commercial plane. I took a vacant seat alongside a personable-looking man, and during most of the trip conversed with him about California. As we were landing at Sacramento, he said, "Governor, I am happy to have talked to you, but I don't believe you know who I am. I am Al Wertheimer. You drove me out of California, but there are no hard feelings because I am established in Nevada now, and my gambling is perfectly legal. I am happier now than I was in California." I said, "And there are no hard feelings on my part. It has been interesting to talk with you." We shook hands and parted pleasantly, although I wondered if anyone had taken a picture of us talking in such a friendly manner. Such a picture could have been embarrassing in a political campaign.

Another notorious gaming place, patronized largely by the motion picture colony but known through reputation and gossip by everyone, was located on Sunset Boulevard in Los Angeles on what was then known as the "Hollywood Strip." It was in unincorporated territory and within the jurisdiction of the sheriff. I spoke to him about it, but he said his men had told him there was no truth to the stories. We then proceeded to put some undercover men of our own in the place. They found big-time gambling offered on a lavish scale. I reported this information to the sheriff, and he promised to conduct raids to establish exactly what was going on. He did this, but each time, shortly before the raiders arrived, the gambling would stop, the paraphernalia would be removed, and the sheriff's men would find only some patrons sitting around conversing in an innocent manner. The report would then be that there was no evidence of gambling. Finally, I was obliged to tell the sheriff that if his deputies could find no gambling, mine could and would do so. He replied that I need not go to that trouble, because he would personally see that there would be no further gambling there. He did, and soon the place ceased operating in violation of the law. The sheriff was Eugene W. Biscailuz. He was an honest officer who cooperated with me in the whole law enforcement program, but he had a burgeoning office that had grown from about twenty deputies when he first took over to more than a thousand in the late nineteen-thirties. His problems of organization were enormous, and he did not know his personnel as one might in a smaller and less changeable department. In addition, the Hollywood crowd was then a sort of sacred cow in the community. It had attained great notoriety throughout the world and had attracted vast numbers of tourists, permanent residents, and business enterprises to the fast-growing Los Angeles metropolitan area. The motion picture industry, therefore, had corresponding influence, and things were overlooked that would not be tolerated in other parts of the community. The sheriff and I were friends and had been colleagues on the State Board of Identification and Investigation for twelve years. We had cooperated throughout that time to break down the barriers that had kept district attorneys, sheriffs, and chiefs of police apart, and we could, therefore, discuss frankly any law enforcement matter.

There were some other places in the state where various kinds of illegal gambling were going on, but a frank talk with the authorities responsible for those areas usually stopped or minimized it to the point where it was of only minor significance. I used this method rather than undertake flamboyant raids because, first, it was the cheapest way to do it—the easiest and in most cases the most effective. Secondly, this enabled me to exercise the new powers of the attorney general in an unobtrusive manner, without alienating the law officers of the state whose good will was needed to organize them into an effective group against the machinations of organized crime bosses who were viewing California with a lustful eye from other parts of the country. In some of the places where illegal gaming operations existed, particularly in the smaller communities, it represented more a corruption of the community than of the officials. Many of the latter told me they would welcome a directive from me to close the places, together with notice that if they did not do so, the state would intervene. They could then go to those who were pressuring for an open town and convince them that unless they complied with the law many people would be in trouble. It is difficult for the uninformed citizen to appreciate the pressure that can be brought to bear on public officials by the business and financial segments of the community when they are determined to have an "open town." This pressure is most effective when the police agencies are pinched, both in the number of their personnel and the salaries paid.

I had experienced some of those pressures as district attorney. When I took office, Oakland was wide open for prostitution, which was directly contrary to the law. No attempt was made to conceal it, and no attempt was made by the police to interfere with it so long as it was carried on in houses that were in police favor.

Within three blocks of the courthouse, there was an entire block occupied by houses of ill repute, and there was a notorious one directly across the street from us. I could have thrown a rock from my office through its windows. It was widely known as Caddy Wells' Parlor House. On investigation, I found that the furniture in all of those houses came from one store at prohibitive prices. However, the purchase of this furniture and undoubtedly other considerations gave such places an informal license to operate, as far as the police were concerned. While these houses were running openly, girls were being arrested in other parts of town and processed through the Police Court, but without any prosecution of the procurers or the male patrons. It was a sordid system, and I decided to attack it with a legal maneuver.

There was a little-used California statute called the "Red Light Abatement Act," which declared that any premises used for the purpose of prostitution constituted a public nuisance, and upon proof of such usage being submitted by the proper authorities the building could be closed and padlocked for one year. I decided to apply that law, and did so by filing suits against all the houses known to be utilized for commercial sex. We closed them right and left. I know it will appear strange, but the first people to complain and to urge me to desist were some of the local bankers and real estate men. They told me that I was closing up Oakland in the nighttime; that the ferryboats carried hundreds of men to San Francisco every evening who spent all of their money for recreation across the Bay, thus depressing the value of downtown property in Oakland. To fend off the businessmen, I told each of them that I was discussing the situation with the grand jury, which was a fact, and then asked if they would testify to what they had told me. Invariably they would say, "Oh, I couldn't become involved in that!" I would then ask them if they would write me a letter stating what they had just told me and making some suggestion concerning the prostitution problem. Most of them would repeat that they could not become involved, but a few said they would. None of them ever wrote, though, and for a long time afterward when I would meet one of them I would say, "You know, you owe me a letter," and he would mumble a promise to write in the near future. On investigation, I discovered that these padlocked premises were all old houses, but when used for prostitution they were bringing unusually high rentals, and were, therefore, able to support larger than normal mortgages. When they were closed up for a year, they became a drug on the real estate market and, therefore, of doubtful security for bank mortgages. Hence the concern of some bankers and real estate men. The Abatement Act was effective for a number of reasons. First, it eliminated one source of police graft. Secondly, it broke a link in the chain between that corruption and the legitimate business world. It made it unprofitable for pimps and other procurers to operate in Oakland. The closing of the houses also operated as a strong deterrent against those who profit greatly in this illicit business behind a shield of respectability. And, lastly, it put at least some of the burden of legal penalties for the prostitution racket on others than the unfortunate women who were enslaved in it.

There was a similar statute known as the Liquor Abatement Act which made it possible to use the same policy against bootlegging establishments. We padlocked scores of them in this manner. It was more effective than to raid speakeasies repeatedly.

I tried at Sacramento to have the same kind of statute enacted concerning gambling houses, but there was too much hidden opposition, and I never could get it passed.

During my years as attorney general, we kept illegal commercial gambling pretty well subdued, with one notable exception. That exception was the booking racket on horse races. It flourished in all of our California cities, large and small, but it took various forms depending upon the vigilance of local law enforcement offers. In some places, bookmaking was as open as a stock market, although the offense was a felony. In other places, it was confined to secret establishments where business was carried on through a battery of unlisted telephones. In some places, almost every cigar store placed bets; in others, runners solicited bets in office buildings, stores, shops, and on street corners. Warren Olney, my assistant, made a thorough study of the situation and came to the conclusion that it was largely through use of the telephone that the racket was carried on, and that if we could curb the phone's use we could practically put an end to bookmaking in California, because its vitality depended upon up-to-the-minute information on each race, and on the secrecy of that information. We took the matter up with the Pacific Telephone and Telegraph Company and its lawyers, Pillsbury, Madison and Sutro of San Francisco, and were told that they did not want that kind of business and would do nothing to stop us from putting an end to it. Olney prepared and filed a complaint seeking an injunction that would prohibit the company from knowingly leasing its wires for that purpose and was also against the lessors. The case was tried before Superior Court Judge Emmet Wilson of Los Angeles, who, to our great satsifaction, granted the requested injunction. We thought we were on our way to beating the racket completely because the telephone company was willing to comply with the injunction, and without their service bookmaking was almost certain to wither. However, the case was appealed and was reversed by our State Supreme Court. I was as much provoked by the way this was done as by the result. On the same day the case was decided, the Court also decided a little matter in which the district attorney of Monterey County had sought to have a Chinese lottery declared a public nuisance. The Court wrote a long opinion in that case, holding that a Chinese lottery did not create a public nuisance. When the Court reached our case, which involved millions of dollars every week, with ramifications all over America, it wrote no opinion, but merely said, "On the authority of (the lottery case), this day decided, the judgment is reversed." Thus, more than two years of hard work went down the drain without a single reason given. I was both shocked and indignant, as I was confident that we were right and that if reasons for the decision had been stated, its injustice would have been manifest to the Court also. But, in keeping with my practice in all my years in public office, I never publicly criticized the courts for a decision against us. For many years I had told young men in my office that we would win some cases and lose others, and that they should not store up bitterness over those we lost. They were entitled for three days to be as angry as they chose to be, but if they carried it beyond that, I said, they were hurting themselves and no one else.

It was too late in my term to devise another statewide program against the bookmakers, so it was necessary for us to play by ear the rest of the time. By pressing local authorities to action, we were able to keep the open betting parlors closed, but only where there was a true zeal to suppress the bookies was there effective enforcement against the batteries of unlisted telephones and runners.

I relate these activities against various kinds of commercialized gambling, not to indicate that it was my major preoccupation as attorney general, but as a demonstration that the commercialization of gambling, bootlegging and prostitution, all of which are so productive of official corruption, was not to be tolerated, and that under the new powers of the attorney general there was a force that could nullify any local arrangements which permitted these operations to exist. Here, I must confess to an ingrained bias against commercialized gambling; not mere betting between individuals, but the big-time, mob-run commercialization of it, because it is corruptive, dishonest in operation, and often cruel in its consequences. I had seen at first hand all of these bad attributes as a youth in Bakersfield and as a district attorney in Alameda County, particularly during the Sheriff Becker regime.

In fairness to the law enforcement officers of those days, I should say that all but a very few did not resent the pressure I put upon them, and some were greatly pleased, as it gave them strong support and an opportunity to resist the local counter pressures that brought such conditions into being. I remember discussing with James Drew, chief of police of Oakland, some lax crime conditions in his city. He listened attentively to me, and, after a few moments of reflection, said, "Wouldn't it be wonderful to be chief of police if our bosses would only give us hell for not enforcing the law better, instead of saying, 'Why are you always picking on my friends?'"

I told him he could tell his bosses—the city commissioners—that if he did not go after law violators, both he and they would be in real trouble. He promised to do so and subsequently did, with the result that conditions changed for the better.

The main thrust of my activities as attorney general was against any intrusion of organized crime. We were well briefed on the rackets that had spawned during the prohibition era in eastern and midwestern cities like Philadelphia, New York, Detroit, Chicago, and Kansas City. We had watched the legislative process at Sacramento to make sure that no laws conducive to mob incursion would be enacted. We had also studied leading mobsters' methods through our police schools at San Jose State College, and were determined that they should not gain a foothold in our state. I preached the doctrine always that the racketeers who plagued the legitimate business people of a community were of no potency until they had established a foothold in the political structure, and that up to that point they could be disposed of as easily as any other garden type of hoodlum. We had proved it in my county when dealing with a free-lot racket, a Business Men's Protective Association, a Cleaner's and Dyer's Association, fake oil mergers, and sundry other shady operations.

To make our law enforcement work more effective, I divided the state into several regions. In each of them, we established an organization of the chiefs of police, the sheriffs, the district attorneys, and later the fire chiefs. We had regularly scheduled meetings in each region, and I made it my business to attend and participate in each of them. At these sessions, we discussed conditions in the area, exposed any evidence of organized racketeering, and exchanged information and ideas for better crime prevention. It was my custom to bring to each region what was going on in other parts of the state. At these meetings, programs were developed and subsequently reported on. I tried to give leadership to them, but not to impose my will on them. Where a program was announced, it was a concurrence of minds and not a decree. This was a happy relationship for me. It stimulated great interest among policing agencies throughout the state and gave me an intimate acquaintance with most of the responsible officers. My communication with them was then on a personal basis. I could pick up the telephone and say to almost any of them that there was a complaint about something or other within their jurisdiction, and suggest that they take a look at it. In the vast majority of cases, they would do so, and remedy the situation if there was anything to the complaint.

By the summer of 1940, when France fell and the Battle of Britain began, we law officers of the state were well organized, functioning, and ready to expand our scope to protect the lives of everyone in times of disaster. We invited the fire chiefs to join us because fire is often the greatest destructive demon, particularly in wartime. They enthusiastically agreed, and from that time on we prepared ourselves for civil defense in the event that a threat of that kind should come to us. We read and discussed the current literature, spotty as it was, on the experiences of Europeans who had been subjected to repeated military disasters.

We all realized the great danger of fires in the event of a bombing or invasion, particularly in California where it rarely rains between April and November, and where a tiny spark in a field or a forest can start a blaze of terrible proportions. This disturbed us greatly, for in such areas there were no local fire stations, and we could rely only on the State Forestry Department with its limited fire-fighting resources. City fire departments were not authorized by law to go beyond their own jurisdictions, and it became quite apparent to us that if we were to have a number of big fires at the same time it could, indeed, spell catastrophe. We proceeded to study the legislation needed to authorize fire departments to move wherever needed, protect the fire fighters in the performance of their duties, and thus make a statewide plan of fire prevention possible. We succeeded in having the legislation enacted as the State Mutual Assistance Act. We then developed a plan for a grid that would enable us in times of stress to move available equipment in any direction to better cover all vital areas.

On December 7, 1941, when Pearl Harbor was attacked, we had a viable organization and program except for the legislative authority to implement it. Governor Culbert Olson immediately called the Legislature into session, and indicated that he intended to put into effect a

Disaster Act passed some years earlier, which would have enabled him to send into the affected areas his own representatives to pre-empt the prerogatives of the local and other state officers in police, fire, health, and rescue services. The act had been passed to take care of local floods, fires, earthquakes, and similar disasters. Its legislative history showed that wartime jurisdiction specifically was eliminated from the bill. I stated in the Governor's Office that I would not abide by any such assumption of power by the governor. There was much hysteria, and some of the leaders of the Legislature questioned my judgment, but as emotionalism subsided and the Legislature saw the unanimity of police and fire services in opposition to the governor's position, it proceeded to set up a Civilian Defense Council, with the governor as chairman and the attorney general as the officer in charge of civil defense activities. I had won the battle but came close to losing the war to the governor because he refused to recognize me in the council, told me nothing about what he had done or intended to do, and would not have his subordinates consult with me. It was a difficult position for me, but I continued to be active with the law enforcement and fire authorities, and with them put through the legislation necessary to make our programs workable.

Lieutenant General John L. DeWitt was then the commanding general of the Fourth Army, with headquarters at San Francisco, and I was in constant touch with him. I kept the law enforcement officers throughout the state thoroughly advised of everything that affected civilian defense. For a long time, we were blacked out at night because of the likelihood of air raids or submarine attacks. California was immediately declared to be a theater of operations after the Pearl Harbor attack, and we were defenseless. Incidents never reported in the news were known by enough people to keep the public at all times aroused as to the danger.

One day a few months after Pearl Harbor, I received a telephone call at my office from the young district attorney at San Luis Obispo, which is midway between San Francisco and Los Angeles. He was greatly excited.

"Attorney General," he said, "something happened here today that disturbs the entire city, and I feel that I must tell someone who might be able to help, so I am picking on you."

His name was Abe Brazil, and I said, "All right, Abe, what is it?"

Early that morning before daylight, he declared, there was a loud detonation that aroused people from their sleep and sent them running down to the seashore from where the sound seemed to come. When they arrived, they were told that a submarine had sunk a tanker in sight of the shore. The people were, of course, perturbed and excited, and they stood there and talked until after daylight. Shortly thereafter, another tanker came along in coastal waters and, in sight of all the townspeople, a submarine surfaced and sank it. There was an air base three or four miles from San Luis Obispo, and it was immediately notified. By noontime, no planes had taken to the air, and it was then that the district attorney telephoned me.

After hearing this, I said, "Abe, did you see all this yourself?"

"I certainly did, and so did half of the people of the city."

I told him that the matter was military and beyond my jurisdiction, but that I would tell Admiral John Greenslade, commander of the Western Sea Frontier, whose headquarters was in the Federal Building only a few blocks from my office. The only thought I had was that communications might have broken down, and Greenslade was not informed of the sinkings. I immediately went to his office and was graciously received by him. He listened attentively to me, and then said:

"Mr. Attorney General, you have been told precisely what happened. Two tankers were sunk, and I am embarrassed to say that there is nothing I can do about it. Confidentially, I have only two destroyers between here and Vancouver, British Columbia. All the rest of the fleet that was not sunk at Pearl Harbor has gone out into the Pacific."

He did not tell me where the fleet's rendezvous was, but it later developed that it was Midway, where one of the most vital battles of the war was fought.

I then asked him why the air base near San Luis Obispo could not have put planes in the air and searched for the enemy submarines. He replied that we had only a few old planes there that did daytime patrol duty, but that it sometimes took hours to put them into action.

At about this time another submarine reportedly surfaced at Goleta, a suburb of Santa Barbara, a hundred miles north of Los Angeles. In broad daylight, it fired upon some oil tanks situated near the coast, causing minor damage. Another sinking of a ship supposedly occurred off Northern California close to the Oregon line, but I had no official information concerning it. There were also many small balloons floated over the Bering Strait by the Japanese and carried by prevailing winds to fall on our forests and prairies. Some landed as far inland as the Rocky Mountain states. What their purpose was, we did not know. It could have been to terrify us, to bolster morale in the Japanese homeland, to test for something else to be dispatched later, or to set fires with incendiary bombs. Our concern was that some of them might land in California and start fires, in which case much of the state would be in danger.

We were told by the military of the danger of invasion and of the great need for comprehensive civilian defense programs.* We, the law enforcement and fire-fighting agencies, took the warning at face value and faithfully followed every instruction and suggestion that emanated from Washington on the subject. But it was not easy for us, as the governor was not in sympathy with our programs, and we were sometimes discouraged by the lack of interest shown by many of our legislators. Their lackadaisical attitude could be attributed to the loose talk of ranking military men in club and social gatherings. Many of these high-ranking Army and Navy officers were made honorary wartime members of the principal social clubs in the cities where they headquartered. In San Francisco, these were the Bohemian, Pacific Union, Family, Olympic, and Press clubs, as well as a number of financial and businessmen's clubs. In these places, at the bar and at the luncheon table, many of these military men would scoff at the entire civilian defense movement, saying it was a lot of folderol and that when the chips were down the military would take over defense of every kind. While they would not repeat this in public, the word spread throughout the business world and through it to the Legislature. This was the same arrogant talk that many high military officers spread around the state prior to Pearl Harbor. It was commonly held that our naval forces could knock out the Japanese Navy by lunchtime on any given day, that the Japanese were not innovative, that they could only copy our methods, that they were far behind us in every military field, and that because of bad eyesight they could not man the essential weapons of successful warfare. All of this was dispelled after Pearl Harbor, but the same arrogance toward civilian defense went on unabated.

In the meantime, Japanese military successes continued throughout the Pacific basin. One of our units composed of Californians was decimated and captured at Bataan and Corregidor, and our people were outraged by much publicized stories of the tortures and sufferings of captured U.S. soldiers. American propaganda portrayed the Japanese as having adopted the Hitlerian theory of a master race, departing from it only in asserting that the *they* were the chosen ones, not the Germans. Published stories of their savagery sadism charged the atmosphere. Over here, the Japanese, largely to retain their culture, lived in self-constituted and closely knit areas. This, of course, had been stimulated also by a considerable amount of racial prejudice that stemmed largely from some of our farming communities. The Japanese were brought to California in the first place as cheap labor, but once here they were too dili-

* Ed. note: During these military briefings there was considerable emphasis on the effectiveness of sabotage activities in the European Theater, the implication being that if the French and other underground resistance forces could be so disruptive, then Japanese loyal to the Emperor might wreak equal havoc on American railroads, bridges, industrial plants, and other vital installations.

gent, capable, and intelligent to remain as common farmhands or railroad workers. They became farm owners, entrepreneurs, and businessmen. This resulted in antagonism against them, culminating in the Federal Oriental Exclusion Act and the California Alien Land Law, both of which caused international complications for decades. On the other hand, Japanese citizenship was not open to Americans nor were our citizens free to buy land in Japan. People of Japanese origin who were born in the United States were acknowledged in Japan as American citizens, but because of the dual citizenship theory of Japan, they were considered to be that country's citizens also. As a result, many Japanese-American boys as they arrived at school age were sent to Japan for their education. They remained there throughout their childhood, and some of them until they had registered for and served as draftees in the military service. They would then return to this country in time to retain their American citizenship. These people were, of course, more Japanese by training, indoctrination, and ideology than the older Japanese aliens who had come to this country at least a quarter of a century earlier, and their affiliation in time of war worried us.

Many Japanese were commercial fishermen, and their boats, like those of other fishermen, went to sea at night. The flashing of lights on such boats, whether Japanese or not, was thought to be a signal to enemy submarines. Military intelligence assured us this was a danger. These anti-Japanese factors and many others of like character were on the minds of Californians at that time. People welcomed the U. S. House of Representatives Committee under John H. Tolan of Oakland when it arrived in our state to take testimony as to whether or not Japanese-American citizens should be removed from California during the war. The atmosphere was so charged with anti-Japanese feeling that I do not recall a single public officer responsible for the security of the state who testified against a relocation proposal. After a conference with the law officers, who agreed unanimously, I testified for a proposal which was not to intern in concentration camps *all* Japanese, but to require them to move from what was designated as the theater of operations, extending seven hundred and fifty miles inland from the Pacific Ocean. Those who did not move by a certain date were to be confined to concentration camps established by the United States Government. Of course, for most of them it was the same as directing their confinement, because the limited time prescribed for removal, the fact that their businesses were turned over to the Alien Property Custodian, the problem of their having no time to look for employment in an unfamiliar part of the country, the language barrier, and the race antagonism occasioned by the war made any other alternative remote indeed. To the credit of the Japanese, not one incident establishing disloyalty occurred prior to the exclusion order, so far as I am aware. After the order, thousands of them renounced any loyalty to the United States and professed a desire to have Japan win the war. These were separated from the rest and placed in the Tule Lake Camp, but how many of them, if any, would have felt that way had it not been for the removal order can only be a matter of conjecture. I have since deeply regretted the removal order and my own testimony advocating it, because it was not in keeping with our American concept of freedom and the rights of citizens. Whenever I thought of the innocent little children who were torn from home, school friends, and congenial surroundings, I was conscience-stricken. It was wrong to react so impulsively, without positive evidence of disloyalty, even though we felt we had a good motive in the security of our state. It demonstrates the cruelty of war when fear, get-tough military psychology, propaganda, and racial antagonism combine with one's responsibility for public security to produce such acts. I have always believed that I had no prejudice against the Japanese as such except that directly spawned by Pearl Harbor and its aftermath. As district attorney, I had great respect for people of Japanese ancestry, because during my years in that office they created no law enforcement problems. Although we had a sizable Japanese population, neither the young nor the old violated the law.

At about the same time we were considering their removal for military reasons, I wrote a formal opinion to the State Personnel Board, telling its members that they could not constitutionally take away Japanese-Americans' Civil Service rights to their state jobs as the commission directed. I know that it seemed ambivalent to protect their constitutional rights in this regard with one hand and deprive them of other rights by removing them from their homes. However, I consoled myself with the thought that the latter was occasioned by my obligation to keep the security of the state. Our entire treatment of Japanese-American citizens during the war was regrettable, yet it would have been infinitely worse had it not been for the ministrations of the relocation director, Dillon S. Meyer, an understanding and warmhearted man.

Recently I had an opportunity to help prevent the recurrence of such an emotional experience. Some years ago Congress gave the United States attorney general the authority even in peacetime to impound persons believed by him to be subversive. This was a broader and far more dangerous power than that used by President Franklin Roosevelt in removing the Japanese from the coastal areas during the War. At the request of the Japanese-American Society in California, I wrote a letter for use before the congressional committee which was studying a bill to revoke the attorney general's authority. The letter was used, and happily the nullifying bill was passed by the Congress and signed by President Richard Nixon.

As time passed, the breach between Governor Olson and me widened. He had caused his Board of Prison Terms and Paroles to parole all but one of the culprits in the Alberts ship murder case after they had served only about four years, and he did it with the suggestion that there was not sufficient evidence to justify the conviction. In addition to trying to freeze me out of the Civil Defense program, notwithstanding the action of the Legislature in making me the officer responsible for the entire program, he vetoed an appropriation of $214,000 for my office to fulfill its obligations under that act.

My relations with the armed forces in the state were excellent, and, with one notable exception, we worked cooperatively with the camp commanders. There were many of them because California was the largest training ground for troops in the nation throughout World War II. Also, it was through the ports of San Francisco, Oakland, Los Angeles, Long Beach, and San Diego that most of the men and supplies for the Pacific area were funneled. New camps with many thousands of raw troops sprang up only a few miles from little cities, and changed the character of life there. New businesses—some good and some bad—flocked there and deluged the authorities with problems they had never been confronted with before. Houses of prostitution suddenly flourished in many towns. There was a new federal law called the May Act which authorized camp commanders to declare that any community within fifteen miles of their posts where such houses were permitted was "out of bounds" for soldiers on leave. Many of the commanders would post notices to that effect on their bulletin boards and publicly admonish the soldiers not to patronize bawdy houses. But they would not take the necessary steps to see that the houses of prostitution were closed, or to pronounce the community where they operated to be off limits. On the contrary, some commanders privately told city managers and chiefs of police that it was necessary to have such places for the morale of the troops. One day the Surgeon General of the United States came to my office and informed me that the troops in California had one of the highest venereal disease rates in the nation. He said it was a serious problem for the armed forces because there were no speedy cures in those days, and the number of absentees because of V.D. interfered seriously with the training of the troops. I told him about the ambivalence of some of the camp commanders in this respect, and assured him that I would do everything possible to bring about compliance with Army Regulations, but that if our efforts were to succeed we must have real cooperation instead of lip service from the camp commanders. I suggested to the commanding general of the region that we bring together in one meeting place all of the responsible officers in both services, and have an agreement that would be understood by and binding on all. The general agreed, and we fixed a date for the meeting in the State office building in Los Angeles, at which both of us would be present. I followed this up by arranging a preliminary meeting with state law enforcement officers to whom I told the entire story. We decided that they could and would close all the places if they had the cooperation of the military. We then had the joint meeting. The general asked me to open with a statement of the facts as I knew them. I did so in very frank terms, and when I finished one of the camp commanders arose and took violent exception to what I had said about the divergent actions of some of the commanders. The general quickly responded, saying that he had made some investigation of conditions, that my statement was justified, and that we were not present to quarrel but to see that there was compliance with federal law. He urged cooperation to that end. Speaking for the Army and to his officers, the general said there would be no more complacency at the cantonments, and I promised for all the law officers present that with the services' help we would keep all the places closed.

As we left, the Surgeon General assured me that if this procedure were followed the situation would be remedied. He said the experience of the armed forces was that ten to fifteen per cent of all servicemen would find a woman to consort with even if it was necessary to jump off a ten-story building; that there were ten to fifteen per cent at the other end of the spectrum who could walk by houses of prostitution without being tempted, but that there were between sixty to seventy per cent who would simply go with the tide. If the houses were open, they would be tempted to patronize them; otherwise, they would get along without them.

He was certainly right in this instance. Within a very short time, the venereal disease rate had dropped dramatically to a point lower than that in most states.

One might think from the foregoing that during my attorney general years almost my total attention was given to law enforcement and civilian defense matters, but this would be far from reality. It should be remembered that I had approximately fifty assistants and deputies to administer, and little could have been accomplished without them. They were a competent and thoroughly loyal group and worked on their assignments with a fervor that was very gratifying to me. I was also greatly aided by the chiefs of police, the sheriffs, the district attorneys, and the fire chiefs of the state. They accepted my leadership in accordance with the new state constitutional powers of the Attorney General's Office and the Civil Defense Act. They cooperated splendidly with me and with each other. In civilian defense, they constituted a built-in organization. Collectively, we discussed our problems, formulated our plans, and executed them in unison. We presented a united front at Sacramento on legislative matters and established confidence in the fact that we were taking seriously the security of the state in the event of dislocation of normal life due to attack from without or subversion from within. It must be remembered that Hitler had boasted that he had no fear of the United States entering the War because he could immobilize the nation with a few telephone calls. A "Fifth Column," or sabotage force, was, therefore, always on our minds and in our planning. So far as subversion was concerned, we cooperated closely with the FBI, which had been placed in charge of the internal security of the nation, and cleared all subversive matters through it. Working through this and other agencies made it possible for me to spend a major portion of my time on organizing the expanded attorney general's offices, assigning projects, bringing our litigation into manageable shape, reviewing opinions of state lawmen, and a myriad of other things in the field of office management.

In doing these things, I was extremely fortunate to attract into the office able lawyers like William T. Sweigert as my chief assistant, Warren Olney as assistant in charge of criminal affairs, Hart Linney as head of the Tax Division, James Oakley and Theodore Westphal as civil deputies, Helen MacGregor as deputy and secretary, Oscar Jahnsen as chief of inspectors, and others of like dedication and character. Vitalizing the litigation calendar was a stupendous job, but it was done and put in good shape long before I left the office. As evidence of the size and complexity of the litigation even after the deadwood had been removed, there were never fewer than two thousand cases on the calendar. Some of it was of a nature that took us to the Supreme Court of the United States—twenty-five times to be exact—particularly when the state was pioneering in the tax field with sales and use taxes. Some of these on the civil calendar were as charged with emotion as the criminal appeals, and in all of them we were obliged to represent the state.

One civil case in particular had challenged my interest before my election, and it took many hours of my time throughout my term as attorney general. It involved the rights of the native Indians of California under the so-called "Lost Treaties" of 1851 and 1852. It exposed a most sordid chapter of California's colorful history and cried out for relief to a stricken people. The case came to my attention shortly after I announced my candidacy for attorney general, when I was called upon by a group of California Indians. They asked me if I would revive a suit on behalf of all the Indians of California that had been filed by Attorney General Webb a number of years before but had never moved. I told them I had no knowledge of the lawsuit or the facts that brought it into existence, but that I would investigate the matter and advise them later. I did study the case, and came to the conclusion that it revealed perhaps the most shocking injustice that had ever come to my attention. I told the Indians that I certainly would activate it, and see it to judgment. The facts that aroused my interest were briefly as follows:

At the time of the Treaty of Guadalupe Hidalgo in 1848, which ended our war with Mexico and ceded to the United States the territory which is now California and several other western states, there were no more than fifteen or twenty thousand people of European extraction in California. The great bulk of the population was native Indians—some 250,000 in number. With the exception of nineteen Mission compounds that were thinly dotted from San Diego to San Francisco Bay, and the Spanish and Mexican land grants in their vicinity, the entire California territory was populated only by a number of tribes of native Indians. It was a quiet, pastoral region and the Indians were mostly a noncombative and placid race. Although gold had been discovered in the foothills near Sacramento a few months before the treaty, word of the discovery had not yet leaked to the outside world, or at least the stampede to California had not yet started. But in the following year, the Gold Rush of '49 catapulted itself upon the sleepy region. A flood of frantic settlers came in search of gold, and would let nothing stand in their way. The Indians who roamed the great valleys were forcibly ejected, and where any resistance was shown, they were hunted like rabbits. Forced into the mountains without a means of livelihood, they started to fight back. The forty-niners then appealed to the United States Government for protection. The government responded by sending agents to California for the purpose of negotiating treaties with the various tribes. The Indians cooperated, and some treaties were agreed upon. The provisions of the treaties demonstrated the domesticity and guilelessness of these native people. In general terms, each treaty provided that the tribe would receive fifty cents or so per acre for an agreed number of acres of the land from which they had been ejected, as well as cattle, horses, hogs, plows, and various farming implements. Each adult woman would be entitled to a number of cooking utensils, some cutlery, dishes, and other small items of household utility. She would also get so many yards of calico, so many spools of thread, needles, pins, and accessories for clothesmaking. One can almost see them today as they sat around in a circle, negotiating for these simple things of life with the sophisticated Indian agents sent by the government to placate them. At all events, they were appeased for the moment. They gave up all right to the potentially valuable lowlands and agreed to live peacefully in the mountains, where living could never be anything but marginal. When agreement was reached, they signed, smoked the traditional pipe of peace, and the agents returned to Washington, where the treaties were lodged with the Senate for ratification. Those occurrences were in 1851–52, and the treaties have never been ratified to this day. In the intervening years, the Indian population in California had withered away until, in 1930, according to census rolls, they numbered only about nineteen thousand. Congress in 1928 passed the Jurisdictional Act authorizing the attorney general of California to sue the United States Government in the Court of Claims on behalf of the Indians of California. The idea was to recover compensation they should have been accorded under those treaties, though reserving to the government the right to subtract all money it had expended for them in the meantime. It was under this act that Attorney General Webb had filed the action mentioned above.

On assuming the office of attorney general, I immediately reactivated the case in accordance with my promise to the Indians. I went to Washington to confer with the appropriate committees of the Congress, the Department of Justice, and the people in the Bureau of Indian Affairs, and with some of the Indians who were in the capital at the time. There I was swarmed over by Indian Claims attorneys or cappers for them who could visualize an enormous fee forthcoming from the lawsuit. Everyone seemed to have a lawyer whom I should associate with me. I did not propose to associate with any of them in the litigation. There had been altogether too many lawyers and agents living off these oppressed people for a generation. The law had imposed a responsibility on me as attorney general, and I proposed to exercise it myself. Inasmuch as I was not acquainted with such cases in the Court of Claims, I did employ a lawyer in the Department of the Interior who was friendly to our cause and who was experienced in that field. He wanted to live in California and was happy to come and accept a deputyship in my office. With him and others on the staff, we did all the pretrial work, and eventually went to trial. I argued the case for the Indians in the Court of Claims at Washington, and an assistant in the Lands Division of the Department of Justice argued for the government. For some reason unknown to me, he showed a bitterness that I have rarely experienced in a courtroom, both against the Indians and against our case. His argument was little more than invective. We had been assigned an hour and a half per side for argument, and when he had used an hour and ten minutes, Chief Judge Richard S. Whaley interrupted him to say, "Counsel, you have consumed more than an hour without reaching the merits. Your allotted time of one and a half hours will not be extended, so I suggest that you get to the merits, if you have any, in the next twenty minutes." Counsel sat down without further argument, and the case was submitted. In late 1942, only a few days before the end of my term, the Court of Claims handed down its decision awarding us something over seven million dollars. This sounds like a substantial sum, but divided among nineteen thousand people or so it would amount to only a little more than $350 for each of them. The award was no larger because the government claimed as an offset every dollar that it had spent for California Indian schools, health, and social services for almost a century. My successor, Robert W. Kenny, was dissatisfied with the award, as was I, and he pursued the matter further. Eventually some of the tribes obtained substantial results, but others are still without relief more than thirty years later. It is a chapter in our history of which we can hardly feel proud.

Having resigned my Republican connections and announced a nonpartisan approach to the Attorney General's Office when I entered the race for that position, I maintained the same neutrality throughout the term. I took no part in Republican politics; nor, in fact, any politics. I was intensely interested in my job and wanted nothing more than to be re-elected as attorney general in order to carry to fruition my plans for making that office the outstanding one of its kind in America—a true instrument of justice and a model for civilian defense. Many people had urged me to run for governor, but I told them I had no interest in seeking that office. Which was the fact. I felt secure as attorney general because there was general praise for our efforts and no one likely to be a serious contender had appeared in the offing. I had no political organization or financial support to rely on, and no personal finances. The Democratic registration was by then almost two to one over the Republican. President Roosevelt was at the height of his prestige, having recently been elected over Republican candidate Wendell Willkie by winning in every state in the Union except Maine and Vermont. We were in a world war and in an atmosphere of "Don't change horses in the middle of the stream." I had a wife and six children and was obliged to remain in the law, for which I was trained, in order to support them. I felt that my opportunities in the legal field would be greater after holding the office of attorney general than after holding any other public position. There was little to attract me to a campaign for the governorship.

However, I felt thwarted at every turn by the incumbent governor. He seemed determined to run the state by decree from Sacramento during the war. In legal matters he bypassed me as attorney general and set aside the plans and programs of the law enforcement, health, and fire-fighting officials of the state, whom I had helped to weld into an enthusiastic and cooperative organization for civilian defense. He refused to recognize me in the State Council of Defense, although I had worked for two years in getting vital forces of the state to take part. He had ve-toed an appropriation bill of $214,000 for my office, and had caused his Board of Prison Terms and Paroles to parole King, Ramsay, and Conner after they had served about four years for one of the most bru-tal murders in the history of my county. The chasm between us was widening, and I could envision sitting in my office with nothing to do for four years in the event we were both re-elected to our respective jobs. All this was terribly disheartening, and it finally reached the point at which I could no longer stand it. Nobody of any substance signified an intention to run against the governor. I thought that Dr. Robert Gordon Sproul, president of the University of California, might be able to beat Governor Olson, and I urged him to try, but he was concerned about the effect it would have on the university, and so declined.

After much inner debate, I left my office one morning, went across the Bay to my home in Oakland, and told Nina to prepare herself for a shock. She inquired about the nature of it, and I told her that, as a last resort, I had made up my mind to run for governor. It was, indeed, a shock, and she asked if I thought I could win. I told her that was not the main consideration; that the governor and I were at loggerheads; that he would not permit me to do the things that the Constitution and laws of the state required of me, and that I would not sit on the sidelines for a term as attorney general while we were in the midst of a war that threatened our very national existence. She said, "All right, if that is the way you feel, you should do it."

I told some of my close friends in the San Francisco Bay area of my decision, and they were aghast. They told me that while they had wanted me to run for governor and had believed I could win, the war had changed their thinking. They now considered it most unwise for me to do so. They enumerated the obstacles that would confront me, all of which I conceded. But, I told them, the war had changed my mind also, and although I previously had been unwilling to run, I now believed I must do so if I was to perform any useful function in the war effort. Reluctantly they agreed to support me if that was my final deci-sion. However, they said a poll had been taken in Southern California and it showed that only about twenty per cent of the voters there were of a mind to back me.

I announced my candidacy on April 10, 1942. From that time on, the press was more interested in my activities. I declared that in two or three days I was going to Los Angeles to review the situation in the southern part of the state. After this information was published, and before I arrived, sixty-five of the so-called "moneybags" of that area convened at the California Club in Los Angeles and solemnly decided that they would take no part in the governor's race, but would devote all their time, energy, and money to electing a conservative Legislature to curb Olson in his next term. Many of these men had urged me over the past two years to run for governor, but this was their way of informing me that I need not look to any of them for help. Actually, I had not asked anyone to assist me financially. Among those present, there was only one who spoke in my behalf. He was a junior partner in a large insurance firm and was filling in for his senior partner, who could not attend the hurried conference. His name was Gordon Campbell, and he was best known as a fullback on the University of Southern California football team fifteen years or so earlier. He performed at this meeting as directly as he played football. He told the rest that they were a bunch of hypocrites; that he had heard many of them say I should make the race, and that it was a cowardly and dishonest thing for them to throw cold water on my candidacy in this manner. His words created some consternation but changed no votes, and the meeting adjourned on this 64-to-1 basis. I did not know Campbell at the time, but we soon became close friends.

After I learned of the meeting, I made a list of about ten businessmen who had been present and who at one time had urged me to enter the race. I visited each in turn, and told them I had not come to induce them to change their minds, but merely to inform them before the election that I knew exactly what had transpired at the meeting. I also emphasized that I had never asked any of them for any financing, and that their action would not change my plans. Their embarrassment was great, and they tried to explain; however, I told them I was not seeking an explanation. I only wanted them to know that I knew of the meeting.

While I did not fully realize it at the time, this was one of the best things that ever happened to me politically. The first public reaction of Governor Olson to my candidacy was that the people of California would not want as their governor a district attorney who was the creature of the moneyed interests of the state. But my action had deprived him of one of his appraisals of me, and, what was far more important, it had relieved me after my election of any pressure based upon campaign contributions from powerful southland intersts.

At the suggestion of Superior Court Judge Fletcher Bowron of Los Angeles, later to be elected mayor of that city at a recall election, I asked Raymond H. Haight, a liberal young Republican, to be my Southern California manager. He consented and, in turn, suggested that we make Gordon Campbell chairman of the Finance Committee in that area. I followed his suggestion, and by great diligence in seeking small amounts he raised about $75,000, which in those days enabled me to make a fairly good primary campaign in that part of the state.

The Republican Party in Southern California at that time was at its nadir, and the few remnants of it were pulling apart rather than together. In visiting the various communities, instead of trying to decide which of the warring factions would prevail at the meetings, I went independently with only an actor friend of mine, Leo Carrillo. He was from an old pioneer Spanish family, and his great-grandfather had been especially prominent under Spanish rule. A noted actor on both stage and screen, he was beloved for the wholesome characters he portrayed as well as for his own humor and likable personality. He was a great storyteller, particularly about events of California history. He was also a lifelong Democrat. He and I would mount the platform alone. He would tell the purpose of the gathering, warm up the crowd with a few stories, and turn the meeting over to me. We made scores of appearances, and finished the campaign without any serious difficulties with discordant local Republican cliques.

We did not start the campaign in Los Angeles or in any of the large cities. Instead, we went into the old Mother Lode country in Central and Northern California. That is the mountain area where gold was discovered in 1848, and to which tens of thousands came by sailing ships and prairie schooner in search of the elusive yellow metal. It is the most historic region of the state, colorful in its physical characteristics and in its folkways. Everything about it is nostalgic. The petty personal clashes that distinguish national and state politics in the large centers of population do not concern the people there. It is a great place to start a campaign for the governorship. Press coverage was as ample as it would have been in the cities; the articles were usually historically backgrounded, full of unusual characters, and noted the size and diversity of California and the importance of its back country life. After ten days of such pleasant campaigning, a candidate feels prepared for the more populous and complex areas.

On my return to San Francisco, the governor and I were invited to debate publicly. We both accepted, and, on the day of the meeting, a large delegation of the CIO, then a decidedly left-wing organization, pre-empted the major portion of the auditorium's front seats and roundly booed everything I said. The moderator offered to close the affair long before the scheduled time, but I said I had come to speak and intended to do so, no matter how loudly they booed me. The debate didn't prove anything, but it did put a little fire into the campaign.

When I came home that evening, I found my wife in tears. While doing her housework, she had been listening to the debate on the radio, and had heard me being booed. This was absolutely new to her, and she thought all was lost.

In California, one of Hiram Johnson's reforms was the abolition of the old convention system of nominating candidates. He substituted the direct primary system, which enabled any candidate to run merely by filing a petition with a number of signatures of members of his party and by paying the filing fee. Also, if desired, the candidate might file for nomination by the *other* party by having a like number of signatures from that party and by paying an additional filing fee. As I recall, the requirement was for a minimum of sixty signatures and a maximum of one hundred and twenty. At any rate, it was easy to fulfill. I filed on both tickets—the Republican and the Democratic. This was common practice for most of the state legislators, congressmen and senators, and many of them received the nomination of both parties. Governor Olson only filed for the Democratic nomination, and accused me of being a hypocrite for filing on both, but there was nothing new about the move. I argued that wartime was no time for partisanship, and if elected I would be a governor for *all* the people, without favoritism of any kind. I pounded this home at every meeting, and pointed out acts and statements that indicated the governor's own blind partisanship. I took him to task for his failures in the Civil Defense field, for his interference with the constituted officers in that same area, for his parole of the shipboard murderers, and for his lack of understanding of California and its problems.† Olson had only been in the state a few years when he was elected to the Senate. Four years later he became governor. He had come from Utah, where he was at one time in the Legislature, and had entered politics in California by espousing the cause of Upton Sinclair in his EPIC campaign (End Poverty in California). My battle cry was to make no small plans for California; all socioeconomic programs should be on the basis of its having a population of twenty million people in twenty-five years. This figure frightened some of my friends, and they urged me to scale it down to fifteen million because that was the prediction of the experts, but I refused to do so, telling them that population estimates for California were for optimists, not experts. Of course, it was a shot in the dark, but it happened that when the census was taken in 1970, twenty-seven years after my first year as governor, the population was twenty million.

† Ed. note: Warren's disagreements with Olson extended to other things as well. Among them was Olson's attempt to appoint a liberal University of California professor, Max Radin, to the California Supreme Court, which Warren successfully blocked as a member of the qualifications committee. Other issues between them ranged from Olson's consistent espousal of leftist labor causes and social programs, most of which Warren opposed on more conservative Republican grounds, to the governor's belief that school children should not be required to salute the flag, whereas Warren ruled, as attorney general, that they could be expelled if they didn't.

It was not a wildly exciting campaign, as Olson's and my trails seldom crossed. The governor confined his activities to his supporters in the big cities. I took my case to the environs of the big cities and to the back country in an effort to give it an all-California appeal. For instance, in Los Angeles County, instead of spending most of my time in downtown Los Angeles where so much divisiveness existed, I encircled it by going to cities like Glendale, Pasadena, Pomona, Long Beach, Santa Monica, Whittier, Beverly Hills, Burbank, and Inglewood, where there was more cohesion and more objectivity and where the political news was as well reported as in the central city. I campaigned very hard in spite of the fact that I had no substantial opposition for the Republican nomination. There was no organization for me in the Democratic Party, but I went where the Democrats were—to the factories, shipyards, canneries, etc.—and told of the need for a nonpartisan state administration during the War. I campaigned as hard and covered as much ground as was possible from April to August, when the primary election was held. When the date arrived and I took a little time to survey the stumping I had done, I realized how much of the state I had failed to cover. California is approximately nine hundred miles long by one hundred and seventy-five wide, and at that time it had over three hundred cities and a population of seven million people. However, the primary election results showed that I had covered it fairly well, for I received practically all the Republican votes, 635,230 to be exact, and 404,778 Democratic votes as against 514,144 for Governor Olson. This was a startling result, and presaged the outcome of the November election. There was no longer any difficulty in building up my volunteer group of campaigners, which was my entire organization. Even the "moneybags" who had scorned my campaign at the beginning wanted to come in on a commanding basis. They said, "Now we will put a good finance committee together and give Olson a real licking." I said, "No, we will have the same little finance committee." "But," they countered, "he can't get any money"—referring to Gordon Campbell. I replied, "If he can't, then we won't have any to spend." And that ended that. By then I had become completely aware of the great favor the financial interests of Los Angeles had done for me in repudiating my candidacy. They had established in the eyes of the people of California that I was not the creature of vested interests, and because most of them were known as contributors to Republican campaigns, this gave credence to my promise to have a nonpartisan campaign. I was not about to give up those advantages. Campbell continued to head up our financing in Southern California, and again he operated as he had in football, hitting hard. Whenever any of the original crowd of sixty-five who had met in the California Club proffered a contribution, he would say, "Did you contribute in the primary election?" and on receiving a negative answer would ask, "Why are you offering to contribute now? Don't think you are buying anything for it, because there is nothing for sale." I gloried in his spunk, and, in spite of his abrasive honesty, he put together a fund that was adequate for our purpose.

One of the greatest strengths in my campaign was the treatment I received at the hands of the press. Most of the newspapers of the state were Republican-oriented, and I had the active support of practically all of them. Most of the Democratic papers also were quite friendly to me, and none of them was bitterly opposed. In the big cities, the only Democratic metropolitan paper was the Los Angeles *Daily News*, and it was not unfriendly. The other metropolitan papers—the Los Angeles *Times*, the San Francisco *Chronicle*, the Oakland *Tribune*, the San Diego Copley chain, and the Hearst papers—all helped me greatly, as did others throughout the state.

Although I had my own quarrels with the governor, I knew enough about politics to realize that those personal issues were not broadly based enough to excite the entire electorate, particularly in Los Angeles, where he had resided. I had lived in Central or Northern California since my very early years, so I looked for every opportunity to indicate some attachment to Southern California and especially Los Angeles.

I remember well my first campaign speech there. In speaking of my devotion to and vision for the future of California, I mentioned that I was born in Los Angeles, not far from where I was speaking. I had supposed it would provoke some interest, but not a single person clapped or even booed. Later in the same speech, I casually remarked that my father came from the little town of Eagle Grove, Iowa, and that brought tumultuous applause. I learned something by the experience, and throughout the remaining years of my political life, when in Southern California, I emphasized my father's boyhood in Iowa and my mother's childhood in Minneapolis, Minnesota, from which many thousands of people had also migrated westward. Midwestern sentiment was always very strong in the southern part of California.

I also learned early in my campaign that my independent or nonpartisan approach to the governorship would be severely tested. The premonition first came in Los Angeles. Although most of those active in the campaign at least gave lip service to nonpartisanship as being a good wartime campaign platform, there were many who believed I should tie myself more closely to the Republican organizations. This first manifested itself in the lieutenant governor's race. There had been a number of Republican candidates, each going his own way in the primaries. A young Los Angeles lawyer by the name of Fred Howser was the winner of the nomination. He had been quite active in younger circles of the Republican Party and as a legislator, and was not enamored of my nonpartisan approach. On the other hand, as soon as we were both nominated he insisted that we have a Warren-Howser ticket. I told his supporters that I could not do so without negating my nonpartisan approach, and this I would not do. Finally, he personally told me that if I did not announce such a ticket, he would announce his withdrawal from the campaign, and say I had double-crossed him. He said the same people who had put him into the campaign had put me into it and that he had a right to insist on our joining forces. I told him that I did not know who put him in the campaign, but I did know that no one had put me into it, that I was a self-starter, and was going to remain independent not only through the campaign but throughout my administration as governor if elected. He did not withdraw, although there were rumblings to that effect throughout the campaign. This did not result in a cooperative atmosphere between the two of us during my administration. At the outset, I told him that if he would let me know what phase of the state government he was interested in I would work out a way for him to be active, but he said that would be "putting him on the spot." I told him to forget about it, and we went our separate ways. At the end of my term, he ran for and was elected a superior judge of Los Angeles County, where he has since served.

My campaign in Northern California went along smoothly almost to the end. Most of my associates and friends were in that part of the state, and it was comparatively easy to develop volunteer organizations in most communities. I had no trouble with finances because three men of outstanding prestige in San Francisco offered to guarantee an adequate campaign fund for Northern California, assuring me that it would all be money without any strings attached to it, that it would come from honorable sources, that I would never be under any obligation for having accepted it, and that all the donors were interested in was an honest administration with a governor who would "call them as he saw them." I had every reason to accept this offer at face value. One of the contributors was a long-time personal and political friend who had originally urged me to run for attorney general, and who had supported in every way my independence in that office. His name was Jesse Steinhart, a distinguished San Francisco lawyer who had been from the beginning a Republican of the Hiram Johnson movement. Another was Charles Blythe, senior member of Blythe-Witter Company, one of the principal investment banking institutions of San Francisco, a man of impeccable reputation as a businessman and civic leader. I knew him more by reputation than by personal association. The third was an executive of the Caterpillar Tractor Company of Stockton and San Francisco, whom I knew only slightly but who was an outstanding businessman with a substantial and growing industrial organization. They suggested that I employ Whittaker and Baxter, a public relations firm, for my publicity. I accepted their offer and suggestion, and had no financial problems during the campaign. My recollection is that we spent about $125,000 in Northern California, as compared with $175,000 in Southern California. That is a very modest amount compared with present-day expenditures, but, as I shall point out later, even that small sum can embarrass a man elected to office on other people's money.

My campaign organization was what today might be called a conglomerate. It was volunteer in essence and composed of many shades of the political fabric. Most of the conservative elements were friendly if not actively for me. On the other hand, an original Hiram Johnson man like Irving Martin, publisher of the Stockton *Record*, a former member of Johnson's Railroad Commission, was my campaign chairman; Al McCabe, an insurance man and formerly Johnson's right-hand man in charge of the Governor's Office, was active among the Progressives. Chester Rowell, publisher of the San Francisco *Chronicle* and formerly of the Fresno *Republican* (he was also one of the organizers of the Lincoln-Roosevelt League, which launched Hiram Johnson into politics), and Marshall Stimson, a long-time Progressive, also supported me vigorously. In addition, scores of prominent independent Democrats who were not active in politics but who agreed with my approach publicly supported me. While the latter had no political following, the prestige of their names was most helpful. My official support in the labor unions was minimal. Harry Lundborg of the Seaman's Union of the Pacific not only supported me personally but obtained the endorsement of his union. With the exception of a few smaller ones, all the other labor organizations were overwhelmingly Democratic and gave their endorsements to Governor Olson. Notwithstanding, as I went around the state, labor men would say to me, "After you are elected governor, and you will be elected, don't be mad at us. You know what happens in politics. Endorsements are not always what they seem to be. He (Olson) has the endorsements, but you will get the votes." It was invariably said with a smile, and I subscribed to it. I was not drawn into a controversy over the endorsements. I tried to appeal to all working people on the basis of my understanding of their problems and my determination to see that their rights were protected and their interests advanced. I stated again and again that I hoped to see the day when every workman would be a member of a union and every employer a member of some association so collective bargaining could become a reality.

In connection with old age pensions, I refused to endorse any of the programs advanced by any of the professional organizations, and we had many of them. On the other hand, I took the position that the average working person, after properly rearing and educating a family, could not have set aside enough money to provide a decent living during retirement in a business world that refused to employ people in their forties and compelled their retirement at sixty-five. I urged that retirement funds be provided by joint contributions of employers and employees throughout the productive years, and that, all having contributed, they be allowed to reap the benefits in retirement, whether they had been able to save much or little in their prime earning period. This was really an extension of the social security principle, which was then a relatively new idea. I urged that the existing old age pension laws be liberalized in a manner that would contribute to that end. This did not satisfy professional pensioners like the "Thirty Every Thursday" people or any of the others. In all the years I was in politics, I never made a speech to one of those groups. Dr. Francis Townsend, a kindly old gentleman, the founder of the Townsend Plan, occasionally would come to my office and urge me to attend some of their meetings, as so many politicians did in those days. I told him his plan (providing negotiable script for the aged through a business tax) could not work at that time, and if I spoke at one of his conventions, many of his people would consider it a tacit endorsement, only to become disillusioned when I failed to urge its implementation. I said I would prefer to risk their displeasure for not appearing rather than their enmity in the belief that I had misled them. His organization never endorsed me, but neither did it fight me bitterly.

I was a pragmatist—not an ideologist—throughout the campaign. In keeping with my plea to make no small plans for California but to do all things in contemplation of a population of twenty million people in twenty-five years, I advocated many steps of what might be called a bread-and-butter nature. These included a sound fiscal policy; the conservation of our natural resources, and particularly the development of our water supply; the expansion of our highway system to better coordinate rural and urban life; the expansion and improvement of public education in keeping with the growth of the state; adequate law enforcement; a dedication to civilian defense and generally to participation in the national war effort, and preparation for a postwar California. Social problems were not in the minds of people during the War, and we could undertake no construction programs because of wartime restrictions on materials and labor.

I was really pressured on only one matter throughout the campaign, and that was the insistence that I announce a Warren-Howser ticket.

More and more old-line Republicans urged me to do it, but I remained adamant. Finally, the weekend before the election, Clem Whittaker of Whittaker and Baxter made such an announcement from our San Francisco publicity office, contrary to my instructions. I was campaigning in a distant part of the state. I called him and told him to close the office and issue no more bulletins. That was my last personal experience with Whittaker, and as far as I know it was his last important political campaign during the years I was governor. This is not to say that I injured his business, as I was thereafter indirectly responsible for his making a fortune. Only two years later, when I advocated a prepaid health insurance program, he was employed first by the California Medical Association and then by the American Medical Association to combat it as a dangerous form of "socialized medicine." Every doctor in the AMA was forced to contribute annually for many years to a fund for that purpose.

I campaigned as diligently as possible in the final election, right up to the closing of the polls, and was rewarded with a majority of 335,000 votes. The thing that pleased me most, however, was the fact that I carried every county in the state except the little mountain county of Butte, which I lost by sixty votes because of a local school controversy in which, as attorney general, I had written an opinion which was not well received by many of its citizens. The victory margin, it seemed to me, was a clear mandate to conduct the nonpartisan administration I had campaigned for. Although at that time the labor unions were strongly Democratic, and Governor Olson had practically all of their endorsements, I had carried every workingman's district.

Having won the election, I lost all of the irritation that resulted from my experiences with the governor and commenced to try to put things together so we could all work in harmony. I do not believe I have ever said anything critical of him since that time, and I should also add that he never went out of his way to injure me. Governor Olson was not a bad man, and I never accused him of being one. He did have a strain of bitterness, and he surrounded himself with some people who played to that trait in his makeup, keeping him upset about anyone who was not of his faction in the Democratic Party or who did not agree with his proposals. I always thought that if our relations had been more direct and if we could have discussed things personally, we could have patched up many of the differences that resulted from our estrangement. But I never saw him, and only rarely his intimates, except at public meetings where their proposals would be made without any prior opportunity on my part to study them, although under the State Constitution and statutes I was their legal adviser. In the four years we were both in the capital, I can remember only one private conversation I had with the governor. That was my first day on the job when I went to his office to tell him I was obliged to investigate and probably prosecute the private secretary of his predecessor. There were many things we should have talked about—civil defense, conservation of water resources, law enforcement problems, prisons, welfare, and others—but we never did.

I never knew how bitterly Olson felt about his experience as governor until the day of my inauguration. The ceremony was in the Assembly Chambers. In the elevator on the way down to the Governor's Office, with him and his sister, my wife and I present, he said, "Warren, if you want to know what hell is really like, just wait until you have been governor for four years." I replied, "Governor, I hope it won't be that bad." His rejoinder was, "Just wait and you will see." We then said good-bye, and with that I took over the office.

On a more cheerful note, when my wife and I reached the Governor's Office for a reception, our children were there and the members of the press took advantage of the situation to become acquainted with them. They asked Earl, Jr., our twelve-year-old, "Earl, whose speech at the Inauguration did you like best?" expecting him, of course, to say he preferred mine. He thought for a moment and said, "I believe I liked the lieutenant governor's best. It was shorter. You know in a warm room like that people don't listen so well to a long speech." The point was well taken, as the lieutenant governor's speech had been about three minutes in length and mine about forty, due to the fact that at this joint session of the Legislature the new governor was supposed to offer a preview of his administration in a "State of the State" message. When they interviewed our seven-year-old, Bobby, he showed them a wallet he had received at Christmas, and called attention to the identification card which carried his name and our new address at the Governor's Mansion, 1526 H Street, Sacramento, California. He then turned the card over and said, "And here is our old address, to go back to when our four years are up: 88 Vernon Street, Oakland, California." Little Bobby may have been reading his California history, for up to that time Hiram Johnson was the only four-year-term governor of the state who had been elected for a second term.

VII

PROBLEMS TO OVERCOME : *Years as a Governor*

My administration as governor began without fanfare on January 4, 1943. We had no Inaugural Ball or other public festivity in connection with it, in keeping with wartime regulations against crowds. This actually pleased both Mrs. Warren and me because we had learned in public life that such events invariably strain more friendships than they make. Ruffled feelings are created among those who believe they should have a more prominent part in the ceremonies and among others who might be overlooked on the invitation list, which could not be unlimited. I therefore took the oath of office before a joint session of the Legislature, delivered the "State of the State" message, held an open door reception in the Governor's Office, to which everyone was welcome immediately after the Inauguration, and then went to work. It all went so smoothly and with such little effort that we followed the same procedure in subsequent elections long after the war had ended.

There were some problems to overcome, however, in moving the family to Sacramento. The Governor's Mansion was in such a dilapidated condition that it was impossible for a large family to move in without extensive alterations. It had been built in 1878 by the Gallatin family as a residence. The head of the family was a prominent Sacramento merchant and a descendant of Albert Gallatin, the famous Secretary of the Treasury and statesman of Thomas Jefferson's administration. When the Gallatins moved to San Francisco, the house was sold to the father of Lincoln Steffens, the journalist who was perhaps the most famous of the so-called "muckrakers" of that period. Steffens had lived there as a boy, and when his family moved from Sacramento, the property was purchased for the state in 1904 by Governor George C. Pardee to serve as the Governor's Mansion. It is a three-story Victorian building with sixteen-foot ceilings and a gingerbread exterior. It is ample in size for a large family but was not habitable when I became governor. None of my predecessors for many years had a growing family at the time of their governorship. As a consequence, they used it very little. The entire third floor was boarded off in 1943 and occupied by bats. One room on the ground floor was a storeroom filled with broken furniture. The rugs and the drapes were moth-infested, the underpinnings of the porches were weakened by termites, and the rotting flooring had holes in it. There were not enough dishes and cutlery of one kind to set a table for six. In sum, it was unlivable. My wife cried on her first visit to it. As a result, I moved into the Sutter Club until the old mansion could be renovated, and left my family in Oakland.

Mrs. Warren then launched a program of rehabilitation. I delegated Oscar Jahnsen, one of my long time colleagues, to supervise the work. They jointly labored for several months at refurnishing it while the construction work went painfully on in spite of a wartime scarcity of materials and manpower. Finally the job was completed only a short time before the end of the school year. Nevertheless, we decided to leave the children in Oakland schools for the remainder of the term. Five of them were in grammar or high school. Jim, our oldest, had finished college and was in the Army. Because of a severe arm injury suffered while playing high school football, Jim had been relegated to limited service and was processing California draftees at the Monterey Presidio at the time of my inauguration. He was so embarrassed by what he considered to be his low status that he declined to ask for a twenty-four-hour pass to attend the event. Later, however, he obtained a reassignment to the 3rd Marine Division and served in the Pacific, to his greater satisfaction, until the end of the war.

When the mansion at length was renovated and refurbished, it was a pleasant place to live. The children enjoyed it, and we lived there happily for almost eleven years.

The Governor's Office also presented some problems when we moved in. Governor Olson had removed every document from the files, and we were obliged to start as if it were the year one in the history of the state. It took a long time for us to learn what the unfinished business of the previous administration was at the time I took over. In the meantime, we received many scorching letters for not responding to prior correspondence that we had no way of knowing about. While it is not unprecedented for public officers to remove all their files upon leaving an office, I have always believed that it is not in the public interest to do so, and have always, on leaving any office, made it a point to make my files available for the needs of my successor.

We faced another starting problem as I took over. The condition of my offices gave mute evidence of the fact that they had been wired for sound so that everything said by anybody in them could be recorded. In the Governor's Office, the listening device was built into a dummy telephone on the desk. In other rooms, it was disguised in other ways. Immediately above the Governor's Office in a secluded room were two large recording machines, capable of taking down simultaneously what was transpiring in the rooms below. The machines, of course, had been removed before my arrival. Still, telltale evidence of them was built into the structure and could be discerned by anyone examining the place.

I had always had an abhorrence of such systems of surveillance, and I did not want anyone to find this one for the first time after I left the office, or to infer that perhaps I had established it. The situation was aggravated by the fact that, some time earlier while the governor was investigating the Legislature with the aid of similar equipment, a microphone had been discovered in the bedroom of the speaker of the Assembly. This and rumors of widespread "bugging" had created an atmosphere of tension and distrust around the Capitol.

In order to end this situation, I called the principal officers of the Legislature to my office and publicly displayed the evidence of bugging to them. I advised them that there would be no surveillance from my office; instead, we would operate in what I hoped would be an atmosphere of mutual respect and confidence. This did much to relieve the tension, and it was not revived during my years as governor.

It might be proper at this point to describe my concept of the relationships existing between various levels of government. My long experience in city and county government and four years as attorney general led me to the conclusion that, within reason, government should be kept as close as possible to the people. I therefore believed in a large degree of local autonomy. The state, I felt, should initiate direct programs of local significance only when problems got beyond the local community's competence or intention to solve them. In state government, I believed in the separation of powers and the autonomy of each of the three branches within its own domain, strengthened by mutual respect between them. I was opposed to any one of the three trying to impose its will on any other. In accordance with this policy, I refused to take any part in the organization of either house of the Legislature. The speaker of the Assembly and the president pro tempore of the Senate were elected by their respective bodies, and I kept hands off. Even when I was asked by those officers about naming some members to certain committees, I declined to give advice saying that was their prerogative and I would try to work with whomever was named. This was not just a theory of mine. It was also a practical conclusion based upon prior experience. I knew enough about our Legislature to be aware that with few exceptions these officers had obtained their positions through the lobbyists and whatever was to be done would result in their dominance. I remembered what a former governor had told me about his experience with the Legislature. He said that the newly elected speaker asked him to supply some names for each of the Assembly committees. He said he complied, but when the committees were announced he found that he had a minority on each and that on every one of them there was a solid majority against him. Nevertheless, throughout the session, whenever complaint was made about committee action, it would be publicized that the governor had participated in its formation.

For many years, I also had watched the trading process between governors and the Legislature. I found that practice to be bad. When the Legislature passed a bill that it would not have passed except as a trading device, and when a governor as a means of barter signed a bill that he would not otherwise have endorsed, then the people would, in all likelihood, have two bad laws instead of one or none. The Legislature had so much more room in which to trade that a governor in that process would usually be receiving only "an apple for an orchard." Hence I let it be known that there would be no more trading; the Legislature would be free to pass its own bills, and I would view each of them on its own merits.

In doing this, I did not impugn the motives of the Legislature, nor did I express any antagonism toward it. I simply put things on the basis that each of us should, as the saying goes, "stick to his last" and we would thereby have better government.

I did not come to the governorship satisfied with the status quo; on the other hand, I had no utopian views as to either government or society. Having witnessed life on both sides of the tracks, I realized that there were many things that called for correction, but I also recognized that California was a new and fast-growing organism and our hope for the future depended on making progress day by day on as many fronts as possible. I considered each day a wasted one if I could not point to some progress made. I did not care to be categorized as either a liberal or a conservative because too many people calling themselves conservatives would consent to no change, and too many so-called liberals would also permit no change unless it was on their often unrealistic terms. Also, there was a not inconsiderable group of legislators who followed the advice of an old assemblyman who had been elected many times. When asked how he assured his constant re-election, he replied, "All you have to do is vote for every social reform, but oppose every appropriation to implement it."

I was enamored of Abraham Lincoln's statement that "I am a slow walker, but I never walk backwards," and desired to live in that tradition. Also, I believed in the progressivism of Hiram Johnson, who had broken the power of predatory interests by opening up our state and local governments so the people could govern themselves through free elections. In fact, I have always believed that if it had not been for the reforms he effected when he was governor, I never would have had the public career it was my privilege to enjoy. I was committed to the nonpartisanship he brought into city and county government. I believed in the civil service he established, putting an end to the spoils system of former days and enabling public employees to live without fear of discharge merely because of a change in administration.

I believed implicitly in the direct primary for all state and local offices, and in the cross-filing procedure for partisan state offices. These were reforms that made it possible for an impecunious young man like myself to launch on a public career that would last half a century. They sounded the death knell of the old-fashioned political boss, and by the time I ran for governor in 1942, he was practically a relic of the past. When I left the office in 1953, I believe there was no one in California who could rightly be called the political boss of any city or county in the state. This, in my opinion, was largely due to the fact that nonpartisanship in local office and civil service throughout the state deprived the boss of the patronage that gave him an organization he could control. Abolition of the convention system, which was made to order for a few big city bosses to control, and establishment of the open direct primary system, which permitted a citizen to run for office without seeking anyone's permission, stripped political machines of the power to limit the choice of the people to hand-picked candidates confirmed by controlled convention delegates.

When I ran for the governorship in 1942, all that was necessary for me to qualify for the ballot was to have the endorsement of my notice of candidacy by sixty voters of my party—any sixty in the state—and to pay a filing fee of $250. This automatically placed my name on the ballot alongside of that of the incumbent governor. And so it remained in the two succeeding campaigns when I was re-elected. By that simple process, all opponents could compete on technically equal terms.

These enlightened procedures permitted every candidate, if elected, to retain his complete independence—unless he bargained it away for the financial or political support of self-seeking special interest groups. Independence was what I most cherished, and I made that the theme of my campaign. My nonpartisan approach apparently appealed to the voting public, if not to the rock-ribbed partisans. The latter tolerated it during my first campaign because they thought it was a good vote-getting "gimmick" in wartime. But after I was elected, many of my supporters said, "We have had enough of this nonpartisan foolishness. Now we will get down to business."

Immediately after the election, I started to prepare my inaugural message to the Legislature. In order to obtain as much advice as possible about problems that should be solved, I wrote letters to each of the Republican county chairmen telling them of the importance of a sound administrative program and inviting their views as to what should be included in it. There are fifty-eight counties in the state and about forty-five did not even acknowledge my letter. A few of the others said curtly, "Cut taxes," or "Don't rock the boat." Only two of the fifty-eight made a considered reply. On the other hand, many of them were already writing or asking to see me about appointments to state office. This annoyed me beyond words. I did not complain publicly, but I told my staff that every request by a county chairman to see me was to be screened by them. If the request concerned a problem of government, I would see the chairman. If it related to a job appointment, the matter must be handled through the staff. This, of course, did not make me popular with the county committees, but it did save me much time and relieved me from many direct confrontations with people whose recommendations for governmental posts were usually not of top caliber. As a result, it became almost a cliché for this kind of politician to say, "It is easier to see the President of the United States than Governor Warren." In general, I made up my mind not to spend time on the trivialities of politics, but to devote every effort to solving the problems of the state—and they were many.

I could see no direct relationship between our problems and national politics, so I maintained only a mild interest in the Republican Party nationally. Many invitations to speak and otherwise participate in political activities in other states were declined. I did everything I could to simplify my job. When I took over, there were three governor's offices in the state: the main office at the Capitol in Sacramento and branch offices in San Francisco and Los Angeles. Believing that a governor can only operate effectively from one properly staffed office, I immediately closed the two branches and opened them only when I was in either city and needed a place to transact some business.

I also made some definite rules, to which I adhered religiously, about how, where, and in what manner the business of the state would be carried on. I took the position that the state provided me an office in which to perform my duties, and it was the only place where that should be done. The use of my home for such a purpose was ruled out, and during the almost eleven years I was governor, I never relented from that decision. Nobody was invited for business purposes, though occasionally a department head or a staff secretary came on an emergency matter. Our family home life was completely separated from governmental affairs. I also let it be known that when I was traveling my hotel must be considered as my home in this regard.

For a while this caused some strained relations. Certain people have a penchant for wanting to talk business to a governor in his home rather than his office. Often they would try to call me at night, and, failing in that, they would call one of my secretaries and explain how important it was that they see me immediately. They would be advised that if they would disclose the nature of the business and it appeared to be of such importance, I would open the Governor's Office and come there; otherwise it must be handled in the regular manner the following day. Invariably, the urgency of the matter would fade in significance. Also, many people refused to believe that I did not maintain a private telephone on which insiders could reach me directly. I know that many of them thought I was not telling the truth, but the fact is that every call for me went through my office in the daytime or through the Capitol switchboard at night. Many people in politics considered it an evidence of status to have the private telephone number of the governor. I had a dislike for unlisted telephone numbers and never had one in my life, with the exception of a Civil Defense number, until I went to Washington as Chief Justice. Then one became imperative because a Chief Justice cannot talk to anyone over the telephone about a case. Throughout my years as district attorney, attorney general, and governor, I was always listed in the telephone book. In Sacramento, it appeared as "Earl Warren, 1526 H Street." This was for the use of Mrs. Warren and the children. It was answered always by the officer on duty at the mansion. If it was for any of my family, it would be routed through to them. If it was for me, it would be routed to my office in the daytime or to the Capitol telephone exchange at night. This created no problems for me and greatly simplified our home life.

I established another rule that also was very helpful to my public relations. I let it be known that there was no back door to my office;

that everyone with whom I had an appointment must come through the front reception room, and that his or her name must appear on the bulletin board available to the press. It is amazing how many people who want to talk to the governor are deterred from doing so by such a simple and straightforward device. So often they believe that the best way to accomplish their objective is through some devious or mysterious approach. Particularly this is true of paid lobbyists. Their way of life is a secretive one. They frequently operate in dark passageways, hotel rooms, and through entertainment of various kinds. Also, because their job is with legislators, they often try to convince them that the best way to get what they want is to disdain the governor and hold back his legislation until their bills are agreed to by him. Too often, the Legislature succumbs to such blandishments and clogs the machinery so that no important legislation is enacted until the closing hours of the term, and then only with the so-called "bugs" that creep into it unknown to the general public, or even to many of the legislators. This is a hidden process that destroys the confidence of people in our system. There is, of course, a place in our government for lobbying activities. They are inherent in the First Amendment right ". . . to petition the Government for a redress of grievances," but this does not include the right to debauch the Legislature or throw monkey wrenches into its machinery.

I had an instance of this very shortly after assuming office. Having campaigned to reduce taxes, as soon as I was inaugurated I appointed a commission to determine what could be done. It did its job and promptly reported that all state taxes should be reduced by fifteen per cent during the War. There was no objection noted, but bills to that effect languished in committee and we could get no action. In the meantime, the bankers introduced a bill to completely change and substantially lower their franchise tax. That bill started to move, so I let it be known that I would not favor picking out one class of taxpayer for preferential treatment while the others were being disregarded. The bankers then sent a delegation to discuss the matter with me. Carl Wente, president of the Bank of America, was their chief lobbyist and spokesman for the delegation. He told how discriminatory the Bank Tax had been, and urged me to view favorably their bill, which had been before several Legislatures. I heard him through, and then said:

"Your people and other groups are really not entitled to any tax relief."

"Why do you say that?" asked Wente.

I told him that I had bills in calling for relief for every state taxpayer, but that banking lobbyists would not let them move; yet none of those lobbyists had ever told me why they were pressing the Legislature not to act.

"They tell me you won't see any lobbyists," he said.

I replied that this was untrue; that none of them had *asked* to see me; that I had no rule against seeing lobbyists, but because I required them to come through the front door and have the interview listed on the bulletin board, they seemed as a group reluctant to come to my office. The bankers' lobbyist then spoke up and said:

"Governor, I wouldn't say all of them are in such a combine."

"You name one that isn't," I challenged.

Mr. Wente thought for a moment and then said, "Governor, do you mean to tell me that is the way people we send up here act?"

"Absolutely, Carl."

He then said, "To hell with it. Let's get some lunch."

It being noontime, we walked across the park and had a pleasant lunch at the Sutter Club, talking about totally different things.

A few days later, my tax reduction bills started to move, and they were soon passed by both houses without opposition.

As evidence of how fast lobbyists work when they want to, I had hardly been seated as governor when they introduced an antilabor bill in the Assembly. Since labor endorsements had been against me during the campaign, they believed I would not veto the bill if it passed. They had it immediately referred to committee and voted out favorably by a rump meeting at the speaker's desk. It was given a second reading and in two days was on the floor for passage. The press called this to my attention and inquired if I favored the bill. I told them I did not; that my administration was not to be antilabor and, furthermore, I would sign no bill rushed through the Legislature in such hysterical fashion.

This was naturally a rebuff to the lobbying fraternity, and there was much grumbling in the corridors of the Capitol. Gordon Campbell, my militant finance chairman, happened to be present when the lobbyist for the milk distributors of Southern California said to a group of legislators, "I guess we put our money on the wrong horse." Campbell, again operating like a fullback, backed him to the wall and said, "So you put your money on the wrong horse? Did you put any money on him before you knew he was going to win? Did you put any money on him in the primary? And if you ever put up *any* money, did you think you were buying something? If so, you were wrong because nothing is for sale. Tell me how much you contributed, and you will get it back right now."

The fellow was thoroughly humiliated and had nothing to say in reply. I do not know if his people had contributed to the campaign, but if they did it was inconsequential because we had no large contributions. There were more people willing to give after the election was over than before. An amazing number spoke to my secretaries, to Gordon Campbell, or to me and said, "I understand you have a campaign deficit and, if so, I would like to make a contribution to help wipe it out." We had a stock answer for such offers: "There is no deficit. We spent only the money we had in hand." That was a truthful answer, not only for that campaign, but also for all my subsequent ones.

The above incident concerning the antilabor bill was an important one for me for putting my administration in perspective. My predecessor, Governor Olson, was friendly to organized labor, and most of its leaders supported him. They refused to take seriously my campaign statements that I knew something about the trials and tribulations of the working men and women of the state, and that I would insist on fairness to them in all things. By the same reasoning, many people believed that because labor endorsements went against me, what I said in that regard was merely campaign rhetoric. This incident caused both groups to reappraise the situation and be more tolerant in their approach to me on such issues. This was of tremendous importance to me because the times had made the Legislature negatively minded. Preoccupation with the War and with the restrictions that came into being because of it prevented serious consideration from being given to social advances or to the construction necessary to keep up with the tremendous growth of the state. On the other hand, people who had complaints rushed to have them remedied. It was, therefore, important in such an atmosphere to have it understood that no elements of our society were to be made scapegoats, and all must be treated fairly.

I had come to the governship with as comprehensive a background for the position as any candidate in the history of the state. My combined nineteen years of service with the Legislature, the city of Oakland and the county of Alameda had afforded me an opportunity to learn about local problems and their relation to state government. My four years as attorney general had allowed me to study how various difficulties should be attacked. It was something of a letdown to learn at first hand how much the war restricted progressive programs. However, I soon adjusted my approach and tried for immediate solution only of those problems which could be dealt with in wartime, while contenting myself with laying the foundation for the solution of those which we would inevitably face at the conclusion of the fighting.

As it turned out, there were plenty of both. My mind was charged with public health, highways, water conservation, civilian defense, education, crime, the Department of Justice, industrial relations, returning veterans, youth, the aging, finances and a spate of other concerns. All of them called for extensive projects to be initiated or regenerated. Because of the long-range character of our approach to them, any attempt to interweave these many subjects into a strictly chronological coverage would result in a tangle of disconnected segments as we picked up first one thread and then another. I shall, therefore, proceed topic by topic, confining myself to the major ones and following each consecutively through my years as governor.

It would be well to start with public health and our mental hospitals, as I had given much thought to both for a number of years, and had seen neither improvement nor widespread public interest in either. I had seen the tragedy of ill health hit thousands of families during the great Depression. For them, there was but one place—the so-called county hospital—and many of those hospitals could better be likened to the "poor houses" described by Charles Dickens.

Commercial insurance companies had stopped writing noncancelable health insurance because of their disastrous experience with it during the Depression years. As related earlier, I had seen fake health insurance companies spread like the measles, and the fakery usually was disclosed only when a stricken family discovered that its policy was worthless. I had seen this kind of fraud countenanced by both local and state officials. I had also found that the insurance commissioner of our state, in spite of innumerable complaints, had never taken any action against any of these crooks.

Many of our counties did not have a public health officer. Our State Board of Public Health was a warring body of political doctors whose main interest was to prevent any public participation in medical affairs. The office of state director of public health was merely a haven for some necessitous doctor on a part-time basis at four thousand dollars a year.

I had worked with several eminent doctors in my county to establish a California Physicians Service. It was meant to fill the void left by the abandonment of this kind of aid-to-the-sick insurance by the big companies. The Alameda County doctors sold the idea to the California Medical Association, but many of the other large county medical associations boycotted it because they objected to any insurance program that interfered, as they saw it, with the direct doctor-patient relationship.

As district attorney, I had much experience with our mental hospitals. At that time, if a person was mentally ill and needed hospital care, it was necessary for some member of the family or another person who knew the ailing one's mental condition to go to the District Attorney's Office, swear to a complaint charging him with insanity, and relate facts leading to the conclusion that he was dangerous to the safety of himself or other persons. If the allegedly disturbed one was uncooperative and refused to go voluntarily to the emergency hospital for examination before a Superior judge, a warrant would be delivered to the police, who would then go to the person's home in a police patrol car and take him forcibly to the emergency hospital, where he would be kept in a cell-like room until disposition was made of the case. In smaller counties where there was no emergency hospital, the unfortunate party complained against would be lodged by the sheriff in jail to await a hearing. If the judge committed him to a state hospital, he would be taken there by the sheriff as if he were a prisoner.

The barbarity of this procedure had so disturbed me that I had already worked for years with enlightened groups to establish civilized procedures for placing mentally ill persons in state hospitals.

But this is not the end of the horror story. Some of our older institutions built in the last quarter of the nineteenth century were regular "snake pits." The buildings were atrocious and much of the help, which was grossly underpaid, was of a migratory nature. These people traveled from one state to another, uneducated, untrained, accustomed to using sadistic methods to subdue unruly patients and leave no clues to the cruelty perpetrated. Escapes were an everyday occurrence, and often if the patient was not apprehended he would be listed as paroled. In 1943, there were about thirty-five thousand in our hospitals and many thousands listed as paroled but with no facilities at home to care for them.

These things were very much on my mind immediately after the election, and I had determined to do something about all of them.

The first thing pressed upon me was the necessity of finding a state director of public health. I had no one in mind, but realized it would take a man of exceptional character and ability to fulfill the requirements. As often happens in public life, when one is greatly concerned and looking for a way to accomplish a particular end, something happens to give him the break he needs.

A few days after the election I started receiving applications for the position of director of public health. Several of them vied for my attention. They emphasized to me something I already knew; namely, that the position could only be properly filled by a person who was trained and experienced in public health administration, as distinguished from a doctor in the private practice of medicine. My advisers told me that there were only a few doctors in the West who were so trained and experienced, and that a Dr. Wilton Halverson of Los Angeles was the best man of the group, but that he would, of course, not be interested because the county of Los Angeles had recently established a new De-

13. During his campaign for governor, Warren revisited the home in Los Angeles where he was born.

14. The undefeatable family, as rival politicians were inclined to regard it.
Left to right: Bobby, Nina, Dottie, Earl Jr., Virginia, Jim, Mom and Dad.
Taken at the Oakland home on Vernon Street in September 1942.

15. As governor of California, Warren liked to present his views directly to the people by means of regularly scheduled radio programs. *(Courtesy Bancroft Library)*

16. Nina and the children gather on the steps of the Governor's Mansion in Sacramento to greet Jim (in uniform) when he returned home on furlough in 1944. (*Bob Handsaker*)

partment of Public Health especially designed for him and had given him Civil Service status, which was the equivalent of lifetime tenure.

I read these letters with great interest, particularly the part about Dr. Halverson, of whom I had not heard up to that time. I proceeded to inquire of a number of people in the public health field, all of whom confirmed the statements of the job applicants, including their belief that Dr. Halverson would not be interested in the state position. I then consulted with a prominent and public-spirited citizen of San Francisco, Lawrence Arnstein, who for years had carried on a crusade at Sacramento for better public health service. He confirmed everything that had been said about Dr. Halverson, and I decided to see if it would be possible to obtain this distinguished man's services.

I telephoned and asked him if he would come to see me. He did so, and I told him of the predicament I was in. Primarily I described for him the very low stature of public health services in California. I did this not to inform him of what I was sure he already knew, but to convince him of my own concern about conditions and my desire to remedy them. In sum, I told him that I understood he had the best health officer's position in the state, and I desired to have him accept the worst job in the state—one where the salary was about half what he was receiving; one that had always been considered a political job; one that had no tenure, one in which he would be subject to being fired at any time; one which up to that time had been looked upon with indifference by both the state government and the public at large. However, I also told him that if he would accept the position and join me, I would give him a free hand to develop the public health office into what it should be, and that I would support him in everything he undertook to do to improve health conditions in California.

He listened attentively, asked a number of questions, and said that if he could have two or three weeks to think about it he would let me know. We agreed to that. In about three weeks, he came to see me, and, to my great satisfaction, said he was willing to accept the position.

I have no doubt that people reading this will wonder why he would do this, and believe I can supply the answer. Dr. Halverson was a devout Seventh-day Adventist. His religion calls for the undertaking of some missionary service in the interest of humanity. While he did not intimate to me that this was the reason or even that he was a Seventh-day Adventist, as I reviewed in my mind his dedication to the public, I could come to no other conclusion.

He remained with me from the day I assumed the office of governor until the day I left. He then became a professor of public health at the University of California at Los Angeles. I believe I can say without danger of contradiction that he elevated the Public Health Service in California from a dismally low level to make it one of the finest in the United States. To this day it has retained that distinction. He was a man totally without guile, and in a plain, simple, and direct manner attacked every public health problem which confronted our state and made progress in all of them.

To indicate how he perceived problems and solved them, two or three months after taking office he came to me and said, "Governor, we have a situation at some of our beaches in Southern California which is dangerous to public health and calls for immediate action." I inquired what conditions he was speaking of, and he said that in three beach cities the ocean water was so contaminated as to be a health hazard to anyone bathing there. I inquired into the reason for this, and he told me it was because of the nearby discharge of the city of Los Angeles sewer system. He said there had been, I believe, two bond issues to remedy the situation but that both had failed, and, as the city grew, conditions became worse. I asked him what the answer to the problem was, and he said, "There is only one answer and that is to close those cities to beach bathing until the situation is remedied."

I knew it would create a furor, and it did, but I told him if that was his judgment, we would close them. The beaches were closed and remained so until Los Angeles held another bond election and established a disposal plant to rid the sewage of its toxic condition. One by one, Dr. Halverson attacked our health problems in a similar head-on manner as long as he was state director of public health.

The state hospitals for the mentally ill were administered by another department through a director, but with a loose organization that left a great deal of local autonomy and enabled each group to operate more or less as a political entity. Immediately upon assuming the office, I undertook to make a personal survey of them, and over a period of a few weeks I visited each hospital. They were then ten in number, and the conditions I found were so appalling that I did not have a peaceful night's sleep for over a month.

Some of the buildings were built in the 1860s, and there were others of temporary construction forty years old which were little better than shacks. In some of the older buildings, there was a center light well that would serve as the flue of a chimney in case of fire below; yet there were bedridden patients on the top floor who would be smothered if there was a fire in the basement or lower floors. I inquired as to when the temporary buildings at Napa had been constructed by the state, and was told they were never constructed by the state; they were refugee quarters for people at the time of the San Francisco earthquake in 1906, and when that need had ended, the state had purchased them.

I then had the state fire marshal make an investigation of the hazards in all of our state hospital buildings. He reported that there were forty-seven buildings in which patients were housed that either were fire or earthquake hazards or both.

I announced that I would never be satisfied until every one of those buildings was destroyed. To make this story short, the last one of them was razed a few months before I left to go to Washington as Chief Justice. It was quite an ordeal to accomplish this, as even the hospital staffs were opposed to the destruction of some old structures on account of the crowded conditions in the hospitals. On the other hand, I knew that the crowding could not be overcome by leaving unsafe buildings standing, for as long as there was a place to house extra patients, the Legislature would have little desire to add new buildings. I therefore made it a policy to destroy those buildings housing the number of patients which could be provided for in every new building immediately after its completion. I do not recall exactly how much money was spent on this hospital construction program, but it approximated two hundred million dollars.

Most of the money was saved and sequestered for that purpose during the War, when our tax revenue from industry was great but could not be spent for construction because of limitations on materials and manpower. It was not easy to protect these accumulated funds until the restrictions were removed. Business groups, through their lobbyists, were constantly pressuring the Legislature to use savings in order to reduce the budget and taxes. This was in total disregard of the growth of our state and our failure to keep pace with that growth during the Depression and the war years. I argued that to commit our savings to current bills rather than future needs would be putting an unjust burden on our youngsters, eight hundred thousand of whom were in the Armed Services fighting a war for us while the younger children were already in overcrowded school quarters, many on a two-shift-per-day basis. If we failed to provide for their growing needs, we would be robbing them of their rightful heritage. I insisted that they would be required to shoulder a sufficient tax burden in the future without paying for a backlog of construction costs, bequeathed to them by our negligence and selfishness. That theory developed into a full-fledged pay-as-you-go policy for me which characterized my years as governor.

I resisted all proposals to finance our building programs through thirty- or forty-year bond issues for the same reason, except where the bonds were self-liquidating, as with the Veterans Home and Farm Loan program, and for water conservation projects. I spoke throughout the state on this issue. The public understood it and the Legislature reluctantly came along with it. By the end of my first term, based upon that experience, I campaigned on the theory that the job of being governor was not a political job but rather a housekeeping job. In support of that statement, I argued that our population was increasing at the rate of fifteen hundred people a day because of new arrivals in the state and the larger number of births over deaths, and that none of these new-comers brought to our state any schools, hospitals, universities, high-ways, water, prisons, jobs, courts, or other necessities. It was, therefore, necessary for us to provide the governmental services for a new city of ten thousand people every Monday morning, including a new public school for at least five hundred pupils every day of the week.

People understood this reasoning and even supported me when I ad-vocated what I chose to call a "rainy day fund." I argued that in the life of every person, family, business, or government there comes a day when adversity of some kind calls for funds in reserve, and that people preparing for such a misfortune say colloquially that they are saving for a rainy day. I insisted that when we could save without raising taxes, we should do so. As a result, we paid off the bonded indebtedness of the state, preserved our surplus for needed construction, and set aside a "rainy day fund" of $75,000,000 to be used only in the event that the national economy should slump and cause our revenues from sales, use taxes, and business taxes to drop accordingly.

It was not long after I left the governorship, however, that it as-sumed the rainy day had or should have arrived, and the fund was used for current expenses. To me this seemed premature, though quite human. It reminded me of a story told of Chief Justice John Marshall over a century and a half ago. Members of the Supreme Court were then living in a boardinghouse which still stands at the corner of 18th and F Streets, N.W., in Washington. The justices were very fond of Madeira wine, and when the weather was inclement they would remain at home and socialize over a few glasses of Madeira, instead of going about three miles to the Capitol where the Court sat. This was rather easy to become accustomed to because at that time there were very few cases on the Court's docket, and the trip to the Court was often difficult because of the poor roads and swampy area between it and the boardinghouse. So that the practice would not get out of hand, they de-cided that they would only imbibe when it was actually raining. One day when the sun was shining very brightly, one of the justices suggested they have a glass of Madeira. When another demurred be-cause of their prior resolution, Chief Justice Marshall went to the win-dow, looked out, and said, "Well, our Court has national jurisdiction, and it must be raining somewhere in the nation."

To return to our mental hospitals, it should be recalled that they were still commonly known as insane asylums. And they were that in every sense of the word. Not only were they overcrowded almost to the point of suffocation, but the treatment was medieval. The number of patients was out of all proportion to the size of the staffs and supporting personnel, both of which, generally speaking, were inferior and had little awareness of modern techniques for treatment. Perhaps they should not be criticized too severely because there was little or nothing to inspire them to rise above that level.

I remember when I went to the Stockton Hospital shortly after inauguration, the veteran senator from that city, Bradford Crittenden, went with me. When I told him how conditions shocked me and what I thought should be done, he said, "Governor, I know you are right, and I do hope you succeed, but these conditions have been here a long time. I have heard other governors say the same thing, but somehow or other conditions remain unchanged."

This strengthened my determination to do something with the mental health system other than to build new buildings. I adopted a battle cry on the issue and proclaimed it loudly and incessantly for almost eleven years. It was, "We will take California out of the asylum age and put it in the hospital age, where emphasis is on prevention, treatment, and cure in place of mere custody."

And I believe we did, although it was a tortuous job. We changed the entire character of the operation. The department was completely revised, even to changing its name to the Department of Mental Hygiene. This was more in consonance with its objective, which was to maintain mental health in the entire community at such a level that the necessity for hospitalizing anyone would be greatly reduced. We proceeded on the theory that our mental hospitals should deal only with the severest cases of mental breakdown; that one of the most effective phases of any mental health program should be outside the hospitals, where contact can be made with men, women, and children before they need to be committed. To assist in this policy, we established outpatient clinics throughout the state—in San Diego, Riverside, Los Angeles, Fresno, Berkeley, Chico, and at the Langley Porter Clinic in San Francisco. These were in addition to the thirteen large state mental hospitals, which were also equipped for outpatient assistance and for voluntary commitment for hospital care. We also established for the first time a hospital for the treatment of epilepsy. In all of these hospitals and clinics, we used the latest methods of treatment and were able, through them, to greatly reduce the length of stay necessary for a patient's restoration to normal life. This program involved construction of housing for more than eighteen thousand beds, three brand-new hospitals, and the acquisition of two large Army General Hospitals at the end of World War II.

Roadblocks were thrown in the way of several of these projects. Some of the counties in Southern California, largely at the urging of real estate developers, opposed the establishment of either mental hospitals or prisons in their jurisdictions. But the most blatant opposition came from medical societies in the communities where we established the outpatient clinics for the prevention of mental illness. In their hysteria against what they chose to call "socialized medicine," they protested that if people needed such help they should go to their own private physicians. They even carried their obsession so far as to oppose the public school training of cerebral palsy children at Redwood City and Altadena.

But we kept on top of the job, and when I left the governorship in October 1953, we were truly in the modern hospital age, with a resident mentally ill population of forty-two thousand and with some ten thousand in their own communities being supervised by our outpatient clinics and social workers.

One of the things that pleased me most was that in 1947 we abolished the barbaric practice of requiring the family of a deranged person to go to the District Attorney's Office and have a warrant issued for their loved one, who would then be handled by the police or sheriff as if he or she were a criminal. We provided by statute that a person could be admitted to a state hospital upon the application of a local health officer, accompanied by the certification of two physicians, and then be treated in all respects merely as a sick person. I was gratified by the progress we made in this field, particularly because we lived without a disaster through a period in which we were compelled to have many patients live in buildings that were definite fire hazards. In those years, there were a number of hospital holocausts in other states, but fortunately none was visited on us. However, the possibility haunted me until the hazardous building was torn down.

Because of these out-of-state catastrophies and, I believe, because of the impact made by the book *The Snake Pit* describing human degradation in a mental institution, *Life* magazine wrote a series of articles on some of the bad ones. While their writers were in Pennsylvania, the governor of that state called me.

"Earl," he said, "I should warn you that when *Life* finishes with us, it is going to your state to investigate your mental hospitals."

I replied, "Please don't do anything to discourage them. An exposé of that kind will greatly help my program to rid our hospitals of any vestige of the snake pit era."

But they never came, and I always supposed that he told them of my reaction and, knowing it, they were not desirous of helping any of my programs. My relations with the Luce publications were never cordial.

The man who was responsible for most of the improvement of California's mental health program was Dr. Frank Tallman, an eminent psychiatrist and administrator from Ohio, whom I obtained in the manner I usually adopted for finding good administrators. I appointed a committee of men and women knowledgeable in the field, and commissioned them to find for me the best available man in the country. They located Dr. Tallman, of whom I had never heard, and recommended him to me. At the time, he was director of the medical hospitals of Ohio. He was not happy there because of an austerity program imposed on him and gladly accepted my offer to be our director of mental hygiene. He was a forward-looking and humane man who had the ability to reorganize and administer our programs under great difficulties. He rendered a splendid service to our state.

While we were improving the state hospitals, we also pressed hard on other fronts in the public health field. California, nearly a thousand miles long, with two mountain ranges paralleling each other almost the length of the state and lacking adequate highways in mountainous regions, had great numbers of people without access to hospital care or even medical assistance. Although we were increasing our medical educational facilities and many doctors were moving to California, few of them were willing to locate in those areas where there were no good hospitals in which they could practice the most modern methods.

Accordingly, I advocated a program that would establish a modern hospital within one hour of travel for every person in the state. We accomplished this by authorizing any area in the state to organize a district with authority to issue revenue bonds for a modern hospital. This was about the same time as the enactment of the Hill-Burton Act by Congress, subsidizing the construction of hospitals throughout the nation by allocating a sum of money to each state to be used for that purpose. We then passed an act appropriating a like sum of money each year to be offered to the newly established districts on the basis of their contribution of one dollar for each two dollars supplied by the joint allotment of federal and state funds. This enabled them to build hospitals for one third the actual cost, and then operate them as a community project through their own chosen directors. These hospitals quickly became an object of local pride, supplemented as they were by newly created state health services and made more accessible by our expanded highway program. Young, forward-looking doctors soon had no hesitation in establishing themselves in the smaller cities, thus providing better medical care for all the people in formerly remote areas. I should emphasize that these hospitals were not for indigents. They were for people who could pay, but for whom there would otherwise be no services in the region in the event of serious illness. There would still be the county hospital for those who could not pay.

The creation of these districts and the financing of them were encouraged by Dr. Halverson, who also completely renovated his own department and organized it in a manner designed to help local health authorities administer their own programs in accordance with state standards and state financial assistance. I set up a Board of Public Health, the policy-making agency, with which he could work harmoniously. He had their cooperation. The new public health functions, which expanded with the schools and all the social agencies of the state, were lodged in six divisions with supervision over fifteen bureaus and three services. Dr. Halverson encouraged all the counties to have alert health departments, and was responsible for getting well-trained men to accept top positions in them. Strangely, the last county in the state to employ a health officer was the small and beautiful Napa County, about thirty miles from San Francisco, where a famous mental hospital is located. This was due to the unswerving defiance of a small town doctor in Napa toward any incursion of the government into medical matters of any kind. At that time, there was a sharp cleavage between public health doctors and the orthodox medical associations. This man adopted the hard line of the medical associations to such an extent that he was able to bootstrap himself into the presidency of the California Medical Association and later the American Medical Association.

Dr. Halverson was effective in bringing related activities of governmental agencies into focus. The University of California at Berkeley conducted important research into matters of public health, and at the suggestion of Dr. Halverson we moved his department to Berkeley, where neighboring buildings for the State Department of Public Health and the University of California School of Public Health were constructed. This seems to have worked cooperatively in the interests of the state to this time. Incidentally, the university named one of its buildings for me (it now houses the School of Public Health), to the chagrin, I am sure, of many of the leaders of the California Medical Association, who carried on a vendetta against me because of my proposal for a comprehensive plan of medical care for the people of California. I could write a great deal more in praise of Dr. Halverson. His services to the state were admirable, including the fact that he chose as his chief assistant Dr. Malcolm H. Merrill, a distinguished public health doctor and teacher who succeeded him as director and made a like contribution to the state for almost fifteen years.

As already indicated, I had given much thought to health problems, and felt the necessity of doing something about them. All my life, I had seen the effects of serious illness in the families of working people. I had seen conditions greatly aggravated in the terrible years of the

Depression. There were enough incidents in my own family to indicate where, but for the grace of God, all of us might have been. My dear mother, over a period of years while I was district attorney, had one serious operation after another. I had watched the daughter of my widowed sister fight death for six years from a hospital bed. I had seen my sister's son invalided home from the Marine Corps in the Pacific during World War II and destined to spend some years in hospitals. The only reason my immediate family was not reduced to the extremities that afflicted so many other people was that my father, by living a Spartan life himself, had been able to take care of medical expenditures. I remembered his experience with his dying brother when he was a young man. I knew these same experiences were being duplicated in tens of thousands of California families every year. The cost of hospital and medical care had even then—more than thirty years ago—advanced beyond the ability of the average family to pay.

I came to the conclusion that the only way to remedy this situation was to spread the cost through insurance. I believed in that principle and carried as much insurance on my life and health as my income would afford. I knew that the commercial insurance companies had stopped writing noncancelable health insurance. I had witnessed the rebellion of county medical societies against their own self-designed insurance program. As a result, I concluded that if anything was to be done to relieve this tragic situation, it must be a public program, and it should be based upon the insurance principle.

In order to avoid excessive costs of collection, we concluded that health insurance should be collected through the Social Security System. After some studies, it was determined that the employers and employees in that system should each contribute one and one half per cent of wages paid by or to them, along with their other Social Security contributions. It was a comprehensive program with provision for those who were indigent.

I believed then and do now that our state would have reaped great benefits from it. No state had such a program, and yet I believed something of this kind was inevitable. In order that the medical profession would know why I was presenting the plan before it was officially announced, I called on Dr. Philip Gilman of San Francisco, president of the California Medical Association, and told him of it. I then publicly announced it in my "State of the State" message in January of 1945.

A few days later the State Medical Society met in Los Angeles and all but declared the plan to be the work of the Devil. Some of the European countries had health programs, and mine was labeled as "Communist-inspired" because Russia took care of her sick, as "Nazism" by others because Germany had long had a health program, and still others called it "socialized medicine" because that was the term used for the English system which so terrified some doctors in this country. Actually, the plan I proposed was in no sense any of these. Ironically it was more like a bill introduced in our Legislature and lobbied heavily for by this same California Medical Association in 1935.

The reason for the change of attitude on the part of these leaders of the medical profession was evident. In 1935, the Depression brought about an abnormal amount of illness. Doctors were busier than ever, but the patients had no money with which to pay their bills. As a result, doctors were hard pressed to maintain their solvency, and their bill, which was ostensibly for the benefit of the working people, was actually advocated as a welfare measure enabling doctors to get their money from the government instead of their impecunious patients. By 1945, however, the situation had completely changed. Doctors were doing a thriving business and were being well paid for their services. As a result, they had no further interest in the patient's problem of paying. The principle of insurance which was by them described as social progress in 1935 had become ten years later, "socialized medicine, Communist-inspired." They reminded me of the people whom Abraham Lincoln said "could not distinguish between a horse chestnut and a chestnut horse."

Nevertheless, they stormed the Legislature with their invective, and my bill was not even accorded a decent burial. It was argued that everyone with medical insurance would be calling doctors about imaginary illnesses, and the fund would be exhausted in no time. As a diversionary tactic, it was said that if we were to have such an insurance program, it should be limited to catastrophic illnesses.

When my original bill was dead, we introduced a "catastrophe" bill, but it suffered the same fate. It was killed with the argument that anyone could obtain medical assistance from a doctor without hardship but it was *hospital* care that was so difficult to obtain and any insurance program should be limited to such care. We soon offered another bill providing for hospital care only. The hospitals were then aroused to believe that the state intended to take over all private hospitals. This was absolutely false, since our bills provided for freedom of choice by patients of both doctors and hospitals. It was then argued that the only way to help needy patients would be to make a cash award to the sick workman and give him the right to spend it in his own way. We tried out this theory by providing that our working people would be entitled to unemployment insurance for sickness as well as economic reasons. This was only a partial attack of the problem, but it encountered similar opposition. However, we were better entrenched on this one because it was to be paid for by a one per cent deduction from the salary of the employees. Again, it was said that nobody would want to work, that false claims would soon bankrupt the fund. However, we won this round, and California became the only state, other than little Rhode Island, to have such a program.

In order to make the system competitive, we permitted insurance companies to assume coverage provided they fulfilled the obligations of the state under the act. Some companies jumped at the opportunity, and prospered greatly in doing so. Contrary to gloomy forebodings to the effect that no one would be willing to work any more and that the fund would soon be bankrupt, it prospered from the beginning. It was not long until we became aware that it was unnecessary to collect as much as one per cent of the salaries of our employed people. I urged the Legislature either to grant additional coverage or to reduce the wage deductions. The insurance companies complained, of course, but they feared the latter more than the former, with the result that we were able to provide for limited hospital benefits in addition to the regular unemployment insurance.

The fund continued to prosper, and I then advocated unemployment benefits for our employed women for a short period before and after childbirth. The opposition was such that I was not able to accomplish this before leaving the governorship for Washington.

Since my experience with these matters, there has been a growing awareness of the need for a national health program, and I was extremely happy to see the federal government initiate one, limited though it is to people over sixty-five years of age. The mounting cost of doctors' fees and hospital care today has reached a point which is prohibitive for the average family, and most people are now convinced, I believe, that we must have a national health program for everyone, based on the insurance principle. The main questions to be resolved relate to the manner of its implementation.

One of the problems I was confronted with as governor was that of our state prisons. They had been a source of irritation for the people and of frustration for most of the governors since an abandoned sailing vessel in San Francisco Bay was converted into our first state prison during the Gold Rush days around 1850. A few years later, San Quentin prison was established, and Folsom prison in the 1880s. These were both maximum security institutions with all the barbarity of medieval days. Prison riots, charges of cruelty, and disorders of various kinds plagued the system. Twice, not long before my incumbency, entire prison boards and once a warden were kidnapped while holding meetings in the prisons. More than one governor had been defeated for re-election largely because of prison scandals.

My predecessor, Governor Olson, endeavored to improve the situation, but the existing conditions were too deeply imbedded to be disturbed. He held public hearings airing charges of cruelty and mismanagement, but the Legislature made no move toward reform except to authorize the construction of a minimum security institution for nonviolent prisoners. It was not completed and was only in partial use at the time of my election.

There were basic reasons for this turbulence. There was no overall management of the prison system. It was supervised by a part-time Board of Prison Terms and Paroles, with a warden often chosen for political reasons operating each prison, assisted by a small paid staff and prison guards of a nondescript character. The other people working in the prisons were the convicts themselves. They performed the clerical work, and even much of the disciplinary function. Some of the wardens selected the toughest criminals in the prison to help them keep order. This, of course, gave the latter great power and great privileges. Prison records could not be relied upon because professional forgers would alter the records to show, for instance, that they were charged with one offense in the courts and convicted and sentenced for another. A petition for a writ of habeas corpus would then be filed in Marin County, where San Quentin was located, or in Sacramento County, where Folsom was, charging an illegal conviction because it varied from the charge for which the prisoner was arraigned. On occasion, they were successful with such a ploy.

While district attorney, I had occasion to break up a ring of forgers that was engaged in changing our county records to conform to altered prison records in order to obtain the release of prisoners. The principal forger was a former convict, and I have no doubt that when he was returned to prison he merely changed his base of operations from outside to inside prison walls.

From my years of experience as district attorney and attorney general, I was convinced that our prisons educated the inmates in crime and hardened them toward society. As governor, I could see a conflict with the existing system coming, and resolved to prepare for it immediately. Accordingly, I assigned one of my lawyer secretaries the task of preparing a bill to completely reorganize procedures for handling prison matters. We consulted with Mr. James Bennett, then director of federal prisons, a forward-looking and humane penologist; Sanford Bates, his predecessor in that position and more recently director of prisons of New Jersey; Rabbi Rudolph I. Coffee of Oakland, a former chaplain in state prisons; and others whom whom we thought might be able to make a contribution.

In a few months this work was completed, and we were prepared for the avalanche of controversy about prison reform whenever it might descend. It came sooner than anticipated, and in a most unusual manner.

One morning I was in my office in the Capitol when I received a telephone call from Chief of Police Charles W. Dullea of San Francisco. He was a friend of mine of long standing who had been most helpful in bringing about the coordination of police activities throughout the state to which I had devoted so much time as attorney general. He opened the conversation:

"Governor, I have some information that will be very distressing to you, and I would like to know how you believe it should be handled."

"What is it, Chief?"

"Two of the most notorious convicts in Folsom Prison have been coming to San Francisco every weekend and staying with women in a hotel here," he replied. "You know one very well. You and I put him away. He's Lloyd Sampsell, one of the yacht bandits."

I did indeed know him, as I had prosecuted and convicted him and one Ethan Allen McNabb for the armed robberies of a dozen or so banks. They were desperate men, and both eventually were executed for later murders. I asked the chief if it would be possible to apprehend them on one of their visits.

"That would be no problem," he said, "because they are here every weekend."

I urged him to arrest them the next time it happened and to give the event the utmost publicity. True to the chief's prediction, they again came to San Francisco the following weekend and were promptly arrested and held for return to Folsom, our recidivist prison where they were supposed to be incarcerated. Because of the previous notoriety given to Sampsell and McNabb, who were known as the "yacht bandits," this arrest attracted much attention in the press.

Sampsell was a handsome young man from a wealthy Los Angeles family who, from an early age, had a penchant for robbing banks. He was arrested and convicted for such offenses in Los Angeles and was sentenced to San Quentin, where he served four years before being paroled. He then teamed up with McNabb, another dapper young ex-convict, and with him robbed several banks without apprehension in the state of Washington. They bought a nice yacht and, outfitting themselves as wealthy young yachtsmen, came to San Francisco and secured mooring space in one of the exclusive yacht clubs, from which they cut quite a swath as free-spending young *bon vivants*. They did not devote all of their time to living in this carefree manner, however. They took time off to rob a number of banks in the Alameda County. Our police were at a loss to know who the culprits were, but the San Francisco police, under Dullea, who was then captain of detectives, arrested them in the apartment house where they were living. A search of the rooms revealed a couple of suitcases stuffed with greenbacks. My District Attorney's Office was immediately notified, with the result that the Berkeley police, who had bank robbery warrants for the arrest of the pair, went to San Francisco to take them into custody.

The San Francisco police, knowing of Sampsell and McNabb's background and their desperation, offered to accompany the two Berkeley officers across the Bay as a security measure. Their offer was declined. When the two officers and their prisoners arrived at the Berkeley Police Station, it was late afternoon and time for a change of shifts. A number of the officers were in the squad room changing clothes, and when the prisoners saw the off-guard disarray, they quickly started to kick and strike the unprepared officers, and in the resulting confusion broke free and fled from the room. There were two hallways, one of which led to the outdoors and the other to a cul-de-sac in the basement. Unfortunately for them, the fugitives in their haste chose the latter. Some of the police recovered their composure in time to pursue them to the dead end and capture them. They were then recognized by everyone as dangerous and resourceful characters. Talk at the jail was that they were standing trial only because it might afford an opportunity to escape. Fearing that they might have stashed away money to hire assistance from the outside, we greatly tightened courtroom security for the trial, which saw them convicted.

Because the institution of branch banking had greatly accelerated bank robberies, and as a symbol of our concern about this type of crime, I had personally prosecuted this and a number of other such cases while district attorney.

The arrest of Lloyd Sampsell during his illegal sojourn away from Folsom was the exact break I needed to do something about the prison system. Having had the bill prepared that we wanted to thoroughly reorganize that system, I immediately called the Legislature into special session for the purpose of advising it and the public of the sordid conditions in our prisons and urging the necessity for a complete change in the interest of public safety. I pledged that if the Legislature would give me this bill's authority, I would take the prisons permanently out of the realm of politics. I promised to fill the very important position of director of corrections through a national examination, with the purpose in mind of obtaining the best man in America for the job. I promised also to appoint, without relation to politics, the very best person I could find to head the proposed Adult Authority, which would replace the existing Board of Prison Terms and Paroles.

The Legislature did not respond with enthusiasm to the proposal because there were a number of sacred cows involved, and some of the

legislators had connections with the system that they considered important to them. However, after a somewhat hectic ten days, good judgment prevailed and the program was adopted with little change. The
newspapers of the state, the law enforcement officers, and the women's
clubs were my unofficial "lobbyists." Without them, we could never
have succeeded. The bill, of course, was not perfect. We had been looking into the future, and such vision is usually subject to adjustment.

As a result, we amended the act from time to time to accomplish the
desired results until by 1953 it was, we believed, structurally sound. In
fact, knowledgeable people said at that time, "The California correc-
tional system should be rated as the best of any of the major states of
the Union."

I was helped in obtaining this reorganization legislation by a committee of experts on prisons, finance, and legislative action, which I had appointed to study penal affairs in California. The final report of that
committee was issued almost simultaneously with the Sampsell scandal
just mentioned. The contents of this report were explicit and, because
of the standing of the committee members and their nonpolitical approach to the problem, carried great weight with the Legislature and
the public. Briefly, what the committee recommended and what we undertook to establish was an integrated prison system with an expert penologist in charge of its administration and with a full-time Adult Authority to fix sentences under the Indeterminate Sentence Law and to
determine paroles. There would also be a Board of Corrections, consisting of the principal officers of the corrections Department and public
members, to determine general policy.

These agencies were designed to replace the nonpaid, lay political
Board of Prison Directors and the Board of Prison Terms and Paroles,
both of which lacked direction of purpose and cohesion and consequently left various institutions almost autonomous and disparate in
their operation. It was our purpose to abolish the "con-boss" system,
which put the toughest criminals in positions of authority over other
prisoners, and to replace the patronage system with Civil Service. This
was coupled with realistic, continuous training programs for institutional
employees, with the idea of recruiting intelligent personnel and affording them an opportunity to advance in the system as vacancies in
higher positions occurred. It was also contemplated that the new system would upgrade the classification and care of prisoners through better feeding, the construction of modern facilities, affording opportunities for education, helping them to acquire working skills, and other
progressive steps. The Board of Corrections on July 1, 1944, issued a
comprehensive statement of policy that guided the department

throughout my years as governor without any discord while we were testing and improving the basic act.

In order to satisfy the Legislature and the public that my request for total reorganization of the department was not politically motivated, I promised to select the director of corrections through a national examination. In compliance with this promise, I set up a committee to conduct the written examination. The members of that committee, after reviewing many applicants, recommended Richard A. McGee, then director of the Department of Institutions for the state of Washington, as outstanding among the candidates. I then augmented the committee with some Californians familiar with prison conditions for the purpose of conducting an oral examination. The expanded committee soon unanimously recommended Mr. McGee. After some extensive interviews with him and after being thoroughly impressed by him, I offered him the position. He told me he would be happy to accept if I would ask Governor Arthur Langlie of Washington for his release. The governor was a friend of mine, and he graciously agreed. I will always remember my final conversation with McGee concerning his employment. I said:

"Mr. McGee, you don't know me and I don't know you. We are accepting each other on faith in a very serious undertaking. I want you to know that as long as I am governor you will never be asked to do anything political, and if you do anything political with our prisons, I will fire you. How is that for an agreement between us?"

He replied with a smile, "That is good enough for me."

We both kept our words, and as a result what had been a nightmare previously—the handling of our corrections system—became a satisfying experience for me.

We built four new major facilities, staffed them with a few good administrators from other states who had taken the examination and with younger men who were developed within the system. After that, we never had a scandal in that department and I never lost a night's sleep for fear of one in my last nine years in office. This was due in the main to the quiet administrative genius of Richard A. McGee. An entire book could well be written about his achievements. Credit for what I believe was as important a contribution as any in my administration must also go to the Adult Authority for the cooperative manner with which it discharged its duties and coordinated them with those of the director. In the hands of lesser persons, there could have been far greater institutional dissension and confusion before our statutes were improved.

To serve as temporary chairman of the Adult Authority, I induced James Bennett to let me have on loan an official in the federal prison system, who helped us greatly through the organizational period. When he returned to his old post, I authorized the Adult Authority to select from its membership its own chairman, although the statute had placed that power in my hands. After the first two years, they selected Walter A. Gordon, one of my original appointees, and continued to re-elect him year after year throughout my administration. Gordon was an able black man whom I had known since his college days at the University of California, where he received All-American recognition as a football player. He was graduated from Boalt Hall and practiced law in Oakland. While in law school, he had been a member of the Berkeley Police Department under Chief August Vollmer, a pioneer in modern police work. Mr. Gordon was a knowledgeable and forward-looking member of the Authority and helped greatly in the upgrading of the system. He later rose higher in his distinguished career, being appointed governor of the Virgin Islands by President Eisenhower, and after a term there became a United States district judge, in which capacity he served until his retirement.

I suppose I had a greater concern for our prisons than preceding governors because, for twenty years before my election, I had been thrown incessantly in contact with their failures. I could see no retrieval of human values stemming from them. Some convicts were subdued to the point that they did not revert to crime, but their subjection for extended periods of time to cruelty, sadism, idleness, and enforced criminal associations usually resulted in broken lives without hope of redemption. Most merely received an advanced course in crime and preyed again upon society when released. It was these repeaters with whom I came in contact as district attorney and as a member of the State Advisory Pardon Board while attorney general. I still remember the frustration I felt so often as district attorney in sending them back to the penitentiary. It was like repeatedly washing dirty linen without being able to remove any of the stains. I was firmly of the opinion that, although imprisonment of the body and mind is inherently brutish, it was a moral imperative to make such confinement as humane and rehabilitative as possible by separating for treatment the psychotic from the rational, the violent from the nonviolent, the sex deviates from the normal, the recalcitrants from the submissive, the confirmed criminals from the casual offenders, and those who seek education or a new skill from the scofflaws.

I believed that, with a proper institutional structure, with enlightened administration by dedicated people, and with the emphasis on rehabilitation in a nonpolitical atmosphere, we could make real progress. We built institutions to enable us to classify all the above types, developed an industrial program to provide meaningful work, initiated educational programs, and created what might today be called "halfway houses" by establishing fire-fighting and forestry camps in our mountainous country. There prisoners soon to be released were permitted to work under almost normal conditions in the great open spaces far beyond prison walls. It was said of our fire fighters that they constituted the best brigade in the nation for that purpose. The forestry camps also rendered valuable service in eliminating pine beetle and other tree infestations. At the time I left, there were about forty of these camps with a normal capacity of eighty prisoners each. They were known as "honor" camps, and the inmates were able to make a little money for their families or for their own use on release. I believe we made real progress, and that belief is one of my lasting satisfactions. We had no prison scandal in the almost ten years that followed our reorganization.

One incident of the improved morale occurred shortly before I left California. Our Women's Institution was located in the mountains near the little village of Tehachapi, about fifty miles south of Bakersfield. There were some five hundred women imprisoned there for crimes ranging from passing bad checks to murder. In July of 1952 there was a massive earthquake in this part of the state. It almost totally destroyed the business district of Tehachapi, and so damaged our prison buildings that they were totally uninhabitable. While the earthquake was still wreaking its destruction—there being scores of convulsions over a period of more than twenty-four hours—we were able to put all of our women in some large circus tents obtained for the purpose. I immediately flew to Tehachapi in my state plane and witnessed buildings, one after another, collapse into rubble from the successive shocks. I went out to the prison, had the women assembled, and talked to them. I told them we did not intend to send extra guards to watch them; that we were relying on them to keep order and care for themselves until they could be moved to our new modern Institution for Women at Covina, which was almost completed. The enthusiasm with which they took this news was good to see. Not one of them tried to escape, and in a week or ten days they were all moved to the new facility, which was not yet completed but which, with their cooperation, was able to house them. As a gesture of my appreciation for their cooperation, I shortened the term of every one in the institution by thirty days. I would have done more, but it would have created severe administrative problems in finding employment and housing for some of those soon to be released.

The prison problem generally is not ended with the release of the prisoners on parole—and most of them are released on parole. There had been many scandals in this department, and at this time there had recently been open warfare between the Board of Prison Terms and Paroles and the chief of police of Los Angeles because of the latter's objection to what he considered early parole and because of the secrecy of the paroles when granted. The chief announced that he would arrest every parolee found in Los Angeles. The Prison Board responded that secret paroles were necessary because of the intransigence of many of the police with regard to the parole system. This sometimes meant that parolees would be hounded out of a town it if was known they were released there.

I thought there was some merit to both arguments, but that a system could be devised whereby every released prisoner could make a new start in life without cost to him and without requiring any political influence. I accordingly recommended to the Legislature a bill entitled Prisoners' Rehabilitation Act. It provided that any inmate after release from one of our institutions might initiate a proceeding for the restoration of his civil rights, which he had lost by his conviction, by filing such a declaration with the county clerk and serving a copy thereof on the district attorney of the county and the chief of police of the city (or sheriff if it was in a rural district). He would thereafter live lawfully for a period fixed by the Supreme Court of California. Its length would depend on the character of the crime he was convicted of. At the end of that period of time, he could serve on the district attorney and chief of police and file with the county clerk a notice of intention to petition the Superior Court for a restoration of his civil rights and a recommendation to the governor for a pardon. The probation officer would then be required to represent him at the hearing. If there were no objection from the district attorney or chief of police, all he need show would be that he had led a law-abiding life, and the judge would restore his rights and recommend him for a pardon. The bill provided that there was to be no charge by any public officer rendered in connection with the proceeding, and it was made a misdemeanor for any lawyer, agent, or provocateur to accept a fee for any service connected with it. This latter provision was opposed by some of the lawyers in the Legislature, but I state publicly that if this provision was not retained in the act, I would veto it if it passed. I wanted the law to enable any man, though penniless, friendless, or without any political influence whatsoever, to be able to restore himself to a respected place in society merely by living honorably. The press took up cudgels for me and shamed opponents of the act into acquiescence. The bill passed; I signed it and announced that everyone desiring a pardon must follow this procedure except where there was a readily proven claim of innocence. While governor, I granted several hundred pardons of this kind, thus killing two birds with one stone in that the bill gave every man a chance to earn a legitimate pardon and at the same time it rid the Governor's Office of any pressure for political pardons.

During the 1944 term of the Legislature, another long-felt need of the state was realized. My friend Robert Kenny, a state senator from Los Angeles County when I became attorney general, ran for and was elected to my vacated office when I became governor. He soon saw the desirability of having a State Department of Justice. Accordingly, we collaborated in the preparation of a bill to accomplish that result. We consolidated with the Office of Attorney General the Division of Criminal Identification and Investigation, which I had headed for many years, the Bureau of Criminal Statistics, and the Bureau of Narcotic Enforcement, which was under the jurisdiction of the governor. The latter was so interrelated with other law enforcement work that I believed it should be in the office of the chief law enforcement officer of the state, the attorney general. The Legislature was not resistant to the idea, and, with our joint sponsorship, the legislation was enacted and California became the first state in the union to have a comprehensive State Department of Justice. Its personnel was incorporated into Civil Service, and although the Office of Attorney General remains elective, the rest has been removed as far as possible from partisan politics. The office was well organized and administered by Attorney General Kenny and, with one exception, it has been capably managed and now is a powerful instrument of government, giving badly needed coordination to the law enforcement agencies of our large state without the sort of centralization that would deprive local communities of the power to enforce the law.

The one exception that I mentioned was during the incumbency of Frederick Napoleon Howser, who succeeded Attorney General Kenny when the latter ran against me for governor in 1946. In that election, I received both the Republican and the Democratic nominations. Howser was a Republican, but I would not support him. He came to my office and asked me why, and I told him it was because he and I did not see eye-to-eye on law enforcement matters and particularly because he had permitted a gambling ship to return after I had gone to such lengths to rid our state of all of them. He told me he would try to close the errant ship. I told him that trying would not be enough, that I was one person who knew it could be done because I had closed all of them before. Of course Howser did not even try. Nevertheless, he was elected attorney general. Immediately thereafter the word was out through the underworld that the state was to be opened up to gambling and other illegal activities. Enough evidence to assure us that this rumor was not unfounded came to our attention. Howser had brought with him two police officers from the Long Beach Police Department, one called Wiley (Buck) Cadell and the other Walter Lentz. They were to be his principal investigators, and it was not long until their intentions became apparent. I told Howser several times that I understood what was going on. He protested that he knew nothing about it, and would take whatever action was called for. But he never did. I then went to the Legislature and asked it to amend the Board of Corrections Act by authorizing the governor to appoint special crime study commissions to assist the Board of Corrections. The Legislature passed the necessary amendment and I appointed five commissions. Their domains were:

Organized Crime
Juvenile Justice
Adult Corrections and Release Procedures
Social and Economic Causes of Crime and Delinquency
Criminal Law and Procedure

They were all important and made valuable contributions, but the most critical commission at the time was the one on organized crime. It was composed of particularly distinguished public servants, including five-star Admiral William H. Standley, onetime Chief of Naval Operations and ambassador to the U.S.S.R.

Warren Olney III was then home from his World War II duty as a Marine officer in the Pacific area. He had just started to practice law in San Francisco. I induced him to become chief counsel and executive officer of the Commission on Organized Crime on a part-time basis. True to his nature, however, it was not long until he was working around the clock. As a result, he eventually caught up with Buck Cadell, who was tried in Mendocino County, convicted, and sentenced to San Quentin for attempting to set up a statewide system of protection for gambling rackets. Walter Lentz later was charged with tampering with a witness in a libel suit brought by Howser. He was acquitted, but Howser lost his suit. This eclipsed the public career of Attorney General Howser, and in his bid for re-election he lost the nomination of his own party. I had known the Republican candidate for a number of years, having engaged in party politics with him, and did not believe he had a background of training or experience for the position, nor did I believe he would give it the nonpolitical administration it should have. The Democratic candidate was Edmund G. (Pat) Brown, who had been district attorney of the city and county of San Francisco for two terms and had greatly improved that office during his tenure. I took no active part in this particular campaign but maintained what might be called a benevolent neutrality toward Pat Brown, who was elected.

My associates and I thought it might be considered an abandonment of our interest in suppressing organized crime to abruptly abolish our commission on that subject. Consequently, I announced that I intended to select another group to follow in the footsteps of that of Admiral Standley. Attorney General-elect Brown at first did not approve of the proposal because he thought it represented a lack of confidence in his law enforcement policies. I assured both him and the public that I had no such reservations. He subsequently agreed, and I appointed another prestigious commission headed by retired four-star general Leroy P. Hunt, U. S. Marine Corps. General Hunt was one of the combat heroes of World War II. I had known him since college days and had considered joining the Corps with him as the nation was girding for World War I. I probably would have done so except that the program under which he entered contemplated a military career, and that did not appeal to me.

The other members of the new commission also commanded respect. With Olney again as chief counsel and executive officer, it, like its predecessor, performed yeoman service. We made Attorney General Brown privy to all the secrets of the commission. Later Brown took our former chief investigator, Harold G. Robinson, who also filled that role with the Kefauver committee, as his deputy director of the Department of Justice to carry on the work. This he did successfully. I believe it can safely be said that whatever might have given the impression that California was a rich field for organized criminals was completely nullified. Attorney General Brown was re-elected in 1954 and twice ran successfully for governor, the last time against Richard M. Nixon in 1962.

The manner in which I was first elected governor and even my years as attorney general and district attorney dictated to a great degree the pattern of my political life as governor.

As already related, I took the position that none of these offices was partisan in nature, and should not be so administered. It was, therefore, not consistent for me to be too closely associated with any political group. On the other hand, every state officeholder should have some party affiliation and should assume some leadership in its councils in keeping with the importance of the office held at the time. I was a Republican and because of the positions I held I was called upon for certain party activities that kept me identified with it. On the other hand, I took no role in city or county party politics or any other political organizations. I kept myself as independent of all of them as it was possible to be. And I never built up a political organization of my own. In every one of my campaigns, I relied on volunteers organized only for that campaign, and when it was over they were disbanded with my thanks.

I claim no magic for the solution of the problems of our state. Government is no place for magicians. The need is for common honesty, independence, governmental experience, hard work, determination to make progress, and a belief that "where there is no vision the people perish."

In order to keep our state government in the hands of the people, I repeatedly told the voters that I aspired to be the governor of California, not its political boss. This, of course, was not popular with many of the Republican central committees, and shortly before my 1950 campaign nine of those committees in the largest counties announced themselves in favor of my lieutenant governor, Goodwin J. Knight, who had been running for governor throughout his entire term of office. In fact, he announced in the fall of 1949 that he was certain that when I realized how completely organized he was throughout the state, I would not file for re-election. Throughout that year, the press badgered me to say whether I intended to run again, and I parried by saying that 1949 was not an election year and I was too busy to consider the question, but when the time was appropriate I would give them the answer.

Practically all the other candidates for state office announced their candidacies and organized their staffs. I deliberately waited until all the "organization" politicians were committed to one or another of them, and then made my announcement and declared my intention to have an entirely volunteer organization. I declined the services of those who had accepted positions of management in the other campaigns, particularly the campaign of Congressman Richard Nixon for the senatorship left vacant by the retirement of Senator Sheridan Downey. I did this not because of antagonism to Mr. Nixon, but because I had seen enough politics to know how some politicians would place one foot heavily in one campaign and the other foot in another, thus putting themselves in a position to shift according to developments, or even to dominate both for any purpose they chose. This was important to me because my lieutenant governor had devoted his four years in office to creating a schism in the party, and I wanted to be sure that everyone in my campaign was loyal to me. In the end, it became of little consequence, because shortly after I announced, the lieutenant governor decided that "for the good of the party" he would only run for re-election to his own position. Nobody filed against me on the Republican ticket for governor.

I named a Los Angeles lawyer whom I had taken out of the military service to be my adjutant general as my campaign chairman in Southern California, His name was Victor Hansen, and he never had been in politics in any capacity. Yet he and the volunteers put together one of the best campaign organizations I had ever had there, and we won the election by more than 1,100,000 votes. My opponent was James Roosevelt, son of the President. I campaigned hard but refrained from engaging in controversy with him. I only remember mentioning him twice during the long contest. When I was asked by the press what I thought of his mother coming to California to campaign for him, I replied, "Well, you wouldn't expect his mother to be against him, would you?" The other time was when he spoke in the auditorium of a public school house to attack me for doing nothing about public education. I was proud of our record with the public schools, but when the newsmen asked me what I thought of his speech, I restrained myself and simply replied, "As far as I can ascertain, Mr. Roosevelt has never been in a *public* school except to make a political speech."

All things considered, it was not a bitter campaign and it left no scars. Mr. Roosevelt was later elected congressman, and during his years there was as strong a supporter as the Supreme Court had in that body. I shall always remember that when his mother died, he invited Mrs. Warren and me to lunch with the family preceding the funeral ceremony.

In the campaign of 1950, as in the others, I spent a great deal of my time in the smaller communities, traveling usually in buses which carried my staff, the newsmen who were reporting my activities, and a few local people who knew the problems of the area. We stopped at many places every day, and I remember one incident that was typical of the informal approaches we made to the voters. We were laying out our plans for a tour of the lower San Joaquin Valley when I noticed on the proposed itinerary that we were passing through a little town of fifteen hundred people without stopping. I inquired why this was, and was told they were all Democrats from Oklahoma and Arkansas, and were for Jimmy Roosevelt. I inquired to see if they had been asked if they would like to have me stop for a few minutes. Told they had not, I insisted that it be done. When they were asked, they said, "If the governor would like to come to our little town we would adjourn school and have a big meeting at the ball park." They did just that, and brought in farmers from the surrounding countryside until we had more listeners than there were in the town itself. I addressed the crowd, telling them how the meeting was arranged, and how silly it was for people to believe that our newly arrived citizens brought political fixations with them; that I was sure they felt the freedom of our political system; that there were no intimidating political bosses here; that they were perfectly free to vote for or against any person or measure on the ballot without fear of reprisal; that I was sure they felt that freedom, as did the older residents of the state, and that we needed the active partici-

17. Though Warren felt at the time that it was prudent to intern Japanese-Americans during World War II to prevent sabotage, he later regretted his part in the action. Here he signs a postwar bill compensating Americans of Japanese ancestry for penalties they suffered under the Alien Land Law. The bill restored rights revoked by the law. (*Courtesy Bancroft Library*)

18. Waving to the crowd at the 1948 Republican National Convention in Philadelphia, Warren accepts his nomination as the party's vice-presidential candidate. Mrs. Warren joins him on the platform. (*Harry J. Coleman, International News photo*)

19. Governors Warren of California and Thomas Dewey of New York chat at a Republican dinner at the Waldorf-Astoria in New York City, in 1952. *(AP photo)*

20. Warren, Dewey, and Senator Robert Taft (R-Ohio) confer in 1948. Warren found Taft an able man but insensitive in personal relations. Dewey seemed more likable, though Warren felt he could have brought more communicativeness and humor to the campaign. *(Harry J. Coleman, International News photo)*

21. Charter Day at the University of California in March 1948: Warren (right) shares a laugh with General George C. Marshall (left) and the university's president, Robert Gordon Sproul.

22. Women's rights were an issue during Warren's governorship years. In 1949 he signed into law a bill requiring equal pay for women doing equal work with men. (*Courtesy Bancroft Library*)

pation of both old and new. I then proceeded to tell them about my program and what I envisioned for all Californians.

I was enthusiastically received by the assemblage, and instructed my staff to advise me after the election on how we prospered in that little town. To my great satisfaction, we carried it by a vote of two and a half to one. And this was in a part of the state where only a few years before I became governor there was great turbulence over the so-called "invasion of the Oakies and Arkies." We had none of this during my incumbency, and for years now these emigrants have been substantial citizens and a sizable percentage of them even affluent.

My most important campaigning was between election years. I would personally go to parts of the state where there were problems and discuss them with those who were concerned, not just politicians, but knowledgeable people without regard to their political affiliations. Then I would invite delegations to come to Sacramento to discuss the difficulties with me whether they were friendly on the surface or not.

I remember one such delegation that came to my office from the CIO. It was militantly Democratic at the time and was highly critical of me because I was a Republican. They demanded to see me for the purpose of setting forth their governmental proposals. I invited them to visit me, and the meeting was held. We spent an entire afternoon reviewing their ideas. Some of them I thought were sound and others not. I told them frankly what I thought of each proposal, and after it was explored I inquired what it would cost, and then listed the figure given. When we had finished with all of them, I added those figures.

"Gentlemen," I said, "many of these proposals in my opinion are desirable, but according to your figures they would cost us three hundred million dollars this year. That is more than the controllable part of the entire annual budget. Where are we to get that kind of money?"

The chairman of the delegation rose and smilingly said, "Governor, that's your problem."

We shook hands amiably all around and adjourned on that note. This, of course, did not reconcile the California CIO leaders to me. All of their endorsements were for my opponent, but it did dissipate much of the bitterness. When the national CIO organization met in San Francisco, John L. Lewis, as its head, invited me to speak and introduced me as a true friend of the workingman. Privately he told me not to be concerned about the rhetoric used against me. I knew that the rank and file of this and other unions felt kindly toward me. The main strength of the CIO was in San Francisco, my own county of Alameda, and our neighboring county of Contra Costa. In every election, I carried all of those counties overwhelmingly. That could not have been done without the good will of the working people of the area.

In all statewide elections, I only had one statewide labor endorsement. That was in 1946 when there was a sharp line of cleavage between the A.F. of L. and the CIO. My opponent, Robert Kenny, was very close to the latter, which enthusiastically endorsed him. That threw the A.F. of L. endorsement to me. The very next year, however, I ran into difficulties with the leaders of that organization. We had been having a number of labor disputes, not between employers and their employees (who had generally resolved their differences through collective bargaining agreements), but between rival unions for jurisdiction over the class of work involved. These intramural fights were destructive of the system of collective bargaining because neither employers nor union labor employees could rely on the effectiveness of their collective bargaining settlements. They might be faced at any time with a picket line beyond which no labor union man would pass. Most of the union leaders, state and national, publicly deplored the jurisdictional strike in principle, but nothing was done about it.

The Legislature considered and passed a bill to prevent jurisdictional strikes. No real fight was made against it, and it was passed by both houses overwhelmingly. When it reached my desk it was vigorously attacked by the unions as a "slave labor" bill. They made a drive to have me veto it. I studied the bill carefully and concluded that it did no more than comply with the public statements of labor leaders against the practice of jurisdictional strikes. I signed it, and was roundly condemned for the action by many of those leaders who had endorsed my candidacy the year before.

Some months before this I had accepted an invitation to speak at the annual convention of the State Federation of Labor (A.F. of L.). When I did not veto the bill, many A.F. of L. leaders urged that the invitation be withdrawn. It was even said that a third of the delegates would walk out if I spoke. The invitation was not revoked, however, and I appeared according to schedule. It was a rather icy atmosphere, but as far as I could see nobody walked out. I spoke about the jurisdictional strike and the bill I had signed, telling them I believed such strikes were destructive of the collective bargaining principle; that they were highly injurious to both employers and employees, and I could see no good reason for perpetuating their existence. I added that it did not seem fair for the forces of union labor to sit quietly while the bill was being passed in the Legislature and then make a massive attack on it when it reached my desk. I was listened to attentively, and when I finished was accorded a respectable, if not thunderous, applause. The tumult subsided thereafter, and I heard little more about the jurisdictional strike legislation.

The lobbyists' practice of lying low while bills they knew could not be stopped in the Legislature were moving toward passage, only to apply their pressure on the governor when the bill was on his desk for signature or veto, was not an unknown technique, as the following will indicate.

The city of Los Angeles, situated as it was in an almost arid part of the state, went to great lengths in marshaling enough water to take care of its growing domestic and agricultural needs. It sought this water in other counties and even other states. Its first forage was in the mountain counties immediately to the north. Under its powers of eminent domain, it acquired the watershed of streams several hundred miles from Los Angeles, showing little concern for the ranchers and small-town people who lived there. After the city acquired the desired land, the former owners became tenants and were often dispossessed of their cattle ranches by the city, which would turn the operation over to a single large agency in order to have greater control of the watershed. Entire town sites were taken for this purpose, and substantial parts of mountain counties became the domain of one gigantic absentee landlord.

Many practices of the city of Los Angeles disregarded the convenience of the local people to the point of ruthlessness. This provoked open rebellion, and the aqueducts carrying the water to Los Angeles occasionally were dynamited. This occurred some years before I became governor, but the intense feeling continued.

During World War II, when landlords were under rent control regulations and were prohibited from raising rents, Los Angeles, believing that as a municipal corporation it was not bound by these rules, decided to increase its revenue by hiking rents from twenty-five to fifty per cent or more on practically every tenant in Bishop, the little county seat of Inyo County. To aggravate conditions still more, the notices were mailed on Christmas Eve. The tenants were all of extremely modest means, fifteen of them being old-age pensioners. Rental fees for struggling local merchants and the weekly newspaper publisher were raised more than fifty per cent. The result of this arrogance was electrifying. Every mountain county in California, whether involved or not—and there were many—demanded legislation that would prevent the populous areas of the state from repeating such acts of tyranny in the future. Emotions ran high, to the embarrassment of Los Angeles, and no great opposition fight was made in the Legislature, with the result that the rectifying bill passed both houses overwhelmingly. However, when it reached my desk, the city made a strong effort to have me veto it. Los Angeles argued that the bill would prevent growing cities from acquiring the water essential for their expanding needs, and that it would unconstitutionally restrict the city in the use of its property.

I announced that we would have a public hearing at which both sides might present their cases. Los Angeles came with its officials and its lawyers; the mountaineers with their old age pensioners, storekeepers, the weekly newspaper publisher, and their legislative representatives. We spent an afternoon hearing legal arguments on one side and human reactions on the other. At the conclusion, being unable to perceive any legal reason for not signing the bill and being impressed by the hardship cases, I signed. The bill did not restrict Los Angeles from seeking new sources of water, and today it is endeavoring to obtain water rights from the Columbia River Basin in the states of Oregon and Washington more than a thousand miles away.

Another instance I have in mind involved a bill to exempt private colleges from state taxation. It was sponsored by a new Roman Catholic archbishop (later cardinal), Francis McIntyre. The argument was that nearly all of the states except California had exempted both private grade schools and colleges from taxation, and California had for many years exempted the grade and secondary schools. There was no fight in the committees or on the floor of either House. As I remember the vote, it was unanimous in the Assembly and drew only one "no" in the Senate.

Notwithstanding this, when the bill reached my desk I received a long, earnest letter from some of my friends in the Masonic fraternity and others urging me to veto it on constitutional and conceptual grounds. They also requested that I give them a hearing. I promptly replied that I would have a public hearing for both sides. However, I soon received a reply withdrawing the request for a hearing. So, without a hearing, I signed the bill, believing it was both equitable and constitutional. Its legality was litigated in the California courts, and, when sustained by the Supreme Court of the state, it was appealed to the Supreme Court of the United States. By that time I was Chief Justice. Because of the above facts, I disqualified myself from participation, and, with me abstaining, the Court upheld the constitutionality of the act.

These incidents are indicative of techniques often used to accomplish a governmental result without fighting out the issue in public.

But to return to my way of keeping in touch with the people as a basis for soliciting their support both in the solution of our problems and in my campaigns, I devised what I chose to call the "town hall" method. Briefly, it was this. Whenever I had under consideration a proposal for the solution of some important problem, after doing the spadework in the department to be affected and after ascertaining what groups throughout the state were interested in the problem, pro and con, I would call a two- or three-day conference in Sacramento, bringing together without regard to political affiliation from one thousand to three thousand concerned citizens from every nook and corner of California.

Their response was remarkable, the more so because each of them paid his or her own expenses.

Beforehand, we would arrange for division of the conference into as many as twenty sections. For each, a chairman, a reporter, and a committee were appointed and briefed on bringing out the views of all those participating. At the opening of the conference, we would meet in general session in the Sacramento Municipal Auditorium. There I would speak and explain why I had called the conference and thank them in advance for any help they might be able to give me toward solution of the problem at hand. Others would then speak on the general topic in question, after which the assemblage would recess to meet in the several sections. Every person attending could select the section or sections in which she or he desired to participate.

Usually on the afternoon of the second day, section reports would be made to another general assembly. On the third day, a composite report would be made, and after discussion and receiving my thanks, the conference would adjourn.

I usually held these mass meetings when the Legislature was in session in order that the delegates might be able to make known to their elected representatives their desires on the subject. This was one of the most important by-products of the conferences.

I called these meetings on a great variety of subjects, such as public health, highways, water, prisons, employment, mental health, conservation, veterans, youth problems, and old age pensions. From some of them such as the youth and mental health conferences, permanent committees lasting many years were established. These gatherings took much of my time and energy, but they were also great educators for me as to both public affairs and people. I was fascinated by them and gratified with what we achieved through them.

This is the kind of politics I engaged in so far as the governorship is concerned. But there is another side to my political activities—national politics—which I shall discuss later. It was somewhat detached from my normal daily routine, which was dominated by state problems.

One of the knottiest of these problems was highways. Our state was growing at an unprecedented rate. The population increased by five million—from seven to twelve—during my years as governor, and this was graphically reflected in the automobile traffic. During the Depression years of the 1930s and the War years of the early forties, there had been little highway construction, but the number of passenger automobiles had increased from somewhat over two million to five million, and trucks had increased not only in number, from a quarter of a million to three quarters of a million, but also in size. Naturally, our highways were both congested and, in the main, inadequate. California is particularly dependent on highways and even at that time had many more automobiles than any state in the Union. Because of the two ranges of mountains running lengthwise down the state, there are fewer railroads than in most large states, and we are compelled to rely heavily, not only on passenger automobiles, but also on trucks to transport our agricultural and industrial products.

During the War, we made extensive studies of our needs, and in 1947 I caused a special session of the Legislature to authorize and finance a highway program adequate to meet those needs. At the time, we were in the group of states having the lowest gasoline tax in the nation—three cents per gallon. We recognized the inadequacy of this income and recommended an increase to six cents as well as an increase in other highway users' taxes. With the new money, we proposed to establish a system of freeways on all our main arteries which would support from four to eight lanes and would eliminate all grade crossings and left-hand turns. The oil companies, which were traditionally opposed to the gas tax as a source of highway revenue, banded together to defeat the bill. They fought desperately, although they were to be the largest beneficiaries of the program. Their lobbyists applied pressure upon the entire Legislature and published untrue and even libelous articles against the proposal and its sponsors. Their principal complaint was that this was gouging the taxpayers for something which was unnecessary. They tried to sidetrack the proposal by advocating bond issues instead of current financing, and even started a movement for toll road financing.

We met them head on with our pay-as-you-go principle, using the counterargument that toll roads were unduly expensive for the average motorist, and with the declaration that we did not propose to have freeways for the rich and run-down secondary roads for the poor.

The special session lasted from January to June, and at times we were told our bill could not pass. During this period, the oil companies raised the price of gasoline three times. Finally, when the third increase was announced, I wired the Department of Justice in Washington, asking for an investigation of the oil companies for violation of the antitrust laws prohibiting price fixing. Such an investigation was announced, and the cohesion of the opposition disintegrated.

We had sufficient votes in the Senate, but it was nip and tuck in the Assembly. I was told by those who were handling the bill on the floor that they were short one vote, but that we could get it if I would sign a certain other bill for one of the assemblymen. I inquired what it provided for, and was told it merely required that canners of horse meat for animal food specifically label their product as horse meat. I had my staff study the bill and, finding it to be desirable, said I would sign it. The Assembly then passed the highway bill by one vote. This was the only time I ever made a trade with a legislator for his vote, but it was for an important one. I never could understand why he was apprehensive about my signing his "horse meat" bill, as it was clearly in the interest of honest advertising and could hurt no one.

Our bill was watered down from a three cents per gallon raise to one and a half cents, but this was not important because we went back later for the remainder and were successful with little opposition. The revenues from this bill were responsible for what I am sure any transportation expert would now say is the finest highway system in the world.

If I were asked what I believe was my strongest forte in government service, I would say that it was the ability to select honest, loyal, and discreet associates who could be trusted with intimate knowledge of what we were undertaking and relied upon to carry on the programs whether I was present to supervise them or not. Perhaps the greatest satisfaction of my many years in office came from the fact that not one of my appointees in a half century was ever accused of dishonesty or of violating his oath as a public servant. Nor was there ever a leak in the confidences that were exchanged in the inner sanctum of my office. This was not the result of only a few at top level being privy to information, because my system of office meetings kept *all* those who were supposed to carry out the programs fully informed.

Excellent staff work, of course, reflected favorably on my various administrations and was more responsible than any other one thing for my re-election to the offices I held.

I had a wonderful group in the Governor's Office. My executive secretary was William T. Sweigert from San Francisco, who had been my chief assistant attorney general. He was a lifelong Democrat and an ardent Catholic, and that caused a few rumbles in Protestant Republican circles for a while, but his fair approach to problems of the office and his generous manner of dealing with everyone soon dispelled any feeling of partisanship or sectarianism, and he supervised the staff work in a way that maintained harmony and progress. Toward the end of my third term, he indicated a desire to go on the bench in San Francisco. I agreed and, characteristically, he asked to start modestly on the Municipal Court. There was a vacancy there, and I appointed him to fill it. Shortly thereafter, I appointed him to the Superior Court, where he served well until appointed by President Eisenhower as a United States district judge in the Northern District of California. He has had a distinguished career there ever since.

A press secretary is a most important staff member for a governor, and I was fortunate in my selection there. Verne Scoggins was a writer for and protégé of Mr. Irving Martin, publisher of the Stockton *Record*, who had been the honorary chairman of my Northern California campaign. Verne had been loaned to me by Mr. Martin during the campaign, and it did not take long for all of us to become aware of his qualities. He knew the politics of the state, its economic problems, and the relationships of urban and rural life. He had been a newspaper correspondent in Sacramento and was well acquainted with newsmakers at the Capitol. Ideally suited by experience for the job, he had the toughness to handle the press in any emergency. I succeeded in obtaining the consent of Mr. Martin to let Scoggins join me, and he managed my public relations for more than ten years, at which time I appointed him a member of the Public Utilities Commission, a position which had been held by his sponsor, Martin, in the Hiram Johnson administration forty years before.

Our method of dealing with the press was simple and direct but well regulated. There were no "scoops." We played no favorites. Whether a newspaper was friendly or not, it received the same information through Scoggins' office or from me in a press conference. I did not see newspapermen in private unless their editors or publishers requested a personal interview for good reason. But I did have two press conferences each week—one morning conference for the afternoon papers the early part of the week and another in the afternoon later in the week for the morning publications.

Some of the correspondents would occasionally complain that we were too tough with our "no individual interviews" policy when their home office insisted that they see me personally. On the other hand, the entire working press felt secure in the knowledge that there would be no exclusives for favorite papers. This was all handled by Scoggins, with little work and no strain on me. I should add that the working press in Sacramento treated me with what I considered to be kindness and generosity throughout my years there.

Shortly after World War II was over, a California Communist paper sent a correspondent to Sacramento to cover the Capitol. The press corps, including representatives of the news services and various newspaper, radio, and television correspondents who determined the admission to that body, refused to admit him because of cold war tensions. He then demanded admittance at least to my press conferences. The members of the corps did not look with favor on the idea because they thought he would make a shambles of it, but Scoggins and I thought it would not be consistent with our democratic policy to deny him that right. Accordingly, we told him he would be welcome. He came two or three times, sat in the rear of the room, asked no questions, and then stopped coming.

My private secretary, Miss Helen MacGregor, had been a devoted deputy during my district attorney and attorney general years. She was a lawyer, and had been secretary for United States District Judge Frank Kerrigan before joining my staff. As my private secretary in the Governor's Office, she managed the many-faceted stenographic and clerical work. She had never been in politics, but was interested through association with the problems that challenged women's organizations of the state—youth, the elderly, education, health, jobs, etc. She employed all the women in the stenographic and clerical phases of our work, about thirty in all. They were selected by her in her own way, without political consideration of any kind. This resulted in a fine group of people who kept our office functioning harmoniously and efficiently.

I had long been concerned about the manner in which death sentences were administered in California. There were some lawyers who made a specialty of bleeding the relatives of condemned men for money to obtain reprieve after reprieve on fraudulent eleventh-hour petitions claiming irregularities in the trial. They would wait until the day before the execution, then ask for a reprieve from the governor in order that they might have an opportunity to thresh out the matter in court. The governor would then obligingly grant a stay of ninety days or more, at the end of which time the man would be sentenced to execution on a still more distant date. This process was frequently repeated, with the result that a man could be led to death's door again and again before he was executed. I believed that if the state did have the right to take a man's life, it was inhuman to do it in such a manner, so I worked out a plan to avoid protracted indecision of this kind.

In California, every sentence to death by a trial court was reviewed in the State Supreme Court whether the conviction was by a plea of guilty or the verdict of a jury. If the conviction was affirmed by that court, it would refer the case back to the trial court for fixing the date of execution not less than thirty nor more than sixty days thereafter. It was at the expiration of this period that the renegade lawyers would make their move. In order to stop this practice, immediately after every death sentence I would ask our attorney general to look into the merits of the case and be able to report to me his appraisal of it by the time the Supreme Court rendered its judgment. At the same time, I directed our prison authorities to study the prisoner, psychiatrically and in any other manner which might bear upon the rightness or wrongness of the judgment. I would receive these reports from the attorney general and the director of corrections immediately after affirmation by the State Supreme Court. I would then immediately study them along with the opinion of the Court, and before there was any action by the lawyers I would make a decision as to whether or not clemency should be extended. If I determined it should be, I would grant it before there was any pressure. If I decided it should not be, I would immediately write to the defendant and his attorney of record and advise them that there would be no reprieves by me, and that any relief sought must be addressed to the courts. This put a stop to most last-minute appeals to the governor.

The following two examples will indicate how I acted to grant clemency. In one case, a young black man jumped into a car driven by a housewife as she finished her shopping in Sacramento. He ordered her to drive to a secluded place where he made her disrobe and then raped her. She was overcome by fear and did not resist. He did not otherwise injure her. A jury very properly convicted him, but sentenced him to death. The attorney general advised me that this was the only case in California where a defendant was sentenced to death for such a crime. I communicated with the trial judge, and asked him if, in his opinion, the same punishment would have been inflicted if the defendant had been a white man. He said, "Certainly not." I then asked if he had any objection to my having the jury interviewed. He did not, so the jury members were questioned, and they were practically unanimous in saying that if it had been a white defendant, they would not have inflicted the death penalty. I then commuted the rapist's sentence to life imprisonment. This was all done before there was any appeal for clemency.

The other illustration is the case of the murder and ravishing of a little girl in the bushes along the Yuba River in one of our interior counties. The child was of an itinerant family camped beside the river. Suspicion fell on an ex-convict who was living in the neighboring hobo jungles. There was independent evidence to implicate the defendant, but the principal witnesses against him were the members of the family of the little girl. Every one of them was of an extremely low mental order. Each had made several statements conflicting with his or her own prior statements and with the testimony of the others. They were all easily swayed by suggestion, and could not repeat the same story precisely. Nobody claimed to have seen the crime committed. It was all circumstantial. The defendant was penniless, friendless, and had no strong defense. I had no doubt of his guilt, but felt sure that if he were executed it would eventually become a *cause célèbre*, and the cause of justice would suffer. I accordingly commuted his sentence to life imprisonment. But because he was an ex-convict, I provided that it should be without possibility of parole. This created quite an angry stir in the little county where the crime occurred, but it soon subsided because I believe the people came to realize the unsatisfactory condition of the evidence.

My successor, Governor Knight, did not follow these practices. On the contrary, he let matters go to the last minute before deciding on them and finally was hoist by his own petard. A condemned man was to be executed at San Quentin, and, reverting to a practice of former days, Knight had a direct line installed between the warden's and governor's offices the night before. The governor, knowing he was to go on a public relations cruise with the Navy the day of the execution, also made arrangements for a ship-to-shore communication with the warden. While on the ship, he received advice of an application for a reprieve. Believing it called for prompt action, he sent a message back to the warden telling him to stay the execution. But the message never reached the warden and at noon the prisoner was executed.

Probably all of this will be irrelevant to life in California by the time this book is published, because only recently the Supreme Court of that state held that capital punishment is prohibited by a provision of the California State Constitution against cruel or unusual punishment. So, unless the people of California restore capital punishment by a constitutional amendment, the 102 men and 5 women who are on death row in San Quentin as this is written will pay the penalty for their crimes in prison instead of by death.*

Besides the staff secretaries already mentioned, I established a departmental secretary who was my liaison officer with the heads of the different departments of state government. He was a sort of unofficial "ombudsman" to see that complaints coming to me about the functioning of any governmental office also reached the head of the affected department and received his personal attention. In addition, he kept me informed on a day-to-day basis of the status of our programs. This was important because I could not be in daily contact with all the the department heads, and yet I must know what was transpiring from day

* Ed. note: The voters of the state expressed themselves in 1972, and it was two to one by ballot in favor of a proposition to restore capital punishment. California's Legislature soon passed a bill making death mandatory for persons convicted of certain crimes. The new law was not retroactive, and no one has been executed under it. However, on July 2, 1976, a United States Supreme Court decision upheld the constitutionality of capital punishment for murder and allowed state court discretion where juries were under the guidance of a judge in deciding whether a defendant should be sentenced to death, but it ruled out mandatory death sentences for murder or any other crime. Soon after, a California county judge declared that the state's mandatory provision was in violation of constitutional rights under this ruling, and at this writing a certain amount of confusion prevails as to the applicability of the death penalty, with many individual cases on appeal.

to day in important matters. We had more than sixty thousand state employees in a myriad of endeavors, and my best means of remaining informed was to have someone on my immediate staff who knew the programs and had access to the department heads for continual briefing.

Incidentally, the state employees were a loyal group and throughout my tenure gave me no cause for concern. They were practically all Civil Service workers, and Civil Service in California was a meaningful and fast-growing organism. I believed in the Civil Service principle because it took employees out of politics for the most part, and relieved them of the fear of losing their jobs with every change of administration. When I was district attorney, at the request of the California State Employees Association, I wrote the formal endorsement of Civil Service which went to every voter at the time it was made a part of our State Constitution. When I became governor, I took steps to make it more effective. In the first place, I instructed my finance committees in northern and southern parts of the state that no contributions would be accepted from state employees, and made a public announcement to that effect. I believe about eighty per cent of the employees were members of the California State Employees Association, which headquartered in Sacramento and had local chapters throughout the state. That organization looked after the interests of state employees. It maintained a lobby at the Legislature, and I dealt with it openly every legislative session in conferences with its board of directors and the members of my Personnel Board, which was the statutory board for employee relations. A number of appointments to that board expired about the same time, which enabled me to reconstitute it in a manner that commanded the respect of the department heads and employees. What had been a political body whose trials resembled kangaroo courts was transformed into a judicious body conducting hearings which accorded due process and expert consideration. The board was manned for the most part by distinguished university professors. These men kept my relations with the state employees and the Legislature on an even keel throughout my tenure.

My departmental secretary, who kept me in touch with all departments, was Merrill F. Small, known by everyone as "Pop"—not because of his age, since he was much younger than I, but because of certain kindly qualities that enabled him to probe into controversial matters without being controversial. He was with me until Senator Thomas H. Kuchel "stole" him from me. When Senator Richard Nixon was elected Vice-President in 1952, I appointed Mr. Kuchel, who was then our state controller, to fill the senatorial vacancy. Kuchel then told me he would be arriving in Washington with no one who had the contacts essential for him to be in communication with the news media and other elements of our state. He asked if he could take Pop Small as his administrative assistant. I knew Pop fulfilled Kuchel's requirements. Before coming to my office, he had published a weekly newspaper in the little city of Quincy, seat of the mountain county of Plumas. He was well known to all the newspaper publishers and had been president of the California Newspaper Publishers Association. Pop was valuable in interpreting them to me and me to them. However, realizing how many people I had prevailed on to let me have associates who were valuable to them, and desiring to have Senator Kuchel became a good senator for California, I said, "Tom, I have stolen so many men from friends of mine to set up my organization that I can hardly object to your committing a little larceny on me." He thanked me, and Pop Small went to Washington.

Senator Kuchel measured up to my expectations. He survived three elections, and was one of the most respected men on both sides of the aisle in the Senate. He was elected by the Republicans as assistant minority leader, which position he filled with dignity and effectiveness. But politics was changing in California, and when there was a complete swing to the right in Republican circles, a demagogue of the first order, Max Rafferty, state superintendent of public instruction, defeated him for the Republican nomination while Kuchel was back in Washington tending to his job. The people as a whole in California, however, would not stand for such reactionary representation for our state, and elected Alan Cranston, the Democratic nominee, who at the time held the same position—state controller—as that from which I had appointed Kuchel to the Senate. Rafferty was also defeated for re-election to his post as superintendent of public instruction, and shortly thereafter left California for Alabama, where he became one of the principal adherents of Governor George Wallace.

I had one other secretary on my staff, a travel secretary who was responsible for all my business trip arrangements, and they were many. While governor, I traveled 250,000 miles in our converted C-47, which was given by the United States Government to the state and reconditioned into an executive plane. I named it the *Grizzly Bear*. With two exceptions, one a trip to Salt Lake City, Utah, for a governors' conference and the other to Corpus Christi for an international ceremony, all of this travel was inside California between 1946 and 1953. I was piloted by three air officers of our National Guard. My other air travel out of California was on commercial lines. I went another quarter of a million miles by automobile, and when taking that mode of travel was driven by various members of the Highway Patrol.

I had several travel secretaries, one of the first being William S.

Mailliard, a young man who had charted his life for public service at Yale. His father, Ward, a highly respected businessman of San Francisco, and his mother, Kate, were dear friends and political supporters of mine. After he had been in my administration in various capacities, I appointed him my travel secretary until he was elected to Congress from San Francisco. He became a ranking Republican member on important committees of the House of Representatives.

Collectively, these staff members did a marvelous job for me, and when I recount any personal achievements, common fairness dictates that these also be recognized as their achievements, because we counseled together on every important issue, and it would be impossible to dissect the results at this late date to determine exactly who suggested the seminal ideas and who the method of operations. One thing is certain—all contributed.

As governor, I was tremendously interested in the University of California, having been graduated from it and from Boalt Hall, its law school. All of our children from their earliest years had expressed a desire to enroll at U.C., and eventually all six of them had graduated—two, Jim and Virginia, from the Berkeley campus; two, Earl Jr. and Bob, from the Davis campus; and two, Dorothy and Honey Bear, from UCLA. I wanted to have the university keep up with the best schools in the country and oriented my administration toward that result. I had been active in alumni offices, and at the time I announced my candidacy for governor was first vice-president of the alumni association and supposedly next in line for the presidency. However, I resigned my alumni office at that time to avoid any conflict of interest.

When elected governor, I gave some thought to the U. C. Board of Regents, because it is the responsibility of the governor to make appointments whenever vacancies occur. It seemed to me that the Board was too heavily composed of bankers, insurance men, and other financial executives and of graduates of the Berkeley campus. The university was showing a need for expansion, and the branch at Los Angeles was becoming restive on that score. I, therefore, undertook to diversify the Board both geographically and as to interest. It is not an easy thing for a governor to do, as the regents' terms are for sixteen years, and normally he would have but four in his own term of office. However, a combination of circumstances assisted me in accelerating that time schedule. As opportunities arose, I appointed two graduates of UCLA, the first to come from that campus—Edward Carter, a prominent department store executive, and Victor Hansen, a Los Angeles lawyer. From the great Central Valley, I appointed Earl Fenston, a Fresno businessman, and Gus Olson, a successful farmer from the Sacramento area. Believing that labor should be represented, I appointed Cornelius J. Haggerty, secretary of the State Federation of Labor (A.F. of L.). There were no academicians on the Board, but I felt there should be, so I appointed Donald McLaughlin, former dean of the School of Engineering on the Berkeley campus and, at the time of his appointment, a world-famous mining engineer. Also, I appointed Dr. Howard Naffziger, a pre-eminent brain surgeon at the Medical School of the University of California in San Francisco, and five-star Admiral Chester Nimitz of World War II fame. Then finally I appointed my long-time friend and confidant, Jesse Steinhart, a distinguished San Francisco lawyer. I also reappointed a few incumbents, readjusting younger men to serve longer terms and the older to serve shorter terms. It was regrettable sometimes that I could not reappoint some of the older men at the expiration of their time on the Board. They had served nobly but were in their middle seventies and a sixteen-year term added to that would be gambling too much on the future.

The governor, by virtue of his office, is president of the Board of Regents of the university. The Board met approximately two days each month at the various campuses, the first day of each session being devoted to committee work and the second to a plenary Board meeting. I deliberately only attended about one third of the meetings because, in spite of my interest in the university's affairs, I did not want to give any impression that I was trying to dominate its management. The State Constitution made the university a separate corporation, subject only to budgetary control by the state. When attending the regents' meetings, I presided as president. In my absence, the Board-elected chairman presided. For most of my years, the university prospered financially, scholastically, and in terms of prestige.

The people of California loved the university, and had good reason for doing so. It had been a great friend to the farmers of the state, and was the basic source of the scientific and technological skills that brought so much war and postwar industry to our economy—without which we probably would have experienced a calamitous unemployment situation in the postwar era.

As soon as World War II ended, service men came to the university by the thousands. The Berkeley campus student population soon exceeded twenty-five thousand. We established a new campus at Santa Barbara and another at Riverside, fully implemented the campus at Los Angeles (UCLA) into one as comprehensive and almost as large as that at Berkeley, and expanded the campus at Davis from a strictly agricultural branch into a full-blown university. With all that, the University of California continued to grow and within a few years after I left, Governor Brown established three more campuses, at San Diego, at Ir-

THE MEMOIRS OF EARL WARREN

vine in Orange County, and at Santa Cruz. During all my years, we kept up with the university's growing needs by constructing the necessary buildings, enlarging the faculties and maintaining their salaries at levels consistent with those of other outstanding universities in the nation.

They were happy years for the school until it and all governmental institutions ran into the witch-hunting disease epitomized by Senator Joseph McCarthy of Wisconsin in his sadistic attacks upon the State Department, the Army, and even private citizens for any association with people of unorthodox or dissenting views. In particular there was hysteria about Communism. It all seems nightmarish now that American Presidents are seeking friendship with Red China, which then and now is the seat of the very Communism that was condemned so vituperously by us in McCarthy's time.

In those days, however, anti-Communist feeling permeated the atmosphere with fear, distrust of neighbors, bitterness, and persecution. The virus struck the university through three members of the Board of Regents—Edward A. Dickson, John Francis Neylan, and Mario Giannini. The first two were former Progressives from the Hiram Johnson era, and had been on the Board for many years, and the latter a recent appointee by me. I had named Mario to the vacancy created by the death of his father, A. P. Giannini, founder of the Bank of America and a great friend and benefactor of the university. I had every reason to believe he would be friendly to the university, not only because of his father's great interest, but also because he was a graduate of U.C. Berkeley and, as president of the Bank of America, he could be of great help on the finance committee. These three regents, who, because of the university's connection with the Los Alamos project in New Mexico, became privy to the development of our atomic bomb secrets, assumed an air of mysticism about it and distrusted with a passion everyone who was not in agreement with them. They let McCarthyism dominate their lives and endeavored to impose it on others. They followed the tactic of seeking out every dissenting voice in the university, and finally induced President Sproul to introduce a resolution requiring all members of the faculty to take a test oath asserting their loyalty, disavowing Communism and disclosing for scrutiny their membership in all scientific and academic organizations. President Sproul, almost immediately realizing that he had been misled into an untenable position, withdrew his support from the resolution. I was not present when the resolution was first offered, but at the next meeting I pointed out that it could do nothing but create dissension in the university and was unenforceable. This caused a split in the Board, and for a year and a half, even until after I went to Washington, the battle raged. Realizing that I would be held accountable to the public for whatever was done, I attended every meeting at which this issue was to be discussed.

My objection to the oath was that a section of the State Constitution establishing the university provided that the faculty should take an oath required of *all* officers of the state "to support and defend the Constitution and laws of the United States and of the State of California" and that no other political requirement should be made of them. The faculty, therefore, like myself as governor, had all taken that oath when employed, and the proposed requirement seemed directly in conflict with, or at least unnecessary in view of, the State Constitution. I argued that even if it should be found not to be violative of the Constitution, it was an abortive action because the only sanction against executing a false affidavit was punishment for perjury, and perjury was defined as falsifying an oath required by law. Because this proposed oath was not one required by law, but merely one prescribed by the Board of Regents, a falsification of it was not punishable. Which meant that if a faculty member were a Communist, he or she could take the oath freely without fear of any penalty for falsification of it. And the atheism of Communists who would not deter them from taking a false oath. The only people then who would be disturbed by the proposal would be those who stood on their rights under the State Constitution, and those who had conscientious scruples against taking test oaths as an interference with their academic freedom.

The press of the state was badly infected with McCarthyism and except for isolated instances like the McClatchy *Bee* newspapers in Sacramento, Fresno, and Modesto, there was little attention given to our anti-oath position. In fact, in most newspapers that position was not fully stated, although much was said about the effort to stamp Communism out of the university. This popularized the oath proposal in many quarters, and I am sure had much to do with securing the support of some of the regents. Some phase of the proposal came up at every meeting, and the vote was usually almost evenly balanced; sometimes we would win by one or two votes and other times lose by the same margin, depending on who the absentees were. My lieutenant governor and the speaker of the Assembly, Samuel L. Collins, were always pulling a strong oar for the oath, and the former often referred to discussions he had with unnamed agents of the FBI to support his position.

The upshot of the whole controversy was that the resolution was adopted, and when sixty-eight members of the faculty refused to sign the affidavit, they were discharged. Many of these were very distinguished professors. They sought reinstatement through a lawsuit against the university. The majority of the regents then employed prestigious special counsel to represent them, but the professors won. I stated that in my opinion the oath would be invalidated by our Supreme Court, and the discharged professors would be restored to duty.

After I became Chief Justice, the California Supreme Court did exactly what I had predicted, and the university was ordered to restore the professors to their positions and pay them their financial losses during the interim.

During all this period, there was a real witch hunt throughout the university for supposed Communists and other subversives. Finally they found one and only one. The reason they found her was that she had been registered to vote as an avowed Communist for some years, and had once run for a local office as such. She was a piano player in a gym class at UCLA.

At one of our meetings on the Davis campus, the debate became very warm. Regent Giannini, in a fury, announced that he was resigning then and there, and that he intended to form an organization of "vigilantes" to rid the university of subversion. That left the Board about evenly divided on the loyalty oath issue. It also confronted me with a dilemma. If I should fill the vacancy with someone who would vote with me, it would be said that the vote was the price of his appointment. If he should vote the other way, it would be said that I was being "soft on Communism," or it might be said I had induced him to vote that way to relieve me of the responsibility of casting the deciding vote. I didn't want to be caught in any of those traps, so I said nothing and left the place unfilled for a considerable period of time. Finally I received a letter from Mr. Giannini saying that after much thought he believed he could return to the Board of Regents and make a contribution to the welfare of the university. I do not know who or what prompted him to write that letter, but I did not want to be mousetrapped that way either. It would look as though I had begged him to return to the Board because of his prominence as president of the Bank of America. Accordingly I replied that I was sorry but I had made other arrangements to fill the position. Shortly thereafter, I appointed Dr. Naffziger who has already been mentioned.

Neylan and Giannini carried their hysteria to such an extent that they deprived the university of badly needed dormitories. They objected to them on the ground that the concept of dormitories was socialistic; that students should be taught to "come up the hard way." I never could understand such an argument because the students were not to live there rent free; the dormitories were to be financed by revenue bonds payable from student rentals, with a state subsidy toward the cost of construction. In two successive state budgets, at my request, the

Legislature made provision for their construction, but Regents Neylan and Giannini, controlling the finance committee, refused to spend the money for that purpose. Finally the Legislature in disgust appropriated the money for other purposes. Since that time, with both of them gone, dormitories have been built on all the campuses, though at several times the cost for which they could have been constructed then.

As an illustration of how much importance the press gave the so-called "loyalty oath issue," one incident might be revealing. The Los Angeles *Times* had supported me since my campaign for attorney general when Mr. Harry Chandler was the publisher. My relations remained cordial with his successor and son, Norman Chandler, until Norman finally became emotional about the loyalty oath and directed his political writer, Kyle Palmer, to write a caustic editorial against me for my opposition to it. As told to me by Palmer, he said, "Norman, don't you believe it would be well for you to have a talk with the governor before breaking off the friendly relations that have existed for so many years?" With some reluctance, after further conversation, Chandler agreed to do so. Both he and I were members of the Bohemian Club of San Francisco, and Palmer, knowing we both planned to attend the annual encampment of the club in its beautiful grove of virgin redwoods on the Russian River north of San Francisco, suggested that perhaps we might discuss the matter in those congenial surroundings. Chandler agreed, and Palmer alerted me to the likelihood of such a meeting.

I was delighted when, at the encampment, Chandler and I could sit in a cluster of giant redwoods, which added a cathedral-like solemnity to the discussion, and quietly debate his concern about radicalism in the university and why he thought a tool like the loyalty oath should be used to screen out subversives. When he had argued his position, I said, "Norman, will you let me tell you my story for a few minutes without interruption and then I will be happy to answer any questions you might have for me?" He agreed. I then reiterated that the whole proposal was fruitless; that it was against the State Constitution, which prescribed the only oath which could be required of the faculty; that there was no statute authorizing such a new oath; that anyone could falsely subscribe to it and be immune from punishment because only the falsification of an oath required by law constitutes perjury; that knowing this an atheistic Communist would have no hesitation in taking it, and that the only ones who would object to it were those who conscientiously believed it would be an abridgement of their First Amendment rights of expression and association as they applied to academic freedom. I told him such protesters believed they were merely protecting the freedom that was guaranteed them under the Bill of

Rights. Everyone, I added, gave lip service to the Bill of Rights as a political philosophy but too many people were unwilling to apply it except where an infringement of it adversely affected them. For example, the slightest infringement on the freedom of religion would arouse all religionists, yet they might be totally insensitive to an abridgement of the rights of others in a different walk of life. The academic and scientific communities, to name two, had an equal concern about their right to pursue knowledge and teach the truth as they found it.

"Your own profession," I went on, "is perhaps the most vigilant in this regard, and the most militant in resisting any incursion on its right to report the news as it discovers it and to interpret it as it chooses. I would think that you would feel yourselves very much akin to the academic community, because you consider yourselves educators in the sense that you go into every home in America for the daily enlightenment of young and old alike. Because of this public service, the government gives you privileges that other citizens do not have. You have the right to send your bulky newspapers and magazines through the mail at low postage rates that are totally out of proportion to those required of other citizens. Now let us suppose that Congress proposed a statute that would deny such mailing privileges to all publishers who refused to subscribe to an oath denying they were Communists and swearing not to use their publications for Communistic purposes. What would your opinion be of such legislation?"

"You know what our opinion would be," he replied.

"I believe I do, but I want you to tell me."

He said, "Of course, we would be against it."

I asked why, and he responded that if publishers subscribed to such an oath, some bureaucrat in Washington would be scrutinizing everything written and would censor it according to his views on whether or not it was in the interests of Communism.

"Norman," I said, "you have just made the case for the university faculty. They contend that if they sign such an affidavit, some bureaucrat or legislator or lobbyist in Sacramento will be constantly looking over their shoulders and trying to find subversion in their teaching, and this would be in violation of academic freedom. And we both know that in the present atmosphere that is bound to occur."

He was silent for a moment and then said, "It looks to me as though there is too much emotion on both sides."

He asked no further questions, and we closed the discussion on that note. A few days later there was an editorial about such undue emotionalism in the Los Angeles *Times*.

The loyalty oath controversy shook the university but did not weaken its foundation. In 1953, when I went to Washington, it was adequately budgeted with between one hundred fifty and two hundred million dollars' worth of new or authorized construction, and was bracketed by the academic and scientific communities of the nation in the highest echelon of American universities.

Our activities in higher education were not limited to the university, but extended to the state colleges, junior colleges, and special schools. Together with the university, they were pointed to as outstanding in statewide education. It was difficult to keep up with the growth. During my years, we established three new state colleges, at Long Beach, Los Angeles, and Sacramento, making eleven in all with an enrollment of 380,000. The junior college system (two-year colleges) was increased to seventy-seven campuses, with a student population of 73,948. This, of course, called for increased construction funds and greatly enlarged faculties, all of which were provided for them, as they were for the university.

The public school system during and after the War years expanded so greatly that it was impossible for many districts to house all their pupils. Many had two shifts and others totally exhausted their bonding capacity for new construction. It therefore became necessary for the state to help all that were in trouble. Immediately after the War, in 1947, we made grants of fifty-five million to distressed districts. This proved to be only a stopgap because the growth continued unabated and, of course, with it the necessity for more and more schools. To fill the need, the state in 1949 adopted the policy of issuing bonds for loans to impoverished school districts to be repaid in thirty years. In that year, bonds in the amount of $250,000,000 were issued and in 1952 another $185,000,00 worth were issued. These bonds, together with the grants, made a total of $490,000,000. It was a lot of money, but the people of California were proud of their school system and were willing to obligate themselves in this manner in order to provide quality education for their children. Fortunately, we had paid off our other bond obligations before they were due. Thus our credit was excellent, and, there being plenty of money available for investments of this kind, we were able to sell our school bonds at fantastically low interest rates.

Another thing that enabled us to keep up with our growth was the fact that we had an architectural division in the state government and, realizing the extent to which construction would be necessary after the War, we kept it busy drawing plans and specifications for our proposed buildings. When the end of the War came, we had not only saved the money to pay for construction, but we had the plans and specifications on the shelf ready to start. When the government was ready to release building materials, it favored those who were ready to begin work. Because we were ready, all that was necessary was for us to call for bids and get under way. We had so many jobs that there were not enough contractors in California to fill them. As a result, contractors came from all over the nation, since their states were not yet ready with building programs. They would come to the offices of my director of finance, James T. Dean, and my director of public works, Charles H. Purcell, and ask the question, "Whom do we see to get this job?" They would be told they need see no one, that all they had to go was file a sealed bid with the statutory bond for faithful performance, and if they were the lowest responsible bidder, they would be awarded the contract. They would then encounter skeptically, "Oh, yeah, we know that, but whom do we see?" Again they would be told there was no one to see, and finally they would say, "Well, where do we get our insurance?" They would be told they would acquire it from any insurance man. The fact was that they didn't *want* the bidding to be honest. They wanted to pay to be on the inside. But they were talking to men who did not play that traditional payoff game. Jim Dean was the soul of honor, plain as an old shoe; a man who had the confidence of everybody. The legislators, whether they agreed with our programs or not, took his word on financial matters without question. He brought into his Department of Finance young men trained in business schools for public service and molded them into an efficient and elite corps. He selected all of them himself and both he and they were apolitical.

Charles Purcell, my director of public works, was one of the great highway and structural engineers of his day. He was lured from another state many years before I became governor to be the state engineer, the highest Civil Service position in the department. He developed our highway system according to the most modern methods known. He had been instrumental in the design and construction of the San Francisco-Oakland Bay Bridge, then the longest in the world, along lines that attracted the attention of bridge builders everywhere. He, too, was positively apolitical, and that was his stumbling block if he had ever previously had the ambition to be director of the department. Whether he did or not, I have no idea. Political directors came and went in administration after administration without any offer of the position to him. Yet I could think of no one for the directorship but him, and a week or so after the election I asked him if he would come to the Attorney General's Office in San Francisco to see me. He came carrying a bulging briefcase. "Charley," I said bluntly, "I want you to be my Director of Public Works. How about it?"

He hesitated, looked embarrassed, and finally said, "My goodness, Governor, I thought perhaps you were going to shift things around, so I brought the things in this briefcase to assist you if it involved my job."

"I suppose there will be some shifting around to be done," I replied, "but I want it to be done by you in your own way. That will be good enough for me. You know the department. I do not, and I do not propose to interfere with you, nor will I permit anyone else to do so. How about it?"

"Well, Governor," he said, "I would be honored to do it for you and will do the best I can."

We agreed not to mention it for a week or two. During that time, I had fun with the newspaper correspondents. I was attending hearings on the budget in the Department of Finance, and would see them daily. They would invariably ask if I had decided on a Director of Public Works, as it was one of the most important positions in the administration. I would say, "Yes," and then they would want to know who it was to be. I told them I was not prepared to announce it, but that my selection was such a logical one, I thought they should be able to guess it without being told. They were so steeped in the practice of appointing politicians close to the governor that not one of them ever suggested Charles Purcell. When I finally announced it to them, they were embarrassed but agreeably surprised because he was favorably known to all of them. He did a wonderful job for me for almost nine years until his death in September 1951.

Men like Dean and Purcell handled millions of dollars without the slightest claim of politics or favoritism being leveled against them. And they were functioning in areas where corruption was not unknown.

While we were doing all this public construction, private construction was keeping pace to provide for newcomers to the state and our returning veterans. Housing projects of all sizes were burgeoning throughout California, many as large as a thousand or more homes. The largest was on a level six-thousand-acre tract of land between Los Angeles and Long Beach where it was said that the foundations for a hundred homes were laid every day, and that the houses were sold by the time the foundations were completed. Most of these tract developers' houses were modest in size, and they were purchased mainly by returning veterans from World War II and later Korea, who were an important new factor in the state's economic and political life.

The story of our veterans is a fascinating one. Before World War II, California had the highest average age of any state in the Union. We had advertised our state so effectively that people who had tired of weather extremes in other parts of the country came to California when they had accumulated enough money to live very modestly. A large percentage of them was either at retirement age or approaching it. At all events, they were beyond the usual employable age. They could maintain themselves as long as they remained healthy, but if they had a serious illness or if their income decreased even slightly, they were in real trouble. Our welfare and old age pension rolls zoomed. Frankly, we were worried because much of this occurred in the Depression years. When the war came along, people from other states came to man our war industries. They occupied all the available housing, and when our million California veterans returned, we needed housing for them. At the same time, tens of thousands of veterans from other states who had trained in California for overseas duty and had formed a liking for the West Coast also returned. By the time I left, a million of them, with their wives and babies, had come to settle. This was both a problem for us and a blessing. It was a blessing because it reduced our average age to a figure considerably below that of most of the other states and it gave us a productive labor pool that was attractive to industry. On the other hand, the influx was so great and so sudden that we were put to our wits' ends to house these people adequately and locate them in jobs. We adopted many programs to facilitate their return to civilian life. We did not follow the practice of some other states in giving a cash bonus to our veterans, because a substantial bonus would have cost an enormous amount of money and much of it would be spent in a short period of time without leaving any tangible benefits.

In keeping with the experience of the state with World War I veterans, we concentrated on helping the new civilians to find jobs, to complete their education, and to purchase a home or a farm. We offered a loan of $7,500 to every veteran for a home or $13,500 for a farm, to be repaid in thirty years at three per cent interest. We supplemented federal funds for them to complete their education. We had apprenticeship programs and on-the-job training for more highly skilled work and a statewide program to locate veterans in both public and private employment. By merging our efforts with the veterans organizations, we were able to cover every community and see that attention was given to the personal problems of every veteran if desired. They responded in kind, and made the transition manageable for us.

Despite our rapid growth and the probability of losing war-related industry, there was no great distress about the economy of the state, and we initiated many programs to stimulate business, industry, and employment. We established for the duration of the postwar emergency a Reconstruction and Reemployment Commission, and sought to distribute industrial plants throughout the state rather than have all of them concentrated in our largest cities. This we tried to accomplish by showing the accessibility of smaller cities, the possibilities for their growth, and the availability there of a stable labor force. We met with considerable success, and this, combined with the general attractiveness of the state to outside capital, made it possible to pass through the immediate postwar period without any depression.

In order to stimulate our economic growth, I induced the Army to release Colonel Alexander R. Heron, who was then in Europe. I wanted him because he had been an able director of finance under Governor C. C. Young, and knew the possibilities of state government in such a project. He also had been an executive with the Zellerbach Paper Company, one of our largest manufacturing industries, and knew the needs of big business. He and his assistant, Earl Washburn, rendered valuable service to the economy, along with my executive secretary, William T. Sweigert, who was a moving spirit and coordinator of the reconstruction program.

We were all proud of the rapid growth of our state, but I realized and often informed the public that all growth is not necessarily good; that we must always have concern for the manner in which we grow, that we must make certain that indiscriminate growth does not destroy either the human values or the natural resources of the state. Today that would be called being humanitarian and ecologically aware. But I was not a biologist, and had never heard the word "ecology" in those days. All I knew was that people must be afforded the opportunity to live in wholesome, natural surroundings, and that we must not dissipate our land, water, or atmospheric resources, or permit slum conditions to develop in our cities.

Years later, in 1964, word came from the Census Bureau that California had passed New York and become the most populous state in the Union. On the plane traveling from Washington, D.C., to speak at a meeting in California, I read in the paper that Governor Pat Brown had announced a three day celebration at which there would be dancing in the streets to commemorate the event. I decided to speak of that suggestion at the meeting. I told them I thought the governor was mistaken in his assessment of the importance of mere automatic growth; that there is no merit in simply being the largest; that the true value of that growth would depend upon how we might develop our state to make life wholesome and purposeful for the greatest possible number of people. I told them that instead of dancing in the streets, we should ring every church and school bell, and call the people of California to the schools, churches, city halls, and other places of public assemblage, there to pray for the vision and the guidance to make California the *finest* state in the Union as well as the largest. I could say this without offending Governor Brown because he and the public knew we were friends and that he, too, wanted our state to be the very best.

In all the years of my governorship, I kept this objective in mind.

We tried to conserve the water of our state by storing the runoff of snow and rain from our mountain ranges so it would sustain the orchards, field crops, and municipalities in our valleys during the hot months of summer. Through the university and our own agricultural projects, we trained farmers to transform arid lands into garden spots. We tried to prevent slums, and, in addition to stimulating the construction of homes, we made possible the redevelopment of rundown areas of cities by replacing sordid living conditions with clean, healthy houses and streets. We built highways so people might go easily to the forested hinterland and to beaches. We bought both mountain lands and beaches for state parks, and made them available to all our people. To restore our waterways to their pristine condition, we established a state antipollution Board and local boards on every river to police further defilement efforts and to eliminate existing pollution. We protected the wildlife of our state by laws and adequate enforcement.

I had a very serious desire to conserve the natural resources of the state and had watched their deterioration with sadness since boyhood. Because I loved the beaches of Southern California, I advocated the purchase of more of them and of some of the beautiful mountain areas for state parks. The rapid population growth of the state made this need quite evident. The Legislature responded, but not to the extent that I had hoped. At the time, we were litigating with the federal government over the ownership of the state's tidelands because of their valuable oil deposits. I wanted revenues from the oil to be impounded in the event we were successful, solely for use in protecting our natural resources either through purchase or through further development of them. The controversy had not ended before I came to Washington, but the revenues from oil leases were being impounded. While I was on the Supreme Court, the state prevailed, but the temptation to spend the money for other purposes was too great, and it eventually went into the general fund. At this time our only major forestry program was for the prevention of fires. This was not a success because the cattle and sheep men were pitted against the Forestry Department, and often deliberately started fires to burn off the underbrush in order to improve the feed for their livestock the following spring.

I sought the advice of Professor Emanuel Fritz of the U. C. Berkeley Forestry Department. With his help and that of others in and out of related industries, we created a new State Forestry Board and established programs for the elimination of tree infestations such as that of the pine beetle. Through legislative authority, we established programs of tree farming to supplant cutting practices that had resulted in tree devastation, and we also established programs for reforestation.

The wildlife of the state concerned me and I set about to make the

Forestry Board a serious conservation agency. After some fumbling because of my lack of knowledge of the infighting between various fish and game groups, I induced to head the program such men as General Henry H. (Hap) Arnold, five-star retired general of the Army, who came to California at the end of World War II, and, after his death, Carl Wente, president of the Bank of America and one of the founders of Ducks Unlimited. Under their leadership, the department was completely reorganized and a nationally recognized leader of game conservation, Seth Gordon, the director of such activities in the state of Pennsylvania, was enticed to California and accepted the directorship of our wildlife programs. Much progress was made under his wise leadership.

When I tried to do something about air pollution, I failed. It seemed to me that if smog made the eyes burn and irritated the throat and nasal canals, as it certainly did, it might bring on more serious conditions that were not yet recognizable. Some universities and medical groups had made certain studies in the area, but these were neither coordinated nor broadcast to the public. I thought it was something about which the state should concern itself. Accordingly, I sent a message to the Legislature recommending that an appropriation be made to the director of public health for the purpose of assembling all pollution information and of making such additional research as might be necessary to determine what the effect of smog is on the health of the people of the state. The reception given to that suggestion was really something. One would think I had robbed the treasury. Los Angeles was the only county in the state where smog was known to be a problem at that time, and the entire Los Angeles delegation rose in its wrath and declaimed, "This is our own local problem and we will solve it ourselves. We are not going to have the state sticking its nose into our business." They were cheered by the lobbyists for the oil refineries, the oil companies selling gasoline, the truckers who fouled the air with the exhaust of their diesel fumes, rubber manufacturers, garbage burners, and other elements of the smog culture. The legislators of the rest of the state were not particularly interested because air pollution was not known to be a problem in their districts, and my bill went down the drain without a hearing.

The irony of the situation is that a year or so after I went to Washington, the farmers and dairymen of Southern California became alarmed over what smog was doing to their cattle and hogs. They went to Sacramento, expressed their fears, and asked that an appropriation be voted so the director of agriculture could do the research necessary to determine what harm was being done and what remedies could be applied. With neither debate nor opposition, the appropriation was granted. I have not followed the smog problem in California closely since that time, except to observe that the so-called "local solution" approach was a failure, and that smog is not only a problem of Los Angeles today, but has spread into a statewide menace that plagues the rural as well as the urban areas.

It should be remembered that during these years we were functioning in a war milieu, and we coordinated our activities with that always in mind. We kept ourselves in close contact and usually in harmony with the Civilian Defense and war agencies of the federal government. Each of these federal agencies had representatives stationed in California, and my departments that were related to their activities were instructed to work with them.

Many states took a different approach. They considered the federal agencies as interlopers and clashed continually with them. This was a constant subject of discussion at governors' conferences. On the Pacific Coast, we governors of Washington, Oregon, and California determined to work with them, and held regular meetings at Seattle, Portland, and San Francisco with their federal and our state opposite numbers in all the various wartime management services to coordinate efforts. The governors personally presided at joint meetings and were able to adjust relationships so as to avoid misunderstandings and confrontations that would inevitably have occurred had it not been for such conferences. As a result, my dealings with these federal agencies were as cordial and constructive as could be expected in emergency activities of that kind. These relationships were particularly helpful to us during the reconstruction period following the war, especially in working out our manpower and materials problems.

We took the entire Civilian Defense program seriously and cooperated with the federal government. In fact, we were told that Governor Dewey of New York and I and our Legislatures were the only ones who went along one hundred per cent with the program. We created a State War Council and later State Disaster Council to carry out responsibilities in this regard. We thoroughly organized the law enforcement and fire-fighting resources of the state to meet war-related emergencies and devised a chain of command to make their actions effective. We received high praise for his work. Thankfully we were never required to call up our Civilian Defense forces to action, but I believe if they had been called they would have given a good account of themselves.

In later years I was to be at times amused and at other times irritated by the deterioration of the Federal Civilian Defense Office. It became a shelter for worn-out political figures, and they were only heard from when some cold war exigency arose. The last time in my experience was during the Tonkin Gulf episode, when I was on the Supreme Court.

The Civilian Defense director called and said he had a matter of urgency to discuss with me. We met, and he told me that, in the event of a nuclear air strike against Washington, he was prepared to have me picked up by a helicopter on the courthouse lawn and flown to a Court rendezvous some place in Appalachia. I asked him if all the members of the Court would be so notified, and he said they would be. I then asked him how our papers and records would be taken there. He said we would be obliged to take care of that ourselves. I reminded him that we had no trucks or other equipment to transport them, and it would be impossible for us even to rent any at such a time. I then asked him how our officers and necessary employees would be transported. He said they would be obliged to find their way to the rendezvous. I told him if the highways were clogged they could not be expected to make it. I then called to his attention the fact that we are only at the Court in daylight hours, and asked him how the plan would work if the enemy were uncooperative and the alarm came in the nighttime. He said the plan was only to be in operation from 9 A.M. to 5 P.M. How would we reach the Court if we were not in the Court building at the time, I inquired. He said we would be obliged to arrange that for ourselves in spite of jampacked highways. I then asked him about our wives, and he replied that no provision was being made for them. Exasperated by that time, I said, "Then I suppose I should call my wife and say, 'Honey, there is an atomic bomb attack to be made on Washington, and I am flying to safety in Appalachia. Sorry I don't have time to come home and say good bye, but it is nice to have met you.'" I told him that I didn't know how the other justices would view the situation, but that I would not be fleeing in his helicopter. Strangely, I heard nothing more about the helicopter or anything else from his office after that.

The job of being governor of California was a multifaceted one. To review all of the facets would make this treatise unduly long, so I must telescope some of them which characterized my administration. In a state like California, whose population grew by five million people during my incumbency, a governor never knows when he goes to bed at night what new problem the morrow will bring. It is a challenging experience, and I was never shocked by new difficulties because, being new, they could be attacked with vigor and with hope of solving them as distinguished from old problems that have become rigidly imbedded in society and provoke only frustration. I believe we attacked all the issues that confronted us and made at least some progress on the vast majority of them. I was not discouraged if we failed the first time because I was not approaching them on the basis of an ideology. I was approaching them pragmatically as they arose, realizing that a start should be made and any advance made in the right direction represented progress upon which to build. I also believed in the adage that "The reach should always exceed the grasp," so if we constantly made some advancement by reaching further toward the ultimate solution than we could grasp, we would always be in the process of working out our problems before they became solidified and beyond solution. Approaching jobs in that spirit, my administration finished with the approbation of some for being "liberal," while others contended that it was a façade for conservatism because it did not neatly fit, in all its actions, into some ready-made leftist ideology. Still others of the Right Wing called it a surrender to the New Deal. But the vast majority of the voters approved, and I accepted that as my mandate. I would like to believe it was a progressive administration.

I was often in trouble with the Legislature because of that body's extremists, as one incident will illustrate.

I agreed with President Roosevelt that we should have a means of bringing about fair employment practices to end discrimination against minority groups. Accordingly, at the first session of the Legislature, I advocated the establishment of a commission to determine how, in California, we might accomplish such equality. At that time, no other state had a Fair Employment Commission, and the President's Commission had no statutory powers. I thought that with the right kind of people on a study commission, we might come up with the right answer. My suggestion died aborning. The people who believed in racial and sexual segregation, of course, opposed it as being "the camel's nose in the tent." Those who were militant on the other side insisted on a strong commission with powers to enforce its desegregation mandates. As a consequence, my proposal died with but few friends.

At the next session, I introduced a bill establishing outright a Fair Employment Commission to deal with the subject. It died from the same kind of pressures. The militants rejected it. They then put their own bill on the statewide ballot as an initiative measure with such radical powers that it turned the friends of a proper commission, including me, against it. The people of California overwhelmingly rejected it, and this set the movement back several years. It was not until six years after I left that such a Commission was established in the administration of Governor Pat Brown.

This is only one example of how progress is prevented or retarded. There were others, of course. I was on tenterhooks with the Legislature most of the time. It was lobby-ridden throughout. In fact, both speakers of the Assembly in my time were not only controlled by lobbyists, but were ultimately prosecuted for corruption. One was convicted and sent to the penitentiary. In the case of the other, the jury disagreed at the first trial and acquitted him at the second. The chairman of the Board of Equalization, an independent elective agency with which both speakers were working, fled to Mexico when indicted and lived there until his death a few years ago.

I was continually in conflict with the lobbyists and fought for legislation to curb them. When I had a bill with teeth in it to restrain their activities, they introduced as a diversionary tactic another which contained high-sounding phrases stating the intention of the Legislature to supervise lobbying procedures, but with no enforcement stipulations. The public reaction in favor of my bill was so strong that it could not be stopped. Both houses adopted it, but at the same time they also passed the lobbyists' bill, thinking they might persuade me to sign it instead of my own. After studying the matter with my staff, we decided that I could, without injury to my bill, sign the other one also—provided my bill was signed last, thereby legally giving it precedence in the event of any conflict between the two.

Up to this point, the reader might gain the impression from some of my statements that I recoiled from being a politician or from engaging in politics. But such definitely was not the case.

After being appointed district attorney in 1925, I became engrossed in public service. I derived great satisfaction from my work and soon realized that I was a politician. As the years passed, I became increasingly attached to public affairs and declined opportunities to leave for more lucrative positions in the private sector. I was never embarrassed by being classified as a politician; in fact, I was proud of it, and openly professed to be. I have known many wonderful people in various activities of government on all its levels, and have enjoyed the friendship of many of them. In fact, I always thought less of a person who sought or held public office and asserted that he was not a politician. It manifested a contempt for the very service he was engaged in, and downgraded the government of which he was supposed to be a smooth-working part. Like any other pursuit in life—such as that of a doctor, lawyer, teacher, or clergyman—it can be honorable or dishonorable depending upon individual performance, and it has been my observation that a man who is ashamed of the position he holds is rarely efficient in it.

Throughout my public career, though, I have been somewhat unorthodox in my ways of reaching for support and in geting things done. While such an approach yielded me more satisfaction than orthodoxy would have brought, it also limited some of my horizons. Had I been in one of the other states where strong party organizations existed under a leadership such as that of Tammany Hall or its corresponding number in other states, I doubt if I could have established myself, let alone succeeded to any appreciable degree.

The things that attracted me were the newly won rights of the people under the liberal administration of Hiram W. Johnson, such as nonpartisanship in local government and in the judicial and educational branches of state government; the direct primary supplanting the old convention system; the cross-filing for partisan offices; and the Civil Service. These enlightened procedures enabled a poor man to seek public office without the necessity of mortgaging himself to a political boss, which until 1911 was essential for holding public office in California. They also enabled a man to maintain his independence in the performance of his duties if he chose to do so, and this was of paramount importance to me. In all the political offices I held, I was willing to stand or fall on my record, but the record had to be fashioned by me. I did not intend to be obligated in a financial way to others for my office, and during the times I ran for district attorney, I accepted no campaign contributions from anyone. It was only when I decided to run for attorney general that it became necessary for me to obtain financial support and then it was something like twenty-five or thirty-five thousand dollars for the statewide campaign, and all the the contributions were small. In that election, I had only to make the primary campaign because I then received all three nominations—Republican, Democratic, and Progressive. Today more than that is often spent in a campaign for county supervisor. Even when I ran for governor, my campaigns were financed to the extent of about $175,000 in Southern California and $125,000 in Northern California. Again, individual contributions were not large, and the total was minuscule alongside present-day expenditures for a similar office. For instance, in a recent election in New York, Governor Nelson Rockefeller reported that he had spent six million dollars to be re-elected.

Even after exercising such relative frugality, I was embarrassed once by my finance chairman in Northern California and once by my Southern California chairman, and was required to fight my way free from their attempted influence. As I mentioned earlier, Charles Blythe, the senior partner of Blythe-Witter Co., investment bankers of San Francisco, was one of the three men who urged me to run for governor, and he undertook to secure the finances for my campaign. I was solemnly told that there would be absolutely no obligations to the contributors; that none of them would ever expect anything from me, and that all they were interested in was having an honest governor. I took these statements on faith, and when I decided to run I appointed Blythe chairman of my finance committee. True to their word, he and his colleagues collected, without any solicitation by me, the money necessary for my Northern California campaign. I mention Northern California separately because in those days it was not feasible to have only one campaign. Because of the size and diversity of the state and the less advanced means of communication, it was necessary to have two distinct campaign managements—one in the North, another in the South.

Shortly after my election, I had occasion to fill a vacancy on the then Railroad Commission, now entitled the Public Utilities Commission, and to appoint a chairman of that body. There was at that time nobody on the commission who was familiar with the needs of the cities, such as consumer interest and effective operation of city-owned utilities. Accordingly, I made a quiet search for such a man, and finally selected the city engineer of Palo Alto, a very well managed city where Stanford University is located. His name was Harold G. (Pete) Anderson. He had been with the city for many years, but was still a young man. I had some difficulty in obtaining his acceptance, because of the danger of his losing credit toward retirement for his years of service with the city. After he was shown that credit for those years could be transferred to the State Retirement System, he accepted. I announced his appointment, and named him chairman of the commission.

Immediately I received a furious telephone call from Charles Blythe saying, "Earl, what are you doing to me?"

"What do you mean, Charley?" I asked.

"Don't you know that I am particularly interested in the Railroad Commission and should have been consulted on appointments to it?" he replied indignantly.

I told him that I had not known of his great interest in it, and besides he had assured me that he would never ask me for anything, and would expect me "to call things as I saw them," which was exactly what I had done. It was not a pleasant conversation, but I thought I had made my position sufficiently clear to terminate the matter. However, this was not to be. Very shortly thereafter, the Pacific Telephone and Telegraph Company announced the sale of a fifty-two-million-dollar bond issue, and sought the required approval of the Railroad Commission. A syndicate was required to handle the bond issue, and Mr. Blythe apparently was to be the head of the syndicate. However, another investment firm sought an opportunity to bid on that stewardship, and made a formal request of the commission to award the job only after competitive bids in accordance with the practice of the Securities Exchange and Interstate Commerce Commission. It developed that in the past our commission had awarded such syndication to Charles Blythe automatically, without bids or competition of any kind. When my new chairman, Anderson, manifested an interest in competitive bidding, Blythe again angrily telephoned me and said, "Earl, you can't do this to me. You know that is my domain. I have handled these bond issues for years, and no one has been hurt. Everybody is satisfied with the way I arrange them."

I told him it was a matter for the commission to handle, and I was sure that Anderson would be fair in the way he did it. Blythe was furious, and the conversation terminated. People then started talking to Chairman Anderson and telling him, "You can't do that. Don't you know that Charley Blythe was the governor's finance chairman?" After hearing much of this talk, Pete came to Sacramento and told me about it. I said, "If you let that kind of pressure sway you, you are not the man I thought you were when I appointed you. You just follow your conscience, and you can't go wrong." He did so, called for competitive bids, and saved the consumers two million dollars. Blythe then called me up, said I was ungrateful and he was through with me. I told him I was going to be impartial in the present case and in the future. He really was through with me, and, for the remaining years of my governorship, was busily grooming my lieutenant governor to run against me.

I ran into another situation in the South after my second election in 1946. Some of my friends suggested that I name Mr. Lee Battson, an extremely wealthy Los Angeles man, as my finance chairman. He was a highly respected man, and I did so. He told me he knew nothing about politics, and didn't want any part of it. I am sure he was telling the truth but, like many other men who collect money in political campaigns, he too assumed a possessive attitude toward his successful candidate. He had ten shares of stock in the Santa Anita Race Track, the largest and most powerful horse racing interest in California. This financial interest was a mere bagatelle to him, but he was a close personal friend of Dr. Charles Strub, the driving force of Santa Anita, and Strub wanted to dominate the policies of the State Racing Board as well as his own track. When there was a vacancy on the Board, Strub, of course, had a candidate, and he had Lee Battson suggest him to me. I could not turn the Racing Commission over to Dr. Strub, so I refused to accept his candidate. I then appointed a man whom I had good reason to believe would not be dominated by Dr. Strub. In doing so, I lost the friendship of Battson, as I had that of Blythe in San Francisco, and for years thereafter he never spoke to me.

Because of these and other experiences demonstrating the influence brought to bear as a result of campaign contributions, I have long been concerned about the future of our governmental institutions if we continue to solicit the enormous sums that have become the norm in all sorts of elections. Our institutions cannot serve their true purpose if they are subverted by the power of money pumped into campaigns or raised to make up deficits.

VIII

I was active in politics throughout my years as governor, but in my
own way. I campaigned as hard as anyone. I tried to please my constituents by working on their problems incessantly, but I gave little time to
political management. I tried to make this clear by stating publicly that
I wanted to be the governor of California—not its political boss. I had
no permanent organization of my own, nor did I rely for election on
any other political body. I took no part in city or county politics, but
endeavored to cooperate in governmental matters with the constituted
authorities regardless of their party allegiance. In campaigns, I believed
in the efficacy of volunteers and built a volunteer force for every campaign, disbanding them with thanks after the election.

I even found it unnecessary to become involved in many state elections because, under our direct primary and cross-filing systems, practically all the candidates for state office sought both the Republican and
Democratic nominations. This eliminated in California the straight
party ticket that characterizes elections in so many states. Also, the fact
that candidates registered in one party were also interested in garnering

votes from the other party in the primaries reduced partisan tensions, and made campaigning largely a personal enterprise. This suited me perfectly, and I profited greatly from it. The Legislature was organized on a bipartisan basis. Members of both parties served as committee chairmen, and the officers were elected with bipartisan support. This relieved me of the responsibility of trying to elect a straight ticket of Republicans and permitted me to run an independent campaign, as did the other state officers and the legislators.

I never tried to purge anyone from office, regardless of how unfriendly they might have been to my administration, and took no part in the organization of the Legislature. There were many times, of course, when I would have been happy to have a more cooperative group in Sacramento, but I was sure that in the long run it would be much better for me to maintain the separation of powers contemplated by the Constitution than to be dependent on a personal or trading relationship. When it comes to a trading game, the Legislature holds most of the cards, and with the aid of the lobbyists can use them devastatingly.

But, as usual, there was another side to the coin, and that was the side of national politics. That called for a little different kind of treatment. While I was attorney general, it was easy for me to remain free from any connection with national politics, and I did so. But when I was elected governor as a Republican, things changed. One of our U.S. senators at that time was a Democrat, and Hiram Johnson, after twenty-five years in the Senate, had no interest in state politics. The leadership of the party, therefore, fell inadvertently to me. I had but one choice; namely, to accept it or to disassociate myself from all connection with it. To do the latter would have been tantamount to throwing away my base of operations, because it was necessary to have a partisan affiliation to compete in any primary election for governor, and under the law it was necessary for any candidate to have the nomination of his own party if his name was to appear on the ballot at the final election. In these circumstances, I informally assumed, without challenge, a moderate leadership by encouraging Republican activities and maintaining an interest in who became Republican state chairman, and in the composition and commitment of the California delegation to the Republican National Convention. I spent little time on these activities, and declined all efforts to project me into the national picture through out-of-state partisan speeches or involvement with political organizations in other states. This was not an easy thing to do, inasmuch as—at the time of my first election—there were only six Republican governors in the United States. The election of Tom Dewey in New York and myself in California was taken as something of a resurgence

of the party, and I had invitations to speak in many states. I declined
them. Dewey was the outstanding candidate for the presidential nomination in 1944, and many politicians believed that I should be his running mate. No matter how vigorously I denied any such desire or intention, the talk persisted. When I decided to enter a state delegation in
the Republican presidential primary, nominally committed to me but
with an announcement having been made that I was not a candidate
and that the delegation was free to vote for any other candidate, speculation about my being the vice-presidential candidate intensified.

The delegation was elected without opposition. The National Committee then invited me to be temporary chairman, and keynote speaker
at the National Convention in Chicago. When I accepted, it became
almost a consensus that I would be the vice-presidential candidate, in
spite of my continued assertions to the contrary. Dewey's principal opponent was Senator John W. Bricker, formerly governor of Ohio. He
and Senator Robert Taft alternated with each other as candidates from
Ohio. Taft was in the embroilment of 1940 with Dewey and Wendell
Willkie, in which the latter blitzed the convention and took the nomination. Nineteen forty-four was, therefore, Bricker's turn. Ohio, being a
large and influential state and the producer of other Presidents and
nominees, considered itself ordained to habitually produce Presidents.

However, I do not believe that Senator Bricker really thought he had
a chance to be nominated for the presidency, as he visited me in
Sacramento before the convention to inquire if I was in earnest in saying that I had no intention of being the vice-presidential nominee. He
said the reason he wanted to know was that if I would not accept the
nomination, he would like to have it. I assured him I could not accept
it, for a reason I had often publicly expressed, and which was simply explained:

In running for the governorship only two years before, I had argued
that the incumbent governor was not sufficiently alerted to the part our
state should play in the defense of our nation or to the problems that
would confront us in the postwar period. I said I wanted to be the wartime governor to prove that such things could be managed more
efficiently, and I promised, if elected, to devote my waking hours for
four years to getting them done. To seek election to a national position
less than two years later would be a breach of faith which I could not
justify.

After I made the convention's keynote speech, it was more or less
generally assumed that when the pressure was really applied I would accept. Even my own California delegation believed that I would and
should relent. On the day of the vice-presidential nomination, Tom
Dewey, already nominated, spent the better part of an hour endeavor-

ing to convince me of the desirability of my being his running mate. When I stuck to my position, he eventually accepted Senator Bricker, who was nominated that evening.

I returned to my job and carried on in the same low key in so far as national politics was concerned. I focused heavily on my gubernatorial duties along the lines just indicated, and at the 1946 election received the nominations of both the Republican and Democratic parties, thus relieving me of any contest at the final election. Time passed speedily, and it was not long before another presidential election came along. This time it was another contest between Dewey and Taft.

At the solicitation of my friends, I entered a slate of delegates pledged to me as a favorite son candidate, but with the statement that I was not seeking delegates from other states, and that my delegates would be released after the first ballot. This was done, and their votes were cast for Tom Dewey, who was nominated. This time, I suppose on account of my refusal to run in 1944, my name was not much in the news as a possible vice-presidential candidate. Charles Halleck, minority leader in the House of Representatives, and Harold Stassen, then president of the University of Pennsylvania, were the names most mentioned. I never gave a thought to the matter because I did not cherish the idea of merely presiding over the Senate as an only constitutional duty, nor was I anxious to leave California, where life and the people had been so good to me.

The night before the morning session that was to nominate a vice-president, I went to bed about midnight, and was awakened from a sound sleep about 2:30 A.M. by a ring of the telephone. Tom Dewey was on the line. He asked me if I could come to his hotel headquarters. After dressing, I went directly there. He was waiting for me, and told me that earlier he had gathered together a number of Republican leaders from distant parts of the nation. They were agreed that I should be his running mate, if I would accept, and he said that would please him also. He told me he could understand why I would not relish merely presiding over the Senate, and that if I accepted and we were elected, he would make the job meaningful by having the vice-presidency play an important role in his administration. We talked the matter over for a half hour or so, and also some of the family problems involved in such a move. Finally I told him I would accept.

Things were different for me than in 1944. I had fulfilled my commitment to the electorate after serving six years. There were only two years left on my second term, and two four-year terms are normally all any governor serves. I did not wish to be a senator or a cabinet officer. There were no other public positions that I looked forward to, and, liking public service as I did, it seemed as though this might be a satisfactory way of topping off a public career. I was then fifty-eight years of age.

I walked back to my hotel, awakened my wife, Nina, at daybreak, and told her the news. I am sure she was stunned, but characteristically she made no complaint, in keeping with her practice of not trying to direct or interfere with any of my political affairs. Her concern was always for my happiness. However, she doubted whether I could be happy with Tom Dewey directing my activities. She was as interested in my independence as I had been through the years, and she considered this a potential inroad on it.

The next morning when the nominations were to be made, Nina and my three daughters went to the Convention Hall. I remained in my hotel. I was told that Harold Stassen was also to be put in nomination. However, this did not happen, and I was nominated by acclamation. I was summoned to the convention for the acceptance and hurriedly went there I had no speech prepared, and I remember opening with the statement, "Now I know how it feels to get hit by a streetcar." One of the columnists said facetiously that he was sure I meant "a streetcar named desire," after the title of a Broadway hit of the day.

That evening I called Sacramento to talk to our boys. Bobby, then twelve, answered the call. I said, "Hello, Bob."

"Hello, Dad."

"How are you?"

"I'm fine. How are you?"

"Fine," I said, "did you hear what happened here in Philadelphia today?"

"What?"

"I was nominated for the vice-presidency."

After a pause, he responded, "Is that good?"

Notwithstanding my wife's misgivings and Bobby's doubts, we played the game throughout. Nina and I were on one whistle-stop campaign train steadily for over a month. We had a special car on the end, from the rear platform of which I talked at eight or ten stops each day. At each of these stations, we would take on some of the local VIPs, with whom I visited between stations. In addition, I was compelled to write a speech to deliver each night in some different auditorium. This I was obliged to do in something of a vacuum. Governor Dewey turned over to me one of his state speech writers for whom he had no place in his campaign, and the National Committee sent me two Hollywood writers who were pleasant fellows but whose forte was writing gags, and I never used Hollywood gags in any of my political speeches All of my people had their own jobs to attend to, so I was stuck with having to prepare a formal address for every night except Sundays. It was quite a grind. In addition, I was entirely separated from the main campaign. As far as I can recall, I only talked to Tom Dewey twice while I was on that train—once when we were in Buffalo, New York, the home of his principal state organizer, whom he considered one of the best in the business. When I was in this aide's city, he was conveniently out of town. He left a small committee to take care of me, and at that night's meeting, in a hall that would hold eight hundred to a thousand people, easily a fifth of the seats were empty. Although I had never had more than a passing acquaintance with the absent head man, I have an idea that he felt neither of us was enamored of the other, and he simply left me to my own devices. I was really provoked. I called Tom, who was in California, and told him, as I remember, "That is a hell of a way to run a railroad." He said he was sorry, and it would be different in New York City. And it was. We were given a rousing cheer both on arriving at and leaving from Grand Central Station, and I spoke to a good crowd at Carnegie Hall.

We had fair crowds throughout our trip, and the people were friendly but without enthusiasm. And so it was on the Dewey part of the campaign. I can understand this because we really didn't talk to the issues currently important to the communities we covered. All of Dewey's speeches were written and ready for delivery before the convention. A few days after the convention, I was invited to the Governor's Mansion in Albany. Senator William F. Knowland, the chairman of our delegation, went with me. We were told the number of major speeches Dewey would make, the subjects and dates of each, and where each one would be delivered. The text for them was already prepared. In addition to this, we were briefed on the manner in which the campaign was to be conducted, and then were left to our portion of it. After Governor Dewey delivered one of these speeches, if he was asked about the subject matter by the press in another city, his stock answer was, "I refer you to my speech on that subject in such-and-such city on October so-and-so."

When he came to California and toured the great Central Valley of the Sacramento and San Joaquin rivers, where people are particularly interested in the manner of development of the water and power of those rivers, he was pressed for an answer as to particular phases of that project. His only reply was to refer them to his speech on water conservation made, I believe, in Oklahoma some weeks before. Some of the press was greatly annoyed, and the McClatchy newspapers, which cover the valley, took the position that they could not support Dewey unless he were more outspoken about his water and power policies. Up to that time, they had inclined toward his election. I called Tom on the telephone and suggested that he discuss the matter with the California press. He refused to do so, but said, "You tell them what you think the policy should be, and I will stick with you on it." I told him they knew what my policies were, but they wanted to know from him what his were. He was adamant, and he lost the state by less than one vote per precinct—about 18,000—but we lost the Central Valley alone by about 200,000 votes.

Nationwide, the press referred to the Dewey campaign as being "tailor-made." It was, indeed, tailor-made, but tailored to fit people of any age, any size, any place, under any circumstances. Naturally, it didn't fit snugly for most. On the other hand, his Democratic rival, President Truman, went out to talk with people about issues they were interested in. He and they communicated, and Truman won. The thrust of his campaign was against the Republican 80th Congress. Dewey defended it, but it was not a popular issue from his standpoint, particularly in the Middle West, where President Truman was able to put the blame on Congress for not arranging for storage space for the farmers' grain crops.

Almost everyone thought Dewey and I would win the election. The pollsters went overboard in their predictions to that effect. Elmo Roper announced about October 1 that a Republican victory was so certain he would discontinue his poll-taking for the remainder of the campaign. When I returned to California, I was told by those in charge that they had closed our headquarters in San Francisco and other cities. This was almost two weeks before the election. I inquired why this had been done, and was told that there was nothing to fight, that the Democrats had no campaign organization, that most of the leaders had deserted the President, and that the Republicans would not contribute any more money toward a foregone conclusion. I expressed my disapproval of this premature action, but it was too late to reopen the various headquarters or rekindle enthusiasm in the disbanded campaign forces. I knew this was dangerous and did my best to counteract it by touring the state and speaking several times each day until the night before the election. We closed the campaign in Oakland, where I had started my political career and where I was still considered to be a favorite. The meeting was in the Oakland auditorium, which accommodated about four thousand people. Although I spoke confidently and for the first time in the campaign said that we would win, I had a strange feeling of doubt when I noticed that there were a few hundred empty seats. I knew that if my friends were truly aroused, we would have packed the auditorium.

The only person who ever expressed real doubt about our election was my wife. About the time we were returning to California from our extended rail trip, she said to me, "Honey, do you really think you will win this election?"

"Oh, I think so. Why do you ask?"

"I don't want to see you hurt," she replied, "but I don't believe you will win this one."

I inquired why, and she said the campaign was not arousing the enthusiasm of the people. It was strange she would have felt that way when everyone else was so sure we would succeed, as I had been in a dozen or so campaigns during our married life and never once before had she expressed such doubts. All the prior campaigns had been successful. It must have been woman's intuition. Nina never engaged in political activities and yet was very sensitive about them in a "feeling" rather than analytical way. We tried to keep our home life detached from my political life. She would go with me to an occasional meeting where it did not disrupt home routines, but she never made a speech, and I am sure she never asked anyone to vote for me for any position.

I can say the same for my children. None of them ever made a political speech for me, but on one occasion I almost gave my daughter Virginia heart failure. I was campaigning in the Wisconsin primaries in 1952, and Virginia accompanied me on the trip when I spoke in the field house of the University of Wisconsin. The place was filled with students. When I was introduced, they commenced chanting, "We want Virginia. We want Virginia."

They kept repeating it while I was waiting to begin my speech. Finally I raised my hand and they permitted me to say, "All right, if Virginia is going to get all the applause, let her make the speech." I then sat down, and my poor daughter almost died. That was followed by a great roar of approval, but as I stood again at the rostrum they permitted me to speak. I carried that congressional district with its two delegates to the Republican National Convention, but I have always had the suspicion that more of them voted for Virginia than for me.

I believe the only one of my children to ask anyone to vote for me was Jim when he was about seven years old. He and his mother were boarding a streetcar when he stopped to ask the motorman to vote for me for district attorney. Unfortunately, the election had been held some weeks before.

Although none of my family made speeches or solicited votes for me, I always considered them my secret weapons. And I believe my opponents did also, for they often said, "We know how to beat Earl Warren, but how are you going to beat that family?" I do not know anyone who got more political mileage from a family that never engaged in politics.

The girls always were ready to attend all the national political conventions and governors' conferences, and did join Mrs. Warren and me on all of them. They took no official part but were usually "adopted" by the people of the news media, and that made life very pleasant for them. They were photographed for the press and television more than I was.

My boys, on the other hand, could not have cared less about such affairs, and never attended one as far as I can remember, although they were always invited. The invitations and the declinations became a family ritual. On each occasion, I would say at the dinner table, "Fellows, Mother and I are going to the Governors' Conference (or Republican National Convention, as the case might be). The girls have said they would like to go, and if you would care to go also, we would be happy to have you." This would be followed by a brief silence and an exchange of glances, after which one of them would say, "Dad, we would like to go, but we promised Sturmer White (or some other school friend) that we would go fishing with him this summer, and that is the only time he can go." I would then rejoin, "Well, of course, you can't go back on an agreement like that. Perhaps you can go with us another time."

Their mother and I understood their lack of interest in such matters, and did not care to press them. I am sure they went fishing or hunting on such occasions because I raised them to be outdoor boys, and they have never lost interest in those activities. Unlike their father, they are excellent shots and fishermen, and whenever I am in California some of my most satisfying times occur when the four of us, with Wallace Lynn, a long-time friend, hunt ducks on his ranch in the Sacramento Valley or go fishing off Mexico in the Gulf of California.

The 1948 election was a close one from the standpoint of presidential electors. A slight change in three key states would have put the Dewey ticket ahead of President Truman and would have thrown the election into the House of Representatives. President Truman had 303 electoral votes, Dewey 189. Truman carried Illinois (28 electoral votes) by 33,612 votes, California (25 electoral votes) by 17,865, and Ohio (25 electoral votes) by 7,107. His total plurality in those three states with 78 electoral votes was 58,584. Had 29,292 people, half that number, voted for Dewey instead of Truman, the latter's number of electoral votes would have been reduced by 78 to 225, and Dewey's increased by the same number to 267. Neither would have been elected, because Senator Thurmond had 39 electoral votes, thus depriving anyone of a majority. In such circumstances, the election procedure moves into the House of Representatives, where each state has one vote. However, close though it was, Truman had a clear majority, and, in accordance with a trite saying in the world of sports, "They pay off according to the scoreboard." It was a great personal victory for the underdog President because so many prominent Democrats had deserted him during the race.

After breakfast at the hotel the next morning, the press asked me to come downstairs for an interview. I did so, and their spokesman said, "Governor, have you an opinion as to why President Truman won?" I said, "Yes." And they inquired, "Would you mind telling us what it is?" "Certainly not; he got more votes than we did." "Thank you, Governor." Charitably, they asked no more questions. I then assembled the family and we returned to Sacramento. One or two of the children were crestfallen, but the others took my defeat in stride, and even appeared relieved. I went immediately to my office, sent a telegram of congratulations to President Truman, and went back to work. This was my customary way of relaxing after a strenuous campaign rather than to lie in the sun at some summer resort. It was my belief that I could better return to normal by a mere change of activities.

Soon after, I received a telegram from the Democratic state chairman telling me that Vice-President-elect Alben Barkley was arriving in Los Angeles the next day and asking if I would like to welcome him at an airport reception. I replied that Mrs. Warren, my daughter Virginia, and I would be happy to do so. They erected some bleachers, a platform to accommodate about fifty VIPs, and arranged for a motorcade into the city. Occurring so soon after the election, the program was not well organized. Only a few people were in the stands, and not more than a dozen, including my party, were on the platform. So many of the Democratic leaders had tuned out on the President that I suspected they were too embarrassed to come. Or it might have been due to a lack of advertising. At all events, the audience consisted mainly of tourists at the airport. The Vice-President-elect and I offered a story or two and an exchange of pleasantries. And that was the reception. The only prominent Democrats I remember as being there were Mrs. Helen Gahagan Douglas and Jimmy Roosevelt. Before the Democratic National Convention, the latter had started a move to draft General Eisenhower for the nomination.

I didn't see Tom Dewey until the Gridiron Club Dinner in Washington about March. He was the speaker for the Republicans. He was more relaxed, genial, humorous, and even folksy than I had ever seen him. I have often thought that if he had displayed a little humor in a relaxed way during his successive campaigns, as he did that night at the Gridiron Club, he might have become President.

There were two minor incidents of that campaign that come to mind. Had they not occurred, the outcome might have differed. In that year, at the time of the Governors' Conference, Dewey was smarting from a disagreement he was having with the teachers in his state. In one of the executive sessions, he made a proposal to raise $150,000 to investigate the teachers' lobby throughout the nation. He insisted that it was the most noxious of all the lobbies, and that it should be exposed by the Governors' Conference. I opposed his suggestion, stating that in California it was more in the public interest than the vast majority of lobbies, and that it would be unwise for us to make a national issue of it and leave unscathed some of the more predatory lobbyists. His motion failed to pass, and because it had been discussed in a closed session, it received no publicity. In our private discussions, he asked me why I was always fighting with the lobbyists in my state, and I told him they wanted to direct the policies of our state government, which I felt was my job, not theirs. He said, "Well, why don't you just call them in, tell them what the policy is, and tell them to conform to it?" I asked if that was what he did, and he said it was. I asked him if they conformed, and he said they did. My response was that if they complied it was because he told them to do only what he knew they were willing to do. This he denied emphatically, and I then asked him if he had ever encountered the oil lobby. He said, "No, but if I ever do, they will get exactly the same treatment as the others." My reply was, "That remains to be seen."

This all sounds as if we were quarreling, but not so. It was part of several friendly and pleasant conversations we had, usually over a sociable drink at the conference.

The point of this story, and evidence that Tom developed a sense of humor after 1948—too late to humanize his campaigns—became apparent one morning two or three years later when I received a telephone call from him at my office in Sacramento. He said, "Earl, do you remember our conversations about the lobbyists in our states?"

"Yes, I do."

"Do you remember what I told you I would do to the oil lobby if I ever tangled with it?"

I replied that I did, and he said, "Well, I was a damned liar. I have a gas tax bill in the Legislature, and the oil lobby just beat hell out of me a few minutes ago."

To return to the teachers' lobby incident, although there was no publicity at the time, someone eventually leaked the story, and Drew Pearson wrote it with flourishes during the campaign, pointing out the difference of opinion between Dewey and me on the subject. I am sure Dewey lost a great number of votes as a result of it because the teachers in California were angry at him, as were many of the Parent-Teachers Associations, and there was like sentiment in those circles in other states. Yet his antilobby stand was not a true reflection of his feelings. He was not antagonistic to the educational process or to teachers themselves. He was merely petulant over some differences between their lobbyists and himself on legislative matters in his state.

The other incident was a very minor one, but I have no doubt that it had a severe impact on voters. As the Dewey campaign train was at one of its whistle stops and the governor was talking, the engineer, in testing the air brakes or for some other reason, gave the train a sudden jerk that unsettled everyone. Dewey impulsively said to the crowd, "They should take that engineer out and shoot him at sunrise." He did not mean that, of course. It was simply an emotional figure of speech, a cliché. Nevertheless, it was a most unfortunate utterance, because it was given wide publicity, and I have no doubt that many people in all parts of the country took it into consideration in making their appraisal of him for the presidency.

I never felt as though I was making any great contribution. I was entirely detached from the main campaign, traveling hurriedly through state after state with which I had no familiarity, and with little guidance. I was so busy making informal whistle-stop talks, visiting with local Republican leaders between stations, and writing a speech for every evening that I had no time for reflection on the progress of the campaign. I was dog-tired most of the time, and I am sure my speeches reflected it, lacking either fervor or stimulation. I was speaking not for myself but for Tom Dewey, and was always conscious of the necessity of avoiding anything that might conflict with his policies.

The result of this election caused the Hearst newspapers in California—and others who were grooming my lieutenant governor, Goodwin J. Knight, to oust me from the governorship—to increase their pressure and proclaim my political demise. As already stated, when the chips were down, Knight abandoned his quest and filed again for his own lieutenant governor's position. The leading Democrat running for governor was James Roosevelt. I cross-filed and, in the primary election, in addition to receiving practically all the Republican votes, I was given 1,000,000 to Roosevelt's 1,100,000 on the Democratic ticket. The final election was almost a carbon copy of the primary, and I won by more than 1,100,000. I might not have run for a third term had it not been for the intransigence of the lieutenant governor. His insistence that I was not a sound administrator and his criticism of my programs led me to believe that he would not have completed my postwar plans even if he could have defeated Mr. Roosevelt, which I doubted. The plans I had made during the war for peacetime reconstruction were being effectuated but had not been completed. We had saved hundreds of millions of dollars for such necessities as hospitals, universities, colleges, and highways, and I could not abide their dissipation by anyone who would not support the policy of "pay as you go."

Again, I had no idea how a third term would be looked upon by the voters because we had had only one two-term governor, Hiram Johnson, in almost a hundred years.

After my re-election as governor in 1950, I continued to stick close to my own job. I made no sorties into other states for political purposes. It was not until some time in 1951 that I gave any real thought to the national situation. I knew that Senator Robert Taft was to be a presidential candidate. He was a perpetual eager runner and made no secret of it. I felt that General Eisenhower would be a candidate also. In 1948, I was told by President Hoover that the general was willing to accept a draft, and that his supporters had a "warehouse" full of campaign materials with which to blitz the convention if the opportunity presented itself. I have no knowledge of the accuracy of this statement, but later, at Bohemian Club encampments where the general was a guest and very popular, the story was current that he had asked people if they thought he could obtain both party nominations. When Tom Dewey announced that General Eisenhower was his candidate, I felt rather sure that Ike would be in the race. Bill Keck, the president of the Superior Oil Company, a vitriolic multimillionaire, was making moves to thwart any delegation I might enter in the primaries, so I took stock of the situation. If his or any other group should elect a delegation, it would align itself with the Republican machinery, and I would become a political nonentity. I therefore came to the conclusion that I would enter a delegation. Some of my friends advised me that unless I announced myself as an actual candidate, I would be accused of running an undercover delegation for one or the other of the principal candidates. I followed their advice, and announced myself as a candidate, though I did so with some trepidation, not because I would be unwilling to be the presidential nominee, but because I thought that while my nonpartisan state administration was a source of great strength in California, it limited my horizon because the other states, with strong party organizations, were not favorable to such politics. Up to that time, I had made no bid for delegates in any other state, and there was no group working for me in any of them. My only chance would be if the two leading candidates would deadlock, and neither concede to the other. I knew that Taft would have a large number because he was always strong in the Southern and Midwestern states, and I was sure that, with Tom Dewey running the fight for the general, they, too, would have a very large block. Harold Stassen, the only other candidate and a former governor of Minnesota, would probably also have a few votes tied up. With our large delegation, a deadlock in the convention might develop, and if it did I could become the beneficiary of it. That was a very outside chance, but it was a chance and I took it without burning ambition or expectation of success. I knew that, having announced in California, I would automatically be put on the ticket in Oregon. In order to give my candidacy a little national publicity, I filed in Wisconsin, one of the earliest of the primary states. I had no connections there, but shortly after my announcement, the well-known LaFollette family declared for me and was most helpful throughout. Senator Taft again was the leading candidate in that state. The other was Harold Stassen. Both of them spent a month campaigning every day, and Taft had the state Republican Party organization behind him. We had a budget session at the time, and I remained with the Legislature in Sacramento every week from Monday through Thursday. Then I would fly to Milwaukee every Thursday evening to campaign Friday and Saturday, returning on Sunday. This was my routine throughout the campaign. It was the middle of winter, and about a third of the time the snow was too deep for me to travel to the outlying places I had committed myself to visit. I spent practically nothing on the campaign except my travel expenses. I had no idea I would do very well, but to my surprise I carried the two congressional districts in Milwaukee and the district which includes Madison, the capital. That gave me six delegates to the convention. Senator Taft took the rest, but I only lost the total vote by twenty-six thousand, and I feel sure that if I had spent a little money and had done some more solid campaigning I could have carried the state without difficulty. The Taft people were so angry at the result that they banished my six delegates and would not even make hotel reservations for them at the convention. We made other arrangements.

After that election, I commuted to Oregon in much the same manner. The only other candidate there was General Eisenhower. He had all the state organization and officialdom as well as the money. It was no contest. He won overwhelmingly—about 2½ to 1 as I recall it. I didn't expect any better, because I spent no money and had no organization. To show they were not unfriendly to me, they voted for me for Vice-President.

When I entered our own primary in California, my determined enemy Keck, having failed to induce any of the other candidates to enter, filed an uninstructed delegation pledged to Thomas Werdel, the congressman from my boyhood city of Bakersfield. It was an extreme right-wing and oil-oriented ticket. Keck and Werdel made a bitter campaign of it, charging me with all kinds of derelictions. They poured a vast amount of money into their effort, particularly in the southern part of the state. Earl Behrens, the political editor of the San Francisco *Chronicle* and dean of the political correspondents at the capital, wrote that they spent a million dollars in Southern California alone. They reccived a substantial vote there, actually carrying Orange County, immediately south of Los Angeles, but did very little in the remainder of the state. In order not to dignify their effort too much, I made a very modest countercampaign consisting of a few speeches, and spent very little money.

When we were selecting our delegation, Senator Richard Nixon, through the intercession of Kyle Palmer, political editor of the Los Angeles *Times*, asked to be a delegate and to participate in the selection of the other members. We consented to having his representative, Bernard Brennan, sit in with us. We made certain that the vast majority of the delegates was loyal to me, but we permitted Brennan to name six or seven of Senator Nixon's stalwart supporters in addition to the senator himself. The entire delegation was then pledged to me. Palmer and Brennan both said it would please the senator very much if we would permit Nixon's campaign aide, Murray Chotiner, to manage a section of the special train we had engaged to take us to Chicago, the seat of the convention. It was understood that he was to have nothing to do with political matters, but would merely arrange the physical details of the trip. He had considerable experience in such matters, and I acceded to that request.

As the campaign was nearing its end, Palmer told me that Senator Nixon had taken a poll among several thousand of his supporters and was intending to announce that a majority of them expressed a preference for General Eisenhower. I told Palmer that was not consistent with the oath that all the delegates had taken to support my candidacy. He said he agreed, and that he had so told the senator. He expressed the hope that Nixon's announcement would not be published, and as far as I know it was not.

The delegation gathered at Sacramento and boarded the special train for the convention. I believe all were present except Nixon, who sent word that he had conflicting engagements in the East. The delegation elected Senator William Knowland its chairman and agreed to the unit rule; that is, they would vote as a unit until and unless released by me. We then boarded the train, and had a pleasant and congenial trip. The night before we arrived at Chicago, Senator Nixon got aboard. He paid his respects to me and said if any of his friends got out of line to let him know. He then visited throughout the train. I do not remember if I saw him again before he left us prior to our arriving in Chicago. Anyway, during the night, the Nixon delegates—but not the senator as far as I know—held caucuses and urged other delegates to vote for General Eisenhower on the first ballot. Some of those who were importuned came to me and asked what the situation was. I told them what I had told the voters: that the delegation was not a front for anyone, and that no matter what happened it was obligated to vote for me on the first ballot at least.

Shortly after my arrival, I visited their hotels and paid my respects to Senator Taft and General Eisenhower. Imagine my surprise when the doorkeeper who admitted me to the general's suite was Murray Chotiner, one of the managers of my train. It was a very close contest between the general and Senator Taft; in fact, I was of the opinion that the senator might have had a bare majority a few days before the final vote was taken. The Taft forces were in complete control of the convention, and it was hardly possible for any but that group to speak. The Republican national chairman of New Jersey was so partisan for Taft that the Taft supporters dominated seating arrangements as well as speakers.

Senator Everett Dirksen and Senator Joe McCarthy made bitter speeches, particularly Dirksen, who treated Tom Dewey, the 1948 standard-bearer, as though he were a pickpocket. As a small example of how arrogant they were, they seated my wife and three daughters in the last row in the farthest corner of the auditorium. It was not until some of the press corps sought my family out for pictures and a complaint was made that they were given reasonable seats. I have always felt that the despotic manner in which the convention was run lost Senator Taft a sizable number of votes and possibly the nomination.

Speculation about the closeness of the contest was so great that it was generally conceded that if our large California delegation were to throw its vote to either Taft or Eisenhower it would determine the issue. There were stories to the effect that, if needed, the Nixon people could accomplish that result. My only statement was that the California delegation would vote for me on the first ballot and then we would survey the situation to see what our future course would be.

The day before the presidential nominations, Senator Taft came to me and told me how much he wanted the vote of my delegation. He said, "This is my last chance." I told him that the California delegation would vote for me. He then replied that either he or Eisenhower would be the nominee. I said that might well be true, but I had told the people of California how my delegation would vote, and that would be done. He asked if there wasn't something I would like in the Administration. He said I could have anything I desired; that there was only one thing that could cause any embarrassment, which was that General Douglas MacArthur wanted the vice-presidency. But he could even take care of that, he said. I told him I wanted no job; that I could go back to California and be happy with the governorship. He then said, "Well, Bill Knowland can have anything he wants." I said, "No, Senator, we will go ahead as we promised." With that he left. I was not particularly enamored of Taft as a candidate. He was an able man, but his sensitivity to human relations was not appealing to me. I doubted if he could be elected President. I could not forget that in 1948, when I was going around the country campaigning by train and we were about to arrive in his home city of Cincinnati, I received a telegram saying he would not be there to see me because he was going to Columbus to attend a meeting of the Republican State Committee. I thought nothing of that, but when we arrived at the railroad station in Cincinnati and there was not a single Republican Party official to meet us, I was really burned up. Of the hundreds of places, large and small, at which we had stopped, Cincinnati was the only city at which there was no one to welcome the vice-presidential candidate's train.

Also, I remember a time in the fall of 1951 when I had a serious operation for abdominal cancer. I didn't advertise the reason for the operation because I would have been a lame duck from then on. They did remove a few feet of my intestines, but the doctors gave me a written report telling what my condition had been, describing what was done to correct it, and assuring me that there was no malignancy left in my system. After a few weeks of convalescence, I was again in harness and recovered my good health. But Dr. Dwight Murray of Napa, the erstwhile Stone Age president of the American Medical Association, and his cohorts called a special session of the AMA before our primary election in order to show their preference for Senator Taft by having him make the speech at the meeting.

At that gathering, word was bootlegged to the doctors present that I was dying of cancer. And thereafter the Taft organizers, though not the senator as far as I know, spread the word throughout the country. I was even told by one of President Hoover's closest friends that, at a dinner with thirty or forty national figures present, Hoover, being an ardent Taft supporter, said, "You don't have to be concerned about Warren. I know the doctors who operated on him. They opened him up, took a look, and sewed him up again." The implications of that kind of story were well understood.

On the first ballot for the presidential nomination, General Eisenhower was short of a majority by only nine votes. Although it was obvious that he would obtain the few that were needed, I refused to release ours for that purpose. I wanted the record kept straight that I would not turn our delegation over to another candidate and would not permit anyone else to do so. Harold Stassen of Minnesota then turned his twelve delegates over to General Eisenhower, who was thereby nominated.

Senator Knowland was a close political friend of Senator Taft, but he was perfectly loyal to me as chairman of the delegation, and held it together as a solid unit throughout. Subsequently, I have often wondered if Senator Taft had not also told Knowland that if our delegation would vote for Taft, he could have anything he desired in the Administration. Being senator from California, the only thing Knowland possibly could have been interested in was the vice-presidency. Had he accepted such an offer and been elected, he would have become President of the United States, because within a year Senator Taft died. I mention this because thereafter my relations with Knowland, political and otherwise, cooled markedly—not to the breaking point, but noticeably.

After the presidential nomination, I was invited by Herbert Brownell, the leader of the Eisenhower forces, to sit down with a group of prominent Republicans and select a vice-presidential candidate. Believing that was already a *fait accompli*, I declined. During the convention and two days before the nomination, John S. Knight, publisher of the Chicago *Daily News*, had written an article about the vice-presidential nomination, the substance of which was that "It's all over but the voting. General Eisenhower will be the next Republican nominee for President with Senator Richard Nixon of California as his probable running mate." I therefore believed that it would serve no real purpose for me to take part in discussing that which had already been decided.

Before leaving, I congratulated General Eisenhower. I told him he would have my unqualified support, and asked him to call on me for anything needed. Mrs. Warren and I did the same thing with Senator Nixon, going to the reception for him and telling him we would attend his homecoming on his return to California. This we did at Whittier, his home city, and Mrs. Warren held one of the two Nixon girls on her lap during the ceremony.

Not long after the Republican national convention, the Veterans of Foreign Wars held a convention in Los Angeles. General Eisenhower was invited to make the principal address, which was to be delivered in the Coliseum. After his acceptance, he notified me and other Republicans that this was to be a strictly nonpolitical appearance, and he wanted us to take no part in the affair. We followed his instructions implicitly. The affair was a complete washout. It was held about five-thirty in the afternoon. But because of the downtown traffic at that hour, the general's motorcade to the Coliseum was routed along a side street. Neither properly planned nor advertised, the parade of cars was little noticed along the route. Only about eight to ten thousand people attended the meeting in a stadium built to accommodate a hundred thousand. Television cameras were stationed on the football field, and the general was directly opposite and facing them. The small crowd of VFWs and their friends sat in the bleachers behind the general and his official escort. As he spoke, he saw nothing in front of him except the television cameras and ninety thousand vacant seats. It was a humiliating and almost ludicrous experience. The general obviously felt embarrassed. I rode with him to the airport, told him that this was no indication of how the people of California felt about him, and promised that during the campaign, which had not yet started, we would fill the stadium for him. We did exactly that sometime later, giving him a rousing welcome.

The general took up his summer residence in Denver, and it was there that he and his intimates planned the campaign. I was invited there to talk with him. We conversed for about two hours on a variety of subjects. He was interested, of course, in his prospects in California. I reported that with a reasonable campaign he should win handily. He was somewhat concerned about a group of proposed electors for General MacArthur, but I informed him that they could only be voted for on a write-in basis, that their names would not appear on the ballot, and that there was no possible chance of their being elected. General Eisenhower continued to be alarmed about this situation, and whenever we met during the campaign, he said he was told that the pro-MacArthur faction might poll a hundred thousand votes and tip the balance between him and the Democratic nominee. On each such occasion, I assured him that nobody could predict how a California election would turn out, but that I would be surprised if ten thousand people would write in thirty or so unfamiliar names on their ballots, as would have been required for a valid vote. At the election, only about three thousand did so. At Denver, Eisenhower also asked me if I thought he should try to see General MacArthur again. I said if I were in his position, I would not do so. Immediately after the convention, the general had sent General MacArthur a cordial telegram, and had received a curt reply saying that he, MacArthur, was not in politics. This in spite of the fact that on the opening day of the convention, General MacArthur had staged an unproductive demonstration designed to stampede the delegates for himself. I told General Eisenhower that I thought it would be demeaning to seek an interview in light of that background. Whether he ever did so, I do not know.

He also asked me if I thought he should go to see Senator Taft. I told him I would wait until Taft made a move, because, after the convention, without congratulating him, the senator had gone to Canada for some weeks, declaring that whether he would support Eisenhower depended on whether they could agree on the issues. I believe the general did visit him, and Taft then announced that inasmuch as the general agreed with his views he would support him.

The general also asked me if I thought he should go to Wisconsin, where Senator Joseph McCarthy held forth, and to Indiana, where

Senator William Jenner was running for re-election as was McCarthy in Wisconsin. I told him that both of these men had shown their contempt for his leadership, and they would probably use a visit by him either to ride on his coattails if they thought it would help them or try to humiliate him if they did not. I made the further suggestion that both of those states seemed to be favorable territory for him, and since he could not visit all the states he could best leave those two to the vice-presidential candidate, who was very friendly with both of those senators. Although he seemed to agree, he did subsequently visit both states. In Indiana, Jenner fawned on him and was photographed for the news media with his arm around the general. In Wisconsin, the situation was worse. In one of his principal speeches there, the general's original text spoke kindly of General George Marshall, the great military leader who had been a sponsor of Eisenhower in his rapid rise from lieutenant colonel to Supreme Commander of the Allied Forces in Europe. General Marshall had been traduced by Senator McCarthy as one of those who had turned China over to the Communists. At the insistence of McCarthy and his followers, Eisenhower at the last moment deleted from his speech the kind words about his leader and benefactor. This naturally created a furor, and had Eisenhower been a less popular candidate the result might have been catastrophic. I had anticipated some such humiliation for him in Wisconsin because earlier in the year, when I was campaigning there, I had been pressured to say something favorable about McCarthy, and it was called to my attention that Senator Taft had spoken of him in glowing terms as a great senator. Although in other states I had openly expresed my dislike for the witch-hunting actions of Senator McCarthy, while campaigning for convention delegates in Wisconsin, I merely stated that I was not a carpetbagger to tell them whom they should elect as their senator, and that I would express no opinion there.

At the request of the general, I once went to Chicago, where he and I discussed various issues on a national television program. Most of my other campaign assignments were in California. I helped in the organization of the state, and traveled with Eisenhower when he was in California. However, I was not a part of the overall management of the national campaign. That was largely in the hands of Governor Dewey and Herbert Brownell. The general made a tremendous impression on his visit to California. The crowds he drew were enormous, and enthusiasm was to the point of idolatry. "I Like Ike" signs were everywhere, displayed by young and old of both sexes with an enthusiasm I had never before witnessed in a political campaign. No one could doubt the outcome in my state. The final vote was:

Eisenhower	2, 897, 310
Stevenson	2, 197, 548
MacArthur	3, 326

At one time during the latter part of the campaign, President Truman visited California on a whistle-stop train schedule. The chairman of the Democratic Committee wired me and asked if I would like to greet the President at the little town of Davis, then the site of our State Agricultural College. The train was there for a brief stop and a rear platform speech by the President on its way to San Francisco. It was not coming to Sacramento, which is fifteen miles from Davis. I replied that I would be delighted to welcome the President to California. At the appointed time, I visited the train. President Truman, his daughter Margaret, and I visited pleasantly, and finally an aide came and asked if I would be willing to be photographed with the President.

Before I could answer, Truman replied, "Now don't you embarrass the Governor. It was good of him to come here to welcome me, and I don't want to take advantage of him."

"Mr. President," I said, "it is never an embarrassment for a governor of California to be photographed with the President of the United States. I will be happy to have it done now. And, if you desire, I will be happy to introduce you to the crowd that is waiting to see you."

He assured me he did not want to compromise me because he knew I was campaigning for General Eisenhower and he for Adlai Stevenson. On my assurance that it was no problem, we went to the rear platform, and, in the presence of a large crowd, I proceeded to introduce him. Looking over the assemblage, I noticed many Republicans from Sacramento, a large percentage of them young people. I also noticed they had signs concealed behind their backs or under their coats, and I was sure these were not complimentary to the President. I therefore commenced by telling how pleased I was that Mr. Truman was paying us a visit; adding that I wished the train could have come to Sacramento so we might give him a more suitable reception; that Californians were always cordial to a President, and that I was sure the audience would be so in this instance. Then I expressed pleasure at seeing the President in such good health and concluded by saying, "And now I will leave you Democrats to your own devices." I shook hands with the President and Margaret and left the train to the crowd's applause. I did not remain in the vicinity to hear the President's speech, but it was reported that he was well received and that the reproachful Republican signs did not appear. Some of our Republican partisans thought this hospitable gesture on my part could well have been dispensed with, but I have always felt that no votes are lost by such an act, and that it would be much better for our country if politics could be kept on a mutually respectful level.

One other incident in the campaign emphasized my view on such matters. Adlai Stevenson, the Democratic candidate, and I were fellow governors at the time of his nomination. I knew him and believed him to be a fine public servant. My girls and his boys were attendants at the governors' conferences, and, being of approximate ages, became quite friendly. Also, in those days, the governors' conferences were vastly different from today. We tried very hard to keep them nonpolitical and were quite successful at it. We did not have conferences of Republican governors and Democratic governors. We kept partisan matters out of our discussions as far as possible. We even went so far as to pass no resolutions unless they were unanimously approved. Most problems of state government and its relation to the federal government were discussed openly, but we stopped short of trying to pass a resolution on a subject if it were decidedly controversial. Preparatory to the national conference, there were usually conferences of the governors of the New England states, the Southern, the Western, and the Prairie states, but not as partisans. It might seem unusually vapid to require unanimity among forty-eight or fifty governors of widely different states, but it was not so difficult as it might appear. This was because we often used the technique of abstention to accomplish the will of the vast majority. As an illustration, during most of my eleven conferences, the question of statehood for Alaska and Hawaii, or one of them at least, was always under consideration. At first, there were only a few ardent supporters of either. I was always a supporter of both. I believed that eventual statehood was at least implicit in their acquisition and that the time for fulfillment had arrived. As successive pro-statehood resolutions were suggested, the number of favorable votes increased. I testified before congressional committees in favor of their admission, and when our cohorts became greatly in the majority, we tried to induce the few dissenters to abstain. Their objections were not always personal but often had to do with politics in their home states. Alaska had more Eskimos, Aleuts, and other Indian tribes than Caucasians. Hawaii had a majority of Chinese, Japanese, native Hawaiians, and other nonwhites, and some governors hesitated to recommend statehood more because of possible political reaction at home than because of personal aversion. We succeeded in inducing them to abstain and the resolutions favoring statehood for both territories unanimously passed the last two conventions I attended. I have no doubt this contributed to the eventual favorable result in Congress.

All of this made for a fine esprit de corps. Our personal relations were cordial, and I wanted them to remain on that basis. It happened that when Governor Stevenson was campaigning in California and came to Sacramento, I was campaigning some other place for General Eisenhower, and could not be there to greet him. I would not have him arrive without some official courtesy shown him, so I tendered the use of my offices while he was there and also the opportunity to speak from the Capitol steps to the crowd assembled in our spacious park. He accepted and was happy with the meeting, which was very friendly. Again, there was a little rumbling from some case-hardened Republicans who were not friendly to me anyway, but I am sure we lost no votes by it. On the other hand, I have no doubt that it contributed to the friendship that grew between Governor Stevenson and Nina and me through the years. We later had some wonderful summer cruises with him through the Greek islands and in other parts of the Mediterranean as the guests of Mrs. Agnes Meyer. It contributed also to other associations, which ended with an all-day outing with him and a few friends only a few days before his untimely death.

As soon as the election was over and General Eisenhower was chosen, I returned to my knitting and stuck pretty close to my governor's job. A campaign year is rather disconcerting whether it is one's own or that of somebody else in which one is participating. There is so much trivia that cannot be avoided, and it is all time-consuming. I was not a part of the new Administration's central organization and only occasionally would receive a call from Eastern headquarters concerning someone under consideration for appointment. The only Cabinet appointment I was asked about was that of a new Secretary of the Interior. I was asked what I thought of Douglas McKay, the governor of Oregon. I replied that I did not know him well because he was a new governor, and I was not familiar with his views on conservation and the protection of our natural resources. But I added that Oregon was a strongly conservation-oriented state, and I would think that McKay probably would reflect the views of the electorate in that regard. I did not say this in an invidious way, but to imply my viewpoint that the man who serves as Secretary of the Interior should have a vision for the development of that great portion of America west of the Mississippi River which is destined to play such a major part in the future life of the country, and that I did not believe Douglas McKay had such a vision.

The other inquiries made of me had to do with sub-Cabinet positions for individuals living in the Far West. I remember one time Herbert Brownell, later to become the Attorney General, phoned to ask if I knew anyone who would be an outstanding chief of the Criminal Division of the Department of Justice. I told him I did, but that I hesitated to suggest him because I had disrupted his legal career so many times to help me, and he had only recently told me at last he had decided to accept a quiet and contemplative position as a full professor of law at Boalt Hall, my old law school at the Berkeley campus of the University of California. I said I hesitated to suggest him because he was always serving good but difficult causes, and I was afraid he would again respond to a call and abruptly end his newly chosen way of life. He urged me to name him because the position was of great importance to the new Administration. I then told him that the man I was thinking of was Warren Olney III, of whom I have already written. I then proceeded to tell Brownell of Olney's selfless dedication and of his absolute integrity, for which I could vouch unequivocally in any situation. As I suspected, Brownell urged my old friend and colleague to accept the position, which he did. Olney served honorably in that post longer than anyone who had held it to that time.

The others concerning whom inquiry was made, and there were very few, were not appointed. I do not know whether they were passed over or whether they did not accept the position. In these circumstances, it would be better not to mention them.

I heard nothing more from the Administration until one morning in early December. It was about seven o'clock. I was still in bed reading when the Capitol switchboard operator called and said General Eisenhower was on the phone and wanted to talk to me.

"Governor," the new President said, "I am back here selecting my Cabinet, and I wanted to tell you I won't have a place for you in it."

I said, "General, I do not want a place on the Cabinet. I am perfectly satisfied with my job as governor, and I could not afford to move my family back to Washington for such a position."

"Well," he said, "I have been giving you serious consideration for Attorney General, but Herb Brownell has been close to me politically in the campaign, and I feel I need his political advice as well as his legal counsel."

"He will make you a splendid Attorney General," I said.

He then remarked, "But I want you to know that I intend to offer you the first vacancy on the Supreme Court."

"That is very generous of you."

"That is my personal commitment to you."

We then passed a few pleasantries about family matters, and the conversation ended.

I immediately told Nina, who asked, "What is the salary?"

I said, "Twenty-five thousand a year."

"How could we take the family back to Washington on that?"

I told her I didn't know. At the time I was receiving that same salary, but the state furnished the mansion, guards, automobiles, drivers, janitor service, one thousand dollars for maintenance per month, an airplane with pilots, travel expenses, and an office staff that was available for many services that one accustomed to them would be lost without. Little more was said about the President's call, and not much thought was given to it, because I had often heard of newly elected officials who promised positions in the indefinite future, only to forget when the jobs actually became open for appointment.

I was not wrong in this instance, because when Chief Justice Fred Vinson suddenly died, the President shopped around for a successor, according to his recollection as reported in his *The White House Years*, pages 226–30. He suggested the position to Secretary of State John Foster Dulles, who chose to remain in the Cabinet, and seriously considered others, who were eliminated for one reason or another. Only then did he decide on me. The general's recollection and mine do not fully agree, but my part in the selection of a replacement for Vinson was so simple that there would be little room for faulty memory.

President Eisenhower and I never discussed our political views except on a public television program during the campaign. My visits with him had always been of short duration, and were discussions about the presidential race. As far as I can recall, I never met the general before the 1952 Republican Convention. At all events, he did appoint me Chief Justice, and I have always been grateful to him for the opportunity that afforded. However, I was sometimes saddened that he was not more understanding of the reasons for some of our Supreme Court decisions in what he privately criticized as the "school segregation" and the so-called "Communist" cases.

Mrs. Warren, the girls, and I went to the Inauguration of President Eisenhower and rode in the parade to the presidential grandstand in front of the White House. It was a very long parade, and I thought the show of military equipment in it was somewhat out of place. It was during the Korean War and the Cold War with Russia, and a flexing of military muscle at such a time for the Inauguration of the President appeared to be unduly provocative.

Neither my wife nor I believe in family arguments, and they have been rare in our household. But she and I had one over the Inauguration, and, believe it or not, I won it. It started over an announcement by General Eisenhower a week before the event to the effect that he would not wear a top hat, that he intended to wear a Homburg. I said that if the President would not wear a top hat, neither would I. Nina insisted that it would be one thing for the President to wear a Homburg instead of a top hat, because he also announced that he would wear a box coat, but it would be quite another thing for me to wear a morning coat without a top hat. My argument was that nobody is supposed to outdress the President on any occasion, and that I would not do it on this one. There was a run on Homburgs, and much consternation was occasioned because it was not a usual headgear for men, but I stuck to my guns, and finally made a bet with Nina that there would not be a half dozen top hats in the whole crowd. We both surveyed the assemblage critically on our arrival, and I soon knew I would win because, as the diplomats assembled on the Inauguration platform, not one of them wore a top hat. Of all the men there, I saw only one so attired. He was the governor of Florida, and with his top hat he wore a tan cravenette coat. Some of the other governors, including Dan Thornton of Colorado, wore five-gallon cowboy hats and a variety of other kinds. So I won that one. To reverse what they say in baseball, "You can't lose 'em all."

We attended the Presidential Ball at the Armory, which was more or less a shambles. Little attention was paid to seating assignments, and everyone took potluck. But the new President was enthusiastically received. There could be no doubt of his great popularity. "I like Ike" was the watchword of the hour.

I returned to my desk at Sacramento and wrestled over the problems of a state with fifteen hundred new people coming to live there every day.

King George VI of England had died in 1952, and his older daughter was crowned as Queen Elizabeth II on June 2, 1953. President Eisenhower appointed me as one of the U.S. delegates to her coronation. It was a very gracious thing for him to do, and I have often wondered what prompted his action. I was not one of the international set and had no particular association with the British Empire. I finally concluded that, knowing as he did how young girls would enjoy such an opportunity, it was a generous act on his part to allow my three daughters to view the spectacle.

And it was a great spectacle. I have never seen anything to compare with the coronation ceremonies. It was a difficult time for me to leave California because we were in the closing days of a regular session of our Legislature. As usual, much important legislation was floundering around in committees or conferences awaiting the rush in the closing days when vital changes can be made without drawing immediate public attention because of the confusion that attends adjournment. I also had some concern about what the lieutenant governor might do in my absence with some of the more controversial bills. Nevertheless, I was happy to go, and Mrs. Warren and the girls were thrilled with the opportunity.

General George Marshall headed the delegation, General Omar Bradley represented the Armed Services, and Mrs. Fleur Cowles, at that time the wife of the publisher of *Look* magazine, and I were the others. We were registered at the Grosvenor Hotel opposite Hyde Park, which was on the line of march. The coronation was to be performed on a Tuesday morning, but portions of the sidewalks and streets along the entire parade route were roped off, and the public was permitted to take places on a first come, first served basis, beginning at five o'clock Sunday afternoon. Before dark that evening, the streets were lined with people who had brought their bedding equipment, food, and whatever else they needed for the forty-eight-hour vigil. They were people of all ages and circumstances, and there were literally millions. To make the situation even more unbelievable, the weather was as miserable as one could imagine for the first day of June. It was chilling cold, the wind blew almost to gale proportions at times, and it rained intermittently throughout the two days and nights. The crowd was undaunted. People kept their places without flinching and with a cheerfulness that defied description. We could hear them throughout both nights. They would sing songs for a time, then there would be silence for a few minutes, while we supposed somebody would be regaling them with a story, then there would be a roar of laughter followed shortly by another song, and so on throughout the night. The noise did not much disturb us because each night official festivities kept us up until about two o'clock anyway, and we were obliged to be up by about five-thirty to be ready for activities the next day. We all had an opportunity to meet the Queen, the Queen Mother, the Duke of Edinburgh, the young Prince Charles (now Crown Prince), and his younger sister, Princess Anne. Receptions they held were in Buckingham Palace. They were not enormous in size, and the atmosphere was informal, with the little prince scampering around as any little boy might do if permitted to attend a reception by his parents. Westminster Abbey, where the coronation took place, could not accommodate all the invited guests who were there from every part of the world. Mrs. Warren and the girls, along with the families of other delegates, saw the parade from a grandstand at Buckingham Palace. It was a spectacular procession, truly regal and without any Hollywood effects. It lasted for several hours and ended at the Abbey. I was extremely fortunate in my seating arrangement. I was directly above General Marshall, who had the place of honor in a forward choir seat. Other chiefs of delegations were in the other choir seats. I remember that directly across from the general were the representative of the Soviet Union, Prime Minister Nehru of India, and leaders of the British Commonwealth. When the Queen Mother came to Washington a few years later, I had the honor of sitting with her at a White House or Embassy dinner. We were discussing the coronation, and I was telling her that I recalled her using various motherly devices to keep the little prince interested in the long proceeding. She asked where I was seated, and, when I told her, she laughed, "You had a better seat than I had." She is a lovely person, and I was delighted to discover that I could talk with her in an informal manner about programs for youth in her country and ours.

I only remained in London for a day or so after the coronation, and then flew back to Sacramento to take care of my legislative problems.

One of the bills that had been kicking around during this session was proposed by San Francisco for a southern crossing of the Bay. It was in opposition to the plan of my Department of Public Works to construct a second bridge close to and parallel with the existing one, which had been built in 1938. We had completed the plans and specifications, arranged for the financing of it without raising the tolls, and were prepared to call for bids. The idea of a much more southerly crossing was rejected by many experts on the grounds that it would cost fifty per cent more to build, that it could not be operated without raising the tolls on both bridges, and that eighty per cent of the traffic to be accommodated originated and ended north of the existing bridge, not south. But there were special interests involved, and when it was known that I was returning from London so soon, they maneuvered the bill authorizing the southern crossing through the Legislature at midnight the day before I arrived home. By the time I reached my office that morning, Lieutenant Governor Knight had signed the bill, believing he had accomplished a great political feat at my expense. I merely said, "Goodie"—his nickname—"you may think you have achieved a great victory for yourself, but if so it has been at the expense of the people around San Francisco Bay. I believe I can say to you confidently that you will not see a southern crossing in the next twenty years. It won't be possible until then." As I write about this episode, nineteen years almost to the day have elapsed since it occurred, and there is still no sign of such a crossing; in fact, many people who were for it then are opposed to it now. Throughout all the intervening years, traffic congestion at peak hours on the Bay bridge has been atrocious, although many millions of dollars have been spent for improvisations on the bridge to increase its capacity.

I left Mrs. Warren and the girls to tour England while I was closing out the legislative session and going through the bill-signing period afterward. In California, all bills not signed by the governor within thirty days after adjournment, excluding Sundays and holidays, die by what is called the "pocket veto." At least that was the procedure in my time. As a precaution against another episode like the southern crossing, I rented a safety deposit box and left in it all the unsigned bills. My trusted assistants retained the keys to the box, thus securing them from unwarranted future signing. Only the original of a bill could be signed into law.

My precaution was not without good reason, for when I returned to England to be with my family, I received a telephone call from the lobbyist of the State Bar. He had secured passage of a bill to give to every litigant the right to one peremptory challenge to the judge in his case; that is to say, the litigant would be entitled to remove the judge without assigning any cause or reason for the action. I was opposed to it, believing it deprived the people of their right to have their elected judges sit in cases before the Court unless they were disqualified for personal bias, conflict of interest, or whatever. I told him he knew I disapproved of the bill, and that I could not sign it. He said he was aware of that, but he had talked to Lieutenant Governor Knight, who would sign it if he could have the original bill. I told him the unsigned bills were all in a safety deposit box, that I was the only one who had access to it, and that the judge-challenging bill was effectively pocket-vetoed. After I resigned, the next Legislature passed the same bill and Knight, who succeeded to my position, signed it.

Mrs. Warren, the girls, and I then traveled through the Scandinavian countries of Denmark, Norway, and Sweden. The weather was delightful, and the countryside was beautiful throughout. Largely because of our Scandinavian background, we were accorded warm hospitality wherever we went. Some of our experiences were unforgettable. For me a high point came in Stockholm during a round of social events, when I was awarded the Swedish Grand Cross of the Royal Order of the North Star.

My mother had been born in the province of Hälsingland, not far from Sundsvall. The farm and the home in which she was born were still in the family. Through the vicar of the church in the area, we were invited to a family gathering at the home. There must have been nearly a hundred relatives there of all ages. We did not know any of them because my mother had sailed from there as a babe in arms in 1866, and had had no connection with any of them since coming to the United States. We were taken to the fjord from which my grandparents had sailed, and were told that until a year or two before our arrival there was an old man who remembered, and often told about, seeing the ship that carried them, their family, and other Swedish emigrants to America. The younger members of the family group were dressed in their colorful festive garments, and we were entertained with the folk dances and songs of the region. We were told much family history that we never had heard before, and, as a departing gift, the vicar, on behalf of our relatives, presented us with a nice leather folder containing a record of the title to the farm, showing it had been in the family at least since 1607. He explained that in all probability it was in the same ownership beyond that date into the dim past, but it could not be established because 1607 was as far back as the archives in Stockholm recorded such matters.

It was not difficult for us to communicate with our relatives, although only a few of our newly found friends could speak English, and our girls and I could neither speak nor understand Swedish. Nina, on the other hand, had also been born in Sweden and her home life, although in California, was typically Swedish. Her father was a Baptist minister, and the Bible was read in Swedish at the breakfast table every morning and in English at the dinner table every night. On Sundays, going to the Swedish Baptist Church, with its various activities, was an all-day affair. Her account of the strict religious life of her family during her childhood always reminded me of a tale about a Scotch Presbyterian who insisted on his children devoting all of every Sunday to religious exercises. Finally, one beautiful spring Sunday morning, the children mustered up enough courage to ask their father if they could go for a walk to see the beautiful flowers and newly adorned trees. "Please, father," they begged of the stern old man. The father thought for a few moments, and then said, "All right, children, you may go for one hour, if you all promise me you will not enjoy it too much."

Nina was not born on the mainland of Sweden, but in the little city of Visby on the island of Gotland in the Baltic Sea. It is a centuries-old place, and is said to be the only walled city of Northern Europe remaining intact today. One of the touching experiences we had at Visby was the reception given us on our arrival at the airport outside the city. Officials were there with garlands for Nina and the girls, but what attracted the most attention was an old Swedish lady who had been the nurse for the Palmquist children on the ship coming to America. Nina, the youngest of the family, who had been only a few months old at the time, was the one to whom she paid most attention. The nurse, on her arrival in the United States, had moved to the state of Washington, and had worked there until she retired on Social Security. She then returned to Visby and was overjoyed to see Nina and her girls. Sentimental stories in the Swedish papers were written about this reunion after some sixty years of separation.

We visited the little Baptist church of her minister father, Nils Peter Palmquist, and when I say little I mean very little. It was not much larger than twice the size of my office in the Supreme Court Building. In the rear and on the second-floor level was the rectory where Nina was born. It was a very small place, but in all respects tidy, clean, and attractive in its simplicity. I can understand why the structure was so small, for the Church of Sweden is Lutheran, and with few exceptions all Swedes belong to the state church. The Reverend Palmquist's Baptist church in California was considerably larger because Swedes who migrated there were an independent lot, not necessarily bound to the Lutheran Church.

One other incident in Scandinavia impressed me greatly. There was pointed out to me at an airport a man cleaning the parking area and mowing a lawn. I was told he was a high government official who was serving in that capacity as a penalty for driving a car after drinking. We were told it made absolutely no difference who was involved, if he (or she) had been drinking and was driving a car, he would be put on a work project like this for thirty to ninety days. They said that it had come to the point where, if a couple went to a party, one would drive the car and the other could drink, but not both. As a result, injurious traffic accidents were minimal compared with ours. The example is something for all of us to think about.

On our return to the mainland of Sweden, we traveled by car through that country to Norway, where we saw many of the beautiful fjords between Trondheim and Stavanger. We stopped at Haugesund, where my father was born. The mayor of the city arranged for a reception in the City Hall of all my father's relatives whom he could muster. Again, we knew none of them because my father also was a babe in arms when he sailed to America about ninety years before. We were happy to see these good people and enjoyed the gathering. Then we visited the little farm from which my grandparents emigrated to America. I could understand why they left. The farm was not only small, but even in summer, when things should look their best, the place did not appear to be very productive; certainly not as much as the cornfields of Iowa where they eventually went to live.

On our way to Göteborg, where we were to board the Swedish liner *Stockholm* for America, we visited Oslo, where I had an audience with King Haakon. He was in his eighties, straight and lean and still playing tennis. He was very friendly. I also visited with Crown Prince (now King) Olav, whom I had once met in California at a Bohemian Club encampment.

Before leaving California for this trip to Europe, I had made up my mind to leave political life but did not want to announce it until my work with the Legislature had ended. However, I believed that I must make my decision known to the people of California immediately upon my return, in order that they might have a reasonable opportunity to select a new governor. The next election would then be only fourteen months away.

I looked forward to a few weeks in Europe, where I had never been except for the days of the coronation. There I wanted to relax and do some thinking about my future, for which I had made no plans. I had no desire to enter the business world for the purpose of making a fortune, although through the years I had been offered positions that paid much more money than I had ever received as a public servant. I had no real desire to practice law privately, because I had been in public service nearly all my adult life, usually as the head of an office which afforded me an opportunity to decide public matters on their merits rather than private matters for the fee involved. I was not sure I could be happy in a transition from one to the other. Furthermore, as governor I had appointed about half the judges of the state, and I wondered if my practicing before them might be an embarrassment either to them or to me. The judges I had appointed were men of sterling character who might even lean over backward to satisfy themselves that they were not being influenced by personal friendship if I were to litigate in their courts.

I was obliged to make a decision because the remainder of my term as governor would pass very quickly, and it would be necessary for me to be gainfully employed in some new capacity. There was no other political office that interested me, and my retirement pay after thirty-five years of service would be something over nine hundred dollars a month. Four of our children were in college. Nine hundred dollars a month does not go very far in such circumstances. As I said earlier, never during my public career did I have any income other than my salary. I had received some $6,500 from my mother's estate, but that had been greatly diminished during my years as governor. The only other financial resource we had was the money from the sale of our home in Oakland, which was the property of my wife, as I had purchased it for her.

All of these things had a bearing on what I should do at the end of my term.

On my way over to England, I stopped in Washington to see Attorney General Herbert Brownell, at his request. I told him of my decision to announce my retirement immediately on my return to California. He then informed me that they were having a difficult time filling the Office of Solicitor General of the United States. A permanent appointment had not yet been made by the President. He asked if I would be interested in it. I told him about my family and financial situation, and said it was a question as to whether I could afford it if it were offered to me. He asked me to consider it while in Europe and advise him if I would accept the Office if the President should tender it to me. I promised to do so.

He then arranged for me to have a short visit with the President and

Mrs. Eisenhower at the White House. It was a social call. No business or politics was discussed. Our conversation was principally about the coronation and how much Mrs. Warren and the girls enjoyed it.

Soon I went to London and joined the family. We traveled throughout Northern Europe as I have already described. I meditated long and seriously about the Solicitor Generalship. The position is probably the most prestigious one in America in the practice of the law. To be the principal lawyer for the United States Government in its most important litigation presents a challenge of enormous proportions. Finally I wired the Attorney General in a sort of self-devised code that he but not others would understand, and notified him that if tendered the position by the President, I would accept.

We boarded the liner *Stockholm* at Göteborg, and had a delightful eight-day passage to New York. This is the same ship that had the tragic collision with the Italian liner *Andrea Doria* between New York and Narragansett three years later. I remember that disastrous occurrence not only because of the terrible loss of life it inflicted, but because of the miraculous survival of the young daughter of noted commentator and television broadcaster Edward P. Morgan, a long-time friend of mine. His former wife, her then husband, and Mr. Morgan's daughter, Linda, were aboard the *Andrea Doria*, and their staterooms were at the exact place where the bow of the *Stockholm* crashed through the side of their ship, killing fifty-one people and maiming scores of others. Many were missing, and it was naturally supposed that she was killed with the others. Two or three days later, she was discovered on the bow of the *Stockholm* under twisted steel and other rubble that came from the shattered *Andrea Doria*. She had no broken bones or visible wounds. When her father brought her to my office one day I could hardly believe my eyes. After that horrible experience, she was a beautiful girl, bright and lively, without the slightest evidence of any such mishap. Her mother's husband was killed in the collision.

Immediately on returning to California, I announced my retirement as planned. One week later, U. S. Supreme Court Chief Justice Fred M. Vinson, without any warning, died in bed in the middle of the night. In a very few days speculation became rife as to who his successor might be. My name was mentioned, and in order to avoid the embarrassment of discussing it with the press and others, I arranged with my friend Edwin M. Carty, supervisor of Ventura County by my appointment and a former mayor of Oxnard and state fish and game commissioner, to take his sons and mine with us on a deer hunt. Our favorite deer-hunting area was on Santa Rosa Island, one of the channel islands off the southern shore of California some forty miles from Santa

Barbara. Much of the island of sixty thousand acres was owned by the family of the late Edward N. Vail and operated as a cattle ranch. They had stocked it with a few mule deer about the turn of the century, and because the family did not hunt and permitted only a very few others to do so, there was excellent sport in terrain as rugged as that of any isolated mountain range. The Vail family was very kind to us and made the Carty family and mine welcome there at any time. We had accepted their hospitality on many occasions and always enjoyed it. This time I went not only for the hunt but also to use the island as a hideout. It had no telephone. Its only communication with the mainland was through a ship-to-shore radio used mostly by coastal vessels and fishermen in the area.

On Friday, September 25, 1953, we received a ship-to-shore message that Attorney General Brownell would like to have me call him in Washington. We sent to Santa Barbara for an airplane which took me to the mainland. There I called the Attorney General. He said he wanted to see me, and asked where I could meet him on Sunday if he flew to California. We agreed to meet at McClellan Air Force Base at Sacramento where my state plane was kept.

When the Attorney General arrived, he told me that the President was thinking about appointing me to the Supreme Court, and wanted to know if I would accept. He said the President would want his appointee to accept an interim appointment in order to be able to start the new term a week hence on Monday, October 4. The President, he added, had communicated with some of the senior justices and was told that there were some extremely important cases on the calendar for the beginning of the term and that they called for a complete nine-man Court. I had no idea what the cases were, and didn't ask. I told the Attorney General it was not an ideal way to leave a state administration of almost eleven years, but if it was necessary it could be done.

Here I would like to correct something I have seen in print to the effect that I was first offered a place on the Court other than that of Chief Justice, but that I refused and said I would accept nothing but the Chief Justiceship. That is positively not the fact. The Attorney General, as I have just related, said the President was thinking of appointing me to the Court and would like to know if I would accept. Nothing was said about my becoming Chief Justice, and I said unequivocally that I would accept. If the President had chosen to appoint some existing member of the Court to be Chief Justice and had offered me the vacancy created thereby, I would have accepted as readily. On the Supreme Court, one position is as important as another. They are all equal. Nothing, as far as I can recall, was said by the Attorney General about keeping our meeting a secret. I suppose that was implicit in the nature of his visit. However, the meeting was not made public, and I heard nothing more until Wednesday morning when I received a call from Washington saying that my appointment as Chief Justice was being announced. I have tried very hard to remember whether it was Attorney General Brownell or President Eisenhower who made the call, but cannot recollect which of the two it was. That might seem strange, but the excitement of the moment, the short notice given for my arrival in Washington, and the fact that at sixty-two years of age I was about to begin an entirely new way of life, three thousand miles from where I had lived and worked during my entire career and in an environment almost totally unfamiliar to me, might possibly account for my cloudy memory of that, to me, pivotal event.*

I had no time to waste, so I started immediately to turn the office over to Lieutenant Governor Knight, who would automatically succeed me. I worked all day and the greater part of the night until Sunday morning, when Nina and I boarded a United Air Lines plane with my then travel secretary, Richard McKinney, bound for Washington.

It was not a trip charged with prideful excitement about my new position. Rather it was one of awe for the tremendous responsibility I was about to assume, coupled with a realization of my own limitations and a sense of sadness at leaving my loyal associates without an opportunity even to express my lasting friendship and appreciation for their devoted support through the years. I knew that, like myself, many of them had no well-formed plans for their future. This was aggravated by the fact that I was sure, for one reason or another, that many of them would not remain in the Administration of my successor. I also had a feeling of deep sorrow at leaving the people of California, who had been so generous toward me throughout my many years of public life.

The clerk of the Supreme Court, Harold P. Willey, and the marshal, T. Perry Lippitt, met me at the airport and escorted us to the Statler Hotel, where they briefed me on my induction, which was slated for noon the next day. That was the limit of my immediate instruction as to my duties on the Court.

My own dislocation was equaled by Nina's. She was obliged to return to Sacramento on Tuesday morning to move out of the Governor's Mansion and make room for my successor and his family. Governor Knight was not too understanding about her task, either. We had sold our home in Oakland because none of us was able to use it and it was too expensive to maintain along with the Mansion. We, of course, as

* Ed. note: According to former Attorney General Brownell, now a lawyer in New York City, Warren's confusion is justified, as both he and President Eisenhower talked by phone with the governor on the same call, and there were other calls by each at that time.

yet had no place to move to in Washington, so she, with very little help, was forced to package, mark, and make orderly disposition of an eleven-year accumulation of household effects for our family of eight. The children were all away from home in college, and she was working against a very short deadline. All in all, it was a nightmare for her for over a month. But she did it as she does everything, efficiently and without complaint. It wasn't until about the first of December that she was able to join me in Washington.

During the time Nina was in California, I was perfectly miserable, and for the first few weeks was practically a prisoner either in the Supreme Court Building or in my hotel room. I was compelled to enter and leave the buildings by devious methods to avoid being confronted by the press, which kept vigils at both places. The reason had to do with a New York scandal involving a notorious labor racketeer who was in one of the state prisons. An effort was being made to have him released, and word of this effort found its way into several gubernatorial campaigns in the eastern part of the nation. There was also a mayoralty campaign going on in New York City, and a few days after I arrived in Washington, Robert F. Wagner, a candidate for the position, referred in either a campaign speech or a press conference to the influence being brought to bear for the release of the racketeer, alleging that one of the principal offenders was "a national figure whose every word or action carries tremendous weight throughout the country." However, Wagner refused to divulge the name of this high official, and that started widespread speculation as to who it might be. The press descended on my office to discuss the matter with me.†

My name, perhaps for fear of libel, was not directly mentioned, but I was sufficiently aware of the techniques of the media to suspect that if I talked to them the best I would get out of the story would be that "Warren denies" that he was the influencing official referred to, leaving the inference that I had been charged with it, which was not the fact. I therefore told Mrs. Margaret McHugh, my new secretary, that I was not available to any member of the press and cut off all calls at my hotel. I did not even leave an opportunity for my wife to phone me. I would call her. Usually I was particularly vulnerable to reporters' calls

† Ed. note: The scandal referred to here centered upon Joseph S. Fay, a former vice-president of the International Operating Engineers Union (AFL), who was convicted in 1945 of conspiracy to extort $368,000 from contractors on the New York City Delaware Aqueduct project. He was sentenced to Sing Sing prison, where he had a parade of politicians and labor leaders as visitors, and much support for his early parole. The New York Supreme Court ruled in 1953 that the New York Parole Board was not required to make the names of those supporters public. Attorney General Brownell was among those who denied that he was Wagner's "high official."

because throughout my years in public service I had cultivated the working press and always made myself available to it in a group conference or through my press secretary. The press in Washington knew that and became persistent, finally resorting to sending me telegrams, some saying they wanted to protect me against any false accusation. I did not reply to them.

After almost a month, I was in my hotel room watching television on the Saturday before the New York election. Mr. Wagner was having a press conference and I listened to it. Reporters reminded him of his prior statement about Washington influence in the prisoner scandal and asked if he would now reveal who the official was. He said that he would not. They then asked him directly, "Was it Chief Justice Warren?" He replied, "Oh, no. I understand he is a very fine man and I am sure he would not do anything like that." I did not know Wagner at the time, but he was elected mayor the next Tuesday, and in two following elections. While he was in office, I came to know him pleasantly in spite of this awkward beginning.

As an anticlimax to the affair, I saw Tom Dewey at a dinner shortly thereafter and mentioned my embarrassment during the recent election. He said, "When I heard your name being bruited around in connection with it, I had the files searched and found nothing that could embarrass you, so I asked Herb Brownell to tell you. Didn't he do so?" I could only say, "No, he must have forgotten about it."

While I am mentioning Governor Dewey, I should add that he was one of the first to call me on the phone to congratulate me on my Supreme Court appointment. After thanking him and having a friendly discussion, I said, "And, Tom, do you know that I finally got a friendly editorial mention from the Chicago *Tribune?*" He replied, "The hell you did! I'm becoming suspicious of you. What have you been doing to get a favorable editorial from the *Tribune?*" I told him I didn't understand it myself, but it was a very short one.

"What did they say?"

"They said: 'Not as bad as Dewey anyway.'"

His response might best be deleted, for he could be as forceful in language as in action.

Our trails did not cross often while I was on the Court. He called on me a few times when he was in Washington, and I invariably talked with him briefly at the annual Gridiron Dinners. In fact, I talked with him at one of them only two or three days before his death. He seemed to radiate health and spoke as though he were in excellent condition. I commented on his good color, and he described the wonderful vacation he was then having in the Caribbean, saying he would return the next morning for another ten days. He talked with brisk enthusiasm and recommended the same vacation for me. Only a few days later he was dead. He was a great governor of New York, a born executive, and would, in my opinion, have made an excellent President.

But I am running ahead of my story. Let's return to the day of my induction as Chief Justice of the United States.‡

‡ Ed. note: Senate confirmation of Chief Justice Warren's appointment was briefly delayed by Senate Judiciary Committee hearings headed by the chairman, Senator William Langer of North Dakota. Langer gave considerable airing to anti-Warren charges and protests by right-wing extremists which had little or no foundation in fact. This brought on a hurricane of indignation from outraged Warren supporters of every political stripe, including the Democratic national party chairman, President Eisenhower, Vice-President Nixon, and new California governor Goodwin Knight. Approval of Warren's nomination soon followed by a Judiciary Committee vote of twelve to three, with three Southern Democrats against. Senate confirmation came on March 1. The Chief Justice, in writing this book, did not feel that the accusations brought against him had enough validity to deserve attention at the expense of other matters.

IX

THE SUPREME COURT YEARS

The day of my induction as Chief Justice of the United States was for me at once the most awesome and the loneliest day of my public career. As mentioned earlier, I approached the high office with a reverential regard and with a profound recognition of my unpreparedness to assume its obligations in such an abrupt manner.

It was completely different from the other offices I had held. Before becoming a district attorney, I had had four years of grooming in that office and had definite ideas as to how it could be improved. On becoming state attorney general, I had many years' background of law enforcement locally, statewide, and nationally. I also knew county government and its relation to the state, and felt prepared to plunge into both the civil and criminal aspects of the job. As governor, my experience in these earlier positions had acquainted me with many of the problems of the state and with ways of tackling them in the best interest of the public. I also knew the personalities involved and the atmosphere in which I must work, and while I did not feel that I had answers to all the issues of growth and war that confronted me, I had a solid background of experience for approaching them.

With the Chief Justiceship, it was quite different. I was not acquainted with Washington or even with members of the Supreme Court. I had known Mr. Justice Tom C. Clark for some years, both in his capacity as Attorney General of the United States and earlier as an assistant in the Department of Justice, when we had transacted important business between the state of California and the federal government. I also knew Mr. Justice Robert H. Jackson, though not as well and not at all officially. I was slightly acquainted with Mr. Justice William O. Douglas, but only through legal gatherings which we both attended at various times. The others I did not know.

In addition to this disadvantage of not knowing many of the justices personally, there was my long absence from the courtroom. Since becoming governor, I had not been engaged in handling legal matters except to study contracts of the state with other parties to see that they were consistent with my policies and to study all bills passed by the Legislature to determine, among other things, if they conformed to the state and federal constitutions.

This last, I thought, would be of some help in judging the constitutionality of measures in question before the Court. During my years as governor, I had signed more than ten thousand bills and vetoed another sizable number, many of them because, in my opinion, they were unconstitutional. In wartime especially, a lot of emotional legislation was introduced against anyone who disagreed with the war or with participation in it.

As district attorney, I had engaged in much litigation, both civil and criminal, and had argued a case in the United States Supreme Court. As attorney general, my work was largely administrative, although I occasionally appeared in court and supervised and collaborated in the writing of briefs in state litigation which sometimes went to the United States Supreme Court and in the writing of opinions to state officers on interpretive and constitutional questions. Most of my practice at all times had been in the state courts. My experience with federal courts had been very limited. With the independent regulatory agencies such as the Interstate Commerce Commission, the Federal Trade Commission, the Federal Communications Commission, and most of the others it was almost nil. All of this lack of experience weighed heavily on my mind as I thought about the fact that in a few hours I would be presiding over the highest Court in the land.

The Court convened at noon in those days, and on the fourth day of October, 1953, I went to the Court building about 10 A.M. First I went to the Marshal's Office and asked to be taken to the Chief Justice's chambers. There I met Mrs. Margaret McHugh, who had been the executive secretary to Chief Justice Vinson and who, to my great good fortune, remained to hold that position with me throughout my time in office. There also were three law clerks—William Oliver, later a law professor at the University of Indiana, who had served with the late Chief Justice Vinson and was held over by him for another year, and Earl Pollock and Richard Flynn, both recently graduated from the Law School of Northwestern University. The last two had reported for work only a short time before my predecessor's death. They later became prominent lawyers in Chicago and Washington, D.C., respectively. Finally, there were two elderly messengers, one of whom died during my first term, the other of whom was retired under the new compulsory retirement act the following year, being over seventy years of age. That was my entire personal staff.

I told them they were welcome to remain with me, and they all consented to do so, aiding in the transition for me. But it was a painful transition. Among my duties were the management of the Supreme Court building and the administration of the Court itself. It was difficult to find out anything from official records about the offices of the Clerk, the Marshal, the Librarian, or the Reporter of Decisions. When I made inquiry about practices or procedures from the officers, I was told there was nothing in writing. Their predecessors had told them it had always been done in a certain way, and they had continued to do it in like manner. Thank goodness, Mrs. McHugh had been with Chief Justice Vinson throughout his tenure, and she knew every facet of staff relationships. As a consequence, the two of us handled all the personnel problems without outside help. The only employee I brought to the Court was Miss Margaret Bryan from my Governor's Office to help with California mail and other matters that depended on a knowledge of people there. She remained with me until my retirement, when she filled a vacancy as secretary to Mr. Justice Clark.

After visiting with staff members for a few minutes, I had Mrs. McHugh take me to the chambers of Mr. Justice Hugo L. Black, the Senior Associate Justice. He welcomed me heartily, and explained to me the procedure in the Conference Room as well as the fact that there were several hundred new cases, some of the gravest importance, which had accumulated during the summer to be preliminarily considered immediately after I was inducted. I, of course, had no knowledge of the records or issues involved in any of them, and no idea of conduct in the Conference Room. I asked Mr. Justice Black if he would manage a few of the conferences until I could familiarize myself with procedures. He graciously agreed to do this.*

* Ed. note: Requests to hear about a thousand cases per year were submitted to the Court at this time. Most were considered first on petitions for *certiorari*, which,

I told Mr. Justice Black how unacquainted I was with the members of the Court, and he volunteered to take me to their chambers and introduce me. They were all equally cordial, but this was time-consuming, and it was not long before I was told that we should gather in the Conference Room so I could take the Constitutional Oath. It is the same for all federal officers and goes as follows:

> "I, Earl Warren, swear that I will support and defend the Constitution of the United States against all enemies, foreign and domestic; that I will bear true faith and allegiance to the same; that I take this obligation freely, without any mental reservation or purpose of evasion; that I will well and faithfully discharge the duties of the Office on which I am about to enter."

This was taken only in the presence of the members of the Court. In robing for the session, I was obliged to use an extra robe that was hurriedly found for me among the effects of the Court in the robing room. I do not know who originally used it, but he must have been a tall man because it was too long for my six-foot-one-inch frame. This almost resulted in my complete discomfiture, as we will see.

Exactly at noon, on an appropriate signal from the Marshal, we marched into the courtroom—Mr. Justice Black in the lead followed by the other Associate Justices according to seniority: Stanley Reed, Felix Frankfurter, William O. Douglas, Robert Jackson, Harold Burton, Sherman Minton, and Tom Clark. In accordance with ceremonial tradition, I brought up the rear. Each went to his proper seat: Mr. Justice Black on the right of the empty chair of the Chief Justice, Mr. Justice Reed to the left, then right and left for the others according to seniority. The seat of the Chief Justice remained vacant while I proceeded to a chair behind the Clerk at the right of the Court.

The Marshal intoned the opening of the 1953 Term of the Supreme Court in this solemn language, as he does at every session of the Court:

> "Oyez! Oyez! Oyez! All persons having business before the Honorable, the Supreme Court of the United States, are admonished to draw near and give their attention, for the Court is now sitting. God save the United States and this Honorable Court!"

---

if granted, means that the Court will decide the case on the merits. It requires a lower court to deliver a certified record of proceedings to the higher court for review. Only some ten to fifteen per cent of the cases appealed actually were heard by the Court, and the number of opinions given averaged well under one hundred and fifty a year.

The first order of business was a statement by Mr. Justice Black on the death of Chief Justice Vinson. Then, while the Justices and the audience stood, the commission appointing me on an interim basis was read by the Clerk as follows:

"Dwight D. Eisenhower

"President of the United States of America

"TO ALL WHO SHALL SEE THESE PRESENTS, GREETING:

"Know Ye: That reposing special trust and confidence in the Wisdom, Uprightness, and Learning of Earl Warren, of California, I do appoint him Chief Justice of the United States, and do authorize and empower him to execute and fulfill the duties of that office according to the Constitution and laws of the said United States, and to Have and to Hold the said Office, with all the powers, privileges, and emoluments to the same of right appertaining, unto Him, the said Earl Warren, until the end of the next session of the Senate of the United States and no longer; subject to the provisions of law."

More of this announcement followed, and next came the Judicial Oath, as required of all federal judicial officers in addition to the Constitutional Oath previously taken in the Conference Room. It was administered to me by the Clerk of the Court:

"I, Earl Warren, do solemnly swear that I will administer justice without respect to persons, and do equal right to the poor and to the rich, and that I will faithfully and impartially discharge and perform all the duties incumbent upon me as Chief Justice of the United States according to the best of my abilities and understanding, agreeably to the Constitution and Laws of the United States.
"So help me God."

I was then conducted to the seat of the Chief Justice, a high-backed chair in the center of the raised bench. It was here that I almost created a major incident by stepping on the overlength robe. Thrown off balance, I tripped over the step up to the bench. It was enough to be noted and commented on by the press, so I suppose it could be said that I literally stumbled onto the bench. However, my discomfiture was somewhat lessened when, a few moments later during the order of business called "Admission to Practice," Vice-President Nixon approached the podium flanked by two old friends of his and mine for the purpose of moving their admission to practice before the Court. The friends were Warren Olney III and Stanley M. Barnes, both Californians and both Assistant United States Attorneys General. Instead of moving their *admission* in the usual form, the Vice-President unconsciously said, "Mr. Chief Justice, I have the honor to move the *nomination* of . . ." It was a solemn moment and his slip passed almost unnoticed, but it did relieve me of some tension.

The first order of business after I took my seat was the presentation to the Court of Attorney General Herbert Brownell by the Acting Solicitor General, Robert L. Stern. According to ritual, I welcomed him to the Court in the performance of his important duties. I never knew why this was the first time he was formally presented, as he had been Attorney General for almost nine months before I became Chief Justice. Nevertheless, I was happy to welcome him because we had been friends in politics for some years and I felt that, as close as he was to the President both politically and personally, he must have been a major factor in my appointment. Contrary to usual custom, President and Mrs. Eisenhower graciously attended the induction ceremony, and I appreciated it very much. They sat with Nina and the families of the other Justices in the box in front of and to the left of the bench.

The session took no more than twenty minutes, after which the Court rose and retired as the Marshal announced a recess for one week.

The President and Mrs. Eisenhower left immediately, before I had an opportunity to speak to them, but later that afternoon we were invited to the White House with Herbert Brownell. Mrs. Eisenhower and Nina visited while the President, Brownell, and I talked in another room. After a pleasant visit, Nina and I returned to our hotel, and the next morning she flew back to California to continue moving us out of the Governor's Mansion.

During the week following my induction, the Court met daily in conference to discuss the appeals and petitions for *certiorari* that had been filed since the Court adjourned the preceding June. This was in order to determine which merited oral argument and which could be disposed of summarily. Without either knowledge of these cases or an opportunity to study them, I played no part in their consideration or disposition. However, for my first written opinion, I took a little case of no notoriety that was argued on the third day of the term; one which should, in my opinion, have received a unanimous opinion all along its route through the courts. But it had not, and, unless reversed by the Supreme Court, it could have resulted in a weakening of the Federal

Longshoremen's and Harbor Workers' Compensation Act, since it threatened to deprive workers of payments due them merely because fellow employees charged by the employer with responsibility for notifying him of accidents and injuries failed to do so. The Deputy Commissioner of the Bureau of Employees' Compensation of the Department of Labor found in favor of the employee; the District Court reversed its decision and enjoined further payments under the Act. The Court of Appeals, by a divided vote, sustained the District Court, and the Supreme Court had granted *certiorari* to review that decision. My opinion was reported on November 9, 1953, the first signed opinion during my tenure as Chief Justice. It unanimously reversed the Court of Appeals and established the claim of the worker (*Voris* v. *Eikel*).

In a matter of hours after first coming to the Court, I learned more about the important cases previously mentioned to me by some of its members. They called for a full Court at the opening of the term and were lumped as the school desegregation cases.

There were five of them, from Kansas, Virginia, South Carolina, Delaware, and the District of Columbia. While the latter was in a somewhat different setting because it did not involve a state law, they all involved the so-called "separate but equal" doctrine as established by the Supreme Court in the case of *Plessy* v. *Ferguson* (1896). That decision declined to prohibit separate railroad accommodations for blacks and whites. It sought to justify racial segregation for almost every movement or gathering so long as "separate but equal" facilities were provided and became known as the "Jim Crow" doctrine. The central issue in each of these school cases was:

Does segregation of children in public schools solely on the basis of race, even though the physical facilities and other "tangible" factors may be equal, deprive the children of the minority group of equal educational opportunities?

The five cases had been argued during the 1952 term before I came to the Court but had not been decided and had been put over for reargument, with a set of specific questions for discussion.

The United States Government, through Assistant Attorney General J. Lee Rankin, supported by a brief signed also by Attorney General Herbert Brownell and other Justice Department attorneys, argued as a friend of the Court in favor of the positions maintained by the black students' lawyers. The first case was argued December 7, 1953, and it was easy to understand why the Court felt it necessary to have a full complement of Justices. The case had been first argued exactly a year before, and failure to reach an agreement had caused resubmission for argument. This would normally indicate a difference of opinion within the Court but without any knowledge by the outside world as to the degree or nature of the disagreement. In these circumstances, there is always the danger of an evenly divided four-to-four Court if any member is absent or disqualifies himself, which means the decision of the Court below is affirmed without opinion from the Supreme Court and without any precedential value.

Some of the cases under review had been decided against the black petitioners in the lower courts on the authority of the much eroded "separate but equal" doctrine of *Plessy* v. *Ferguson*.

To have affirmed these cases without decision and with the mere statement that it was being done by an equally divided Court, if such had been the case, would have aborted the judicial process and resulted in public frustration and disrespect for the Court. The Court was thoroughly conscious of the importance of the decision to be arrived at and the impact it would have on the nation. With this went realization of the necessity for secrecy in our deliberations and for achieving unity, if possible. Accordingly, we proceeded in a manner somewhat different from that in the average case. Perhaps it might be well to outline our normal way of proceeding in the conference. That procedure is not a secret, though what is said and done beyond the final results as given in the United States Reports is confidential and should not be disclosed.

Our usual manner of proceeding was as follows: When the briefs of the parties were all filed, the case was placed on our calendar for argument. Enough cases were listed for two weeks because throughout the year we heard arguments for that period of time and then recessed for two weeks to work on the opinions that were assigned to us for writing. When I assumed office, we heard cases argued Monday through Friday; later I changed the schedule to Monday through Thursday. On Saturday morning, we held a conference on the cases heard during the week. The procedure was very simple. In each case, the Chief Justice would, in a few sentences, state how the case appeared to him, and how he was inclined to decide it. Then, beginning with Justice Black, the senior Justice, each would speak his mind in a similar manner. He might only say, "I look at it the same way the Chief does and come to the same conclusion," or he might say, "I view the case differently. It seems to me this is the real issue, etc.," defining it. Or, "I believe it is controlled by the case of *So-and-So* v. *So-and-So* (citing precedent), and that brings me out the other way." Then we proceeded down the line until everyone had spoken briefly in this informal manner. During all of this, nobody was interrupted, and there was no debate. If we were all of one mind and no one desired to say anything more, the case was ready for assignment for the writing of the opinion. The Chief Justice always assigned the opinion to be written if he were with the majority. If he were not, the senior Justice who was with the majority made the assignment. If, after the first canvassing of the Court, as I have described it, there was a difference of opinion, the case was open for debate. We did not observe Robert's Rules of Order or any other definite procedure. It was a self-disciplined affair, each Justice deferring to the speaker until he was finished. The discussion proceeded in an orderly manner until all had spoken as much as they desired. If they were ready to vote, we did so at that time. In voting, we reversed the process and first called upon the junior member, going up the ladder with the Chief Justice voting last. I have tried diligently to learn when and why this procedure was first adopted, but without success. It is one of those things that grew up in the dim past and has been carried on without question. The reason assigned by some is that by voting first the junior member is relieved of casting the deciding vote when the other eight members are in a four-to-four deadlock. I suppose that is as good as any other reason. We then moved from case to case in this manner until all had been decided. The conference started at ten o'clock, and, with the exception of a half hour for lunch, which had been ordered beforehand and was always on the table in our dining room directly above the Conference Room, we continued throughout the day until we had discussed all our cases. Usually we adjourned shortly after five, but often not until after six. On rare occasions we recessed until Monday morning to complete our work.

During these conferences, no one was in the room except the Justices —not a secretary, a law clerk, or even a messenger. If it were necessary for anyone to contact us, it was done by written message and a knock on the door. When there was a knock, the junior member of the Court answered it unless he was speaking at the time, in which case some other Justice would respond. We had a telephone in the room, but I have no recollection of its ever having been used during a conference while I was on the Court.†

The Justice to whom a case had been assigned for the writing of an opinion would, on his own time, prepare a draft, have it printed in our own print shop in the building, and distribute it to all the members of the Court. If they all agreed, it would be reported in open Court at the next session by the opinion writer, who might read or summarize it as he chose. If any Justice desired to dissent, he prepared his draft and circulated it to all the members, any of whom might join it or, if they desired, write and distribute their own dissent. Also, we had what is

† Ed. note: Reliable sources have it that on at least one occasion the traditional knock on the door and delivery of the message were solemnly observed to carry World Series scores to the Chief Justice, an inveterate baseball and football fan.

known as a concurring opinion. Often Justices arrived at the same conclusion as the majority, but reached it by different routes. They, too, might write an opinion and have it recorded with the others. When all the Justices had either written or joined an opinion, but not before, the case was ready to be announced to the public. If a Justice should, for any reason, feel disqualified, he could recuse himself and that action was also reported with the opinion.

This whole procedure is substantially the one still followed today.

It is all a very secretive method of operation, and many people wonder why this is so; why we do not have open hearings on our discussions as Congress is supposed to do. But if one stops to think about the consequences of open hearings, it is easy to understand the necessity for such secrecy. Many Court decisions have a strong impact on the economy of the nation, or at least some part of it. Because, as a rule, the Court deals only with the facts of the given case, such reverberations might not even be known to us in our complex and conglomerate economy. If premature word were to escape from the Conference Room as to the outcome of a case, dire results might follow. Those with the unauthorized information might prosper greatly while the uninformed might be bankrupted. Some of our cases radically affect the stock market. For instance, when the Court in an antitrust case dissolved the existing relationship between the giant General Motors and Du Pont companies, the stock market was markedly affected, and if someone had been allowed to have advance notice of the decision, he could have made an enormous but illegitimate profit at the expense of the uninformed. The same result could occur in the divestiture of large bank mergers or international conglomerates, as in recent federal actions involving the International Telephone and Telegraph Company. Although this security was a matter of constant concern, I can say with great relief that there never was a leak during my sixteen years on the Court. In fact, I only heard of one suspicion of a security breakdown in the years immediately preceding mine, and it turned out not to be a leak but rather a case of someone's correctly guessing the outcome of a case after psychoanalyzing the members of the Court from their past decisions in related matters. I believe the cases involved were the Gold Clause cases. They were of tremendous importance to the economy of the nation and were bound to have a profound effect on the stock market.

In those days, opinions were not released to the public until after an announcement was made at the Court. In this case, as soon as the writer of the opinion started to read it, a lawyer in the courtroom went to the telephone and directed his stockbroker to sell (or buy) for him, thus creating a mild flurry on the market. It was thought for a time that there must have been some advance notice, but the lawyer's act turned out to be legally innocent. He was thoroughly familiar with previous decisions of the Court and the way each Justice voted on them. He believed he knew their voting patterns well enough to be able to anticipate the way the case was to be decided by knowing who had written the majority opinion. His surmise was correct, and that was all there was to it. When I became Chief Justice and was made aware of this danger, we changed the system so as to deliver to the press copies of every opinion the moment its announcement was commenced. This gave everyone an equal break on the news.‡

To return to our method of handling the school segregation cases, we were all impressed with their importance and the desirability of achieving unanimity if possible. Realizing that when a person once announces he has reached a conclusion it is more difficult for him to change his thinking, we decided that we would dispense with our usual custom of formally expressing our individual views at the first conference and would confine ourselves for a time to informal discussion of the briefs, the arguments made at the hearing, and our own independent research on each conference day, reserving our final opinions until the discussions were concluded.

We followed this plan until the following February, when it was agreed that we were ready to vote. On the first vote, we unanimously agreed that the "separate but equal" doctrine had no place in public education. The question then arose as to how this view should be written —as a *per curiam* (by the Court) or as a signed, individualized opinion. We decided that it would carry more force if done through a signed opinion, and, at the suggestion of some of the Justices, it was thought that it should bear the signature of the Chief Justice. I consented to this, and then the importance of secrecy was discussed. We agreed that only my law clerks should be involved, and that any writing between

‡ Ed. note: Newspaper accounts of the day indicate that courtroom doors were locked during the reading of this decision and only afterward, when they were unlocked, was there a stampede for the phones. However, the lawyer to whom the Chief Justice refers may have had a system of signals or other means to transmit the news to someone outside.

At any rate, the point is made that individuals should not be allowed to have the advantage of prior knowledge of Supreme Court opinions.

The Gold Clause cases resulted in four decisions in 1935 which in effect backed up congressional and New Deal devaluation of the dollar and removal of the United States from the gold standard. This caused a flurry of buying on the stock market as those who had taken money out of the country rushed to again purchase American securities. Five-to-four decisions reflected the general tension over the cases. Further reflecting their importance, President Franklin D. Roosevelt had a special telephone line run from the Supreme Court building to the White House so he could learn immediately which way the ruling went.

my office and those of the other Justices would be delivered to the Justices personally. This practice was followed throughout and this was the only time it was required in my years on the Court. It was not done because of suspicion of anyone, but because of the sensitiveness of the school segregation matter and the prying for inside information that surrounded the cases. It was thought wise to confine our communications to the fewest possible people as a matter of security. Headway being made in conference was discussed informally from time to time, and on occasion I would visit with Mr. Justice Jackson, who was confined to the hospital, to inform him of our progress. Finally, at our conference on May 15, we agreed to announce our opinion the following Monday, subject to the approval of Mr. Justice Jackson, who was still recuperating from a heart attack which had incapacitated him for some time. I went to the hospital early Monday morning, May 17, and showed the Justice a copy of the proposed opinion as it was to be released. He agreed to it, and to my alarm insisted on attending the Court that day in order to demonstrate our solidarity. I suggested that it was unnecessary, but he insisted, and was there at the appointed time.

It was a momentous courtroom event and, unlike many other such events, it has not lost that character to this day. I have tried to describe the scene in Chapter I.*

There was another side to the coin in these five segregation cases, which all raised the same central issue and four of which are compendiously referred to as *Brown* v. *Board of Education of Topeka* (1954). In the *Brown* decision, we decided only that the practice of segregating children in public schools solely because of their race was unconstitutional. This left other questions to be answered. For instance,

---

* Ed. note: When Earl Warren took over as Chief Justice, the Court was quite divided. Justices Black and Douglas usually took a strongly liberal view in their opinions; Justices Jackson and Frankfurter were more conservative; the other Justices fluctuated in between. In addition, there were personality conflicts which provided a certain amount of bristling discord and admittedly has been beyond Chief Justice Vinson's powers to settle.

Warren has been given all credit by some historians for bringing greater amity and unity to the Court, at least for all-important racial decisions. Other observers, including the Chief Justice himself, have been more modest in their estimate of his harmonizing influence, holding that nothing could unify such differing spirits unless they individually *wanted* to be unified for a particular purpose. Memoranda in the Warren files for his Court years indicate that the Justices themselves gave Warren much credit for his leadership. A note to Warren from Mr. Justice Frankfurter on the day of the *Brown* decision says:

"Dear Chief: This is a day that will live in glory. It's also a great day in the history of the court, and not in the least for the course of deliberation which brought about the result. I congratulate you."

And from Mr. Justice Burton: "To you goes the credit for the character of the opinions which produced the all-important unanimity. Congratulations."

could plaintiffs bring court actions as *class* actions for all who were similarly situated or should persons actually joining in the action be entitled to relief only for themselves? What court should determine the decree in each case? For what reason could there or could there not be any delay in obeying the Court's mandate and to what extent? All such questions we continued until the next term, inviting the United States and all states affected by our decision to file briefs and argue if they desired to do so.

These cases, postponed because of the death of Mr. Justice Jackson, which left an eight-man Court, came on for argument from April 11 to 14, 1955, with the newly appointed Mr. Justice John M. Harlan in attendance. At the time of Mr. Justice Jackson's death, John Harlan was a recent appointee to the Court of Appeals of the Second Federal Judicial Circuit. President Eisenhower nominated him to the Supreme Court on January 10, 1955, but those were the investigative days of Joe McCarthy, and Harlan was not approved by the Senate until March 17 because of the silly bulldozing he was given as a result of having been a Rhodes scholar, which some right-wingers vaguely associated with red-tinged "internationalism."

Solicitor General Simon Sobeloff, in response to the Court's invitation, argued for the United States on behalf of the petitioners as a friend of the Court. The attorneys general or their assistants of the states involved in the litigation argued for their states, which included Arkansas, Florida, Maryland, North Carolina, Oklahoma, and Texas. All opposed school desegregation.

The principal arguments on this phase of the case, as well as in the original proceeding, were made by John W. Davis for the states and Thurgood Marshall, now an Associate Justice of the Supreme Court of the United States, for the plaintiffs' side. The arguments, for me at least, took a strange course. One might expect, as I did, that the lawyers representing black school children would appeal to the emotions of the Court based upon their many years of oppression, and that the states would hold to strictly legal matters. More nearly the opposite developed. Thurgood Marshall made no emotional appeal, and argued the legal issues in a rational manner as cold as steel. On the other hand, states' attorney Davis, a great advocate and orator, former Democratic candidate for the presidency of the United States, displayed a great deal of emotion, and on more than one occasion broke down and took a few moments to compose himself.

Again the Court was unanimous in its decision of May 31, 1955, reaffirming its earlier opinion of May 17, 1954, by asserting the fundamental principle that any kind of racial discrimination in public education is unconstitutional, and that all provisions of federal, state, or local law requiring or permitting such discrimination must yield to this principle. Recognizing that because full application of these constitutional principles might require solution of a wide variety of local school desegregation problems, school authorities were given the primary responsibility for elucidating, assessing, and solving such problems. However, it was stipulated that courts would ultimately have to consider whether the action of school authorities constituted implementation in good faith of the governing constitutional principles.

We discussed at great length in conference whether the Supreme Court should make the factual determinations in such cases or whether they should be left to the courts below, deciding finally to leave them to the latter, subject, of course, to our review, because they were getting closer to the problems involved, and were in a better position to engage meaningfully in the fact-finding process. As guidelines for them, we directed that neither local law nor custom should be permitted to interfere with the establishment of an integrated school system, and that the process of achieving it should be carried out with "all deliberate speed" —a phrase which has been much discussed by those who are of the opinion that desegregation has not proceeded with as much celerity as might have been expected. These people argued that the Supreme Court should merely have directed the school districts to admit Brown and the other plaintiffs to the schools to which they sought admission, in the belief this would have quickly ended the litigation. This theory, however, overlooks the complexity of our federal system, the time it takes controversial litigation to proceed through the hierarchy of courts to the Supreme Court, the fact that the administration of the public school system is a state and local function so long as it does not contravene constitutional principles, that each state has its own system with different relationships between state and local government and that the relationship can be changed at will by the state government if there should be a determination to bypass or defeat the decision of the Supreme Court. Evidence that such evasion would occur came immediately in some of the resolutions and laws initiated by certain states. In this, they were encouraged by the so-called Southern Manifesto, signed by over a hundred Southern representatives and senators in the Congress of the United States. It urged all such states to defy the Supreme Court decision as being against their way of life and their "good" race relations, and to use "all lawful means" to make the decision ineffective. So reinforcing was this Manifesto to Southern defiance that the doctrine of "Nullification"—first advanced by John C. Calhoun of South Carolina, discredited more than a century before and made forever inapplicable by the Civil War Amendments—was revived by Southern governors, legislators, and candidates there for public office. The doctrine, in simple terms, argued that states have the right to declare null and void and to set aside in practice any law of the federal government which violates their voluntary compact embodied in the United States Constitution. The doctrine, of course, did not prevail, but the delay and bitterness occasioned by it caused inestimable damage to the extension of equal rights to citizens of every race, color, or creed as mandated by the Fourteenth Amendment.

With courage drawn from this profession of faith in white supremacy by practically every Southern member of Congress, together with oft-repeated congressional speeches and statements to the effect that no nine honest men could possibly have come to the conclusion reached by the Court in *Brown* v. *Board of Education,* excited and racist-minded public officials and candidates for office proposed and enacted every obstacle they could devise to thwart the Court's decision. This was aggravated by the fact that no word of support for the decision emanated from the White House. The most that came from high officials in the Administration was to the effect that they could not be blamed for anything done to enforce desegregation in education because it was the Supreme Court, not the Administration, that determined desegregation to be the law, and the Executive Branch of the government is required to enforce the law as interpreted by the Supreme Court. Bernard Shanley, the personal counsel of the President, in an effort to allay Southern animosity against the Administration, was reported in the press to have said in a speech that the *Brown* case had set race relations in the South back by a quarter of a century. The aphorism (dear to the hearts of those who are insensitive to the rights of minority groups) that discrimination cannot be eliminated by laws, but only by the hearts of people, also emanated from the White House.†

† Ed. note: *Brown* v. *Board of Education,* then, was for all practical purposes a two-part decision. The first, in 1954, announced overthrow of the *Plessy* v. *Ferguson* principle that separate accommodations for races could be provided so long as the accommodations were equal—as in fact they rarely were. *Brown I* said the right and constitutional thing to do was to integrate *all* public educational facilities. No more fiction about "separate but equal." *Brown II,* in 1955, put teeth in the earlier ruling which, as events proved, was only gumming on the school integration problem because of the determined resistance of the white South.

Brown II insisted that integration of public schools be undertaken "with all deliberate speed." It put the burden on local educational systems to comply and on local courts to enforce compliance where it was wanting. Still the South resisted. Deliberate speed could be deliberately slow, and nine years later only a small percentage of the black students in the South were attending school with whites. It wasn't until 1964 that the Civil Rights Act and such cases as *Griffin* and later *Bradley* said that *any* further delay in desegregation of schools was intolerable under the Constitution and would be met with federal action.

One effect of the Brown decisions was to show blacks that they need no longer be supplicants for equal rights dispensed at the white man's whim; the Supreme Court

A few years later, Governor George Wallace was emboldened to stand at the entrance to the University of Alabama, and, in the face of the Deputy Attorney General of the United States, who had read to him the order of a United States district judge directing the university to admit a black student, shout in defiance, "Segregation in the past, segregation today, segregation forever."

The Court expected some resistance from the South. But I doubt if any of us expected as much as we got. Nor did I believe that there would develop in the Republican Party, which freed the slaves through the Civil War and the Thirteenth Amendment and granted them all the attributes of citizenship through the Fourteenth and Fifteen Amendments, a Southern strategy which had for its purpose a restriction of such rights in order to capture the electors of those states and achieve the presidency. I, for one, thought it would be wonderful if, by the time of the centennial of the Fourteenth Amendment (1968), the principle of desegregation in *Brown* v. *Board of Education* could be a

---

had decreed that they were fully entitled to such rights according to the law of the land. This inevitably led to ever more insistent individual and class action demands by the black community.

As a result, during the decade between *Brown I* and the Civil Rights Act, several legal props were added to the ideal of racial equality, and one of these was supplied by the Court's decision in *Cooper* v. *Aaron* in 1958. This case, which Warren Olney called "a landmark," was largely brought on by Arkansas governor Orval Faubus' intemperate actions.

By passing state laws that circumvented federal ones and by engineering events so that violence would result from efforts to bring blacks into white schools, Faubus and the Arkansas Legislature sought to counteract the integration order of *Brown*. When a token group of black children sought to enroll at Central High School in Little Rock, Faubus used the National Guard to forcibly prevent them from entering. The Little Rock School Board asked a federal district judge to postpone the Court-ordered desegregation of that area's schools, claiming it was hazardous to public safety. The judge refused. It was an ugly time of glistening bayonets, hate-filled mobs, red faces and screamed epithets, a time of deep crisis when bigotry stood up nakedly and defied social progress and the nation's highest court. The rest of the United States watched with mixed feelings.

President Eisenhower invited Governor Faubus to visit him at his summer home in Rhode Island, where they discussed the problem at great length and apparently amicably—because at the conclusion Faubus returned to Little Rock as defiant as ever. This created such an uproar throughout the country that the President finally reacted. He federalized the Arkansas National Guard, putting it directly under his command, and sent special troops to help keep order. This broke the resistance of Faubus and the Little Rock mobs.

"Even then," Warren lamented, "there was no direct appeal from the White House to obey the mandate of the Supreme Court." Warren was especially incensed that any state governor should try to tell the Court what was legal or illegal about school desegregation, which Faubus had sought to do.

Cooper v. *Aaron* held that state government resistance and resulting unrest was no excuse for failing to desegregate. It also rejected the notion that integration programs should be suspended long enough to allow various states to test their legal validity in the courts.

reality throughout the land. And I still believe that much of our racial strife could have been avoided if President Eisenhower had at least observed that our country is dedicated to the principle that . . .

> We hold these Truths to be self-evident, that all Men are created equal, that they are endowed by their Creator with certain unalienable Rights, that among these are Life, Liberty and the Pursuit of Happiness . . . (Declaration of Independence)

With his popularity, if Eisenhower had said that black children were still being discriminated against long after the adoption of the Thirteenth, Fourteenth, and Fifteenth Amendments, that the Supreme Court of the land had now declared it unconstitutional to continue such cruel practices, and that it should be the duty of every good citizen to help rectify more than eighty years of wrongdoing by honoring that decision—if he had said something to this effect, we would have been relieved, in my opinion, of many of the racial problems which have continued to plague us. But he never even stated that he thought the decision was right until after he had left the White House.

I have always believed that President Eisenhower resented our decision in *Brown* v. *Board of Education* and its progeny. Influencing this belief, among other things, is an incident that occurred shortly before the opinion was announced. The President had a program for discussing problems with groups of people at occasional White House dinners. When the *Brown* case was under submission, he invited me to one of them. I wondered why I should be invited because the dinners were political in nature, and there was no place for me in such discussions. But one does not often decline an invitation from the President to the White House, and I accepted. There were several people present at this particular one. I was the ranking guest, and as such sat at the right of the President and within speaking distance of John W. Davis, the counsel for the segregation states. During the dinner, the President went to considerable lengths to tell me what a great man Mr. Davis was. At the conclusion of the meal, in accordance with custom, we filed out of the dining room to another room where coffee and an after-dinner drink were served. The President, of course, precedes, and on this occasion he took me by the arm, and, as we walked along, speaking of the Southern states in the segregation cases, he said, "These are not bad people. All they are concerned about is to see that their sweet little girls are not required to sit in school alongside some big overgrown Negroes."

Fortunately, by that time, others had filed into the room, so it was

not necessary for me to reply. Shortly thereafter the *Brown* case was decided, and with it went our cordial relations. While Nina and I were
occasionally invited to the White House after the decision for protocol
reasons when some foreign dignitary was being entertained or were invited to some foreign embassy for a reciprocal honoring of the President, I can recall few conversations that went beyond a polite "Good
evening, Mr. President" and "Good evening, Mr. Chief Justice."

Some Southern states, and Northern areas as well, have used every
conceivable device to thwart the principle of the *Brown* case, and they
have been successful in preventing full compliance or even that degree
of compliance sufficient to create good will between the races. Because
of these drawbacks, some people are of the belief that the Court's
decree was a failure, but the fact is that real progress has been made.
However, the tragedy of the situation is that because of the resistance
die-hard segregationists have made, advances have come about only
after torrid litigation or after federal legislation which has emphasized
the unfairness of the white supremacy theory to the point that deep bitterness against whites is felt by all minority groups—blacks, Chicanos,
Puerto Ricans, Asians, and American Indians. That, too, can be
remedied whenever we all realize the importance of the Thirteenth,
Fourteenth, and Fifteenth Amendments to the Constitution in granting absolute equality of citizenship to "*Everyone* born or naturalized in
the United States . . ."

Some more recent cases decided by the Supreme Court emphasize
that these patterns die very hard. Despite the Court's condemnation of
the principle of racial segregation and outlawing of it in public schools
in 1954, it was not until 1962 that the separation of blacks and whites
in state courtrooms was likewise outlawed. It was not until 1964 that a
black witness was given the right to be examined by counsel in the
same spirit of deference accorded to white witnesses. It was not until
1968, over one hundred years after the passage of the civil rights statute
on which the Court belatedly relied, that blacks were determined to
have the same rights as whites to live where they choose. Despite an old
holding by the Court that systematic exclusion of Negroes from juries is
unconstitutional, that problem still persists. And it was as late as 1969,
after I had retired from the Court, that Mr. Justice Black was moved to
say in the case of *Alexander* v. *Holmes County Board of Education*
that ". . . there are many places still in this country where the schools
are either 'white' or 'Negro' and not just schools for all children as the
Constitution requires." In Justice Black's view, there was "no reason
why such a wholesale deprivation of constitutional rights should be tolerated another minute."

These examples illustrate the fact that harmony in race relations is not simply or easily achieved. No matter how comprehensive and clear the law is on this subject, there will always be bigots to promote tensions and patterns of resistance. But the vast majority of people must realize by now that racial equality under law is basic to our institutions and that we will not and cannot have peace in our nation until the race issue is properly settled. We have, it bears repeating, thirty-four million members of minority groups whose civil rights have not been but must be fully respected. That calls for a combination of effective law and good will. In the absence of both or either of these elements, we can only expect chaos. If there is one lesson to be learned from our tragic experience in the Civil War and its wake, it is that the question of racial discrimination is never settled until it is settled right.

To know how far toward equality of citizenship we have traveled since 1954, we must know from where we started at that time. A thumbnail description of the status of black persons in the Southern states at that time will give some indication of the progress made. To do this, it is necessary to go back to the Civil War and the three Constitutional Amendments that followed it. That horrible war and the Thirteenth Amendment abolished slavery forever throughout the Union. The Fourteenth Amendment made the slaves and all others born or naturalized here citizens of the United States and of the states where they lived, with all the privileges and immunities of that citizenship and of the right to due process of law and equal protection of the laws everywhere in the nation.

The reconstruction of the nation was undertaken in accordance with these principles for a period of ten years until 1876. When the Democrats in the Tilden-Hayes affair traded the presidency to the Republicans for the muting of the newly acquired rights of the black people who had so recently been enfranchised, the Supreme Court then, in keeping with the national mood, in one case after another, beginning with the Slaughter House cases and the Civil Rights cases, limited the rights of the blacks until finally the case of Plessy v. Ferguson held that the states could by statute separate blacks from whites in public transportation providing the accommodations were equal. This was the doctrine upon which the "Jim Crow" treatment of blacks was premised; and the so-called "black codes" developed, until by the 1940s the South was almost as much an area of apartheid as the Republic of South Africa. The doctrine of separation of the races was honored to the nth degree, but the "equal" part of the equation was totally disregarded. Southern states required separate entrances, seating arrangements, and exits to all public facilities, separate waiting rooms in rail, water, and air facilities, whether public or private, separate drinking fountains everywhere. Segregation was enforced at all places of public entertainment, including public parks, beaches, playgrounds, libraries, auditoriums, and circuses. States provided for separate telephone booths, school textbooks, elevators, barbershops, and taxicabs. Whites and blacks were prohibited from competing with or against each other in athletic contests, or even from playing with their own color group in close proximity to similar activities by a group of the other color. In some states this principle was extended even to boating, fishing, or the playing of games such as checkers. There was segregation in the hospitals, prisons, mental institutions, and nursing homes. Even ambulance service was segregated. In this respect, I recall after the *Brown* decision, in one of the Southern cities a little black girl was critically injured and lying on the street. Someone called for an ambulance, but unfortunately for the little one she was refused ambulance service because the ambulance which responded was for whites and not for blacks. Blacks could not live except in restricted areas, could not work except at menial tasks, could not join white labor unions, were not given equal pay for equal services, and were denied any promotion that would put them in competition with or in the same status as white workers.

Blacks were prevented from voting or otherwise participating on any level of the government under which they lived by devious devices, such as the Grandfather Clause, which denied a person the right to vote unless his grandfather had been qualified to vote. That clause for many years excluded all blacks because slavery had barred their grandfathers from voting. The poll tax was used in a restrictive manner against blacks, as were the good character clauses and those prescribing educational qualifications. Black college professors who had qualified in the academic world as doctors of philosophy were denied the right to register as voters because of an inability to read and understand the Constitution or to pass an educational test administered by a sometimes almost illiterate election official.

They were not even permitted to worship God in the same building as whites, although they worshiped according to the same Bible and the same textual interpretation. Many black people went to jail because of the assertion of this right. There was a story current in Washington when this right was being tested that I cannot forget. It concerns a black man who attempted to enter a white church one Sunday morning. He was stopped at the door by a church official and told he could not enter. The black replied that he was not there for the service, that he was an employee of the church and was there to make some necessary preparation for the service. After cross-examining the black severely, the official yielded and said, "All right, you may come in to do your work, if you promise me that you will not pray while you are in here."

There are many other equally demeaning indignities imposed on blacks, some of which must be attributed to the courts. Tens of thousands of them have been sent to prison for life without a lawyer to represent them, often after being the victims of atrocious third-degree methods compelling confessions to avoid further cruelty. The whole race for a century was degraded even in the courtroom, where they were compelled to be segregated. They were systematically excluded from jury service, and in many places where the black population was substantial, even the oldest residents could not recall and the court records did not show that any black had ever been on a jury panel. Their testimony was not received according to the same standard as whites. There were counties where it was almost unheard of for a black to prevail in litigation where only the testimony of blacks was pitted against that of whites. Not only were they segregated and sworn to tell the truth as witnesses on different Bibles, but they were further demeaned by the manner in which they were addressed by both court and counsel. White witnesses would, of course, in keeping with good manners, be addressed as Mr., Mrs., or Miss in the giving of their testimony, but no black witness would be so addressed. With them, it was always Willie or George or Smith or even "boy" with males and Mary or Gertie, etc., with females. A lawyer or judge in many Southern courts would not want to have his social standing affected by treating blacks as equals in the courtroom.

The record of the courts in racial matters has been no better than the American pattern in education or anywhere else. Shortly before I retired, a case illustrating this sad state of affairs came to the Supreme Court from Alabama. It was typical of practice in the state courts there whenever both white and black witnesses testified. As best I can reconstruct it, the white lawyer addressed white witnesses in the case in the customary manner, using Mr., Mrs., or Miss as a routine courtesy, but finally a black woman was called to the stand to testify. The white lawyer asked her, "What is your name?" She replied, "Miss Mary Hamilton." His next question began, "Mary, what do you do?" She interrupted, "My name is *Miss* Mary Hamilton." He then commanded, "Mary, answer my question." She turned to the judge and said, "Judge, do I have to answer the question unless he addresses me properly?" The judge replied, "Answer the question." She then said, "I refuse to answer his question until he addresses me properly." Without hesitation, the judge said, "You are in contempt of court. I sentence you to five days in jail and fine you fifty dollars." That is the entire record in the case. She served the five days in jail, but was then befriended by the

NAACP, which appealed for her and carried the case to our Court after the courts of Alabama had affirmed her conviction. We reversed the case, but in the meantime she had not only suffered much courtroom indignity, but had languished five days in jail.

About the same time, we had two other cases pointing up the same kind of discrimination. We dealt with them in like fashion. One of these was from the state of Virginia. In that case, a black man walked into a courtroom and sat quietly in the center section rather than in the space set apart for blacks. The judge, noticing him there, ordered him to come up to the bench and told him to sit in the black section. The man said nothing and stood before the Court with his arms folded. When he failed to move promptly, the Court sentenced him for contempt. Now this was in a court of law in a state immediately adjoining the District of Columbia, where people are expected to have faith in our pledge of "One Nation indivisible under God, with liberty and justice for all."

To indicate how thoroughly this bigoted treatment is ingrained in some of the states, my colleague Justice Thurgood Marshall told me of an occurrence that involved Mrs. Constance Motley, a distinguished United States district judge in New York and before that an able trial lawyer, who argued a number of civil rights cases in the Supreme Court of the United States. The incident occurred during a trial that drew the attention of the press. Mrs. Motley, who is black, apparently made a favorable impression in behalf of her client on the reporter for a certain newspaper and he referred to her in his article as "Mrs. Motley." But, said Justice Marshall, that was quickly changed. Her name appeared as "Mrs. Motley" in only one edition of the newspaper. Thereafter the paper always referred to her as "the Motley woman," according to the custom of referring to all colored women, regardless of their cultural or professional qualifications, in that demeaning fashion.

Of all the indignities, I suppose the most macabre one is that blacks could not even lie in peace and at rest in the same cemetery as whites. This was poignantly brought to general attention when cemeteries in the South refused to allow the bodies of black soldiers, killed in action in our present unfortunate war, to be buried in white cemeteries. It took the intervention of the Federal Courts to overcome this ghoulish discrimination in a recent case.

Oppression solely because of color appears in so many unrelated forms that it is often forgotten that they all more or less stem from the paraphrased doctrine of "separate but unequal," which was the real meaning of the Supreme Court decision expounded in *Plessy* v. *Ferguson* in 1896. Many people are unaware of the progress that has been made in areas other than education since *Brown* v. *Board of Education*.

Now black people, by Supreme Court decision or congressional action, have equal use of public parks, beaches, golf courses, auditoriums, and other public facilities. They have access on the same basis to all forms of public transportation—land, water, and air. In other words, Jim Crow is legally dead. Blacks have the right to eat in the same restaurants as whites, live in the same hotels and apartments, patronize theaters and other forms of entertainment and recreation, and buy property where they desire. They can vote in elections, run for public office, and participate in government as they wish. And, of course, every school child is entitled by law to an education in an integrated public school system on equal terms with all others. To protect these rights they have direct access to the federal courts through government and private actions. While most people are of the belief that all of these rights have been decreed by the courts, such is not the case. *Brown* v. *Board of Education* and its progeny took away some of the limitations on Congress established by earlier cases such as the Slaughter House cases, the Civil Rights cases, and *Plessy* v. *Ferguson*. Responding to its newly recognized power, Congress, at the suggestion and with the support of Presidents Kennedy and Johnson, enacted the Public Accommodations Act of 1964 and the Voting Rights Act of 1965. Gains in all of these areas have been great, and under normal circumstances would have done much to span the gap between the races. But they have not yet achieved that goal because of the bitterness with which every stride forward has been fought by racists, extreme right-wing groups, and blind adherents of the status quo.

To their credit, President Eisenhower and his successors have cooperated with the Congress in establishing and extending the life of a Civil Rights Commission, which has functioned as a watchdog over our constitutionally or statutorily protected civil rights, particularly as they relate to minority groups and the otherwise underprivileged. The Commission, under the chairmanship first of Dr. John A. Hannah, president of Michigan State University, and more recently of Father Theodore M. Hesburgh, president of Notre Dame, has made a notable contribution to the cause of equal rights. It has worked quietly but persistently and its reports point up with clarity the conditions that call for rectification still.

An extremely touchy matter that has arisen out of the need to integrate schools is that of busing. Governor George Wallace of Alabama injected it into a presidential campaign, and others from Berkeley to Boston have catapulted the "busing issue" onto the American public. Opponents hold it to be an undesirable principle whereby the courts are determined to wrench children from their neighborhoods and put them on buses for hours every day all over America in order to bring about a proportionate balance of black and white children in the schools. They have even argued that this must be prevented by depriving the courts of their constitutional jurisdiction.

This, however, is a complete distortion of the situation.

The Supreme Court has never held that there must be exact racial balance in the schools or that long-distance busing is desirable. Until recently, it has never recognized busing as a principle, only as a tool for the courts to use where the authorities have been reluctant to carry out the desegregation called for by *Brown* v. *Board of Education*. That decision was aimed at affording all children an equal opportunity for a good education, nothing more.

I believe that most parents would prefer having their children attend a school within walking distance of their home. They recognize, however, that it often becomes necessary or at least desirable to have pupils transported to a more distant school in order to better educate them. Busing is only one means to accomplish proper results when others have failed or been denied. There is much merit in a suggestion of Father Hesburgh's to the effect that "busing" can properly be used to transport underprivileged children to better schools but not the opposite; he would leave poorer schools to the bulldozer.

The Supreme Court has been quite consistent in advancing the cause of desegregation when pertinent cases have come before it. At this writing, although there have been nine changes in membership since the *Brown* case, there has been unanimity in all but a few peripheral matters which eventually worked out to the same end.

There was but one event that greatly disturbed us during my tenure, and that was the aforementioned Little Rock case (*Aaron* v. *Cooper*) which gave Governor Faubus the national spotlight. We were all of one mind in that case, which has already been discussed, but Mr. Justice Frankfurter called our attention to the fact that there had been a number of changes in the membership of the Court since *Brown* v. *Board of Education*. He suggested that in order to show we were all in favor of that decision, we should also say so in the Little Rock case, not in a *per curiam* or in an opinion signed by only one Justice, but by an opinion signed by the entire Court. I do not recall this ever having been done before. However, in light of the intense controversy over the issue and the great notoriety given Governor Faubus' obstructive conduct in the case, we thought well of the suggestion, and it was done.

After the decision was announced, Mr. Justice Frankfurter informed us that he had many friends in the Southern states, and that he intended to reach them by writing and circulating a concurring opinion of his own, to be officially filed at a later date. This caused quite a sen-

23. Dwight and Mamie Eisenhower campaign in California in 1952 as Warren smiles from the front seat. A Nixon cap is also in evidence. (*Courtesy Bancroft Library*)

24. Chatting with President Dwight D. Eisenhower in the Oval Room of the White House in 1953. (*UP Telephoto*)

25. President John F. Kennedy is sworn in by Chief Justice Warren during the inauguration ceremonies, March 20, 1961.

26. The governor goes fishing. With son Bob he examines a catch of swordfish at La Paz, Mexico, in July 1949. *(Dorothy Gunn)*

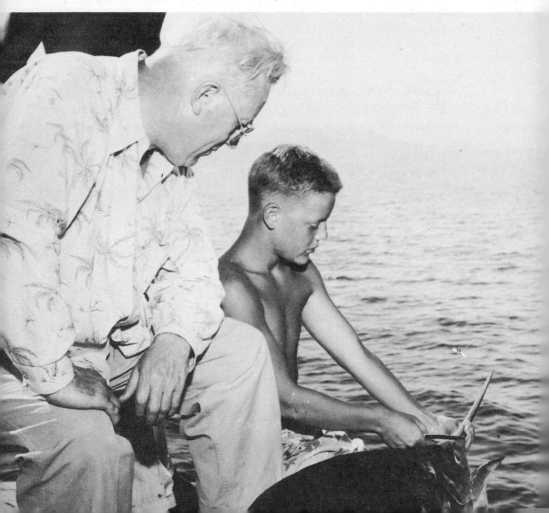

27. An inveterate sportsman, Warren displays the results of a day's duck hunting in December 1960 with Governor Pat Brown of California (left), Pat's son, Jerry, later to become governor of the same state, and old friend Wally Lynn.

28. During a visit to the Sacramento *Bee* newspaper in 1973.

29. A friendly discussion with ex-President Harry Truman, Mrs. Truman, and President Lyndon Johnson in January 1966.

30. Chief Justice and Mrs. Warren at a White House party in 1967 with President and Mrs. Lyndon Johnson, Senator and Mrs. Hubert Humphrey. (*Kevin S. Smith*)

31. The Warren Commission. Warren sits in the middle, flanked by other members of the President's appointed body to investigate the assassination of President John F. Kennedy. His colleagues are (left to right): Representative (later President) Gerald Ford, Representative Hale Boggs, Senator Richard Russell, Senator John Cooper, former CIA heads John J. McCloy and Allen Dulles, and general counsel J. Lee Rankin. (*Ackad photo*)

32. President Tito of Yugoslavia takes Warren and Mrs. Agnes Meyer for a drive at his island retreat on Brioni in August 1962. Mrs. Tito beams over the Chief Justice's shoulder.

33. Mrs. Warren's favorite portrait of the Chief Justice, taken in 1967. (*National Geographic Society*)

sation on the Court, because it was our invariable practice not to announce the decision in any case until all of our views had been expressed. Nevertheless, he circulated such an opinion prior to the Court's announcement. Afterward, some of the Justices stated that they would never permit a Court opinion in the future to be made public until it was certain that the views of all were announced simultaneously.

Many people despair as to the integrative effectiveness of *Brown* v. *Board of Education* because it has not been a complete success. They fail to recognize the great impact it has made in educational and other fields and in its stimulation of Congress to legislate for equal rights.

All of the various segregation case decisions went hand-in-hand with the principle of *Brown* v. *Board of Education*. Those decisions related not only to blacks but equally to all racial groups that were discriminated against. In fact, I reported a case of jury discrimination against Mexican-Americans, now styled Chicanos, two weeks before the *Brown* case in *Hernandez* v. *Texas* (1954). In that case, the defendant had been convicted of murder over his protest that people of his class had been systematically excluded from jury service as far back as anyone could remember. Fourteen per cent of the population of the county had Latin names, yet the state stipulated that:

> . . . for the last twenty-five years there is no record of any person with a Mexican or Latin American surname having served on a jury commission, grand jury or petit jury in Jackson County.

The state contended that this and other acts of discrimination did not violate the Constitution because the Fourteenth Amendment bore only on the relationship between blacks and whites. We hold that it applied to "any delineated class" and reversed the conviction. And so it must go with any such cases. They apply to any class that is singled out for discrimination. Most of our cases have involved blacks, but that is because there are more of them; they are more widespread and have been the most discriminated against.

Tortuous as school desegregation has been, the effect the *Brown* case had on various apartheid practices was stupendous. The federal courts made meaningful many spin-offs from it, and with minor exceptions those courts met every test in following the Supreme Court. I have no doubt that when history appraises this difficult era, the real heroes to emerge will be the federal district judges and the judges of the Circuit Courts of Appeals in the southern and border states. Without meaning disparagement of any others, I believe it would be fair to single out for special commendation the judges on both levels in the Fifth Circuit, comprised of the states of Alabama, Mississippi, Louisiana, Georgia, Florida, and Texas, and those in the Fourth Circuit, comprised of Maryland, Virginia, West Virginia, North Carolina, and South Carolina. The Fifth Circuit produces more litigation than any of the other ten circuits in the nation, and for obvious reasons far more civil rights litigation than any of the others. During much of the crucial integration period, it was admirably presided over by Chief Judge Elbert Parr Tuttle of Atlanta, Georgia, who guided his able colleagues on the Court skillfully and courageously through its most difficult period in the past century. The same can be said for Chief Judge Simon E. Soboloff of the Fourth Circuit, who with the vast majority of his colleagues gave strength to the cause of equal rights in the remaining Southern states.

The reason I speak in such high praise of the Southern federal judges is that we of the Supreme Court merely *declared* the constitutional principle prohibiting segregation because of the race. We left those judges the job of *implementing* it in a region where three centuries of slavery and invidious segregation had case-hardened a way of life that permitted no deviation from the theory of white supremacy. District and circuit courts were the closest to the problem and knew the changes that could reasonably be made to accomplish the desired result. Faced with violent criticism in some places, they responded nobly. I have been told by some judges involved that on their visits home after some of their decisions, friends of many years, on seeing them approaching, would deliberately and obviously cross to the other side of the street to avoid greeting them. Not only they but their families were often humiliated in a variety of ways.

I recall one incident at a Judicial Council Meeting of the Fourth Circuit where the judges, in executive session, were reporting on conditions within their jurisdiction. One of the newly appointed district judges said, in substance, "After my decision in a recent school desegregation case, one of the statesmen of our region said in a public speech that, before having any evidence in the case, I sat down with the Negro plaintiffs and wrote the judgment which I ultimately rendered in their favor. Now, if I had done that, it was something for which I should be impeached. But, of course, I did no such thing. I am not asking this council to do anything in the matter, but you all have had more experience than I, and I would like to know if you have any advice for me."

There was silence for a few moments, and finally Judge Morris A. Soper of the Court of Appeals said, "It wouldn't make any difference to me whether the son-of-a-bitch is a statesman or not. I would seek him out and tell him in public that he is a goddamn liar."

That ended the matter peremptorily. I feel sure Judge Soper would have done just that. He was then over eighty years of age, and was as vigorous as a man many years his junior. He was from a former slave state which was completely conditioned to the Southern culture, as was the younger judge who asked the question, and it was difficult for him personally to accept some of the changes brought about by the *Brown* decision. On the other hand, as a federal judge, he accepted the legal interpretation of the Supreme Court. He did so without deviation, and I am sure the accusation that a judge conspired with one of the parties to prejudge a case was so abhorrent to him that he would not have let it go unchallenged.

Although the courts were the triggering force in destroying the old "separate but equal" fallacy, Presidents Kennedy and Johnson and the Congress are entitled to a fair share of credit for making meaningful the rights guaranteed by the Civil War Constitutional Amendments. In this connection, it must be remembered that in a number of early historic cases the Supreme Court narrowly interpreted those Amendments and eventually announced the "separate but equal" doctrine of *Plessy* v. *Ferguson*. That was used to open the door to all manner of discriminations, without leaving an opportunity to prevent them. In 1957, Lyndon Johnson, then the majority leader of the Senate, sponsored and had passed the first Civil Rights Bill in many decades. It was not an omnibus bill, but it pointed the way toward the public accommodation and voting rights bills that were later sponsored by President Kennedy and carried on to passage by President Johnson after Kennedy's assassination.

Busing is a false issue, and the reason I say that is because it has been blown out of all proportion. I suppose few parents in the nation like to see their children bused to school for any reason, but we are told that for reasons other than to achieve racial equality over forty per cent of our children in the kindergarten, elementary, and high schools are bused to and from school every day of the school year. We are also told that no more than one per cent are being bused by court order to prevent racial discrimination. In most cases, the courts have used the tool of busing because all other judicial efforts to implement *Brown* v. *Board of Education* have been frustrated by the intransigence of the community. Let us assume that in a case or two the lower courts have exceeded sound judgment, those cases are subject to review in the Supreme Court, and it has not set any rules in that respect which would inhibit quality education. I feel sure there are very few people who would deliberately take a child from a superior school and send him to an inferior one—that would be punishment of the child—but the possibility of interchanging students where the authorities deliberately maintain two grossly unequal standards on the pretense of equality in order to prevent desegregation could be a strong incentive to equalize them. Our goal is for equal opportunities for a good education, regardless of race, color, creed, or economic status. This, at a minimum, should be the heritage of every American child, and the essential tools to accomplish the result should not be taken from the courts, if we expect justice to be achieved through them.

Throughout my years as Chief Justice, I made it a practice not to read the "fan" mail concerning our cases, whether it arrived before or after decisions had been announced. Several reasons prompted this practice. First, it would be highly improper to discuss a case with anyone orally or in writing before our decision was made public. Secondly, at such times it would also be wrong to read mail advocating a decision either way. One might be unconsciously influenced, particularly if there was a great predominance of opinion favoring one side. Thirdly, a Justice should not try to explain or defend, or to acknowledge praise or criticism for a decision in such manner. The Court's opinion itself is a studied conclusion based on the issues involved and speaks for itself better than any informal discussion of it later. It is printed in the United States Supreme Court Reports and cannot be added to or detracted from except through future litigation on the same subject matter. I therefore concluded that if I were not to acknowledge such mail it would be better not even to read it. Accordingly, I instructed my secretaries simply to file it without calling my attention to it. I only remember deviating from this practice once, and that was in the *Brown* case.

The reason I did was that my secretary advised me that the mail was not heavy, and I wondered why this should be so. I was told that in the Rosenberg treason case, which was decided about three months before my arrival on the Court, mail to the Court was delivered in large sacks, each containing thousands of letters. I thought *Brown* was probably destined to bring about a similar reaction.

Probably it was mere curiosity about two months after the decision that caused me to ask to see the accumulated mail on the case. I remained in the office one Saturday afternoon to read it. To my surprise, there were only between six and seven hundred letters. And they were almost equally divided pro and con. Some of them were very bitter and excoriated us for the decision. Many were from clergymen complaining that it was contrary to the Bible and to the word of God. Some said that if God had intended all people to live together, he would not have made some black and some white, that he would not have separated them in different parts of the world. Still others thought that it was contrary to the Christian religion because if Christ had not been for segregation he would have taken a black man as one of his disciples. Others contended that it was pure Communism; that we were trying to "mongrelize" the nation. There were also letters from clergymen on the other side, saying that the *Brown* decision was in keeping with the Fatherhood of God and the Brotherhood of Man, a demonstration of the dignity of the human spirit and in keeping with the Biblical injunction to do unto others only that which you would have others do unto you. Many of the favorable letters, of course, stressed that it was in keeping with the words of our Declaration of Independence. Still others felt it was a heartening demonstration of democracy at work.

Most of the critical letters were from the Southern states, but a number were also from my own state of California. I was not surprised that they were on both sides of the question, but was again amazed at the comparatively small quantity of them. I mentioned this to some of my colleagues, and my recollection is that they said their mail was comparable to mine. This intrigued me because I was accustomed to reading of a single congressman receiving huge amounts of mail for days on a single bill. I have since learned that people do not write to Supreme Court Justices as they do to their legislators. They apparently follow that old admonition to the effect that if you don't like something, "write your congressman about it." Perhaps that is where most of the adverse mail on the *Brown* issues was directed, because there were plenty of congressmen making speeches that denounced us. We were called everything from illiterate to dishonest.

Then I was singled out by the John Birch Society for special treatment. Along highways throughout the nation, they rented large billboards saying "Impeach Earl Warren" and signed "John Birch Society." This continued until about six months before my retirement, when they abandoned that project and transferred their activities to others whom they considered "un-American." I was about to say they transferred their *wrath* against me to others, but it really wasn't wrath; in my opinion it was a public relations stunt. It was carried on for thirteen years as a means of collecting funds for their organization. As they well knew, we were functioning in a controversial and highly emotional area. Almost every day that we reported our opinions, there might be some losers as a result of the decision who would feel inclined to help finance any organization that opposed the Court. All they needed to know was what organization was active in that respect and that their names would not be publicized. The John Birch Society accommodated such people. Ironically, it was organized and operated somewhat like the

Communist Party, with secret "cells" whose membership lists were closely guarded from the public. Its hierarchy culminated in the dictatorship of Robert Welch, a wealthy, retired candymaker living in Boston. Its battle cry was against Communism, and it seemed to feel that the objective of every President from Woodrow Wilson to Lyndon B. Johnson was the consummation of international Communism. Some were described as conscious actors in the conspiracy and others as puppets in the hands of the bankers and other financial evil genii. In one of its official publications, even President Eisenhower was described as a conscious agent of Communism. The Society claimed a very large membership but only a few were ever identified. It was not a grass roots organization, and was financed by people of means who, among other things, objected to paying the taxes levied against them. The income tax was one of the Birch Society's principal "whipping boys," and many people in the higher money brackets contributed to the Society because of its claim that taxation was a principal weapon of Communism and its objective of limiting taxes to twenty-five per cent of income.

In the 1964 campaign for the presidency, there was a movement in the Republican Party to disavow any support given by the John Birch Society because of its venomous attacks on former Presidents of both parties and because of its clandestine method of operation. However, candidate Senator Barry Goldwater said he would not repudiate anyone who was for Goldwater; that he knew, without naming them, many fine Americans who were members of the John Birch Society, and that he was for any organization that was against Communism. The organization, using the device of making people hate some group by blaming that group for the ills of the nation, as Hitler blamed the Jews in Germany, chose the Supreme Court as the object of its attack. Partly, this was because the Court cannot engage in a running political defense of its actions. The Society needed a symbol; it chose me with its billboard campaign of "Impeach Earl Warren." I never was disturbed by it at the time, because the hundreds of thousands of dollars the members spent on the signs consumed most of their energy and resources. They knew, as does everyone else, that the only way a Justice of the Supreme Court can be removed is by an impeachment resolution of the United States House of Representatives, followed by a trial in the Senate. In all the thirteen years the campaign continued, nothing of that kind was attempted. Consequently, I recognized it for what it was—an expression of dislike on the part of vested interest groups who were offended by the Court's interpretation in various cases that came before us. These groups included: some people who felt hurt by our decisions regarding the federal income tax; monopolists who failed to convince us that antitrust laws as written by Congress should be diluted to the point of ineffectiveness; a few big oil and gas men who were pained when two bills favorable to them were vetoed because of fraud (one by President Truman and the other by President Eisenhower) and who then attempted to have the Supreme Court grant them the same rights through ingenious and devious litigation, and a number of people who were so frightened by Cold War propaganda that everyone who disagreed with them was suspected of being a Communist—or at least, in McCarthy jargon, a deluded "Commysimp." Joining these groups were those who were so concerned about violence and so-called "crime in the streets" that they believed accusations that the Supreme Court was "soft on crime" whenever it ruled in favor of an alleged criminal whose constitutional rights had been violated.

It was not difficult for me in such circumstances to view those "Impeach Earl Warren" billboards as ludicrous. I never was inflamed by them, and in passing one of them I could even smile as I surveyed the surroundings and speculated as to why it was placed at that particular site. Sometimes I thought I could discern the reason and other times it seemed to me that they simply had some left over and placed them haphazardly about. It was not so easy, though, to convince my wife that the signs should provoke a smile. In all my years in politics in California, I had never been subjected to any such treatment. I was cordially received there wherever I went and perhaps both of us were somewhat spoiled. However, before the signs started to come down, Nina, too, could pass them with a degree of equanimity.

My friend, Senator Thomas Kuchel, took the floor in the Senate and delivered a seething rebuke for the Birch Society's clandestine activities. He was widely acclaimed for his forthright speech because too many legislators were afraid of the concealed power of the organization.

Another longtime friend of mine who lent me support was California state senator Thomas M. Storke, publisher of the Santa Barbara News-Press. He was outraged when the impeachment signs went up. He said, "Earl, I'm going to take them on." I urged him strongly not to do so because, as I told him, it would not stop them, but on the contrary would advertise them and give them the publicity they sought. Senator Storke was eighty-seven years of age at the time, and had been operating his newspaper since the first day of the twentieth century, when he bought an old publication with a few hundred subscribers for twenty-five hundred dollars. He immediately became a champion for the city of Santa Barbara, and most of the good things that happened to it were initiated by him, including the establishment of the Santa Barbara campus of the University of California. He was a Californian of early days—a rancher, a horseman, an early Westerner in every sense of the word—whose antecedents had founded Santa Barbara and built the Presidio there in 1776.

When Tom Storke decided to do something, he did it. He announced in a front page editorial that he intended to tell the world of the chicanery, the cowardice, and the un-American character of the John Birch Society. He stated that he did not intend to spare any words; that he invited them to sue him for libel if they chose to do so; and that he was financially able to respond to any judgment for damages they might obtain. This latter statement was not an idle boast, because in a very few years he sold the newspaper for $9,200,000 cash, reserving to himself for the remainder of his life the editorship emeritus at a very substantial salary. He then did exactly what he said he would do. He took the hide off the Birch organization; wielded cudgels for me and for Senator Kuchel, and blasted the members for the un-American guile and secrecy of their activities. He never was sued for libel. On two different occasions, however, both he and I were hanged in effigy from the flagpole of the city's beautiful courthouse. Santa Barbara is a lovely place, but there was a sizable number of undisclosed Birchers there. In recognition of Tom's courage, which so many others lacked, he was acclaimed nationwide and received the Pulitzer Prize, the Nieman Prize of Harvard, and other awards.

The *Brown* case and the changes that it brought about caused many people to believe that it was the most important case of my tenure on the Court. That appraisal may be correct, but I have never thought so. It seemed to me that accolade should go to the case of *Baker* v. *Carr* (1962), which was the progenitor of the "one man, one vote" rule. Perhaps an explanation here would give an understanding of this view. I start with the premise that *Brown* v. *Board of Education* was of tremendous importance, and made a great impact on the life of the nation. On the other hand, the principle it declared of equal educational opportunities for all races was grounded solely on the Fourteenth Amendment to the Constitution, without benefit of legislation by Congress. This was not entirely a fault of Congress, as the Court, by its early decisions, had limited the scope of the Fourteenth Amendment, particularly by the "separate but equal" doctrine of *Plessy* v. *Ferguson*. *Brown* lashed at three centuries of slavery and its remnants based on the white supremacy theory, and was naturally resented bitterly in those parts of the nation where blacks were not even accorded the right to participate in government. On the other hand, if Congress had passed remedial legislation a generation or more before having to enforce *Brown*'s integration provisions, the blacks and other minorities would have achieved their rights by the middle of the twentieth century, and much of the emotional heat undoubtedly would have been avoided.

Now let us consider *Baker* v. *Carr*. That case arose in Tennessee, which was one of the most malapportioned states in the Union, although the legislatures of more than forty states were so unbalanced as to give people in certain parts of them vastly greater voting representation than in others. In Tennessee, for example, although there had been a conspicuous shifting of population from country to city, districts retained the same voting strength in the State Legislature that they had had for more than sixty years. Representation was distorted to the point where one district had only a few hundred voters while another embraced tens of thousands, yet both districts were given equal weight in legislative decisions. The situation approached the "Rotten Borough" era in England, where a few families were given parliamentary power equal to that of thousands of people in other parts of the country, thus bringing government to a very low estate until remedied. Tennessee had more small districts than large ones, and the representatives of those districts would not vote to redistrict the state to bring about fairer distribution of voting power because it would cause some of them to lose their seats and to relinquish control over the larger metropolitan areas. Neither would they vote to change or implement the State Constitution, and it could not be changed unless a measure to do so were submitted to the people by the Legislature. As a result, the cities and suburbs, where most of the people lived, had little to say about the manner in which they were governed They were deprived of an opportunity to do many of the things that were essential to their orderly development.

This situation was not unique to Tennessee. It applied in some degree to most of the states of the Union; in fact, only two, as I recall, had equitable representation in both houses of their legislatures. I remember Mr. Justice Black, who had been in public life for half a century, telling me that as far back as he could remember every governor in Alabama had run on a platform to equalize representation in the Legislature, only to be stymied by that body. In the state of Georgia, under what was called the Unit Rule, the great city of Atlanta had little more weight in the election of the governor and other state officers than one of the smallest counties. I was informed by another Justice from one of the more populous states that a lobbyist for some large interests told him that in order to stop any legislation disapproved by his clients, it was only necessary for him to control the votes of nine senators, and they could be from the least populous counties.

To all of this, our Supreme Court had in the past contributed. Because of timidity, it made change hopeless. It refused to enter or to permit lower federal courts to consider any litigation seeking to remedy unequal apportionment, on grounds that it was a political problem to be handled by political agencies of the states. Mr. Justice Frankfurter insisted on this, and resented our entering what he chose to call the "political thicket," contending that it would involve the courts in matters outside their rightful domain. But in *Baker* v. *Carr*, Mr. Justice Brennan wrote for a majority of the Court that the question of whether people underrepresented in their government were being deprived of equal protection of the laws was a justiciable one, subject to the jurisdiction of the courts. From the doctrine of that case developed the "one man, one vote" rule, and in the space of a very few years it covered the entire spectrum of representative government—federal, state, and local. While occasionally some aberrant piece of litigation, occasioned by self-interest, violates the principle of "one man, one vote," the doctrine has been accepted nationally and now regulates our political life. The reason I am of the opinion that *Baker* v. *Carr* is so important is because I believe so devoutly that, to paraphrase Abraham Lincoln's famous epigram, ours is a government of *all* the people, by *all* the people, and for *all* the people. It is a representative form of government through which the rights and responsibilities of every one of us are defined and enforced. If these rights and responsibilities are to be fairly realized, it must be done by representatives who are responsible to all the people, not just those with special interests to serve. In sustaining this principle in a case involving legislative representatives, I expressed it in this way:

> The right to vote freely for the candidate of one's choice is of the essence of a democratic society, and any restrictions on that right strike at the heart of representative government. And the right of suffrage can be denied by a debasement or dilution of the weight of a citizen's vote just as effectively as by wholly prohibiting the free exercise of the franchise . . .

And:

> Legislators represent people, not trees or acres. Legislators are elected by voters, not farms or cities or economic interests. As long as ours is a representative form of government, and our legislatures are those instruments of government elected directly by and directly representative of the people, the right to elect legislators in a free and unimpaired fashion is a bedrock of our political system. (*Reynolds* v. *Sims*, 1964)

Perhaps I should explain how I happened to write the opinion in some of these state legislative cases. My own state was one of the most malapportioned in the nation. After the 1920 census, when it became apparent that Los Angeles was outstripping the remainder of California in population, concern arose as to whether it would dominate all the other counties. Under our system at that time, the State Constitution provided for equal representation in both houses. There were eighty members in the Assembly and forty in the Senate. The Constitution further provided that in order to maintain the Legislature on a basis of equality it must be reapportioned immediately after each decennial federal census. We also had a constitutional provision known as the initiative by which the voters might submit legislation or Constitutional Amendments directly to the people by filing a petition with the Secretary of State bearing the signatures of eight per cent of the number of votes cast for the Office of Governor at the last election. Upon certification of the Secretary of State that the required number of valid signatures had been filed with him, the legislation proposed in the successful petition automatically appeared on the ballot. If voted for by a majority of the voters it became the law, either as a statute or a Constitutional Amendment, depending on the stated purpose for which it was submitted. That procedure was followed in changing the representation in our Legislature. The proposed law provided that the eighty members of the Assembly should be elected strictly according to population, but that the forty members of the Senate should be so distributed that no county would have more than one senator and no senatorial district would cover more than three counties. This plan was submitted as a Constitutional Amendment and approved overwhelmingly by the voters, and for a quarter of a century was used as our method of apportionment. It was called the "Federal System of Representation" because of its resemblance to our United States House of Representatives, which is based on apportionment by population, and our Senate, which was a fixed geographic representation regardless of population.

By the time I became governor, Los Angeles had about four million people, San Francisco about 800,000, Alameda (my county) about 750,000. Each of these three largest counties had but one senator each. On the other hand, a senator also represented some of the sparsely populated mountain counties with a three-county senatorial district of less than a hundred thousand people. Los Angeles tried two or three times through the initiative process to increase its voting power in the Senate, but each time almost every county in the state voted against such proposals out of fear of being dominated by Los Angeles. The last attempt was made in 1948 when I was governor. The state was functioning well at the time, and I gave a statement to the press opposing the change. There was no constitutional issue raised, merely a question of fair representation for the larger counties. Because most of the large counties except Los Angeles were against the proposal, I joined with them in opposing it. It was frankly a matter of political expediency.

I thought little more about this until *Baker* v. *Carr* came to the Supreme Court on the constitutional question of whether each voter was being given equal protection of the laws. I concluded that it *was* a matter for the courts to decide when I saw what effect disproportionate representation had in Tennessee and remembered my California experience.

There followed a spate of legal attacks against the makeup of legislatures in several states. One of those states was my own. I was led to the conclusion that it was unconstitutional to overweigh the value of some voters and underweigh the value of others. I then decided that rather than merely join the opinion of one of the other Justices, after having taken the political stand I had in California, I should now squarely face up to the question from a judicial viewpoint. Accordingly I assigned the state malapportionment cases to myself, knowing that this would create much comment in California. I wrote the opinion in *Reynolds* v. *Sims*. It held that our form of government required fair representation; that fair representation meant equal representation in which one man's vote had the same value as every other, and that legislatures not elected on that basis were unconstitutionally organized.

Naturally this created much controversy, most of it provoked by those who would lose their positions by the redistricting the ruling necessitated. The Council of State Governments opposed it to the point of proposing a Constitutional Amendment that would negate the decision.‡ Many states endorsed this proposal, but how close they came to making it effective is not known because some states did not agree to the resolution as written and substituted or added language of their own. Others withdrew their original approval. Whatever the number of states wanting a Constitutional Amendment, the proceeding was carried out almost in secret, with virtually no one opposing it. Just about the only notoriety given to the move would be a three- or four-line item on possibly page nineteen of the daily papers, announcing that the Legislature of State X had passed a resolution calling for a constitutional convention under Section V of the Constitution.

The only method ever used before this to amend the Constitution

‡ Ed. note: This proposal would have allowed states to amend the Constitution without going through Congress or a constitutional convention. Instead, two thirds of the state legislatures could propose an amendment and it would be adopted if three quarters of the legislatures then voted for it.

was submission by both houses of the Congress for a specific Amendment. That procedure was well understood by the nation, but the Amendments submitted to annul the decisions of *Baker* v. *Carr* and its progeny came under the portion of Article V which authorized Amendments "on the application of the Legislatures of two-thirds of the several States," etc. This procedure had never been attempted in the history of the nation. Congress had not enacted any procedure in the event of its use, and it was not at all certain whether a convention called in this manner would be limited to consideration of the particular Amendment suggested or whether it might be used to amend the Constitution to any extent it happened to choose.

At the same time and in the same manner, two other Amendments were proposed, one of which would have destroyed the effectiveness of the Supreme Court of the United States. It would have set up a "Court of the Union" composed of the fifty Chief Justices of the State Supreme Courts, with authority to review and overrule any decision of the United States Supreme Court in cases involving federal-state relations. The Court of the Union would convene upon the application of a certain number of states. This, of course, would have changed the character of our national institutions and would have impinged upon the Supremacy Clause of the Constitution (Article VI) to an uncharted extent in the enforcement of federal law as interpreted by the Supreme Court under Article III. The relevant portion of Article VI (Section 2) reads as follows:

> This Constitution, and the Laws of the United States which shall be made in Pursuance thereof; and all Treaties made, or which shall be made, under the Authority of the United States, shall be the supreme Law of the Land; and the Judges in every State shall be bound thereby, any Thing in the Constitution or Laws of any State to the Contrary notwithstanding.

In spite of the grave implications of these two proposals and a third which does not need discussion here, there was no national debate on the subject. The resolutions of the state legislatures were quietly moved along without the discussion they deserved. The American Bar Association was inert, thereby giving aid and comfort to supporters of the proposals. In spite of the ABA's plethora of sections and committees, not one of them undertook discussion of the legal issues with which the proposals were infected.

It can reasonably be said that one man, Arthur Freund, a prominent lawyer of St. Louis, was more responsible than all others combined in finally bringing the danger of the proposals into public view. When it looked as though either or both of these amendments might succeed in obtaining the endorsement of the requisite number of states, Freund made a one-man crusade of the issue. He wrote to legislators, lawyers, scholars, and newspapers until finally a few of the important newspapers of the country took cognizance of the situation, wrote articles about it, and pointed up its dangers. Only then did the movement die aborning.

The American Bar Association reacted to the state proposals as it did to the anticourt activities of Senator Joseph McCarthy. Its weight and influence during those years were with him and his anti-Communist hysteria and his diatribes against everyone who did not join him in his unsubstantiated attacks.

The Court was under attack by powerful interests nearly all the time I was there. The first storm came after *Brown* v. *Board of Education*. Most of the Southern legislators joined the Southern Manifesto, a statement condemning the decision, arousing the people to thwart it, and pledging themselves to employ all possible means to that end. There were fulminations on the floors of both houses, and threats to apply the dead hand of nullification. The Court received no support of any kind from the American Bar Association as we were pilloried and reviled. I was personally held to be a modern-day Thaddeus Stevens.* Such heated criticism, in spite of the lip service more recently given to the *Brown* ruling, has never subsided. To this day, every decision enforcing the equal protection or due process clauses of the Constitution in civil rights cases is the occasion for some people in Congress to assail the Court for the abuse of its function and the exercise of naked power.

Throughout the McCarthy era, we were under attack for being "soft on Communism" because we prevented rabid congressional committees from "exposing for the sake of exposure," from establishing "guilt by association," and from compelling witnesses to implicate themselves without regard to Fifth Amendment protection against self-incrimination. Even some of the lower courts joined in the witch-hunting.

In one such case, a federal judge sentenced a witness to prison for one year for refusing to name associates with whom he was in college fifteen years before. The inquiry was to show that he had fraternized

* Ed. note: Thaddeus Stevens was a Whig and later Republican leader of radical persuasion in the mid-1800s, much disliked by the South. He opposed the Fugitive Slave law, introduced the Fourteenth Amendment, advocated the confiscation of property in Confederate states, and led impeachment proceedings against President Andrew Johnson.

with students who were said to have been Communists at that distant time.†

I mention this example to show the extent of overzealousness that was rife in those days, and something of the human suffering it could cause.

Yet we continued to be assailed from every quarter for the Court's stand against such abuses. There was even legislation proposed, sponsored by Senator William Jenner of Indiana and later by Senator John M. Butler of Maryland, which was designed to divest the Supreme Court of jurisdiction in some of the "subversive activities" fields in which the McCarthy group was most interested. Some of this legislation, evoking as it did the atmosphere of Cold War hysteria, came dangerously close to passing.

General Eisenhower had campaigned in favor of the powerful oil and gas interests of the Southern states, particularly Texas, and promised that if elected he would see that the producers were kept free of federal regulation. The perimeters of this were far-reaching. Tens of millions of people throughout the country were dependent upon the oil and gas of the Gulf states as it came to them through interstate pipelines that reached to the Great Lakes and to both the North Atlantic and Pacific coasts. A federal hands-off policy was to be accomplished through congressional action exempting the sales of the gas and oil from regulation by the Federal Power Commission, which had been established to control interstate activities of the electrical, oil, and gas industries. Such a maneuver had been attempted in the administration of President Truman through a bill introduced by Senator Robert Kerr of Oklahoma, one of the advocates of big oil and gas interests. Because of irregularities in the passage of the Act, the President saw fit to veto it.

† Ed. note: The case referred to here is one in which the lower court judgment eventually was reversed. A number of cases of this kind found their way to the Court during Warren's tenure, culminating in *Sweezy* v. *New Hampshire* and its companion case, *Watkins* v. *U.S.*, both decided on the same day in 1957. Four Justices at this point were of the opinion that persons had a right not to testify when government investigative bodies exceeded their authority in their zeal to convert witnesses into informers or to establish guilt by association. Said the Chief Justice in his opinion on *Sweezy*: "The core problem is the same: to find a way to protect the constitutional liberties of individuals against unjustified encroachments through legislative activities without impeding the legislative process." Since the Justices at this time generally found for the individual against the encroachers, it brought them nose to nose with Senator McCarthy and other professional witch-hunters. Later, in the *Barenblatt* v. *U.S.* case (1959), the Court seemed to grow more cautious and back-pedal a bit by affirming the conviction of a Vassar instructor who had refused to answer questions about Communist associations. Chief Justice Warren, however, firmly joined Justices Black, Douglas, and Brennan in dissenting from this majority opinion.

After the election of President Eisenhower, the bill, with his blessing, was again introduced, and again passed. However, corruption raised its familiar head, and it developed that bribes were offered to legislators to vote for the bill. President Eisenhower, despite his original espousal, then vetoed it. Questionable conduct revolved largely around representatives of the Superior Oil Company, which had crossed my trail in former years. With two strikes on them, the oil and gas people did not take a chance of striking out. The Kerr bill was never introduced again. Instead, they shifted their ground to the courts, and sought by a series of cases to have the Supreme Court grant them the questionable benefits they had sought (and failed) to achieve through the Kerr bill. The Supreme Court was not responsive to this approach, and in all of the cases denied the relief sought.

Then came a suit brought by the government against the El Paso Gas Company for monopolizing the gas industry in all the Western states. The Court decided with the government, and against a merger desired by El Paso, but after the decision the government capitulated and joined in the endeavor to nullify the Court's mandate. Again, the Court did not accommodate El Paso and sent the case back to the lower trial court twice to have its mandate implemented. Thereafter the matter was taken to Congress in an attempt to nullify the judgment of the Court which had confirmed the government's original allegation of antitrust violation.

It is natural that these interests should be front-runners among those who would discredit the Court, and they have been somewhat effective. For many years, they have financed groups and individuals through their so-called "educational foundations" and have assailed the Court in scores of broadcasts and writings in which they talk about the need for law and order, protection against Communism, and anything else that has popular appeal. Strangely, they say nothing about the poor, downtrodden oil and gas industry and its tendency toward monopolistic practices.

While this was going on, the Court also incurred the wrath of the electric power interests. As almost everyone knows, the Tennessee Valley Authority is the *bête noire* for the private power sector of the economy. Established in the Roosevelt administration, it has so far survived claims that it is Communistic, Socialistic, and the mortal enemy of private enterprise. However, in 1952 General Eisenhower campaigned on a pledge to contain TVA so it could not in future encroach on private enterprise. When elected, he set up an interdepartmental committee to accomplish this result. Unfortunately, the "dollar-a-year man" who was appointed to make the survey and draw the terms of the contract which followed, awarding the Dixon-Yates combine rights in preference to

TVA, was disclosed to have a personal financial interest in giving the award to Dixon-Yates. Consternation followed, and the issue became so hot that President Eisenhower, on behalf of the government, canceled the contract because of this conflict of interest. Dixon-Yates then sued the government for damages for breach of contract. The case came to the Supreme Court. We decided for the government, but the thing I most remember about the argument was that after Solicitor General Lee Rankin, with his customary candor and straightforwardness, argued the conflict of interest issue and the cancellation of the contract, counsel for Dixon-Yates read a letter from the President saying it was the greatest contract of its kind which had ever been executed. This decision did not endear us to the electric power industry.

The breakup of the association between the giant General Motors Corporation and the Du Pont interests, although our action was in accord with the contention of the government that the connection was a violation of the antitrust laws, created a sensation. Legislators of both parties rushed to pass legislation relieving the parties of any of the legal consequences of their violations, and amended the tax laws so as to minimize any tax loss.

This case and the fact that we interpreted the antitrust laws very strictly gave us a bad name with big business. I was with the majority most of the time in sustaining the provisions of the antitrust laws. I always disliked monopoly and the more I saw of business and government the more committed I became to the theory that the greatest danger to our private enterprise system is monopoly. I therefore felt that whenever Congress determined that certain conduct was monopolistic and proscribed it, it was our solemn duty to enforce such legislation without equivocation. This was not a popular attitude in many business circles, and it put us in conflict with some of the railroads when we held up the gigantic merger of the Pennsylvania and New York Central railways into what is now known as Penn Central, and with the banking industry when we ordered some of the biggest banks to dissolve their monopolistic mergers.

We also were heavily attacked by many people, particularly legislators, when we declared compulsory prayers in the public schools to be unconstitutional.‡ I vividly remember one bold newspaper headline

‡ Ed. note: A key case in this regard was *Engel* v. *Vitale*, in which the daily invocation of prayer promulgated by the State Board of Regents for New York State public schools was declared unconstitutional by the Supreme Court. This, and a series of religious liberty cases in which decisions went against everything from obligatory Bible-reading in public schools to the requirement that public officials swear to a belief in God, caused the Chief Justice, a staunchly religious man, to be bitterly assailed by those who took the Court's actions to be antireligious.

saying, "Court outlaws God." Many religious denominations in this same spirit condemned the Court, although most of them have receded from that position. Scores of Constitutional Amendments and legislative bills were proposed in the Congress to circumvent the decision but were later abandoned when the public came to recognize that the ruling was not an irreligious one. Rather it tried to maintain the separation of church and state guaranteed by the First Amendment.

History is replete with evidence of terrible wars between different denominations of the Christian religion. In Philadelphia in the last century, bloody strife, murder, and arson were rampant because of a controversy over whether the Protestant or Catholic Bible should be used in public school devotions. The majority of us on the Court were religious people, yet we found it unconstitutional that any state agency should impose a religious exercise on persons who were by law free to practice religion or not without state interference. Among other things, this assured that conflict between religious factions could be avoided.

Because the Court, over the years, sought to make our criminal procedures conform to the relevant provisions of the Constitution and be a reality for the poor as well as the rich, it was made the target for widespread abuse. Many of these cases dislodged old law enforcement practices that had become tarnished with brutal intimidation of prisoners and suspects along with other injustices. Because police and indignant citizens were overwhelmed with the wave of violence that flooded the land, they found in the Court a stationary target and made us responsible for the increasing crime rate. We were "soft on criminals," they said.

Their attack centered on the case of *Miranda* v. *Arizona*, in which we held that before a prisoner—as distinguished from one who is being questioned in the merely investigative process—can be interrogated by police, he must be informed of his constitutional rights as to the purpose of the arrest and of the fact that he is entitled to have a lawyer present during questioning if he desires one. We also declared that the defendant must be told that if he cannot afford counsel, the state will provide same free of charge, and that he cannot be compelled to talk, but that if he does, anything said can be used against him. There was really nothing new in this except to require police and prosecutors to advise the poor, the ignorant, and the unwary of a basic constitutional right in a manner which had been followed by Federal Bureau of Investigation procedures for many years. It was of no assistance to hardened underworld types because they already know what their rights are and demand them. And so it is with all sophisticated criminals and affluent prisoners who had ready access to their lawyers. However, because so many people who are arrested are poor and illiterate, short-cut methods and often cruelties are perpetrated to obtain convictions. Hence a large percentage of police officers and prosecutors rebelled against such an articulation of a defendant's rights by the Supreme Court.

A sizable proportion of the American people, too, groping for a reason for so much criminal activity in our disturbed society but overlooking the root causes the crime—such as the degradation of slum life in the ghettos, ignorance, poverty, the drug traffic, unemployment, and organized crime (often made possible by the corruption of law enforcement officials)—joined in placing the blame on the courts and particularly on the Supreme Court. This formed part of the basis for the so-called "law and order" campaign of 1968. It was a one-sided affair because courts cannot debate the wisdom or propriety of their decisions, and the wildest and most emotional charges often go unchallenged.

This resulted in much proposed legislation in the Congress, and a great deal of castigation of the courts in congressional committees and on the floor.*

The House of Representatives became extremely critical when we granted *certiorari* to review a decision of the Court of Appeals of the District of Columbia which confirmed the House's action in excluding Representative Adam Clayton Powell from its membership. His expulsion occurred in spite of his valid election to a seat from New York and his possession of the three constitutional requirements for the position: citizenship, qualifying age, and residence. The House employed special New York counsel and claimed that our exercise of jurisdiction to review an act of Congress refusing to seat an elected member of that body was an unwarranted confrontation of one of the three branches of government by another. They contended that the decision of Congress was not reviewable in any court. We eventually held, in an opinion written by me only one week before my retirement, that the House of Representatives had exceeded its constitutional powers in excluding Powell from membership by the requirement of only a majority vote. Correct procedure called for expulsion from membership for misconduct only after a trial and by a two-thirds vote. Powell had, after all, been seated according to the wishes of the voters of his congressional district.

This action of the Congress, though clearly beyond that body's constitutional powers, was provoked by the flamboyant, abrasive, and in-

---

* Ed. note: In recent years the Burger Court has modified the *Miranda* protections somewhat in specific decisions involving such things as the resumption of questioning of a prisoner after a reasonable length of time, the treatment of grand jury witnesses, and the possible impeachment of defendants who change their testimony from that originally given arresting officers. But, by and large, the erosion has not been extensive.

solent actions of the congressman. It also had racial overtones because Powell was black. Although other members of Congress have been charged with corruption in the courts and even convicted and sentenced to imprisonment, the House traditionally has permitted them to go unscathed as congressmen, even to the extent of permitting them to retain committee chairmanships and control vital legislation.

I have enumerated these different areas of decision and the enemies they have created for the Court, not as a complaint against their disapproval of us, but merely to show that the Supreme Court, if it defies the status quo, is bound to build up a formidable array of dissenters in powerful places. I hope the Court can always be criticized as publicly and as forcibly as desired. Justices must live with their judgments and be judged by them, not only at the time of their rendition, but through the indefinite future.

Not all judges and lawyers agree that the courts should be powerless to answer unfair criticism. They believe that the bench's power of punishment for contempt should be expansive and almost without limit. However, one of the things that the Supreme Court has done in recent years is to limit contempt proceedings to certain definite categories, and to limit punishments after a trial so they conform to the principles of due process. This, in my opinion, is essential to the preservation of a humane administration of justice that eschews arrogance.

In discussing the practice of courts punishing for contempt, it should be mentioned that nearly all the more severe punishments were imposed on people who were poor or for one reason or another were unpopular in the community. A classic example was that of a woman witness in the West Coast trial of a number of unimportant members of the Communist Party. The witness was being interrogated about her association with others who were alleged to have been connected with Communist activities. She stated to the Court that she was willing to testify as to her own actions, but that she would not be an informer against others. After testifying, she was asked eleven questions such as "Did you know A or B, etc.?" all of which she refused to answer. At the conclusion of the trial, the judge summoned her before him for contempt of court for failure to answer the questions, and angrily sentenced her to serve one year in prison for each separate refusal. The sentences were to be served consecutively, thus resulting in an aggregate of eleven years of imprisonment for contempt of court, all this without a trial by a jury or even by a judge who was detached from the incident and presumably free from bias.

This was at the height of the Cold War era when the hysteria created by Senator McCarthy was abroad and many people—in fact, a large segment of our citizenry—were inflamed against anyone who espoused the political philosophy of Communism or was suspected of associating with anyone who did. As a result, the Supreme Court was soundly traduced for setting aside this outrageous conviction and for reversing the convictions of the defendants in the case on the ground that the government had failed to show any illegal acts on their part; it had merely discovered that they advocated Communism as a political philosophy. Many politicians made anti-Supreme Court sentiment a basis of their campaigns for election, and some with long careers in high office maintained their tenure by such an appeal.

In a free country, people who feel that they or the public generally have been injured by an act of government have a right to complain. It is a right protected by the First Amendment's guarantee of freedom of speech and the press and by the right "to petition the Government for a redress of grievances." It is a therapeutic right because, if it is denied, government is no longer responsible to the will of the voters who are supposed to run our institutions through their elected representatives. Although federal judges are not elected, the principle applies equally to them as well as to the officers of the legislative and executive branches.

The judging process is particularly vulnerable to such fault-finding because in every case the judge decides for someone and against someone after a courtroom confrontation which invokes self-interest and emotion as well as reason in the reaction of the parties. A person who becomes a judge should understand that protest is one of the constituents of the process, and if he cannot adjust to it he should not undertake the job. To use the admonition of President Truman, "If you can't stand the heat, stay out of the kitchen." Criticism becomes normal, whether the judging is in a courtroom or on an athletic field. How many times have we heard at a baseball game the booing of the umpires even before they have been called upon to make a single decision? This is not ill will but merely a demonstration of the public's right to place blame.

The Supreme Court is particularly subject to criticism because most of its decisions are, as they say in athletic events, "close calls" and "judgment calls." Also, as a case wends its way to the Supreme Court, it becomes charged with emotion from the publicity given it and the discussion that follows. In addition, the questions presented to the Court are public questions which normally affect large groups of people. Add to these things the fact that its decisions are final, and one can easily see why the Supreme Court would attract more criticism than other courts. Also, the criticism becomes effective because it is a one-sided affair. Justices must take it in silence, leaving it to the people to form their own opinions concerning the Court's actions. This limita-

tion and others make the life of a Justice of the Supreme Court an aus-
tere one, yet I could generally accept denunciation as a part of the job
without resentment, except for one phase of it. That phase was the
treatment the Court received from the American Bar Association,
which I shall now discuss.

X

FORMIDABLE DISSENTERS: *The Court and Its Castigators*

Throughout the years of the McCarthy era and the desegregation period, the American Bar Association almost never had a kind word to say for the Court. On the contrary, it did much to discredit us. For years, it joined supporting Southern racists who accused the Court of arrogating power to itself because of its civil rights cases, particularly the *Brown* decision, and of being soft on crime and Communism.

This I thought was one organization from which the Court had a right to expect an enlightened appraisal of its work and a public defense of it where such support could be justified. But this was not forthcoming. One incident will show not only how it failed to support the Court but also how the ABA threw the full weight of its organization against our actions in a way designed to discredit us throughout the world.

The Association decided for its annual meeting in 1957 to make a pilgrimage to London where we, with the English Bench and Bar, might jointly express our devotion to the principles of common law which had developed there and had become the foundation for the legal institutions of both countries. I was approached by the president of the Association, Mr. David Maxwell of Philadelphia, and asked if I would lead the pilgrimage. I told him that Mrs. Warren and I had some overseas travel contemplated for the summer vacation, but he was insistent that it was most important for this historic goodwill mission of the American Bar to be headed by the Chief Justice of the United States. Reluctantly I consented and revised our plans for the summer.

As the time for departure came closer, I was told that they were thinking of inviting Vice-President Nixon to join the caravan, and was asked what I thought of the idea. I replied that I had no objection, but that if it were done, the character of the visit to England would be radically changed; it would then become a political rather than a legal affair, and there would no longer be any necessity for me to be there. I said this because the political pot was boiling as to whether Vice-President Nixon was to succeed President Eisenhower. Governor Rockefeller and others were very much in the news as possible Republican successors to the President. Knowing the mild interest of the news media in common law and their intense interest in national politics, I felt sure that the participation of the Vice-President would completely subordinate the legal purpose of the convention to a political one. I do not know whether the Vice-President was invited or not, but a news story was leaked from the Association to the effect that because of personal animosity I had been instrumental in barring him from attendance at the convention.

As to the convention itself, the principal business was done in New York, leaving only the filing of a few committee reports and the ceremonial affairs for the British meeting.

One of the committee reports filed the first morning in London was a publicity "blockbuster" on "Communist Tactics, Strategy and Objectives." It told little about those matters; rather, it was a diatribe against the Supreme Court of the United States, charging it with aiding the Communist cause in fifteen recent cases. It listed the allegedly pro-Red cases, giving biased outlines of their facts and the Court's holdings, then arguing that they gave great joy and comfort to the Communists. Finally, it recommended that Congress enact legislation to protect the nation from the effects of these sinister Supreme Court decisions. It concluded with the following:

> If the courts lean too far backward in the maintenance of theoretical individual rights it may be that we have tied the hands of our country and have rendered it incapable of carrying out the first law of mankind—the right of self preservation.

This became the theme of the convention so far as public interest was concerned. The press gave full coverage to it, and I was badgered by reporters the remainder of my stay in London for a reply to it. However, I gave no statement because I did not go across the Atlantic to engage in a bitter controversy within the group of which I was supposed to be the leader. We were declaredly there on a goodwill mission to testify to the unity of the two nations in preserving freedom under law. The Paris edition of the New York *Herald Tribune*, which circulated throughout Europe, was typical of the coverage. In its main article on page one on Friday, July 26, 1957, under the headline "BAR ASSOCIATION TOLD HIGH COURT WEAKENS SECURITY AGAINST REDS" and subheads "NEW LAWS TO PROTECT U.S. ASKED" and "DELEGATES ACCEPT COMMITTEE VIEW," the opening paragraphs indicate the thrust of the story:

> The policy-making body of the American Bar Association accepted without protest here today a report stating that recent Supreme Court decisions threaten the right of the United States to "protect itself against Communist subversion" and that "serious consideration" must be given to corrective legislation.
>
> The House of Delegates, the association's assembly of 236 policy-making members, heard former United States Sen. Herbert R. O'Conor, Md., cite reasons why a six-point legislative program must be erected against the new "resilience" of American Communists . . .
>
> The six-point legislative program asked by Mr. O'Conor's special Bar Association Committee on Communist Activities generally would undo, if enacted, the legal effect of 15 Supreme Court decisions in the last 15 months.

Following this in the newspaper was a long dissertation on the report itself. This was the "great news" of our trip to the home of the common law. I have never said so before, but in my opinion it was saved for the occasion for the sole purpose of achieving some publicity because there was so little else at the convention to arouse the news media.

After that, I was more or less a pariah and several snide articles concerning me appeared in the press. They were of no importance to anyone else, and are not worthy of repetition here, but were designed to show that I was not only discredited by the Bar of the United States but was myself annoyed by the customs of England. This last insinuation was positively untrue. I was cordially treated by the English people, from Her Majesty the Queen and Sir Winston Churchill to the rank and file of the British Bar.

Never before have I discussed any phase of this affair, although I have been asked many times to divulge the story. I tell it here because it is indicative of the disservice the American Bar Association did to the Supreme Court, and I have no hesitancy in saying now that it was done designedly to besmirch the Court and to gain publicity for an otherwise rather unproductive convention. I say this because the Association apparently was later ashamed of it, and did not include it as given in its permanent report of the proceedings of that year. Volume 82 of the Reports of American Bar Association, 1957, carries a report of the convention. On page 179, it offers only an insipid summary of the committee action under the heading "Communist Tactics, Strategy and Objectives," and concludes with this statement: "The full report of the Committee which was received and filed appears on Page 328." Turning to page 328, we find a truncated version of that report, leaving out the castigation of the Supreme Court and concealing the real import and purpose of it.

There was no reason at all why this committee report should have been left for London. It could have been disposed of in New York. There was no debate on it, no action taken on it except to file it, but the implication was left that the American Bar Association approved of it, as indicated by the subheading of the article above referred to in the *Herald Tribune*, "Delegates Accept Committee View." This view was permitted to stand and no official of the Association said a word to dispel that impression. It was not until the last night of the convention, at the banquet in Guild Hall, when Sir Winston Churchill spoke in high terms of the Court, that anything was said to soften the blow.

The committee report in glowing terms praised the Commission on Government Security, headed by Loyd Wright, a former president of the American Bar Association. It, too, was a scare document insinuating throughout that the Supreme Court was legally responsible for a resurgence of Communist activity in the United States, and ending with a recommendation that all Court personnel be screened as to their loyalty. This meant that they should be passed upon by the FBI before the Court would be entitled to employ them.

The only other ABA committee report of any notoriety was that of the Individual Rights Affected by National Security Committee (page 340, Annual Proceedings) recommending that the district courts be empowered to send people to jail summarily for contempt if they failed to answer questions of the Un-American Activities Committee of the House of Representatives. It approved H.R. 259, which would have accomplished this purpose without the benefit of indictment or jury trial.

It, too, was a rebuke to the Supreme Court for having held in *Watkins* v. *United States* (1957) that although the Congress has broad powers of investigation to assist it in determining what legislation should be enacted, it has no power to expose people for the mere sake of exposure.

The combination of these reports did much disservice to the Supreme Court, both at home and throughout the world. They were extreme right-wing documents in the spirit of Senator Joseph McCarthy, and aroused many people who were terrified by the "Red scare" hysteria of the Cold War. The Court was flayed thereafter by many on the floor of Congress, and Senator McCarthy himself said, "I will not say that Earl Warren is a Communist, but I will say he is the best friend the Communists have in America." When the John Birch Society started its publicity campaign to "Impeach Earl Warren," it prompted one extreme right-wing commentator and lecturer to tell a New England audience, "I would not impeach Earl Warren; I would lynch him."

To my knowledge, no one prominent in the American Bar Association condemned these things. The mood of the moment, I am sure, prompted many people to agree. Others, while thinking such anti-Court overreaction was rather bizarre, treated it only humorously. But can you imagine the uproar that would have followed if the same things had been said about the President, the Vice-President, the speaker of the House or some prominent senator?

All this was, of course, stimulation for Dan Moody and similar broadcasters who sang a daily song for the sanctification of the Texas oil tycoons and other sacred cows of the right wing, and it was also a boon to religious bigots like Gerald L. K. Smith and military fanatics turned politicians like General Edwin Walker of Texas, who purveyed their own brands of vilification.

After the ABA convention in London, Mrs. Warren and I took a month to travel through Ireland, Scotland, and England, returning the latter part of August on the S.S. *United States*. During this tour, we traveled alone and with few official commitments, which made it very refreshing. The leisure time also afforded me an opportunity to reappraise my association and experiences with the American Bar Association, and to determine what my future conduct with relation to it should be.

By the time I arrived back in Washington, I had concluded that I could no longer be a member of an organization of the legal profession which would ask me to lead fifteen thousand of its members overseas on a goodwill mission and then deliberately and trickily contrive to discredit the Supreme Court which I headed.

Accordingly, I wrote a letter to Mr. Charles R. Rhyne, the newly elected president of the Association. In the letter I resigned from the ABA, stating my reasons. I did not want to make a great public controversy over it, and accordingly did not make the letter public. I sent it to him marked "Personal and Confidential" to insure that it would reach him first. This is a partial quote from the letter, which has never yet been made public:

> After giving the matter most serious consideration, both before and after the London Convention, I am convinced that my continued membership in the American Bar Association would not contribute to the welfare of the Association or of the Court of which I am a member. I, therefore, resign with the following brief explanation of my reasons for so doing.
>
> The Association is composed primarily of practicing lawyers, and the members should be free at all times to say and do whatever they consider to be in the interests of their practice. This involves full discussion of the decisions of all our courts. Such a course inevitably leads to differences of opinion concerning the wisdom of those decisions. This calls for debate, and if the Association is to fulfill its purpose, it should always be in a position to criticize those decisions without the embarrassment of the presence of the Chief Justice of the United States, who is partly responsible for the most controversial of them. His presence would, of necessity, cause embarrassment to some, because the bar of the nation, if not the general public, knows that the members of the Supreme Court cannot with propriety engage in public debate when their decisions are challenged, and that they must live in silence with what they have written regardless of what might be said in derogation thereof . . .
>
> [Ed. note: The Chief Justice goes on to describe the circumstances of the offensive report, as already related, and then concludes in the letter:]
>
> This [attack on the Court], as I am sure must have been anticipated, was the most widely publicized action of the Convention. It conveyed the thought to the world that in the *unanimous* opinion of the American Bar, the Supreme Court of the United States is advancing the cause of Communism, is unworthy of its heritage and, therefore, must be thwarted by the other Branches of Government. If that is the opinion of the Association, it is, of course, its right to say so. Moreover, it

would be its duty to say so. But the Chief Justice, who is part and parcel of the Court, and who bears his share of responsibility for its actions, should never be put in a position where he can be represented as either subscribing to the condemnation or of being too timid to say even a single word in defense.

These are my own personal views. Membership in the Association being an individual matter, I have so treated it in taking this action, and have not discussed it with any of my associates . . .

I shall continue to cooperate with the American Bar Association in every worthy enterprise. As you must know, I have a high regard for you, and I anticipate that you will give to the Association a forward-looking administration of which all lawyers can be proud. If I can be of assistance to you in accomplishing that end, you have but to call on me.

In a few days, I received the following letter from him:

With reference to our discussion of your letter of September 3, I have now obtained a copy of the transcript from the House of Delegates and it reads as follows:

CHAIRMAN RHYNE: Because of the requests that have been made to the Chair, I would like to call the attention of the House to a notice to editors that has been placed on the press desk over here, to this effect:

"Reports of Committees and Sections of the American Bar Association, prepared for submission to the House of Delegates, represent the views of the Committee or Section reporting, and are NOT to be construed as the official policy of the American Bar Association.

"In the case of those reports preceded by specific resolutions calling for approval of the House of Delegates, action by the House on such recommendations becomes official policy of the Association."

As you all know that is in accordance with Article XII of the Rules.

This notice was on the press desk at the time of the making of the report to which you refer. It is also my impression that the report was summarized rather than read in full to the House, but I want to check the official transcript against the report as released to the press by the Chairman on that point.

Since your letter was labeled "personal and confidential" I have labeled this note that way also. Before presenting your resignation to our Board of Governors which, as I informed you, is the only body authorized under the American Bar Association's Constitution to act upon it, I would appreciate a written authorization from you. Otherwise, some member of that body is almost certain to inquire by what authority I am revealing something that was written to me in confidence.

I have already expressed to you how much I deeply regret your decision and my hope that you will reconsider before the October meeting of the Board.

I promptly replied as follows:

This is in response to your letter of September 6th concerning mine of September 3rd.

By labelling my letter "Personal and Confidential," I had no intention of limiting your use of it. I merely marked it in that manner so that it would be sure to come to your attention first.

I then gave no more thought to the matter, believing that I was no longer a member.

The next year the ABA convention was held in Los Angeles. Because it was in my own state, I was invited to make a speech there. In order to establish that my resignation was not a matter of personal pique, I agreed to appear, and to speak as I did annually to the American Law Institute on the state of the judiciary.

It was a great mistake. While there with four other Justices of the Supreme Court, I attended a dinner given by one of the committees, and without warning Chief Justice John R. Dethmers of the state of Michigan, a vitriolic fellow, gave the U. S. Supreme Court a lambasting the like of which I had never heard. That, of course, attracted the news media and produced reportage highly derogatory to the Court.

That was the last meeting of the ABA I ever attended, but it is not the end of the story.

A few months later, Mr. Joseph D. Stecher, secretary of the American Bar Association, from his office in Chicago announced to the press that I had been dropped from membership in the Association for "nonpayment of dues." This was absolute libel. On September 3, 1957, my dues were paid up until August 1958. It then came to light that an obscure and little known rule of the Association provided that the resignation of a member must be approved by the Board of Governors, and that for some undisclosed reason they had not accepted mine the previous year. At the February meeting in 1959, the Board of Governors did accept my resignation but did not make my letter public, and their announcement was hazy. Mr. Ross Malone of New Mexico was president of the Association. On his trips about the country, he blew hot and cold depending on where he was, until I finally wrote telling him that I at least wanted a letter from him which I could show to my children proving ". . . that their father had neither welched on his dues nor lied about his resignation."

Almost six months later, I received a reply. It was equivocal and left the matter open to other unfavorable implications, so I wrote the whole experience off as a bad one. I could, of course, have made public my original letter of resignation, which would have settled the matter, but I did not desire to initiate another public controversy, which could only hurt the Court and the Association. So I remained silent.

A few years later, Mr. John D. Randall of Iowa, then president of the ABA, came to my chambers and said he hoped I would rejoin the Association. I told him that was not possible, and I reminded him of the way they had handled my resignation. He told me he was not familiar with the situation, but that he would interest himself in it and report back to me. I said that I did not care to make a public controversy over it, but that, as I told Mr. Malone, I did not want my children to believe that their father had been dropped for nonpayment of dues or for some other reason that could not be disclosed. In due time, I received a forthright letter which I appreciated and which served my purpose.

In summary, it said that Mr. Randall had personally examined the files of the Association and had ". . . concluded that the Association inadvertently has created a most undesirable picture with reference to [my resignation] and that you have been placed in a most embarrassing situation without any fault on your part whatever."

Mr. Randall's letter went on to say that I was a member in good standing at the time of my resignation and that the inaction of the ABA's Board of Governors ". . . sprang from its hopefulness that you might withdraw the resignation." He explained that Mr. Rhyne and the members of the Board had misinterpreted my "personal and confidential" marking on the resignation letter of September 3, 1957, had therefore neglected to file the letter in the official records of the Association, and this had led to confusion that resulted in Mr. Stecher's unwarranted statement that I had been dropped from the rolls for non-payment of dues.

"Fairness to you causes me to write this frank appraisal of the matter," wrote Mr. Randall graciously, "and to extend our sincere regrets, with the hope that you will accept the same in the spirit in which it is extended."

I then forgot about the matter, and heard nothing more about it until Mr. Edward L. Wright of Arkansas became president of the Association in 1970. I do not know what prompted him to review the incident, but I received a letter which concluded: "The purpose of this personal letter is not to reopen an old and unpleasant subject; rather, my only desire is to memorialize in a single writing the fact that your termination of membership in the American Bar Association came about solely from your voluntary resignation effective September 3, 1957."

This, too, I appreciated because it was unsought and was, I am sure, written only in a spirit of fair play. I, of course, wrote thanking him for his interest in the matter and for the fairness of his appraisal.

This is the first public disclosure of the facts of my resignation from the American Bar Association, and I do not write now to create fresh controversy. Few people will care about my personal situation, but it really is an important factor in the appraisal of the Supreme Court by the public. If the Court cannot rely upon the main national body of the legal profession to treat it fairly in times of stress, whether it be the Communist scare, the racial question, the "law and order" crisis, or the so-called "strict constructionist" theory of the Constitution, it is, indeed, defenseless against the most powerful and reactionary interests in the nation.

I have spoken sharply of some of the ABA's leadership, but I do not mean to impugn the motives or actions of all of its presidents. Some of them were very fine, generous-spirited men who, left to their own devices, would have done much more for the welfare of the public as well as the legal profession. But each of them has but a few months of actual leadership and little opportunity to change the course of the organization or the predispositions of its bureaucracy. The ABA has been developed over the course of many years in the image of powerful commercial and geographical interests that are too influential to disturb. I have long thought it is unfortunate that there are not two broadly based national legal organizations, one openly oriented toward the commercial and industrial interests and the other committed to human rights for all people regardless of race, color, political views, or economic status. I do not suggest that either should separate itself from any phase of the legal spectrum, but that each, with deference to the other, could state its major objectives without assuming to cover the entire field of the law. The ABA attempts to embrace the entire field, only to black out on some areas, as it did at this critical time in the late 1950s when human rights were being infringed upon and later when the malapportionment of legislative bodies was an issue. As an example in addition to the instances I have cited of its public repudiation of the Supreme Court, the ABA failed in its work sessions to even consider the basic principles of civil rights or the Bill of Rights. Finally, a proposed resolution (page 120, ABA Report, 1957) to express the disapproval of the Association for inflammatory attacks against the Supreme Court was disapproved by the committee to which it was referred, and tabled without discussion. This is not the role for a national association of lawyers to play. An association dedicated to human rights could not avoid such a responsibility. Two organizations such as I have suggested could exist in healthy competition without injuring each other.

This has been a long dissertation about the powerful interests the Court offended and the abandonment of it by the American Bar Association, but I believe it all points to the reasons why the public opinion polls for years have shown that only a minority of the public—percentage-wise only in the low thirties at times—believe in the job the Court is doing. It demonstrates the old axiom that constantly dripping water will wear away stone. If the Court had been given credit by the ABA for integrity when it was accused of being dishonest in its efforts to insure equal rights for minority groups, or when it was accused of subversion in its endeavor to give the same constitutional protection to the most currently despised groups as was accorded those well stationed in life, or when it was accused of being soft on crime, or when it insisted that the poor were entitled to legal counsel as well as the rich, or when it was flayed as a Godless group of men because it held that state-prepared and compelled prayers for children in the public schools violated the First Amendment provision for the separation of church and state, or when it insisted that under our system of government one man's vote should have the same value as that of any other—if it had been conceded credit for having a certain integrity and constancy in its defense of these constitutional causes, however unpopular they might be with the powerful and privileged, then I am sure that the opinions of a sizable proportion of the people would have been more tolerant. In the absence of any such credit-giving, the Court could expect nothing different from the harsh reaction it got from those who were influenced by the ABA.

But the principal question this situation raises is how the Supreme Court should react to all such attacks.

Some candidates running for office have successfully made the Supreme Court their whipping boy in discussing Communism, crime in the streets, the erosion of religious training, vested interest in governmental representation, and other problems. The Court then has the choice of doing what Mr. Dooley said ("The Supreme Court follows the election returns") or removing itself as far as possible from the political tumult of the times and dedicating its efforts to:

> . . . a more perfect Union, establish justice, insure domestic tranquility, provide for the common defence, promote the general welfare, and secure the blessings of liberty to ourselves and our posterity . . .

as provided in the Preamble to the Constitution.

Every man on the Court must choose for himself which course he should take. Conformity to the wishes of the powerful would be the easiest by far. To habitually ride the crests of the waves through the constantly recurring storms that arise in a free government, always agreeing with the dominant interests, would be a serene way of life. It is comforting to be liked, and it would be pleasant to bask in the sunshine of perpetual public favor. As tempting as that might be, I could not go that way. Of necessity, I chose the latter course because that is the only means by which I could find satisfaction in my work. So many times in life the only permanent satisfaction one can find comes from bucking an adverse tide or swimming upstream to reach a goal. The fulfillment of that goal, according to my lights, rested in the discharge of my constitutional oath of office to ". . . support and defend the Constitution of the United States against all enemies, foreign and domestic . . ." and the judicial oath to ". . . administer justice without respect to persons, and do equal right to the poor and to the rich . . ."

As everyone knows, individual members of the Court did not always agree with the result achieved in many cases. But I want to say here, without equivocation, that I do not ascribe to any Justice who sat and disagreed with me on any occasion a lesser dedication on his part to support and defend the Constitution than I claim for myself. Our disagreement often stemmed merely from differing interpretations of its general words. In speaking of my adherence to the Constitution, I do not register myself with whose who, in the political jargon of today, classify themselves as "strict constructionists." That is a spurious issue. There has been an avalanche of dissembling in support of the term, but I have not heard anyone who uses it as a shield define it. Neither have I read of anyone in the history of the Court who can safely be said to be a strict constructionist. I shall have more to say about "strict construction" in another context.

Neither do I agree with the so-called doctrine of "neutral principles."

It, too, is a fantasy and is used more to avoid responsibilities than to meet them. As the defender of the Constitution, the Court cannot be neutral, whether it is judging litigation between individuals, between the government and an individual, or between branches of the government. The Court sits to decide cases, not to avoid decision, and while it must recognize the constitutional powers of the branches of Government involved, it must also decide every issue properly placed before it.

Over a century and a half ago, Chief Justice Marshall said of the function of the Supreme Court:

> It is most true that this court will not take jurisdiction if it should not; but it is equally true, that it must take jurisdiction if it should. The judiciary cannot, as the legislature may, avoid a measure because it approaches the confines of the Constitution. We cannot pass it by because it is doubtful. With whatever doubts, with whatever difficulties a case may be attended, we must decide it if it be brought before us. We have no more right to decline the exercise of jurisdiction which is given, than to usurp that which is not given. The one or the other would be treason to the Constitution.

These words have not been successfully challenged, and I have tried to live within their concept.

The problems that confront the Court in these days are so complex and their special circumstances are so far beyond the vision of even the wisest of the Founding Fathers that it would be impossible to find specific words in precedent cases to justify every decision reached. The Founding Fathers were aware of this. They contemplated expansion of the Union under changed conditions and wrote the Constitution as broadly as possible to permit adjustment to such changes. That monumental document consisted of approximately five thousand words, not much longer than an average modern magazine article. Yet it is still serving our highest ideals today, and present-day Americans—210 millions of us with our manifold problems—are able to live in freedom under its far-seeing principles.

To me, therefore, it is understandable that honest men devoted to that great instrument would apply its provisions in a somewhat different way to ever-changing conditions. And that is exactly what has happened throughout the history of the nation. It is what makes "strict construction" a ludicrous term in this context.

Only two years after John Marshall was appointed Chief Justice, he and the Court were in great trouble with Thomas Jefferson because in his landmark decision of *Marbury* v. *Madison* (1803), Marshall held that executive action was subject to judicial review. The party of Jefferson, with his support, undertook to remove the Justices responsible for the decision, and in the following year, Justice Samuel Chase was impeached by the House of Representatives, not for "treason, bribery or other high crimes and misdemeanors," as provided in Article II, Section 4 of the Constitution, but for intemperate political criticism of the Administration in his instructions to a grand jury. He was acquitted after a trial in the Senate. He is the only Justice in the history of the Supreme Court to have been impeached, but there is little doubt in the minds of historians that had he been convicted a similar fate awaited Chief Justice Marshall and his colleagues; not for "high crimes and misdemeanors," but for disagreeing with the Administration.

Thomas Jefferson never recanted on his enmity, and twelve years after he left the presidency he wrote: "The judiciary of the United States is the subtle corps of sappers and miners constantly working underground to undermine the foundations of our confederated fabric. They are construing our Constitution from a co-ordination of a general and special government to a general and supreme one alone. This will lay all things at their feet . . ."

Later Marshall had similar problems during the Andrew Jackson administration; yet today he is the most towering figure in our judicial history.

Chief Justice Taney, following Marshall from 1833 to the Civil War, had severe difficulties through the outgrowth of the troublesome slavery question.

And even in this century the two Roosevelts brought the force of their Administrations to bear against the Court. Theodore Roosevelt castigated the Court publicly for not following his policies, and advocated the recall of controversial decisions of the Supreme Court by popular vote. Disappointed because Justice Oliver Wendell Holmes, his first appointee and one of the giants of Court history, failed to support his position in an important antitrust case, he was reported to have complained that he might as well have appointed someone with a backbone of macaroni.

Franklin D. Roosevelt, angered by decisions of the Court during his Administration, sought to have Congress increase the number of Justices by adding one for each Justice over the age of seventy, of whom there were then six, thus enabling him to bring the number to the maximum of fifteen as fixed by the bill. Called by its proponents the Court Reorganization Bill and by its opponents the Court Packing Bill, it was killed in committee and did not reach the floor in either house.

Every man who has sat on the Court must have known at the time he took office that there always has been and in all probability always will be controversy surrounding that body. It is inherent in the Court's work. Accordingly, he must have been prepared for attacks upon it. I venture to express the hope that the Court's decisions always will be controversial, because it is human nature for the dominant group in a nation to keep pressing for further domination, and unless the Court has the fiber to accord justice to the weakest member of society, regardless of the pressure brought upon it, we never can achieve our goal of "life, liberty and the pursuit of happiness" for everyone.

Perhaps, therefore, before discussing my own approach to the problems of the Supreme Court which have provoked the most feeling, it might be enlightening to explain in nonlegal terms what the jurisdiction and the procedures of the Court are. I say this because in the news media the Court is often portrayed as a mysterious body operating behind a veil of secrecy, and the general public is led to believe that its "mystique" is beyond the comprehension of normal individuals. This is far from the truth, and after sixteen years on the Court and several in retirement, I am prepared to say that its processes are more available to the public than those of the other branches of the government—the Congress and the presidency.

The reason its activities are not better known is because the media does not consider the Court's work newsworthy until it makes a decision which stirs emotion on the part of great numbers of people on the losing side. Then the media gives a superficial judgment which is often wide of the mark, and leaves the matter to the public in that unsatisfactory condition. This is largely because news gatherers are not deeply concerned with the proceedings before the Court until decision day; their homework is thus generally inadequate. During the years I was on the Court, I could count on the fingers of one hand those news gatherers who devoted full time to reporting on Supreme Court work, while across the park in the Capitol and down the mall at the White House there were scores of qualified reporters all the time. Those were in addition to the numerous others who covered various departments of the government such as State, Defense, Commerce, HEW, etc.

The Supreme Court has very limited jurisdiction. This should be stated at the outset, because so many people are of the opinion that if the members of the Supreme Court do not like anything that exists in the nation, they simply reach out, drag it before them, and decide the issue in accordance with their own predetermined ideas. How far wrong such a concept is can be shown by the Court's limited jurisdictional range. Practically the only original authority the Court has is in cases between states on boundary disputes, conflicting rights on interstate waterways, and some few taxation issues that must be decided. Other minor matters in which the Court could take original jurisdiction have been extended by Congress to the concurrent jurisdiction of the lower courts, and are normally required to be commenced there. Because the taking of testimony by a Court of nine men would be a clumsy procedure, a special master—either a retired judge or justice or outstanding lawyer—is appointed to hold hearings to ascertain the facts and report his findings to the Court. After the party states have had an opportunity to file briefs and argue orally about these findings, the Court makes its decision. This original jurisdiction is, therefore, an exceedingly small part of its workload, rarely amounting to more than one or two cases a year.

The remainder of that workload is in the appellate process over two classes of cases—those coming from the Federal Courts of Appeals and those coming from the highest courts of the states having jurisdiction over the subject matter. There are two methods of seeking review in the Supreme Court, through direct appeal and through the writ of *certiorari*. The latter is the outgrowth of an ancient practice, but in our procedure it simply means a writ issuing from the Supreme Court calling up the record from a lower court for review. All cases from the United States Courts of Appeals are made subject to this kind of review, as are all cases from the highest court of a state where such court has decided a federal question of substance not previously decided by the U. S. Supreme Court or has decided it in a way that is potentially not in accord with applicable decisions of that Court.

There are also procedures for direct appeals from both federal and state courts, but because of statutory changes the differences between the two proceedings are being minimized to a degree that will enable us for the purpose of this discussion to treat them as one.

In either procedure, the records in the courts below are brought to the Supreme Court and made public for any interested person to scrutinize. Briefs are then filed by the litigants to convince the Court that it either should or should not hear oral argument in the case. These, too, are public records for the interested public to see, as, of course, is the opinion of the court below. The decision of the Court as to whether the case is of sufficient importance to hear oral argument rests entirely within the discretion of the Court based upon the records already filed. If it decides to hear argument, the appellant will file a brief stating the precise question involved, citing the portions of the record that sustain his position, the applicable law, and his argument to convince the Court that the judgment below should be reversed. The appellee, trying to sustain the judgment of the court below, in like manner files his brief in opposition. The appellant then is entitled to file a brief in rebuttal. All of these briefs are public documents open to inspection. The case is then on the Supreme Court docket for argument. All arguments to the Court are open to the public, and much of the time the courtroom is crowded with lawyers, representatives of the news media, and members of the general public. With the argument concluded, the case is submitted to the Court for decision.

From this point until the decision of the Court is announced to the public, the decision-making process is, of necessity, confidential. In this phase of its work, the Court is limited to the issues presented by the record in the court below, the opinion of that court, the written and oral arguments of counsel, and the independent research of the Justices and their staffs. Throughout the process and, indeed, throughout the time the case is filed in the Court, it would be highly unethical for any Justice to discuss or even listen to anyone discuss the case or suggest any way of deciding it. Efforts to do so on the part of any outsider could well be treated as contempt of Court. The Court is thus relieved from all the pressures that are put upon the members of the Congress, on the heads of departments of the Executive Branch and on the White House itself to bring about certain results. There are no lobbyists importuning the Justices to serve the purpose of their employers, no emotional constituents to placate, and no news media seeking premature information on any case. Throughout the decision-making process, members of the Court are left to their own consciences in the quiet of their chambers to reflect on the facts and the applicable law, except for any discussion they might have with their colleagues on the merits of their cases.

In the sixteen years I sat on the Court I had only one personal experience of a deliberate attempt to surreptitiously influence the action of that body. It began on the afternoon of Wednesday, March 12, 1969. I was working alone in my chambers when I received a telephone call from Mr. Justice Brennan asking if I were free to see him. He was in his chambers, so I told him to come right in. In a few moments he arrived with Mr. Jack C. Landau of the Department of Justice, with whom he had just had a conversation in his office. He thought I should also hear it.

Justice Brennan later told me that he had met Mr. Landau as a reporter covering the Court for a newspaper chain, and had written a letter to the Harvard Law School recommending him for a Nieman scholarship, but did not know that he was then in the employ of the Department of Justice. Mr. Landau had called Justice Brennan's secretary this day, asking to see the Justice on a very important matter. In about ten minutes, Mr. Landau arrived at the Court building and was ushered into Brennan's chambers with the following result as stated to me by the Justice in the presence of Mr. Landau:

Mr. Landau said that he had recently been appointed Director of Public Information for the Department of Justice. He was calling on a mission for Attorney General John Mitchell which the latter regarded as most important. The department, it seemed, was very much upset about a story which would appear in the New York *Times* the following day. The story concerned the results which would follow from a decision of the Court on Monday, March 10, 1969 (which I will discuss later). He said that the Attorney General, the Solicitor General, and others in the Department of Justice read the opinions as meaning that the transcript of any conversation, whatever its content, which had been obtained by illegal electronic surveillance would have to be turned over to the defense in a court trial. Based on this interpretation, other agencies—the CIA, the FBI, and the Department of State—had voiced alarm that this would require discontinuance of any criminal prosecution that might involve transcripts of electronic surveillance on any Embassy located in Washington. He said that electronic surveillance and monitoring of every Embassy (about 125 at that time) in the city was taking place and had been carried on for a good while. This information had not been made known to the Court before the cases were decided because the Department of Justice had assumed that the recent appointees to the Court, who had been with the Department of Justice, had knowledge of the practice and would have fully informed the Court of the situation. He said that most of that day the Attorney General, Solicitor General Erwin Griswold, and others of the department had been discussing how to get this information to the Court, and that they thought the department had been at fault in not conveying word before the cases were decided.

Justice Brennan then told Mr. Landau that his statement that every embassy in Washington was "bugged" was the first time he had ever heard any such thing. Landau replied that there had been considerable talk in the department as to how to disclose the information to the Court, that it would be most embarrassing to our foreign relations officially to admit the practice, and that, therefore, it could not be made the subject of a formal petition for rehearing or other document to be filed with the Court. He said that the possibility of the Attorney General personally coming to see the Chief Justice was discussed but rejected on the ground that some undisclosed protocol procedure would be required. He said that having the Solicitor General visit me was also rejected on the ground that it would be improper for one counsel to see the Court without the knowledge of other counsel in the case. It was finally decided, Landau went on, that since he had known Justice Brennan for some time, he should ask him for an appointment. The Attorney General wanted to emphasize that the department was at fault, and that he would do anything at all that would help the Court avoid a congressional reaction which might either lead to a Constitutional Amendment or some legislation to curtail the Court's jurisdiction.

It was at this point that Mr. Justice Brennan had told Mr. Landau that he should see the Chief Justice. Landau objected, saying he "would be terrified." Justice Brennan insisted, however, and they came to my office as I have related.

When I invited them to be seated, Mr. Landau asked if he might remain standing, as he was under considerable tension. Justice Brennan took a chair and went over the conversation just described that had taken place in his chambers. He added that he had understood Mr. Landau to say that the President was also concerned in the matter. However, Mr. Landau interrupted to say that he only meant to convey the information that the White House had asked for advice as to what answer the President should give if asked about the *Ivanov* and *Butenko* cases (which had prompted all this alarm) at his press conference scheduled for March 14.

When Mr. Landau confirmed the remainder of his conversation with Justice Brennan, I said that I had no information of any such surveillance, and had recently read an official government pronouncement in the newspapers which alleged that there were only twenty such surveillances in the entire nation. I told Mr. Landau that, in light of that announcement, I had been surprised at the elaborate and expensive illegal wiretapping used in the recent *Katz* case to overhear telephone conversations of a relatively minor gambler. After some interrogation about whether the Solicitor General had full knowledge of this widespread surveillance and about the fact that there had been no mention of it in the cases before us, it was apparent that this young man was only being used as a mouthpiece for others more sophisticated who would not dare to fulfill a mission of this kind. I did tell him, however, that his call was a highly irregular one, and that the cases we were discussing as well as all others would be decided only on the record before us.

We then closed the interview, but before leaving, for reasons I do not thoroughly understand, he repeated that the Attorney General (John Mitchell) wanted me to know that he would do anything in his power to head off any congressional inquiry that might lead either to a Constitutional Amendment or to some legislation to curtail the Court's jurisdiction. Why he should repeat this statement when there was nothing of the kind pending in the Congress I do not know, unless it reflected an undisclosed objective of the new Administration.

When Mr. Landau left, Mr. Justice Brennan and I discussed for a few moments this outrageous attempt to influence a Court action and the almost unbelievable information that had been given to us. We felt that we should not be the sole possessors of it, and I decided immediately to call a conference of the entire Court.

When we were assembled, all the members of the Court being present, I told them that I had asked them to meet, not for the purpose of deciding any matter or even to discuss it, but for the purpose of transmitting to them some information that had come to Mr. Justice Brennan and me. Justice Brennan first related what occurred in his chambers between Mr. Landau and himself, and I reported what was said by the three of us in my office. I then asked the Justice if I had accurately reported our joint experience. When he substantiated that I had, without another word being uttered by anyone, I said, "The conference is adjourned," and we all returned to our chambers. I took this summary action because I did not want to discuss any phase of the *Ivanov* or *Butenko* cases in light of what had just happened.

In about an hour, Mr. Justice Brennan again came to my chambers and said that he had just received another call from Mr. Landau, who told him that the Attorney General wanted the Chief Justice to know that he had overstated his case to us, and that it would be more correct to say that they had only forty-six of the embassies permanently wiretapped and the remaining ones only occasionally. I felt no need of communicating this correction to the Court because it had no bearing on the purpose for which I had called the earlier meeting.

The importance of this surreptitious attempt to influence the Court can only be assessed in terms of what immediately preceded and followed it.

On March 10 the Court had decided the case of *Alderman, et al.* v. *United States*. It also included the cases of *Ivanov* v. *United States* and *Butenko* v. *United States*, both from the Third Circuit. All three came to the Court from felony convictions and involved the claim of illegal surveillance through wiretapping by the federal government. After their convictions, it was discovered that one of the petitioners' places of business had been wiretapped by the government. The government sought to have the Court accept its *ex parte* determination that "no overheard conversation in which any of the petitioners participated is arguably relevant to this prosecution." The Court refused to accept such a self-serving determination, and remanded the case to the District Court for a judicial hearing and decision. The government then moved to modify the order to permit it to submit the transcripts to the Judge to view them *in camera* (in secret). On this motion, the Court held that the margin of error was too great to permit a judgment in such a manner, and that the case should be returned to the District Court for a determination on evidence as to (1) whether the wiretap was illegal, and (2) if so, whether its use had contributed to the prosecution, in which event the injured defendants would be entitled to see the transcripts of their conversations.

The government knew at the time of this incident that there were a dozen other cases raising the same issue which were being held for action similar to whatever should be taken in the *Alderman* and *Butenko* cases. In all of them, the Attorney General admitted wiretapping, but would not admit that the conversations heard were of assistance in the prosecutions. They were all important cases, but those that were best known to the public involved heavyweight champion prizefighter Cassius Marcellus Clay, Jr., now known as Muhammad Ali, James R. Hoffa, president of the Teamsters Union, and *Ivanov* v. *United States* and *Butenko* v. *United States*, both of the latter concerned with alleged Russian spies.

The Department of Justice knew that these cases would be on the docket of March 24 and, having an identical issue, would normally be accorded the same treatment as in the *Alderman* case. Undoubtedly consternation over a result that would be adverse to wiretapping was the reason for the unusual approach to the Court by Mr. Landau for the Department of Justice.

On Monday, March 24, with only one dissent, all of the cases were accorded the same treatment as *Alderman, et al.* The rulings were contrary to the position of the Attorney General (*Giordano* v. *United States*). The sole dissenter was Mr. Justice Black, but his dissent had nothing to do with any pressure from the government. It was his belief that Fourth Amendment protection against unreasonable searches and seizures did not apply to wiretapping, and in the case of *Katz* v. *United States*, shortly before, he had expressed his view on that issue in detail.

I have often wondered since that time whether I should have brought the intrusion to light by making it a public issue. I say this because I feel certain that if we had decided with the government in those cases it would have been considered by the Department of Justice as the password to intrude into our decision-making process whenever it had a poor case on the merits. On the other hand, I concluded that it would serve no good purpose to have a confrontation of the Court and the new administration, particularly one that had campaigned against the Court on the charge that it was soft on crime. It would have smacked of vindictiveness and reprisal. I also thought that perhaps, because Attorney General Mitchell's private practice had been largely confined to dealing with public bond issues, he was not yet fully acquainted either with the constitutional doctrine of separation of powers, which was designed in large part to protect the independence of the judiciary, or with the illegality of searches and seizures without a warrant. However, I later viewed instances of his department dismissing criminal cases to avoid exposing the contents of illegal wiretapped conversations and of his penchant for wiretapping and bugging without a search warrant merely when in his arbitrary judgment, it might affect internal security. Then I had recurring doubts concerning my decision.

I believe this event can now be described for the first time without disturbing governmental relations, because as I write this it is several years since I retired from the Court, Mr. Mitchell has resigned, and the Supreme Court has recently circumscribed the power of the Attorney General to tap telephone wires without judicial sanction. Also, it might be of some interest to the public because there was undoubtedly a resurgence of wiretapping by the government, as evidenced by the Watergate episode and related cases.

But to return to my thesis that the judicial process as it functions in the Supreme Court is more open than that of either the legislative or executive branches of the government, I would like to repeat that the entire record of any case upon which the Court must make a decision is on file and open to public inspection. The same is true of the briefs upon which it must rely in deciding the issues raised. In addition to the arguments being made in open court, a transcript of them can be inspected in our library five days after their delivery. Thus, the only thing kept from the public until finalized is what the decision is to be and when it is to be made. Furthermore, this does not cause a great delay because normally reaching a decision takes but a few weeks and in troublesome cases a few months.

On the other hand, when a bill is introduced in either house of the Congress, there is nothing to indicate what brought it into being. The hearings are too often conducted secretly; chairmen of the committees have dictatorial powers as to what can reach the floor for action; lobbyists and other pressure groups ply their trade secretly; and bills are reported for action by committees without the right by the main body to improve them through amendments. They must take the bill or leave it as it comes to them from the committee as the result of secret hearings.

The executive branch of the government proceeds in an even more secretive manner and insulates its prerogative by stamping any written record of its activities which it desires to conceal from the public with the word "classified," making it a felony to divulge the contents to the public.

I write this general analysis of the processes in the other branches of the government not for the purpose of suggesting that they are subservient to sinister secret influences, but in answer to those in and out of government who constantly refer to the Supreme Court as *the* secretive branch of the government.

The separation of powers in the Constitution and the necessity for keeping an open mind which will enable one to judge without prejudice any problem that might come before him limits a Justice's social contacts and his expressions of opinion on all public questions. This was a particular shock to me when I came to the Court because for a third of a century I had held public offices where the formulation and the expression of ideas on public questions were a part of my daily life. Throughout all those years, I was in contact with the news media and with people who were involved in some public problem. Nevertheless, I completely changed my activities on coming to the Court. I cut off all connection with the members of the press who had been so friendly with me through the years, and refrained from all public discussions. For years in Washington, I received at least one invitation a day to a cocktail party and sometimes two or three. I went to none. My wife never drank and did not like cocktail parties, so that was not a grave deprivation for us. The only deviation from this practice was when an embassy of a nation where I had traveled gave a reception commemorating its independence or some other important national event. I attended some of those, and I had a system which worked splendidly in such cases. I would arrive about five minutes after the announced opening time. There would be very few people present. I would go through the receiving line, pay my respects to the Ambassador, his wife and his nation, and go to the room where the guests were gathered. From there in a few minutes I would leave the building without partaking either food or drink. Shortly after, I would be home for dinner because we lived close to most of the embassies, and I could have a drink there before dinner if I wanted one.

Any greater participation in such affairs is fraught with danger for a Justice. There is always someone present to provoke a discussion on some controversial question, and a "listening post" to report in the news media any unwary remark made by a public figure. I had an experience of that kind which was embarrassing. It occurred at a dinner on the twenty-fifth wedding anniversary of Naomi and Barney Nover, two long-time friends and journalists from the West. There I met Mr. Earl Mazo, who had recently published a book on the life of Richard Nixon. He asked me how I liked it. I told him I had not read it but had read a review of it, and that I did not like an apparent statement in the book that I had tried to stop Richard Nixon's political career because of my disapproval of his campaign tactics against Helen Gahagan Douglas for the Senate. Mr. Mazo said that he had offered me an opportunity to refute the statement, but that I would not grant him an interview to discuss it. I told him it was an old political canard which had been bruited around in some political circles for years but was not true. His friend, a newspaperman who was later presidential assistant to Nixon, Clark Mollenhoff, rushed out and filed a copyrighted article in which he said I had called Mr. Mazo a damned liar. This, like the story under discussion, was not true. It was a good commercial for the Mazo book, but nothing else. I was taught better manners than that, and I am quite sure that never at a public affair during my half century of public service have I called a man a damned liar whether he was present or not. For weeks after this, newspaper reporters would attempt to open interviews with me by saying, "Tell us about that Mazo affair." I would not respond, but it was awkward and shows how a person can be mousetrapped into irrelevant and controversial matters in Washington.

When we came to the capital, we fully intended to buy or build a home. I foolishly let that fact be known, as a result of which we were plagued by real estate agents. I had no time for them, so I pushed them off on my wife. Nina heroically dealt with them, but finally cut off all contacts after being greatly embarrassed on a number of occasions. They had been told that we wanted to live in the District because I abhorred the wasted time and traffic congestion involved in commuting from the suburbs. Nina finally discovered that some of them were going to District homeowners and asking them if their homes were for sale. When the answer was in the negative, they would say, "Well, the Chief Justice is crazy about your house. Will you allow Mrs. Warren to see it, and we will find out what he is willing to pay for it?" Neither of us knew of such ploys at the time, but Nina eventually found out that she had visited two or three houses under these false pretenses. During the same period, she attended a women's luncheon where she met the owner of one of the homes she had viewed, and the latter in passing mentioned the price she was asking. To Nina's astonishment, it was fifty per cent less than the agent had quoted. That was the end of our house hunting, and we even abandoned the thought of building. Inflation was upon us, and, with the exodus to the suburbs, property values in the District were not stable. These things, coupled with the help problem in Washington, caused us to look for a close-by comfortable place where domestic services would be supplied. We settled on the Sheraton-Park Apartment Annex and a seven-room apartment which has served us well. For a while our daughters, Virginia and Dorothy, were with us, but both were married later, and we have been alone since. The Annex is a part of the Sheraton-Park Hotel, but is only connected with it by a corridor of about two hundred yards in length. It is still the residence of many men in government. Vice-President Agnew lived there, as did Vice-President Johnson until he purchased a home. Senators Lehman of New York, Holland of Florida, Lodge of Massachusetts, Carlson of Kansas, Percy of Illinois, former Speaker Joseph Martin, Secretaries of the Treasury Anderson and Connally, and others also have lived there at various times.

Through all the years we have spent in the nation's capital, we have never boarded the "Washington Merry-Go-Round," and our social life is quite limited. However, during my active years on the Court, we attended many protocol dinners at the White House and the embassies. We accepted practically no invitations to private homes because that called for reciprocation, and that would crowd our evenings and so could not be accommodated to my work. I worked almost every night to some extent, even on nights when we attended a White House or embassy dinner. Even at that pace, I never felt as though I was abreast of my reading. I am not a fast reader of important materials, and the amount of such reading at the Court is colossal. When I first came to Washington I wondered how I would ever get through it. At that time the Court met at noon, recessed for lunch for thirty minutes at 2 P.M., and then sat until 4:30. This was the procedure Monday through Friday while hearing the cases argued. Then on Saturday morning at ten o'clock, we would convene in conference and, with the exception of thirty minutes for lunch, would continue until our work was completed —until five, six, or even seven o'clock. Upon adjournment, I would give the orders to the clerk of the Court so he could prepare them for the Monday session. This was a backbreaking schedule for me in particular because I always had administrative work to occupy my morning hours. The work had to do with management of the Court, which is the responsibility of the Chief Justice, the affairs of the Judicial Conference of the United States, of which I was the chairman, and incidental activities of the Smithsonian Institution and the National Gallery of Art, of which I was chancellor of the Board of Regents and chairman of the Board of Trustees, respectively. I also needed time to confer with my three law clerks, who worked so closely and confidentially with me. I had little free time to work undisturbed on my opinions and to prepare for oncoming cases. This left only the off hours for such work, and there were precious few of them.*

I felt this workload presented an impractical situation, and sought ways and means of remedying it. Two of these seemed apparent to me. Starting the sessions of the Court at noon was an anachronism. It had begun with the establishment of the Court in 1789, when there was no automobile or rail travel and even before the paving of streets. There

* Ed. note: Additionally, the Chief Justice, always an avid outdoorsman, served as a member of the Board of Trustees of the National Geographic Society. Though rewarding, the job put a further demand on his time.

was reason for it then because the uncertainty of weather and street conditions made it difficult to assemble the Court and its attachés before noon on many occasions. Also at that time the Court calendar was very short, and would permit a leisurely pace. But in the middle of the twentieth century, all these conditions were changed, and it seemed to me that there was no reason why we should not conform to the almost universal practice throughout the nation of opening sessions at 10 A.M. I made the suggestion, but changes are not made quickly in historic and prestigious institutions like the Supreme Court. There is something sentimental about practices rooted in history, even though their time has passed, particularly when they have resulted in a pattern of life. The idea of a new schedule was not received with enthusiasm at the beginning, and I did not initiate it peremptorily. Instead, I kept it on a back burner, but referred to it from time to time. Finally all agreed and the change was made without incident. Some out-of-the-District lawyers were obliged to come to Washington the day before their scheduled appearance, but that adjusted itself quickly, and I am sure the 10 A.M. opening now has general acceptance. It was a boon to me because it gave me the entire morning to devote to the legal work of the Court, leaving matters of administration and conferences with my law clerks until after adjournment. It made my work more orderly and effective. My practice was to take home briefs, memoranda, etc. every night. I would do whatever reading conditions would permit before retiring about midnight. My daughter Virginia gave me a combination alarm clock and radio which awakened me each morning at seven o'clock to the accompaniment of soft and soothing music that was an agreeable change from a harsh alarm bell. I became very much attached to that musical program. I would read in bed until eight-thirty, then arise, shave, have my breakfast, and be ready to leave for the Court by nine-thirty. At that time of the morning, by proceeding through Rock Creek Park to avoid traffic lights, we could be at the Court building normally in fifteen minutes. The reason for this schedule was that from seven to nine o'clock the traffic congestion was often intolerable, and it would take at least three quarters of an hour. The city of Washington had not been laid out to accommodate automobile traffic. Streets have been modernized very little since the French architect Pierre L'Enfant designed them by commission from President Washington in 1791. To better distribute the traffic, starting times for some hundred thousand government employees were staggered at half hour intervals beginning at seven o'clock and ending at nine. As a result the morning crush was greatly lessened. To avoid the same problem in the afternoon, the release times of the employees were at four, four-thirty, five, five-thirty, and six. To conform to this situation, I always remained at the office until after six, and thus was able to reach home in fifteen minutes. I had a car and a driver, which was a godsend, as fighting traffic congestion for me is as enervating as a hard day's work.

In view of the fact that no Chief Justice or member of the Court had ever previously had a government car, it might be of some interest to know how I became the possessor of one. When Nina and I came to Washington, we did not have a personal car because mine had been furnished by the state of California. In Washington, when we attended a public affair Mrs. McHugh would hire a limousine for us. On one such occasion shortly after our arrival, we were to attend a White House dinner and she made arrangements for the limousine service. But when the car arrived at our hotel, I was surprised to see that it was a station wagon with large lettering that said "Washington National Airport" boldly appearing on its front, rear, and sides. The driver said he had erroneously been instructed to take us to the airport, and he had brought this car to take care of the baggage.

At the White House, there was the usual group of press photographers and reporters at the entrance. They saw the car and after dinner asked me how I happened to come in so public a conveyance. I told them the story, and they wrote little articles about it. Many people in and out of government were surprised that the Chief Justice of the United States did not have an official car because there were many hundreds of such cars on the streets of Washington. All of the principal executive officers and sometimes people in the third or fourth echelons had them. This was also true of the Legislative Branch, including the chairmen of important committees. These, with the numerous military vehicles, made public cars on the streets a sizable part of the traffic. A number of the congressmen and senators asked me if I would like to have them introduce a bill providing a car for me. I told them I would prefer that they did not because I did not wish to be seeking something for myself which was not accorded to the other Justices. Later, Senator Styles Bridges of New Hampshire, chairman of the Senate Appropriations Committee, phoned and asked if I would object to his offering an Amendment to provide the Chief Justice with a car when he presented a massive appropriations bill. I told him I would not object. He did so, and it passed without discussion. I always appreciated this action, and am of the opinion that if the lack had not been publicized in that accidental manner I never would have had a car and a driver. One must know the parking situation in Washington to understand what a problem it is for a government official to drive his own car to public affairs in all kinds of weather and find a place to park. The reason I doubt that I would ever have had a government vehicle except for this short-cut procedure is because I tried for years to obtain cars for the other Justices. They needed them for the same reason I did. Some needed cars even more urgently because of their age. When I came on the Court, Mr. Justice Frankfurter was seventy, Mr. Justice Reed was sixty-eight, Black sixty-six, Burton sixty-five, Minton sixty-three, Jackson sixty-one, Douglas fifty-five, and Clark fifty-four. I was sixty-two. Jackson died of a heart attack the first year I was in Washington, as had Justices Rutledge in 1949 at fifty-five and Murphy in 1949 at fifty-nine. Chief Justice Vinson died in 1953 at the age of sixty-three. Also, Chief Justice Stone was stricken on the bench while hearing arguments and died the same day in 1946. The constant pressure on the Court was so great that men of that age should not have been driving cars in the traffic congestion of Washington. For several years I tried, as I say, to have Congress appropriate money for a car and driver for the other Justices. The Subcommittee of the House, at the insistence of its dictatorial and revengeful chairman, John J. Rooney of Brooklyn, each time rejected the request with a cutting jibe until the Justices finally suggested that I save the Court embarrassment by forgetting it.

I learned that by adding a week of argument in the fall and about two weeks in the spring, we could limit our argued cases to Monday through Thursday, and have our conference on Friday without slowing up on the calendar. There was general acceptance of this idea, and it was made effective at the beginning of the 1955 term. I am sure this lightened the burden for all the Justices as it did for me. I do not know whether there is any connection between the two, but since that time there has been but one heart attack (Frankfurter) while there had been a succession of them and of strokes in the years immediately preceding my incumbency.

Some of the columnists, knowing of my interest in sports, and particularly football, surmised that my purpose in doing this was to enable me to go to football games. This was entirely wide of the mark because I believe, outside of the Army-Navy game in Philadelphia to which I took the entire Court and their wives for a number of years, I never attended a Saturday afternoon football game in Washington. Anyway, practically all of the colleges in the city had abandoned football at that time.

On the other hand, I was a confirmed Saturday morning worker. Throughout my public career, I went to the office on Saturday, not for scheduled appointments, but to be able to do some reflection. There was little time for it otherwise. I also liked to take care of some loose ends of the work with members of my staff whom I had not been able to consult during the week. It was not driving work, but satisfying because it enabled me to view in perspective many things that otherwise would have been at tag ends. I did not require my staff to be present, but Mrs. McHugh was always there. I told her many times that it was not necessary for her to do so, but if I came to the office she was always there on my arrival, for which I was most grateful.

I thought that my attendance record was pretty good because I missed only one day in sixteen years. That was on a day of arguments, and I was too sick with a one-day flu bug to get out of bed. Her record was better. She was never absent on a business day throughout my sixteen years on the Court. My law clerks, although not required to do so, usually were there on Saturday because they knew I would be available to talk over their work with them. It was always a "freewheeling" session to discuss whatever any of us thought was important. About half past one, the law clerks and I would leave the Court building and walk uptown to the University Club or the National Lawyers Club for lunch, where we would spend a couple of hours socially. I remember one year when I had two particularly large law clerks: Henry Steinman, a graduate and varsity basketball player of the University of California at Los Angeles, and R. Gordon Gooch, of equal size from the University of Texas. Someone reported, and the newspapers printed, that I could be seen walking uptown with my two bodyguards. This was particularly amusing to me because I never had bodyguards on any of my jobs; first because I never wanted to live that way, and second because I did not believe they could protect me if someone was bent on killing me. At our luncheon sessions, we would discuss anything from a legal principle or a football game to some of my past experiences in politics. These Saturday afternoon sessions continued without break throughout the years and made our relations very personal. I always dreaded to see the end of the Court term, because it was our practice normally to retain each clerk for but one year. I hated to see them depart and felt somewhat as I did when my own boys left home to go to college. I wanted them to have the opportunities that would open up to them by leaving, but I did not like to give up such close association and companionship.

XI

THE PRESIDENT'S COMMISSION: *Investigating the Kennedy Assassination*

On Friday, November 22, 1963, the Supreme Court was having its regular conference. We had just returned from luncheon on the floor above, when, a little after 1:30 P.M., I received a typewritten note from my secretary, Mrs. McHugh, saying, "The President was shot while riding in a motorcade in Dallas. It is not known how badly he is injured."

The Court, shocked beyond words, immediately adjourned. There was little said, but I believe each of us, stunned by the news, repaired to a place where he could receive radio reports of the tragedy. I know that is what I did. In perhaps a half or three quarters of an hour the news came that the President was dead. It was almost unbelievable, and was particularly poignant to us because we had all seen John F. Kennedy in the White House in his youthful vigor about thirty-six hours before, when he had held a reception for the Supreme Court. On that occasion, the members and their wives were invited to join the President and Mrs. Kennedy in their private living quarters on the second floor for refreshments while the other guests were gathering below. We could not forget how friendly and happy the occasion was, and how he was scheduled to leave for Dallas the next morning. We jokingly admonished him to be careful "down there with those wild Texans." Of course, the thought of a real disturbance of any kind was far from our minds. It was a delightful affair for us, one that would have been stamped permanently on our memories even had there been nothing tragic to follow.

Later, on that Friday afternoon, we were informed that Vice-President Johnson, while in Texas, had taken the oath as the thirty-sixth President of the United States, and that he and Mrs. Johnson were returning to Washington on the presidential plane with Mrs. Kennedy and the body of her husband. The plane arrived at Andrews Air Force Base about six o'clock. The public was not to be admitted to the base, but we were among those who were asked to be present. With heavy hearts, Nina and I attended.

It was a heart-rending sight to see a saddened new President and the fallen President's widow, still in the bloodstained clothes she wore after her mortally wounded husband had slumped in her lap, descend from the giant Air Force plane. We watched as the body was lowered into a waiting ambulance. President Johnson addressed a few words concerning the great tragedy that had beclouded our country. There was no other ceremony. Nina and I paid our respects to him and returned dejectedly to our home.

The next few days are not clear in my memory. I made no notes at the time, but as nearly as I can recall I spent much of that night and Saturday glued to the television screen listening to the wild stories and rumors which permeated the air. I watched and heard the same things repeated time after time. It was sickening, but there didn't seem to be anything else to do.

The only thing that broke the gruesome television reports during the day was a visit Nina and I made, by invitation, to the White House Saturday morning with the other Justices and their wives to view the casket in the East Room. I then returned to the Court, and spent most of the day waiting for some information about what was to happen in the next few days. The entire governmental plant was closed. It was as though the world had stopped moving.

About nine o'clock Saturday evening I was startled from my numbness by a call from the White House. It was Mrs. Jacqueline Kennedy, asking if I would make a short talk in the rotunda of the Capitol the following day at the ceremony for her husband as he lay in state there. I was almost speechless to hear her voice personally asking me to speak at the ceremony. I, of course, told her that I would do so. After our brief conversation, I undertook to compose something, but it was simply impossible for me to put thoughts on paper. Accordingly, I went to bed around midnight, postponing until morning the writing of the statement I must have for the ceremony at one o'clock the next afternoon.

It was again difficult to write in the morning, but there could be no further delay. I was still struggling with the words at 11:20 A.M. when my daughter Dorothy came running into my study and said, "Daddy, they just killed Oswald." A little annoyed, I said, "Oh, Dorothy, don't pay any attention to all those wild rumors or they will drive you to distraction." She replied, "But, Daddy, I *saw* them do it." I rushed into her room in time to see a replay of Jack Ruby shooting President Kennedy's assassin, Lee Harvey Oswald, on her television set.

This confounded my writing effort even more, but I had only a little more to do, and managed to complete the statement shortly thereafter. I then enlisted the services of Nina to type it for me. She was ready to leave for the ceremony, but quickly typed it, after which we hurriedly departed. From midtown to the Capitol, traffic was restricted because of the vast crowds already assembling to view the casket in the Capitol Rotunda where it was to lie in state until the funeral service the following morning. Through the helpful assistance of a number of policemen along the way, we were able to arrive at the Capitol on time. It was a simple and highly emotional ceremony. The three speakers were the veteran John W. McCormack, speaker of the House of Representatives; Senator Mike Mansfield, majority leader of the Senate, and myself. The talks were all short. This is what I had ground out so laboriously:

> There are few events in our national life that so unite Americans and so touch the hearts of all of us as the passing of a President of the United States.
>
> There is nothing that adds shock to our sadness more than the assassination of our leader, chosen as he is to embody the ideals of our people, the faith we have in our institutions, and our belief in the Fatherhood of God and the brotherhood of man. Such misfortunes have befallen the Nation on other occasions, but never more shockingly than two days ago. We are saddened; we are stunned; we are perplexed.
>
> John Fitzgerald Kennedy—a great and good President, the friend of all people of good will; a believer in the dignity and equality of all human beings; a fighter for justice; an apostle of peace—has been snatched from our midst by the bullet of an assassin.
>
> What moved some misguided wretch to do this horrible deed may never be known to us, but we do know that such acts are commonly stimulated by forces of hatred and malevo-

lence such as today are eating their way into the blood stream of American life. What a price we pay for this fanaticism!

It has been said that the only thing we learn from history is that we do not learn. But surely we can learn if we have the will to do so. Surely there is a lesson to be learned from this tragic event.

If we really love this country; if we truly love justice and mercy; if we fervently want to make this Nation better for those who are to follow us, we can at least abjure the hatred that consumes people, the false accusations that divide us and the bitterness that begets violence. Is it too much to hope that the martyrdom of our beloved President might even soften the hearts of those who would themselves recoil from assassination, but who do not shrink from spreading the venom which kindles thoughts of it in others?

Our Nation is bereaved. The whole world is poorer because of his loss. But we can all be better Americans because John Fitzgerald Kennedy has passed our way; because he has been our chosen leader at a time in history when his character, his vision and his quiet courage have enabled him to chart for us a safe course through the shoals of treacherous seas that encompass the world.

And now that he is relieved of the almost superhuman burdens we imposed on him, may he rest in peace.

After the brief ceremony, the multitude in the Capitol and the thousands who continued to line the streets for the remainder of the day and night eventually passed through the Rotunda to pay their final respects to the fallen thirty-fifth President of the United States. The press reported that the line extended for forty blocks.

The following morning, members of the Court assembled at the White House. We joined the heads of state, Prime Ministers, and other distinguished representatives of more than a hundred nations, members of the Cabinet and of our Congress, and the Kennedy family for the solemn funeral trek to St. Matthew's Cathedral.

Behind the casket was a saddled but riderless horse with a sheathed sword across the saddle and boots reversed in the stirrups, representing, according to custom, the loss of a leader. Heading the six-block march to the Cathedral was Mrs. Kennedy between the two brothers of her husband, Robert and Edward. Following them were President and Mrs. Johnson; then the rest of the dignitaries who had gathered for this mournful occasion from all over the world.

The walk seemed longer because of the slow, muffled rolling of the drums. My thoughts were largely of the stricken Mrs. Kennedy and the fortitude she was showing in her grief. I could not understand how she stood it.

At the Cathedral, Richard Cardinal Cushing, who had married the President and Mrs. Kennedy and had baptized their children, met the procession and ushered the casket into the church.

After the ceremony, which lasted about an hour, the caravan formed again; this time in cars for the long trip across the Potomac River to the last resting place of John Fitzgerald Kennedy in Arlington Cemetery. Hundreds of thousands of grief-stricken citizens silently stood along the route and watched. There, after a brief committal service conducted by Cardinal Cushing, Mrs. Kennedy lighted the Eternal Flame at the head of the grave, and the throng, still stunned by sadness, dispersed and went silently to their homes.

Government must go on no matter what impediments confront it, so everyone was at his or her station on Tuesday morning. That is not to say that government was normal. It was not. The thinking of most Americans was chaotic. The killing of Oswald by Jack Ruby while he was in the custody of the police at their headquarters in Dallas simply compounded the confusion. It gave rise to the wildest kind of rumors and speculations. Amazing stories by supposed witnesses were published along with theories predicated on them, and most of the theories had to do with imagined conspiracies of various kinds. Many agencies announced the probability of holding public investigations independent of the others. The Dallas authorities fed everything, good or bad, to the news media. The attorney general of Texas proposed having an open hearing before a justice of the peace, which meant television, radio, and newspaper coverage, regardless of how disjointed or circus-like this atmosphere for a trial might be. Several committees of the Congress were flirting with public hearings that would proceed in similar manner. The result would have been chaos. The world was ready to believe almost anything, and indeed it did.

The federal government, with the FBI, the Secret Service, the CIA, and other agencies, had no clear jurisdiction of the subject. They were in the investigation merely by sufferance of the local and state authorities of Texas, because at that time it was not a federal crime to assassinate a President, or to murder the assassin as Ruby had done. Either was a state crime, as were other cases of murder.

The public was becoming restive because the alleged assassin was dead, and the killing of him had been witnessed by more than a hundred million people over television. Things were moving to a crescendo when on Friday, November 29, there was a request to my office for a conference as soon as possible with the Deputy Attorney General, Nicholas Katzenbach, and Solicitor General Archibald Cox. I agreed to see them immediately, and they arrived in my office very shortly thereafter.

They informed me that President Johnson, in an effort to bring order out of confusion, had determined to establish a bipartisan commission of outstanding people to investigate the entire affair and report the true facts regardless of consequences. They said that because in this country we do not have posthumous trials, there was no way to determine with accuracy what had happened, other than by a fact-finding commission. The President, they said, wanted to know if I would serve as chairman of such a commission. I told them I thought the President was wise in having such a commission, but that I was not available for service on it. Because of past experiences of that kind in the history of the Court, we had discussed the propriety of taking on extrajudicial appointments and, although we had never voted on it, I was sure that every member of the Court was of the opinion that such appointments were not in its best interests. I told Katzenbach and Cox that I had more than once expressed myself to that effect for several reasons. First, it is not in the spirit of constitutional separation of powers to have a member of the Supreme Court serve on a presidential commission; second, it would distract a Justice from the work of the Court, which had a heavy docket; and, third, it was impossible to foresee what litigation such a commission might spawn, with resulting disqualification of the Justice from sitting in such cases. I then told them that, historically, the acceptance of diplomatic posts by Chief Justices Jay and Ellsworth had not contributed to the welfare of the Court, that the service of five Justices on the Hayes-Tilden Commission had demeaned it, that the appointment of Justice Roberts as chairman to investigate the Pearl Harbor disaster had served no good purpose, and that the action of Justice Robert Jackson in leaving Court for a year to become chief prosecutor at Nürnberg after World War II had resulted in divisiveness and internal bitterness on the Court. I asked the Deputy Attorney General and Solicitor General to convey my respects to the President, but to tell him that, consistent with my own beliefs and of those of the other members of the Court as I understood them, I must respectfully decline the honor. I then suggested a few names of persons whom I thought might serve well the purpose of the President. The conference ended on that note.

I considered the matter closed. However, about three-thirty that same afternoon I received a call from the White House asking if I could come to see the President and saying that it was quite urgent. I, of course, said I would do so, and very soon thereafter I went to his office. I was ushered in and, with only the two of us in the room, he told me of his proposal. He said he was concerned about the wild stories and rumors that were arousing not only our own people but people in other parts of the world. He said that because Oswald had been murdered, there could be no trial emanating from the assassination of President Kennedy, and that unless the facts were explored objectively and conclusions reached that would be respected by the public, it would always remain an open wound with ominous potential. He added that several congressional committees and Texas local and state authorities were contemplating public investigations with television coverage which would compete with each other for public attention, and in the end leave the people more bewildered and emotional than at present. He said he was satisfied that if he appointed a bipartisan Presidential Commission to investigate the facts impartially and report them to a troubled nation that the people would accept its findings. He told me that he had made up his mind as to the other members, that he had communicated with them, and that they would serve if I would accept the chairmanship. He then named them for me. They were:

Richard B. Russell, Democratic senator from Georgia since 1933 and former governor of that state; chairman of the Senate Appropriations Committee;

John Sherman Cooper, veteran Republican senator from Kentucky, a former judge of that state, and United States Ambassador to India;

Hale Boggs, Democratic assistant majority leader of the House of Representatives. A member of the House from Louisiana since 1946;

Gerald R. Ford, member of the House of Representatives since 1948 from Michigan. Chairman of the Republican Conference Committee.*

Allen W. Dulles, former foreign service officer, and director of the Central Intelligence Agency under President Eisenhower from 1953 to 1961.

John J. McCloy, Assistant Secretary of War from 1941 to 1945; president of the World Bank from 1947 to 1949; U. S. Military Governor and High Commissioner for Germany from 1949 to 1952. Coordinator of U.S. disarmament activities since 1961.

* Ed. note: Warren died before Ford became President.

I knew all of these men to be distinguished and honorable men; I believed they would be accepted as an able and conscientious commission.

I then told the President my reasons for not being available for the chairmanship. He replied, "You were a soldier in World War I, but there was nothing you could do in that uniform comparable to what you can do for your country in this hour of trouble." He then told me how serious were the rumors floating around the world. The gravity of the situation was such that it might lead us into war, he said, and, if so, it might be a nuclear war. He went on to tell me that he had just talked to Defense Secretary Robert McNamara, who had advised him that the first nuclear strike against us might cause the loss of forty million people.†

I then said, "Mr. President, if the situation is that serious, my personal views do not count. I will do it." He thanked me, and I left the White House.

I am sure he felt the importance of the assignment in those extravagant terms to the day he died, because when Nina and I were having dinner with him and Mrs. Johnson on December 12, 1972, at the time of the opening of his civil rights papers, he said, "Chief, of all the things you have done for your country, the most important was your work with the Commission on the assassination of President Kennedy."

That he felt a great urgency at the time is further indicated by the fact that he immediately made the appointments by Executive Order No. 11130 as of that date, and the press release announcing it was heard over the radio by Mrs. McHugh shortly after she arrived home from the office. Nina heard it before I arrived home for dinner. This was the announcement:

Immediate Release   November 29, 1963
Office of the White House Press Secretary

THE WHITE HOUSE

The President today announced that he is appointing a Special Commission to study and report upon all facts and circumstances relating to the assassination of the late President, John F. Kennedy, and the subsequent violent death of the man charged with the assassination.

The President stated that the Majority and Minority Leader-

† Ed. note: A Gallup poll at this time indicated that more than half the American people believed that more than one person was involved in the assassination. The percentage overseas was undoubtedly much higher.

ship of the Senate and the House of Representatives have
been consulted with respect to the proposed Special Commission.

[The names of members of the Special Commission followed.]
The President stated that the Special Commission is to be instructed to evaluate all available information concerning the
subject of the inquiry. The Federal Bureau of Investigation,
pursuant to an earlier directive of the President, is making
complete investigation of the facts. An inquiry is also scheduled by a Texas Court of Inquiry convened by the Attorney
General of Texas under Texas law.

The Special Commission will have before it all evidence uncovered by the Federal Bureau of Investigation and all information available to any agency of the Federal Government.
The Attorney General of Texas has also offered his cooperation. All Federal agencies and offices are being directed to
furnish services and cooperation to the Special Commission.
The Commission will also be empowered to conduct any further investigation that it deems desirable.

The President is instructing the Special Commission to satisfy
itself that the truth is known as far as it can be discovered,
and to report its findings and conclusions to him, to the American people, and to the world.

Congress immediately undertook to implement the Order, and
passed a resolution by December 10, which became Public Law 88-202
when signed by the President on December 13, 1963. It accorded the
broadest powers to the Commission for obtaining testimony. The President directed every agency of the government to withhold nothing
requested by the Commission or anything else that would be of assistance. We were all of the opinion that this direction was scrupulously
followed by all the agencies. I doubt if any Commission could ever
have better cooperation than ours received from the federal government,
from the state and local agencies of Texas, and from law enforcement
agencies in other parts of the country whenever we sought it. Not a single barrier was raised against us. The interested congressional committees and the Texas authorities all refrained from having any conflicting
public investigations, so we proceeded with very little discord.‡

‡ Ed. note: Some official discord came later, however. When the Commission's
report eventually was published, FBI Director J. Edgar Hoover charged that it was
unfair in its criticism of his agency for not acting on knowledge the FBI had obtained that Oswald was in the area and dangerous. Warren had insisted that the
condemnation be included in the final report, over Congressman Ford's objections.
Hoover later supported the report in general.

The Commission first met on December 15 and decided that our staff would be independent of the several government agencies involved, and that while we would carefully review their reports and investigative records with selected lawyers, we would not duplicate the investigative process itself unless it should become necessary to do so to ascertain the truth. We assessed our task and agreed that we were not a prosecuting agency, that we were not to conduct an adversary proceeding of any kind, but on the contrary were merely a fact-finding body. We were conscious of the fact that Jack Ruby would be tried by Texas authorities for the murder of Oswald, and that we should not create an atmosphere which would make it impossible for him to have a fair trial. Because of that and because the nature of our investigation was such that we could not develop the evidence in the orderly way it is presented at a trial, we decided to hold our hearings in private executive session. Each witness could have his counsel present with the right to object to questions or to engage in the questioning of the witness. We also agreed that if any witness asked to be examined in public he must be accorded that right. (There was but one who made the request, Mark Lane, and he testified at an open hearing.) It was agreed that no witness should be under any restraint in discussing publicly what transpired at the taking of his testimony. Consequently, a number of the witnesses did have press and television interviews after their appearances before the commission.

We invited the president of the American Bar Association, Mr. Walter E. Craig, to take part in the hearings and to advise us if in his opinion, the procedure conformed to the basic principles of American justice. He did participate, either attending personally or sending a representative, and he offered helpful advice. We made the same offer to the president of the American Civil Liberties Union. Although that organization did not actively participate, we did counsel with their people from time to time.*

* Ed. note: According to minutes of early staff meetings, presided over by Warren, the Chief Justice was scrupulous in seeing that witnesses' constitutional rights were protected. This, of course, was to be expected from one who, as a Supreme Court Justice, had been a frequent defender of individual rights against bullying investigative agencies. Since the Commission was out to dissolve unfounded rumors, not encourage them, he cautioned staff members against asking witnesses questions that were not susceptible of proof and would lead to mere speculation on the witnesses' part. It was Warren who headed off suggestions that witnesses be restrained from talking to the press. He especially warned against leaks from the Commission itself which might feed the already raging fires of supposition.

One such leak had to do with Robert Oswald's testimony before the Commission to the effect that his brother Lee may have been a Russian secret agent. This somehow had reached an alert New York *Times* reporter. Another seepage, originating with the same fraternal source, had it that Lee Oswald had contemplated an attempt

Because neither the members of Congress nor I intended to relinquish our regular jobs during the lifetime of the Commission, it was decided to look for quarters in the Capitol Hill area. Our first meetings were held in the Archives Building, but there was not room there for our entire work force.

We decided to ask Mr. J. Lee Rankin, former Solicitor General of the United States under President Eisenhower, to become chief counsel for the Commission. He was a lawyer of rich experience, impeccable character, and with an understanding of human relations that fitted him superbly for the job. As would be expected of one who has such qualifications, he accepted the responsibility and was sworn in on December 16, 1963. We were then in business. Within a very short time, he had recruited a staff of fourteen lawyers from all parts of the nation, half of whom were men of outstanding ability and accomplishment in the private practice of the law, and the other seven younger men of more limited experience but well trained, highly intelligent, and with adequate legal experience to guarantee superior workmanship in the field for which they were recruited. He also arranged for liaison representatives from the Departments of Justice, Treasury, Defense, State, Internal Revenue Service, General Services Administration, and other agencies.

Fortunately for us, General Services Administration located adequate space—two floors—for us in the new building of the Veterans of Foreign Wars, which is diagonally across the street from the Supreme Court Building and only a short distance from the Capitol. It afforded us ample room to preserve our working papers and records, which we had decided to place in the National Archives on completion of our work. This was later done.

During our entire ten-month term of service, reports from the various investigative departments flowed in to us. As evidence of the number and size of those documents, the FBI through the months submitted to

---

on the life of Richard Nixon when the Vice-President visited Dallas in April of 1963. He had also threatened to kill Eisenhower. Commission members were doubtful about Robert Oswald's credibility and were reminded that he had a stake in any income that might accrue from magazine, newspaper, or other offers for such sensationalistic disclosures.

Still another early problem of the Commission was the report that when Lee Oswald was arrested, he had with him an address book containing the name, telephone number, and license number of an FBI agent. The FBI had omitted to mention this in one of its subsequent reports. Speculation arose among Commission staffers as to whether Oswald might have had some FBI connection, and there was some nervousness expressed in a meeting about asking J. Edgar Hoover, the Bureau's formidable chieftain, if one so violent and bumbling and, in the words of one staffer, "not too bright," could be on the payroll. No such connection between Oswald and the FBI was ever shown to exist.

us 2,300 reports totaling approximately 25,400 pages and the Secret Service 800 reports totaling 4,600 pages.†

The Commission started taking testimony on February 3, 1964. We arranged to have the hearings so far as possible when the Supreme Court was not sitting, and I was able to attend the taking of testimony from practically all the important witnesses. The Commission, as a body, heard 94 witnesses; 395 were questioned in depositions by our legal staff; 61 supplied sworn affidavits; and 2 gave statements. Everyone who claimed to have any significant knowledge of the assassination or was thought to have such information was examined.

The 888-page Report of the Commission was filed on September 21, 1964, ten months after the assassination. Accompanying it were twenty-six volumes containing all the testimony resulting from the investigation. The Report and its supporting evidence are to be found in public libraries throughout the nation and in capital cities of the world.

The facts of the assassination itself are simple, so simple that many people believe it must be more complicated and conspiratorial to be true. If the sole responsibility of the Commission had been to determine who shot and killed President Kennedy, it would have taken very little work; the time-consuming and painstaking job was running down the wild rumors.

Both during and after the lifetime of the Commission, some people were making money by writing or lecturing on their notions of who had killed Kennedy and why, not only around our own country, but throughout Europe as well. These speculative lectures, interviews, and writings fell on fertile soil in many places, particularly abroad, where assassinations so often were brought about by intrigues of the "palace guard" to effect a change of ruling power. In my summer travels around the world, I found a conspiratory theory to prevail almost everywhere I

† Ed. note: Warren asked the FBI not to release its voluminous report until the Commission had time to review all the facts in the case and evaluate them. Before the Commission's report was finished, some 552 witnesses had been heard or their statements read. Total cost of the Commission, for the statistically minded, was some $1,200,000, with about one fourth going for salaries. Its concerns were multitudinous and sometimes spun off from the investigation itself. Records of its meetings in the National Archives reveal that the members, though firmly guided by the Chief Justice, were not always in harmony. For example, some thought Marina Oswald, in her testimony, was less than honest with the Commission, but Warren blocked further questioning of her because he felt it would do no good. The members also worried about a book she was writing, about the trustworthiness of various attorneys and agents, about repercussions resulting from various news breaks, about unanimous agreement among the commissioners with all of the body's findings (Senator Russell in particular being more suspicious than the others of Oswald's possible conscription as a Soviet agent during his stay in Russia). One member, Representative (later President) Gerald Ford, later wrote a book about his impressions of the investigation, which went somewhat against the grain of Warren's feeling that the Report should stand for all of them without individual elaboration.

went. One of the lecturers and writers, who claimed to have knowledge of a conspiracy between Oswald, Ruby, the slain officer J. D. Tippitt, and others, and said he could produce the names of people who could prove it, was twice called before the Commission and questioned about the matter, but refused to give us any information. The last time, in order to make certain that we had all the facts, we brought him back from Europe to testify, but again to no avail. Yet he continued to write and lecture on the subject to his financial benefit.‡

Many people in this country believe in the conspiracy theory because they are of the opinion that a crime of this magnitude could not be committed by one disoriented man. They look for an Alfred Hitchcock or Perry Mason mystery in every crime. But they overlook the history of American presidential assassinations. Outside of the Lincoln assassination, which was a conspiracy—the outgrowth of bitterness resulting from the Civil War—none of the others was ever proven to be more than the act of the individuals who fired the shots.

The report of the Commission concerning the various assassinations reads as follows:

In the 100 years since 1865 four Presidents of the United States have been assassinated—Abraham Lincoln, James A. Garfield, William McKinley, and John F. Kennedy. During this same period there were three other attacks on the life of a President, a President-elect, and a candidate for the Presidency, which narrowly failed; on Theodore Roosevelt while campaigning in October of 1912; on President-elect Franklin Delano Roosevelt, when visiting Miami on February 15, 1933; and on President Harry S. Truman on November 1, 1950, when his temporary residence, Blair House, was attacked by Puerto Rican Nationalists. One out of every five Presidents since 1865 has been assassinated; there have been attempts on the lives of one out of every three.

In all but one of those instances, the assassin was the sole perpetrator. In each of them, the killer was tried and found to be either guilty

‡ Ed. note: While the Chief Justice tried to remain outwardly aloof from comment on the smörgåsbord of conjecture that was spread before the public, he sometimes expressed his ire in private. New York attorney Norman Redlich, an assistant counsel for the Commission, wrote Warren to advise him that he, Redlich, had provided some information which had been grossly falsified by author Edward Epstein in a book called *Inquest*. Inaccuracies and distortions were claimed, and Redlich then proceeded, point by point, to refute key parts of Epstein's book. He got back from the Chief Justice a letter of sympathy. It included a line that became almost a Warren theme song as the Oswald theoreticians proliferated: "We can expect much writing of this kind from charlatans and lazy writers who will not take the time to analyze all the papers to determine what the facts actually are."

or insane. They were all misfits in society. In the assassination of President Kennedy, the situation was the same.

Lee Harvey Oswald had been a misfit all his life. His father died two months before Lee was born on October 18, 1939. The boy never lived in a stable home, and at the age of three he was sent to an orphanage where his older brother and half brother had preceded him. A year or so later his mother was married for the third time, in 1945. That marriage was also short-lived; it ended in divorce, after several separations and reunions, in 1948. In 1952 he and his mother went to New York, where they lived with his half brother's family until they were asked to leave after Lee pulled a pocket knife and threatened his sister-in-law. He then became a constant truant from school, and was charged with being "beyond the control of his mother insofar as school attendance is concerned." He was remanded to Youth House for three weeks for psychiatric observation, where he was diagnosed as having "personality pattern disturbance and schizoid features and passive-aggressive tendencies." He was then placed on probation and referred to a child guidance clinic. He was described as "a seriously detached, withdrawn youngster —detached from the world because no one in it had ever met any of his needs for love." He admitted to fantasies about being powerful and sometimes hurting and killing people, but refused to elaborate on them.

On his return to school, he became a disciplinary problem, and his mother took him to New Orleans, where he finished the ninth grade and then dropped out to work for a year, after which he joined the Marine Corps in October 1956. He was a "loner" in the Corps, had two disciplinary proceedings on minor matters, but was discharged under honorable conditions, at his own request, a few months before his regularly scheduled separation date, ostensibly to care for his mother, who had been injured in an accident.

However, almost immediately after his discharge, he went to Russia and tried to renounce his citizenship. When the Russians would not accept him, he reportedly attempted to commit suicide on October 21, 1959, by slashing his wrist. His act was discovered, and he was hospitalized. He was never admitted to Russian citizenship but was permitted to remain in the country, and was sent to Minsk as a factory worker. Less than eighteen months after his defection, he opened negotiations with the United States Embassy in Moscow looking toward his return to the United States.

He was nineteen when he went to Russia with such bravado and twenty-two when he returned, thoroughly disillusioned by his experience, but still not enamored of the United States, although he struggled desperately for credentials enabling him to return.

While in Russia, on April 30, 1959, he married a nineteen-year-old

Russian girl with a seventh-grade school education and union apprentice training which qualified her as a pharmacist. She worked in a pharmaceutical warehouse preparing and packing orders. On February 15, 1960, a baby girl was born to them, and after months of effort he finally obtained the necessary papers from both the Russian and United States governments. The couple, with their newborn baby, left the U.S.S.R. by ship, arrived at Hoboken, New Jersey, on June 13, 1960, and almost immediately went from there to New Orleans.

From that time until the assassination, he lived a nondescript life, either quitting various jobs or being discharged for inefficiency or incompatibility. He lived largely on unemployment compensation, and often left his wife and child to the charity of friends. She bore a second baby girl one month before the assassination. He was without friends or associates, an absolute "loner" wherever he worked. He attempted to assassinate Major General Edwin A. Walker by shooting at him in the dark from an alleyway in the rear of the general's home. The shot barely missed the general's head. This further strained his marital relations when he confessed the attack to his wife.

Not only did he leave his wife destitute, but he had no money himself. Friends helped her, but aside from trying to keep him in jobs they had no sympathy for him. He tried once more to go to Russia through Cuba, but neither the Russians nor the Cubans would have anything to do with him. This angered him greatly. His wife, Marina, was of the opinion that he never intended to go back to Russia, that he ostensibly wanted to make the trip via Cuba but actually intended to remain there and leave her and the little girls in this country. He was a complete malcontent, best described by his wife after the assassination, when she said in her broken English: "When Lee in the United States, he no like the United States; when he in Russia he no like Russia; when he come back to United States he no like United States; he like Cuba; when Cuba no take him, he no like Cuba. I guess he only like on the moon."

I have written this much about Oswald's background simply to show that he was a total failure in everything he undertook; that he was incapable of working or living satisfactorily with anyone. Although of reasonable intelligence, he had no skills, and had a disposition and orientation that would not enable him to plan, counsel with or take orders from anyone. This bears directly on his capability as the alleged focal point of a conspiracy of the magnitude dreamed up by some people. The foregoing is only a shorthand statement concerning Oswald; the whole story is related in the Commission Report and in the volumes of testimony supporting it.

The news media and many other people for years have importuned me to discuss publicly the subject matter of the Report, but I have always declined to do so for two main reasons. First, because the Report and the evidence are both available either in the libraries or through millions of published copies to anyone who desires to inquire into the facts. They tell the story much better than I could possibly do it in any short space or public discussion. Second, because I believed the Report at the time it was made and nothing has transpired to change that belief. In this respect, I wish to say that not one single witness, one document, or one artifact has been produced to provably discredit it. To our best knowledge, the facts remain precisely as reported, and, that being true, the conclusion must remain the same. Of course, fiction writers and readers can conjure up hypothetical questions as to all human acts, but in order for the answer to be of any value, the facts upon which the question is based must actually exist and not be chimerical.*

In the assassination of President Kennedy, there are no facts upon which to hypothesize a conspiracy. They simply do not exist in any of the investigations made by the Federal Bureau of Investigation, the Secret Service, the Central Intelligence Agency, or the Departments of State, Defense, and Justice. The last was headed by the late Robert F. Kennedy, brother of our assassinated President, who certainly wanted nothing short of the truth. In addition, the authorities of the state of Texas, of the city of Dallas, and law enforcement agencies of other cities throughout the country were anxious to be helpful in every possible way. All of this was supplemented by nine months of arduous work

---

* Ed. note: Throughout the inquiry, the Commission in general and Warren in particular were bombarded with mail. Much of it was denunciatory. People could not seem to believe that the Commission—although it had Warren, Dulles, former Solicitor General Rankin, and other experienced people serving it who knew a covert operation when they saw one—would be able or willing to get to the bottom of the deep wells of intrigue they imagined to be operating in this case. Critical letters came from everywhere, even from private citizens in Russia. Marguerite Oswald wrote to demand that her late son be designated "alleged" or "accused" whenever he was referred to by the Commission. Not all were unfavorable, though. Jack Ruby's lawyer and doctor sent letters thanking the Chief Justice for his humaneness. Doctor Emanuel Tanay, calling Ruby "a psychotic person," said, "On the one hand you showed him the respect and acceptance he so desperately is striving for, and on the other you held [up] the mirror of reality to him."

Many of the letters, books, and articles attacking the Commission challenged the "single bullet theory," which had it that the bullet which wounded Governor Connally had first hit President Kennedy. Independent tests by the FBI, by CBS News, and by Dr. John Lattimer, as well as the autopsy, Kennedy's clothing, and other evidence, strongly supported this explanation and negated the "multiple assassin" theories which argued that bullets also came from in front or from the side of the death car in an incredibly synchronous fusillade. Anyone objectively examining the evidence reviewed by the Commission must conclude, as Warren did, that the single-bullet theory is more convincing by far than any other description of events that day in Dealey Plaza.

by our own staff of outstanding lawyers independent of all of these official agencies. And none of us could find any evidence of conspiracy. Every witness who could be found was examined, and it is revealing to note at this late date—nine years after the Commission Report was filed—that not a single contrary witness has been produced with convincing evidence. Practically all the Cabinet members of President Kennedy's administration, along with Director J. Edgar Hoover of the FBI and Chief James Rowley of the Secret Service, whose duty it was to protect the life of the President, testified that to their knowledge there was no sign of any conspiracy. To say now that these people, as well as the Commission, suppressed, neglected to unearth, or overlooked evidence of a conspiracy would be an indictment of the entire government of the United States. It would mean the whole structure was absolutely corrupt from top to bottom, with not one person of high or low rank willing to come forward to expose the villainy, in spite of the fact that the entire country bitterly mourned the death of its young President and such a praiseworthy deed could make one a national hero.

I believe it is fair to say that all doubters, except those who wrote or lectured for money while deliberately using false hypotheses, were led to believe that the various rumors and distortions occurred because there was no judicial trial of the assassin. I can understand this because in the other presidential slayings there was a trial, a conviction, and, with the exception of the Lincoln assassination, the matter was laid to rest. Here there could be no trial because Oswald was dead; hence the Commission.

I have related above the reasons why I have not carried on any discussions about the Report of the Commissions, and I do not propose to do so now because the Report itself gives all the data in better form and, of course, more fully than I could possibly relate it here. On the other hand, I will give my own appraisal of what kind of murder trial it would have been.

As district attorney of a large metropolitan county for years, I personally prosecuted many murder cases and guided through my office scores of others. With that background of experience, I have no hesitation in saying that had it not been for the prominence of the victim, the case against Oswald could have been tried in two or three days with little likelihood of any but one result. To substantiate that statement, I will quickly review what we would have been able to prove in a murder case.

Lee Oswald, a disoriented, willful and violence-prone young man of barely twenty-four years, a failure in everything he undertook, alienated from the rest of the world wherever he might be, with almost no friends or funds, insisted that he would have a place in history and bragged that "in twenty years he would be Prime Minister." On March 13, 1963, he purchased the assassination weapon, an Italian Army rifle with a telescopic sight, for $21.45 from a mail order house in Chicago under the name of A. Hidell. He had it sent to a post office box in Dallas, Texas, which he had rented under that same fictitious name. In another transaction, Oswald had earlier bought from a Los Angeles mail order house the .38-caliber Smith & Wesson revolver with which he murdered Officer J. D. Tippitt shortly after the assassination of the President, and which had been delivered to the same post office box in the name of Hidell.

On April 10, 1963, after leaving an incriminating note for his wife on his dresser in the event he should be arrested, he had attempted to kill Major General Edwin A. Walker, shooting the rifle from an alleyway in the darkness and barely missing the general's head. He later revealed the attempt to his wife.

Oswald obtained a job at the Texas School Book Depository warehouse on October 16, 1963, through the intercession of friends of his wife with whom he had left her and the babies destitute. At that time, although it was known that President Kennedy intended to visit Dallas, it was not known what the program for him would be or even if there would be a motorcade. The route which the motorcade would travel was announced only shortly before the event itself.

On November 21, Oswald unexpectedly went from Dallas to Irving, where his wife, Marina, was staying and remained there overnight. In the morning, without the knowledge of others in the house, he packaged his rifle, which was stored there, and went to work in the car of a neighbor, telling him there were curtain rods in the package. He told the same story to others at the warehouse, where he worked during the morning trucking cartons of books around the sixth floor of the Depository.

At noontime everyone but Oswald left the floor for lunch, and at twelve-thirty when the presidential car passed by the Depository, there was nobody on the sixth floor but him. He had moved some of the book cartons both to shield him from view and to give him a place on which to rest his rifle while shooting. As the President's car, occupied by John F. Kennedy and Mrs. Kennedy in the back seat and Texas Governor John Connally and Mrs. Connally on the jump seats, rolled on by, Oswald fired three shots. Two of them struck the President, one of them fatally wounding him, and one of the three also wounded the governor. People on the street in front of the building saw the rifle protruding from the building and a man shooting.

The motorcade was passing at the rate of eleven miles per hour, and during the period between the shots the President's car was from 175 to

260 feet from the assassin, making him an easy target for any person trained with a rifle. Oswald had qualified as a marksman in the Marine Corps, and he was known to have practiced with this rifle with live ammunition and on "dry runs." The four-powered telescope on the rifle contributed greatly to its accuracy, particularly against a moving target. Professional witnesses testified that it was an easy shot.

As police surged into the building, they encountered Oswald on a lower floor, but were told by a foreman that he worked there; hence he was not hindered. He immediately fled from the building, the only one of the work force to leave. He hurried to board a bus some distance from the Depository, but when its progress was retarded by the traffic, he suddenly left it and hired a taxi to drive him to a corner within a few blocks of his rooming house, from which he walked home. He was there only a short time, during which he changed clothes and picked up his .38 Smith & Wesson revolver and the belt and holster for it. He then struck out on foot across town until he was stopped by Officer Tippitt, who was patrolling the streets in response to a radio message about the assassination. This was about 1:15 P.M. As the officer stepped out of his car and moved to talk to him, Oswald drew his revolver and shot Tippitt four times, killing him instantly. Many witnesses saw and identified Oswald as he fled from the scene.

Going through a parking lot, he threw his jacket under one of the cars. It was identified later by his wife and by others who saw him wearing it at the time of the shooting. He fled about eight blocks from the scene and ducked into a moving picture house without purchasing a ticket. The attendant called the police, who arrived shortly and proceeded to question the six or seven people inside. When they approached Oswald, he said, "Well, it's all over now," and immediately struck an officer between the eyes with his fist, drawing his revolver at the same time. They struggled until three other officers subdued Oswald, disarmed him, and took him to the police station.

Now to return to the sixth floor of the Depository where the original shooting had occurred. Three empty cartridges were found on the floor near the window from which witnesses said the shots came. On the same floor behind some book cartons was the rifle from which they had been ejected. It was the rifle which Oswald had purchased under the name of A. Hidell. The paper in which it had been packaged as curtain rods was also found there. Two witnesses who were on the fifth floor immediately below the window had heard the cartridges hit the floor as they were ejected from the rifle at the time of the shooting.

The above details concerning Oswald and his part in the assassination were established as fact during exhaustive hearings in which many hundreds of reports and statements were studied and appraised.

The evidence developed and the complete lack of conflicting proof to support any other alternatives led the Commission to conclude that Oswald murdered both President Kennedy and Officer Tippitt, and attempted to do the same to Officer M. N. McDonald, who undertook to arrest him in the theater. We could find no evidence to show that anyone else took part in the killings in any way, and so determined that Oswald was the sole perpetrator.

As to the various conspiracy theories advanced, they tended to fall into three categories. There were those who thought the assassination was plotted by Russia and/or Cuba as a part of the Cold War. There were those who held it was a conspiracy of rich Texas oilmen and other extreme right-wingers to effect a sort of coup d'état, getting into high places persons who were more favorable to their interests. And thirdly there were the general theorists who simply had a feeling that the crime was too terrible and of too great a magnitude to have been conceived and carried out by one lone individual.

The first two groups were diametrically opposed to each other, yet both joined in criticizing the Commission for not finding that there was a conspiracy. None of the critics could point to any evidence that they or the Commission possessed to establish a conspiracy or to identify who these other guilty parties might be. They relied on rumors and assumptions. The third group relied only on a morbid feeling of doubt. The reason that all of these theories coalesced in frustration was that there was nothing but conjecture to substantiate them.

I remember an occasion when I was in Lima, the capital of Peru. Our ambassador, J. Wesley Jones, asked me if I would have a press conference to discuss the Report of the Commission. I told him I did not have such conferences at home. However, at his urging and because of the doubts expressed there, I consented to do so. There must have been seventy-five persons who attended. I doubted that they were all newsmen, but I subjected myself to their questioning for about an hour, in the course of which all three types of conspiracy theories were raised. As far as I could determine, everybody there believed there must have been a conspiracy of some kind. I could understand that mentality because, traditionally, assassinations in the Latin American nations could effect a change in government. As the questioning slowed down, I finally said, "Now let me ask you a question. How many of you have read the Commission's Report?" There was an awkward silence. Not one indicated that he had. I then said, "You could have read it had you desired to, because we sent copies to your libraries and to some government officials." With that the questions ceased and we adjourned the conference. We parted with everyone friendly and smiling and temporarily subdued, but I had the feeling that I had not changed a single mind among them.

In the last few years, although conspiratorial theories have borne no fruit, an attack has been made on the fact that pictures of the badly mutilated head of the President taken for the doctors at the inquest do not appear in the records of the Commission now on file in the National Archives. It has been contended that the reason these pictures were not filed was because they would show that the shots which struck the President did not come from behind and above him.

While I have never before entered into that discussion, I feel that it is appropriate to do so here because I am solely responsible for the action taken, and still am certain it was the proper thing to do.

The President was hardly buried before people with ghoulish minds began putting together artifacts of the assassination for the purpose of establishing a museum on the subject. They offered as much as ten thousand dollars for the rifle alone. They also wanted to buy from the family the clothes of Oswald, his revolver with which Officer Tippitt was murdered, various things at the Depository, and they were even making inquiries about the availability of the clothes of President Kennedy. They also, of course, wanted the pictures of his head. I could see in my mind's eye such a "museum," preying on the morbid sentiments of people and perhaps planting seeds of assassination in the minds of some deranged persons who might see opportunity for personal notoriety or expression in assaulting yet another President. I saw the pictures when they came from Bethesda Naval Hospital, and they were so horrible that I could not sleep well for nights. Accordingly, in order to prevent them from getting into the hands of these sensationmongers, I suggested that they not be used by the Commission, but that we rule on the convincing testimony of the Naval doctors who performed the autopsy to establish the cause of death, entry, exit, and course of the bullets. I also suggested that, in order to avoid any charge of destroying evidence, we send the pictures to the Department of Justice with the suggestion that they be shown to nobody except with the consent of the Kennedy family. This was done, and they are preserved there for any useful purpose to which they might be put.

Sometime in the latter part of President Johnson's administration, when the aforementioned charge was made, he set up a Board of outstanding pathologists from various parts of the country and submitted the pictures to them for comparison with the findings of the doctors at the National Naval Medical Center on which the Commission had relied. That Board confirmed the findings of the Commission.

While this has not entirely stilled talk of the possibility of other shots having caused the death of President Kennedy, it should be sufficient proof for any reasonable reviewer of the facts. It should be apparent to anyone that the Kennedy family would not want to withhold from public scrutiny anything that would tend to establish the truth about the assassination of their loved one.

I should also say that the procedure adopted by the Commission was the one commonly used in criminal court to establish cause of death. In such circumstances, the court would not permit the prosecution to exhibit such a revolting picture because of the prejudice it would instill in the minds of the jury.

In addition to my recommendation for the conditional impoundment of the pictures, I also recommended that the Justice Department exercise its powers of eminent domain under the Constitution for the purpose of taking for its use all the artifacts of the assassination—the weapons, clothes, exhibits, etc. This was done, the government paying to the rightful owners just compensation for them. In my opinion, it is better that there are not today sideshow barkers at circuses or local fairs throughout the country emotionalizing over such relics and inducing morbid thrill-seekers to relive the assassination of President Kennedy with the aid of pictures of his disintegrated head.†

† Ed. note: During the ten months in which the Warren Commission was meeting, the Chief Justice carried on his Court duties as well. It was a burdensome time, and one of lingering sadness, for Warren had much admired Kennedy and the spirit he brought to the land. The Report's critics were many and shrill, and they often forgot that the Commission, at Senator Richard Russell's insistence, did not say that Oswald was the only assassin. What it did say was that ". . . the Commission *has found no evidence* that either Lee Harvey Oswald or Jack Ruby was involved with any person or group in a conspiracy, domestic or foreign, to assassinate President Kennedy" (italics ours). That should have mitigated the heat, but it didn't, and Warren was exhausted by the time the fact-finding body disbanded.

While a Senate Intelligence Committee investigation in 1976 asserted that the FBI and CIA failed adequately to pursue certain leads in the case or to provide the Warren Commission with their fullest relevant information, the Committee also stressed that it ". . . has not uncovered any evidence sufficient to justify a conclusion that there was a conspiracy to assassinate President Kennedy."

EPILOGUE

The foregoing were the last pages Chief Justice Warren wrote for this book before his death. He had intended to provide further material and put a finer finish on what is here. Left incomplete was writing that would have expanded on his Court years and covered his additional duties as Chief Justice, such as the administration of the federal court system, guidance of judicial conferences and his chairmanship of the Boards of the National Gallery and Smithsonian Institution. He was a member of the Board of Trustees of the National Geographic Society. He also planned to write briefly of his travels and his work with the World Peace Through Law organization, which gave him its World Jurist Award in 1971 and its Human Rights Award in 1973.

And, assuming that he might have yielded to the nudging of his editors, he would have applied the wisdom acquired during his many years of public service to some comments on the contemporary American scene—the future of the Court after his departure, the Watergate scandals and the depreciation of national ideals that it reflected, the need for reform in financing political campaigns, and the cause of international justice, among other matters.

This further writing, regrettably, was not to be. But a few editorial remarks designed to fill in some gaps and round off his life story might be appropriate.

Warren enjoyed traveling. In his later years on the Supreme Court and while in retirement, he made almost annual trips to various parts of the world, often in connection with conferences on aspects of international law. J. Lee Rankin, former Solicitor General of the United States, once said, "When you travel, you realize this is the best-known American in the world. The new nations of Asia and Africa call him a saint—the greatest humanitarian in the Western Hemisphere since Abraham Lincoln."

His wife, Nina, went with him, and together they felt enriched by the widening of their horizons. Mrs. Warren was in the habit of sending picture postcards to members of the family who had stayed behind, each card dated and containing a scribbled impression of the place from which it was sent. When the Warrens returned home, they collected the cards and these, when added to the notes in her journal, gave them a graphic record of their travels. Since her husband was often totally absorbed in official business when abroad, it was a family joke that he once said, "Of course Nina has to go along. If she didn't, how would we know where we'd been?"

Places they visited included West Germany, where they met the mayor of Berlin, Willy Brandt; India, where Prime Minister Nehru entertained them and Warren was impressed with the Indians' high regard for American constitutional law; Britain, where they lunched with Prime Minister Harold Macmillan; Italy, where they attended the coronation of Pope Paul VI; Australia, where a meeting was arranged for them with Prime Minister Robert Menzies; Yugoslavia, where their host, driving a golf cart as they sped around his estate, was Marshal Tito; and many other countries, hardly the least among them being Russia, Israel, and Greece.

During his retirement years, Warren also traveled extensively within the United States, often as a speaker on college campuses. He enjoyed meeting the students and exchanging ideas. Sometimes he would combine these trips with his favorite recreations, fishing and duck hunting, when he could get together with old West Coast friends such as Wallace R. Lynn and hotel man Ben Swig.

For all his exposure to the world, his affability, and his strong leadership in public affairs, Warren actually was a very private person. At any rate, as he says in this book, he avoided most social affairs in Washington, D.C. His nonworking hours, never plentiful, were spent in large part with his family, which was and is numerous, happy, and long-lived.

Earl Warren was an anomaly in the American governmental system. He stood for all the storied nineteenth-century virtues: hard work, personal integrity, direct action with a boomer philosophy, rock-firm independence. As such, he fitted into no one's pocket, not the Eastern establishment's nor the Western conservatives', nor that of any President's administration during his long Court tenure. This largely explains why, in his pre-judicial years, he did not go further up the national political mountain, on the treacherous slopes of which such almost disingenuous probity can be a handicap. But once picked up and dropped near the top, as if by helicopter, when Eisenhower suddenly appointed him to the Supreme Court, he had a chance to exercise his virtues with considerable effect on the national scene.

Above all, he was resolute in bringing about improvements in the protection of the consumer at the mercy of monopolistic corporations, the suspected lawbreaker at the mercy of the police, the minority group member at the mercy of white-dominated school and political systems, the nonreligious at the mercy of organized religion, the protester at the mercy of whatever forces would suppress his or her small voice. In this resolve to see that the weak received their constitutional due as well as the large and strong, he was often a steadier of the more timid members of the Court as they came to decisions which sometimes jolted the entire United States power structure.

Warren's philosophy would fit more comfortably into the political climate of the seventies than it did into his own time. He abhorred the kinds of proliferating bureaucracy, of intimidation by pressure groups, of under-the-table dealing by elected officials, of spying and side-stepping critical issues and generally behaving corruptly, wastefully, and ineffectually that were growing and spreading in government during his Court years and which culminated in Watergate. These things greatly offended his sense of efficiency as well as morality, for Warren was a pragmatic rather than an idealistic reformer. Certainly he felt the freshening winds of rebellion when they began to blow with the student movement of the sixties, but he was no mere weather vane; those same reforming airs, inherited from Hiram Johnson, had been propelling him for years. They followed him into the Court, and, as Justice Abe Fortas wrote:

"The fact is that the Warren Court was both the product and the producer of a profound moral, ethical, and constitutional revolution. It functioned in times when the demand for a full measure of human rights had become insistent."

Warren was never one to shirk the power and responsibility that were his as the leader of the nine men who were final arbiters of constitutional law for some two hundred and ten million Americans. His boldness in liberal—he would merely have termed them "fair"—Court decisions brought on the wrath of those who felt either betrayed or threatened by them. They traduced him for arrogating power for the Court and bending the law to fit his own view of it. Some, as we have seen in this autobiography, went all-out for his impeachment. To Warren, this was palpable nonsense. He knew that he had no desire to use his influence for any purpose but to uphold the rights and principles guaranteed to all American citizens under the Constitution.

Responding to various accusations which still rankled during his retirement, he wrote the following in a preliminary draft of some pages that were to be included in this book but had not been inserted before his death:

"Critics have accused me and other Justices of coming to the Court with a predetermined intention of centralizing all power in Washington in order to change and control social and economic patterns of American life.

"I believe, of course, that constitutional decisions of the Court in the past are entitled to great respect. But when time has proved that they are wrong because they deny constitutional rights to the people or any part of them, then they should be reconsidered and changed. This is not to say that when I came to the Court it was with any idea of centralizing power in federal government by invading the province of state governments. It is not reasonable to expect that at the age of sixty-two one who had lived and acted in government with certain principles for a third of a century would without reason reverse his way of life and endeavor to uproot the things he had long believed in."

There are those who believe Warren underwent a dramatic change after his elevation to the Supreme Court had eliminated any need to please the voting constituency in his home state. But, as this book attests, he did not significantly alter his basic beliefs, which were rooted in his hard-working, injustice-hating, proletarian childhood. When he did act in seeming contradiction of those beliefs, as in voting on the side of police wire-tapping in the *Irvine* case and on the side of a college Board of Regents that deprived a doctor of his right to practice in the *Barsky* case, he adjusted, as if with the aid of a humanistic gyrocompass, to a more liberal course soon after.

It is one thing to feel that one is morally right, another actually to be so judged by history. For example, a recent President evidently believed that anything is morally permissible if it helps one to attain what one sees as righteous ends—such as getting elected or gaining power over one's political rivals. The difference between this outlook and Warren's is that Warren insisted that both the means and the ends be morally justifiable.

Warren had such faith in the workability of legal institutions, so long as fundamental precepts of fairness and equality for all were adhered to, that he urgently wanted to imbue everyone with an acceptance of international law as the most logical answer to war and other impediments in mankind's painful road toward self-mastery. One of the most regrettable omissions of this book is that he was not given time to put his thoughts about world law and the means of expediting it into the manuscript.

Always one to plan ahead, to recognize needs before they became mass frustrations, he said in a keynote speech given at a World Peace Through Law conference in Athens:

"It is even more important for us to devote our greatest effort toward having a body of international law than it is to make improvements in our domestic law—important though some of those changes may be. I say that because we have already ordered our thinking in the field of domestic law . . . But not all people have yet recognized the absolute necessity for having a court of international law with jurisdiction to decide current world problems and the means of enforcing judgments."

To develop a body of universally acceptable legal principles and procedures whereby all people can count on achieving a peaceful and equitable settlement of their differences—that is surely a job that calls for Earl Warrens of the present and future. Or better still, since his kind is so rare, it calls for his love of peace and equality at law to be spread among all peoples and joined with his capacity for constructive activism.

ACKNOWLEDGMENTS

For their various contributions during the preparation of this book, the editors, in behalf of the late Chief Justice Earl Warren, would like to express their sincerest gratitude to the following:

Mrs. Nina Warren, for her loving support throughout the project and for the loan of many of the pictures used.

Mrs. Margaret K. McHugh, former executive secretary to the Chief Justice, who lent invaluable assistance before and after his death.

Mr. Warren Olney III, former Assistant Attorney General of California, counsel for the Warren Commission and later director of the Administrative Office of the U. S. Courts under Warren, for his great help with the California years.

Ms. Willa Baum, director, and Ms. Amelia Fry, project director, and the fine staff of the Regional Oral History Office at the University of California, Berkeley, for aid in checking out facts and for making ROHO's excellent interview materials available.

Mr. Theodore Eisenberg, former U. S. Supreme Court clerk, now an attorney in New York City, for his reading of and advice about the book's Supreme Court material.

Mr. Verne Scoggins, former press secretary to Warren when he was governor of California, for checking over the sections on those days.

Mr. John Daly, former newscaster and a friend and son-in-law of the Chief Justice, for his help in reading and commenting on the completed manuscript.

The staffs of the U. S. Supreme Court Library, San Francisco State University Library, and the University of San Francisco Law Library.

None of the above is in any way responsible for inaccuracies that may appear in this book. We are extremely thankful for the time and effort they so generously gave.

The editors

INDEX